EMERGENCY INDEX

EMERGENCY INDEX
AN ANNUAL DOCUMENT
OF PERFORMANCE PRACTICE
VOL. 4

COPYRIGHT 2015 UGLY DUCKLING PRESSE
ISBN 978-1-937027-55-1
ISSN 2376-4287

EMERGENCY SERIES EDITORS

YELENA GLUZMAN & MATVEI YANKELEVICH

PUBLISHED BY

THE BROS. LUMIÈRE FOR
UGLY DUCKLING PRESSE
OLD AMERICAN CAN FACTORY
232 THIRD STREET, #E-303
BROOKLYN, NY 11215
>WWW.UGLYDUCKLINGPRESSE.ORG<

DISTRIBUTED BY

SMALL PRESS DISTRIBUTION (US)
INPRESS BOOKS (UK)

FUNDED IN PART BY

A GRANT FROM THE NEW YORK STATE
COUNCIL ON THE ARTS AND SUPPORT FROM
DONORS, SUBSCRIBERS, AND PARTNER
ORGANIZATIONS

PRINTED IN THE USA BY

MᶜNAUGHTON & GUNN (SALINE, MICHIGAN)
ON 100% RECYCLED PAPER

DESIGN

DON'T LOOK NOW!
AND KATIE GAYDOS

TYPESETTING

KATIE GAYDOS

TYPE

AKZIDENZ GROTESK & ORATOR

FOR MORE INFORMATION

>WWW.EMERGENCYINDEX.COM<

EMERGENCY INDEX

AN ANNUAL DOCUMENT OF PERFORMANCE PRACTICE

VOL. 4
documenting 2014

SUPPORT FOR THIS ISSUE OF INDEX
was provided by a grant from
The New York State Council on the Arts
with the support of Governor Andrew Cuomo
and the New York State Legislature

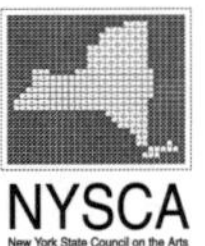

NYSCA
New York State Council on the Arts

CONTRIBUTIONS TO INDEX ARE TAX-DEDUCTIBLE
www.uglyducklingpresse.org/donate

A LIFETIME SUBSCRIPTION TO INDEX IS AVAILABLE
www.uglyducklingpresse.org/subscribe

<u>INDEX VOL. 4 MASTHEAD</u>

EDITORS
Sophia Cleary
Yelena Gluzman

CONTRIBUTING EDITORS
Luke Arnason
Adelaide Bannerman
Linda Frye Burnham
Oron Catts
Corina Copp
Steven Durland
Louise Hickman
Branislav Jakovljevic
Pekko Koskinen
Kristen Kosmas
Olga Kudrina
Claudia La Rocco
Anya Liftig
Caden Manson
Katie McGowan
Sawako Nakayasu
Esther Neff
Rob Ray
Ben Spatz
Sara Wintz

PARTNER ORGANIZATIONS
Bodega Philadelphia
Grace Exhibition Space
Issue Project Room
Live Art Development Agency (UK)
Movement Research
NY Public Library for the Performing Arts
NYU Dept. of Performance Studies
Presentaatio ry (Finland)
PS122
Spread Art

PUBLISHERS
The Bros. Lumière for
Ugly Duckling Presse

MANAGING EDITOR
Matvei Yankelevich

ASSOCIATE EDITOR
Katie Gaydos

COPYEDITOR
Alena Jones

PROOFREADERS
Nicholas Fuenzalida
Clarissa Kerner
Claire LeDoyen
Karen Szczepanski
Emma Wippermann
Allie Wuest

INDEXING ASSISTANCE
Christina Aushana
Nick Bell
Matthew Dewey
Emily York
Sean York

WEB MASTER & REDESIGN
Andrew Ross

WEB ASSISTANCE
David Baillot

ORIGINAL WEB DESIGN
Playtime Collective

WEBSITE
www.emergencyindex.com

EDITOR'S NOTE

EMERGENCY INDEX VOL. 4, comprises 196 submissions and captures a robust range of radical performance. Whether the work is a celebration of queer identity or an indictment of white supremacist patriarchy, many of these performances rely on liveness to transmit the urgency of their messages. Performance introduces a frame through which artists develop strategies of experience, circumvent exclusionary or oppressive language systems, and find ways to speak together.

The task of self-documenting these types of works can sometimes seem counter-productive, or even violent, as though putting words to a performance diminishes its awesome, live, fleeting power. I must resist that notion in my own practice and in working on this project because ultimately, I believe that way of thinking unnecessarily truncates the longevity of how performance can keep *doing* beyond its initial emergence.

Something I am realizing in reviewing this past year's volume is the absolute requirement that artists speak to each other. One way of sharing our ideas—and listening to others—is through reading these texts. But further, with *INDEX* as a resource, the conversation can continue–it can grow; email contacts are printed on the left-hand-side page. If you let it, this book can become a connector between you and others. Peruse the pages chronologically, or use the index to find people who are doing and thinking about things you are interested in, want to debate, or parse out. Strike up a conversation about something that resonates with you. Reach out. Collaborate. Mobilize. In *INDEX*, everyone is cc:ed.

Worst-case scenario is that this book is simply entertainment, something our readers flip through on the toilet. Best-case scenario is that this book acts as a resource to connect artists, thinkers, activists and others to engage with each other beyond their studio, home, school, residency, or city. As we continue to publish these yearly volumes and amass an archive of practitioners working in performance, we expand the network of individuals that may be available to us all as friends, supporters, collaborators, or mentors. *Emergency INDEX* is a growing conversation; it's not only a book–it's a community, a process, a possibility.

—SOPHIA CLEARY, CO-EDITOR
AUGUST 2015

HOW TO READ THIS BOOK

FOR MORE THAN 30 YEARS, one of the most hotly-disputed issues in performance has been that of documentation. Acknowledged as, at best, a conflicted endeavor, and at worst, a betrayal of the very essence of performance, documentation has been problematized while performances have proliferated. Meanwhile, hundreds of thousands of performances have come and gone, witnessed only by the people in the room, or on the street. And though we can argue about the advantages of such a condition, it does make a rather unique situation: performance has become a field whose practices are largely invisible to itself.

To respond to this situation, we began with a simple idea: to create an annual periodical allowing the people who made performances in that year to document their work in print. We would not curate these entries on the basis of their genre, their popularity, their location, or their perceived quality. All performances were eligible, as long as they identified themselves as performance and were performed in the year of publication.

In its non-curatorial approach, *Emergency INDEX* is indebted to the legacy of *High Performance* magazine (1977–1998) and their "Artist's Chronicle," a section of the magazine in which performance artists were openly invited to send descriptions of their recent works—the result is a surprising document of performance in the late 1970s. Famous works appear alongside one-offs, celebrated artists next to unknowns. From this democratic hodge-podge comes a fascinating snapshot of an emergent form.

Emergency INDEX is not, however, concerned solely with performance art. We believe that the broad, confusing field of performance has evolved into a similarly emergent situation, and we hope that our contemporary re-imagining of the "Artist's Chronicle" can help make visible the breadth of contemporary performance.

Because each annual edition of *INDEX* will include dance, therapy, poetry, protest, rehabilitation, scholarly research, theater, conceptual art, advertising, and many other fields utilizing performance, we feared simple descriptions would be opaque to those who are not familiar with the histories and problems of a particular field. So we asked authors to articulate not only what they made, but why they made it—to describe the problematics driving their work as well as the performance itself. Instead of focusing on the inevitable misrepresentation of describing the performance as *experience*, these documents endeavor to describe the choices, tactics, and techniques used to pursue a specified aim.

Each yearly volume contains hundreds of performance descriptions. For all we know, the pages of *Emergency INDEX* may provide the only print documentation of some performances described herein; certainly, for most, this is the only printed description written by the performance's creators for no purpose other than documenting the work.

While eschewing traditional curation and designing the book with equal space for every performance, we do not wish to imply that the works documented in this book are equivalent through their self-identification as "performance." On the contrary, rather than emphasizing the category, the book aims to underscore the variety of the works themselves. Moreover, instead of being discouraged by the disparity between the descriptions (necessarily reduced to language) and the performances they inevitably misrepresent, we have decided to cheerfully use the materiality of language itself to provide yet another channel of information.

That is why the back-of-the-book index is a salient feature of this book. By cross-referencing and indexing the language used by authors in their descriptions, we hope to leave a document not only of the performances themselves, but also of the language used when talking about performance.

You are holding in your hands a simple, flexible, physical, and time-tested technology. It allows for chance encounters, unplanned adjacencies, sudden epiphanies, as well as casual browsing and concerted searching. We hope that *INDEX* will serve as a useful tool and an inspiration for those to whom performance matters, to whom it is a persistent thorn, who look to performance as a means or as an end.

In short, we are tremendously excited for you to get lost in the labyrinth of *Emergency INDEX* and to find many threads to guide you through its pages.

PERFORMANCE DOCUMENTS

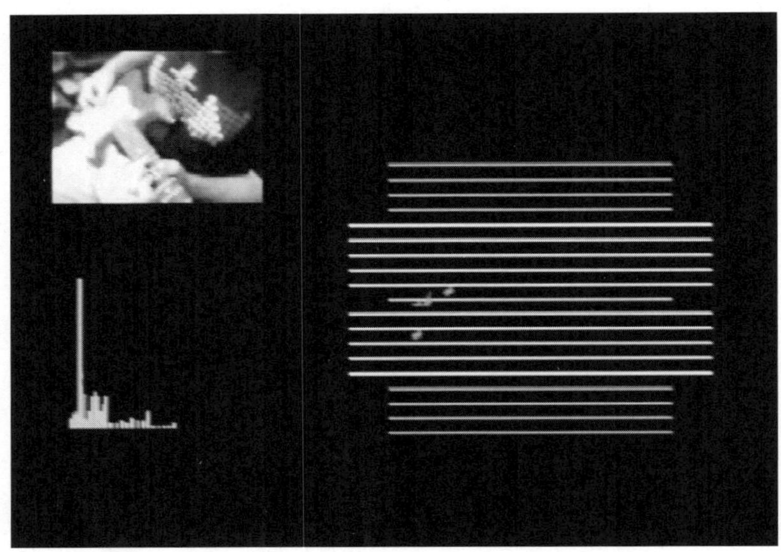

UNWINDING THE EARTH
first performed on January 1, 2014
performed once in 2014

JUDSON

New York, NY
pump.org.in

UNWINDING THE EARTH
JUDSON

Initially, I create software in Java to analyze audio from a live audio/video feed. Then, for the camera, I perform a piece (I composed for this project) for guitar. The noise (the most forceful of a complex wave, consisting of multiple frequencies) from the microphone is translated into music notation. These scores are then performed by a virtual string section (one bass, three cello, four viola, eight violin) available to Java and broadcast from the computer (stereo) audio output channel.

Where the lone computerized string section would immediately sound like chaos, the audience member watches the performance and hears the guitar part (from a spatially distinct location) simultaneously with the computer output (from another spatial location). This encourages the audience member's perception (likely exceeding capacity) to amass stimuli as a single entity. Insofar as the audience member interprets the visual scene as coherent and comes to feel the guitar part as coherent, the computer part (as a facet linked to the other parts) is no longer a series of random pitches at random intervals. As an appendage, conspicuously lacking coherence itself, it might be lent coherence from other organized stimuli.

What precisely constitutes musicality? I am not concerned with the well-worn question, "is it music?" Rather, I am investigating an elusive border between experiencing a sensation of hearing music (to be attended to), and that of noise. Moreover, by such experimentation, I am hoping to discover the neural mechanism by which we distinguish gestalt groupings (objectively arbitrary) of the intertwined sensory impulse streams worth further attention, from irrelevant signal noise.

In other words, the binding problem of how we might know that the redness and roundness of a ball are features of the same thing is solved. The binding problem assumes that all entities are bound (in some ideal plane we often call reality), and that we humans passively detect the holism. My proposal here is that features are disembodied and reassembled in the mind and that holism only exists for the sake of our biologically limited cognitive machinery (the brain).

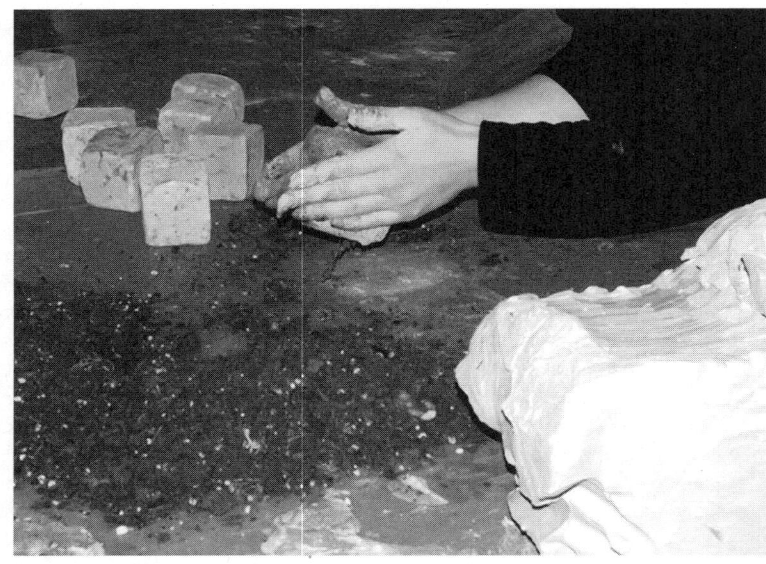

COMPULSIONATTAQUE

first performed on January 4, 2014
Panoply Performance Laboratory, Brooklyn, NY
performed six times in 2014

ANAÏS HERAUD

Germany

lab@anaisheraud.com
anaisheraud.com

COMPULSIONATTAQUE
ANAÏS HERAUD

As the audience enters the gallery, I bring five long and heavy packages into the space with the help of the organizer. They have the shape of a human body and are wrapped in black plastic bags tied up with rope.

(...)

The audience is invited to go outside in the street where I'm maintaining an iron bar horizontally between my stomach and a road sign. Five strips of white fabric are hanging on the iron bar. They are held down by the weight of small pieces of gray clay attached to their ends. The word "Compulsion" is on each strip which swings slowly with the movement of my body. I gently bring down the whole apparatus to the floor. The words on the fabric slowly deform into a heap.

(...)

We reenter the space. Out of a block of gray clay and soil, I build small cubes until they look like paving stones. I throw them over the heads of the audience and they crash into and stick to the wall behind them. I repeat that action several times and invite the audience to throw these objects as well. I open plastic bags that contain snow (it is snowing outside) which has kept the imprint of the packaging. With black spraypaint, I write on each pile of snow the word "Attack." It melts slowly.

(...)

compulsion...compulsion...compulsion...ATTAQUE

This performance is part of a broader research called "CompulsionAttaque." I am interested here in investigating the complexity of the effects that go through my body in situations of tension during demonstrations. I am interested in focusing on the shared experience of inner revolt: the intimate, the personal, the first creative impulse or desire for change.

I have started to research widely on forms of revolt and how it finds expression in language. I collect banners, flags, memories and pictures of demonstrations that I have been involved in or which were documented. These elements become the materials which I will react to during the live act.

How can feelings such as constraint or compulsion be physically experienced and take form in the sensible world? How does one put voice and words into action? How can I relate the individual feeling to the shared action and to a possible artistic gesture?

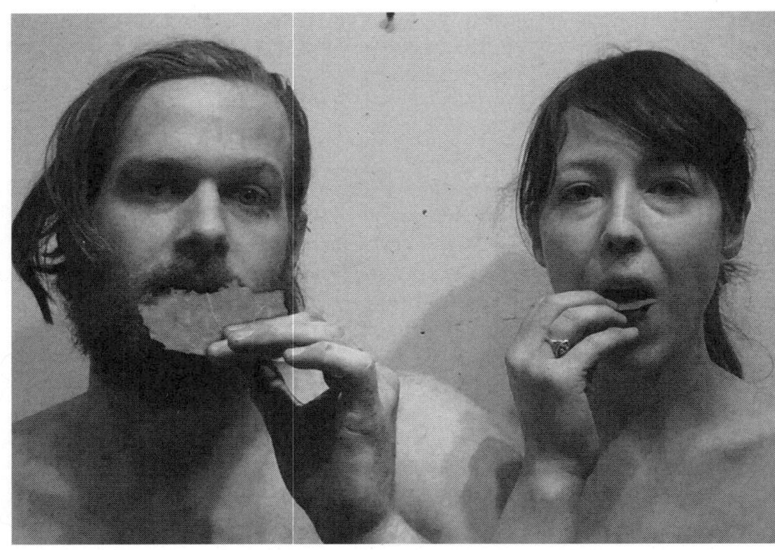

WE ATE LEAVES FROM A MOON TREE

first performed on January 12, 2014
artist's studio, Chicago, IL
performed once in 2014

SARAH BELKNAP / JOSEPH BELKNAP

Chicago, IL
info@sarhandjoseph.com
sarahandjoseph.com

WE ATE LEAVES FROM A MOON TREE
SARAH BELKNAP / JOSEPH BELKNAP

Humans have different responses to the actual vastness or complexity of many situations. Handed a tool and asked to perform a task, a signature can be distinguished. We all have a signature, a fingerprint, a biometric. Inside that biometric is knowledge that stems from a singular source, DNA—a score layed out into infinity. But is mathematical poetry still poetry? Was it always meant to be that seed of a tree on Earth that traveled to the Moon?

We ate the leaves of a failed experiment. NASA sent seeds of trees to our Moon to test this or that—relative to germination atmospheres and gravities. Then a seal was broken and the seeds no longer were viable to the experiment. A certain astronaut did not lose the poetry of that situation and took the seeds as a pet project. He planted them around this country, in some of the most humble places. We are tracking them down. They are Moon Trees. This plant has BEEN there. We consume the plant—as in the parable of Adam and Eve—to inherit the knowledge of the plant. Knowledge through ingestion. Knowledge of the Moon. What the Moon knows. The stories the Moon knows. The Moon in our body.

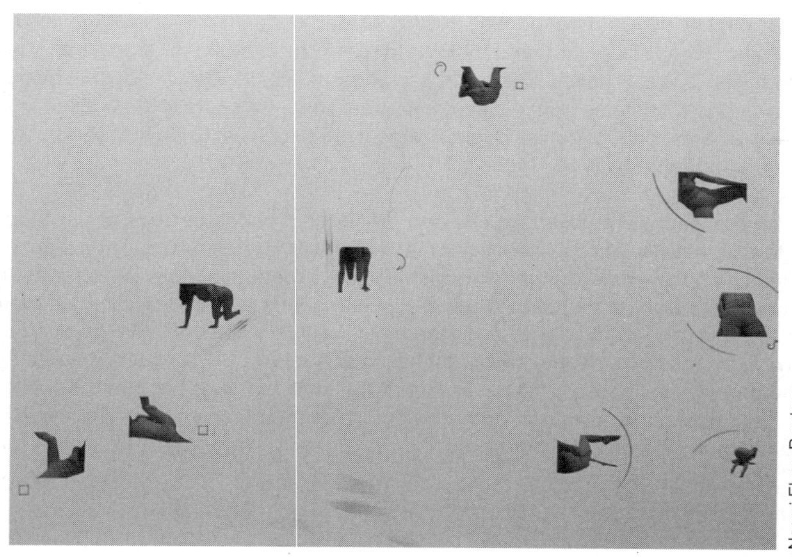

BEAVER

first performed on January 14, 2014
Center for Performance Research, Brooklyn, NY
performed twice in 2014

NAOMI ELENA RAMIREZ

Brooklyn, NY
naomi@naomielenaramirez.com
naomielenaramirez.com

BEAVER
NAOMI ELENA RAMIREZ

"Beaver," a graphic score and performance piece, investigates the gestural language of the sexualized female form as it is represented in the tradition of the fine art nude, pornography and mass media, in an analytical manner within the conceptual fine art exhibition space. "Beaver" interrogates the following questions: How do cultural representations of female sexuality in advertising, mass media and mainstream pornography affect how female sexuality is expressed both individually and collectively? How do phenomena like "slut-shaming" and the threat of sexual violence delineate, thwart or promote female sexual self-expression?

Culling imagery from mainstream pornography and movement improvisation, the resulting piece asks these questions through gestures and movement performed by a female body in a nude leotard and leggings. Passing through positions appropriated from porn magazines, laborious repetition, physical manifestations of the fear of sexual violence, gestures of self-appraisal and groping and female sexual self-pleasure, the female body re-performs the images seen and learned through mass media as the norms of female sexuality. The performance interrogates the impact of these norms through repetition that de-fetishizes the sexuality performed. Seated on three sides of the performance space and in close proximity to the performer, the audience must contend with a living, breathing body performing positions usually mediated through photography or video. The sexuality of the work is performed confrontationally. The intimacy of live performance does not allow the viewer an un-interrogated gaze.

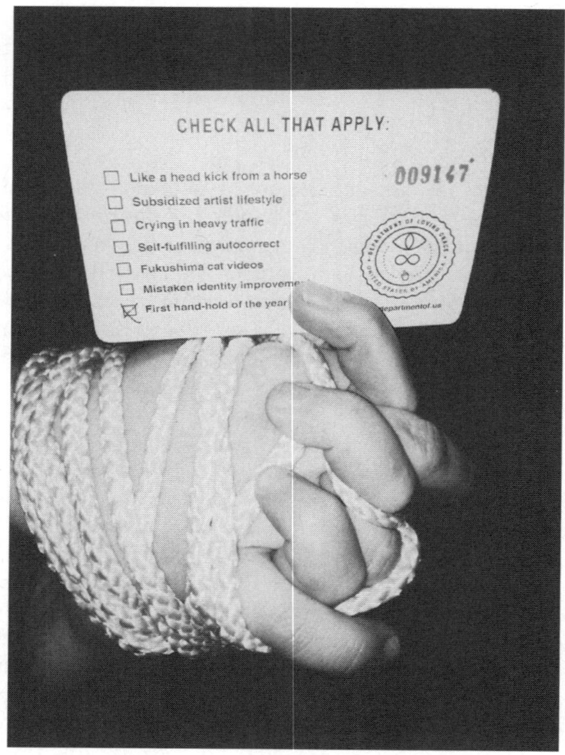

Joel Gregory

WE WERE BOUND TO DO SOMETHING STUPID IN PUBLIC (ATTACHMENT CAN BE PROBLEMATIC)

first performed on January 16, 2014
Yerba Buena Center for the Arts, San Francisco, CA
performed once in 2014

FKU TWIN$ / EMJI SPERO, JUDY BALS

San Francisco, CA
judyfanniebals@gmail.comw

WE WERE BOUND TO DO SOMETHING STUPID IN PUBLIC (ATTACHMENT CAN BE PROBLEMATIC)

FKU TWIN$ / EMJI SPERO, JUDY BALS

Go to a cultural event as a couple with hands tied together for the entirety of the event. Be together and mean it. Adapt to the difficulties and pain of attachment. Enjoy the extreme togetherness of being consensually tethered. Mingle and engage as normally as possible.

The assumption is that couples are supposed to do this sort of thing. Taken to its logical extreme. Like some perverse, self-inflicted attachment therapy, where rage and despair are replaced with *hygge* and nurtured codependency as the objects of focus.

NOTABLE INCIDENTS

i. Unintentionally disrupted one of the event's planned performances with the inflexibility of our bond. A masked performer selected one of us to be an audience participant without realizing we were bound together. Both of us approached, the performer put their hand up and told us, "Only one." We showed the performer our ensnared fist. The performer responded, "Oh. Fuck." This drew laughter from the audience. The performer sent us away upon fully understanding our condition.

ii. We were pleased to have opportunities to feel kind and accommodating given our artificial, manufactured helplessness:

a. I'm your "right hand man," in the bathroom. I've been waiting all night for you to ask me to wipe your ass.

b. Fetching things from pockets, opening doors, etc. We felt mildly disgusted with ourselves for being so pleased.

iii. Shaking hands with friends and hugging new acquaintances inadvertently became a group activity. This was received with varying degrees of disinterest, amusement, pleasure and, at least once, horror.

iv. While watching the film, our arms had to be propped up uncomfortably on the armrest. This gradually grew more painful. At times our fingers became cold, at other times, numb. We managed the pain by adjusting our position and the rope, massaging each other's palms, fingering the tight sweaty space between our hands. Approximately 3/4 of the way through the film, the pain became all-consuming. Viewing an experimental film in this condition was an experience akin to listening to Metallica at full volume with the heat turned all the way up in the car. Let's do that too.

FINDINGS

i. The discomfort of our attachment grew with time.

ii. We could not do the thing that was for "only one" because we are two.

iii. We were advised by an observer that there are less painful ways to bind flesh with rope. Mistakes are clear in retrospect.

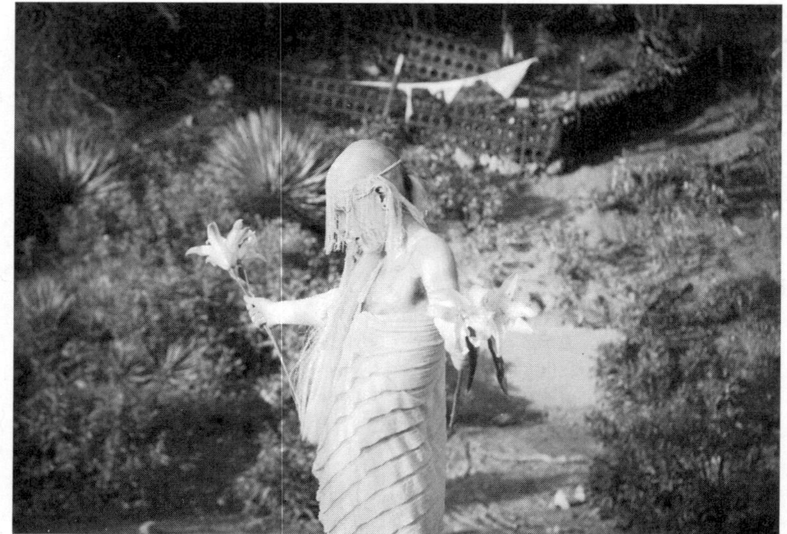

Los Angeles Nomadic Division

GABRIEL
first performed on January 19, 2014
The summit of Mount Disappointment, San Gabriel Mountains, CA
performed twice in 2014

JAMIE ROSS

Montreal, Canada
jamieross.org

GABRIEL
JAMIE ROSS

"Gabriel" is a site-specific performative project based on my intimate written communications with a man named Gabriel imprisoned in a California Correctional Institution in the Antelope Desert. For years, I wrote to Gabriel, who mailed drawings, dozens of letters and once, a photograph. He would send me meticulously shaded pictures of teddy bears and tattoo flash designs and I would send him photos of landscapes I had traveled in, and of chosen family. Erotic fantasies developed as one of us would take up and embellish a story of the other's; this is how the two of us came to know each other.

In one of his letters to me, Gabriel wrote about a fantasy he had in which we are both lifted into the air by an angel from our respective homes and unite in his namesake mountains that he could see from his cell window: the San Gabriel Mountains. There, we unite and alight, set down on the barren peak and make love.

From a crossroads at the edge of a massive fire scar on Mount Disappointment, so named for the discovery that it is not the highest mountain in the chain, I slowly danced an elaborate sunset ritual of visibility—a reminder that Gabriel is remembered and that one day incarceration may be abolished. Using this site, an hour outside Los Angeles, I employed elements of western ritual magic to invoke the Archangel Gabriel's spirit, explore our sexual unification and to enact the empowerment of the man's spirit.

The fantasy was performed again on the hill of Tepeyac in Mexico City a month later, to connect the collective fantasy with the land of Gabriel's birth.

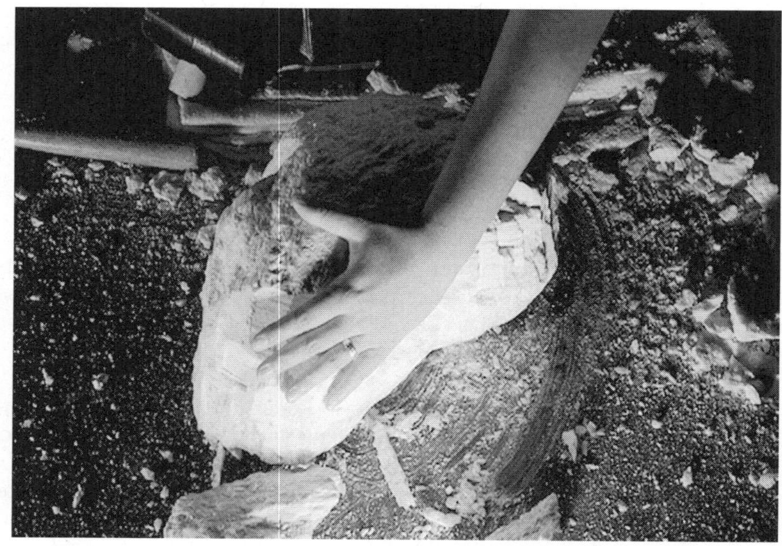

PRESENT TENSE SERIES
first performed on January 24, 2014
SAVVY Contemporary, Berlin, Germany
performed once in 2014

CHIARA CARTUCCIA
Duan Yingmei, Jill Orr, Nathalie Mba Bikoro, BBB Johannes Deimling, Omar Ghayatt, Zhou Bin

Germany
chiara.cartuccia@gmail.com
savvy-contemporary.com

PRESENT TENSE SERIES
CHIARA CARTUCCIA

What does it mean to take into analysis the present of performance art, if performance art itself never exists outside the present time? Performance art is a flux, but it does not run in a linear way. Instead, it builds systems of vortexes.

Performance art is always present, but contains in itself the long breadth of the past and the possibilities of the future. When completely aware of its inner temporality, a performance resembles the dialectical image described in Walter Benjamin's unfinished work *Passagenwerk (Arcades Project)*: "Every present day is determined by the images that are synchronic with it: each 'now' is the now of a particular recognizability. In it, truth is charged to the bursting point." Like the Benjaminian dialectical image, the performance artist's gesture operates within a present that is the living stage of the encounter between what has been and what is yet to come.

Performance art can appear in many different places, but constantly occupies the same space, the space of the encounter between the gesture and the eye, the voice and the ear. The space of the "here and now." Performance art has no structure, no general rules, but is a heterogeneous, multiple, continuous chain of new and renewed presences.

Present Tense Series was a composite program meant to investigate practices and theories of contemporary performance art through a series of live performances, artist talks and screenings, with the final aim being to open up a significant, fruitful discussion about this particular field of artistic production, which eschews any codification and possible classification.

The program, conceived for SAVVY Contemporary, brought together some of the most interesting performance artists from four continents, involving them in an open dialogue, in the context of which the gallery served as a catalyst of energies and ideas. Present Tense Series did not follow any curatorial ideology, no theoretical preconceptions have to be put at the base of this path. The key factor in the choice of the invited artists has been the necessity to always propose projects that refer directly, and meaningfully to the reality of present times, in all their complexity and mutability.

Featured artists were Duan Yingmei (China), Jill Orr (Australia), Nathalie Mba Bikoro (Gabon), BBB Johannes Deimling (Germany), Omar Ghayatt (Egypt), and Zhou Bin (China).

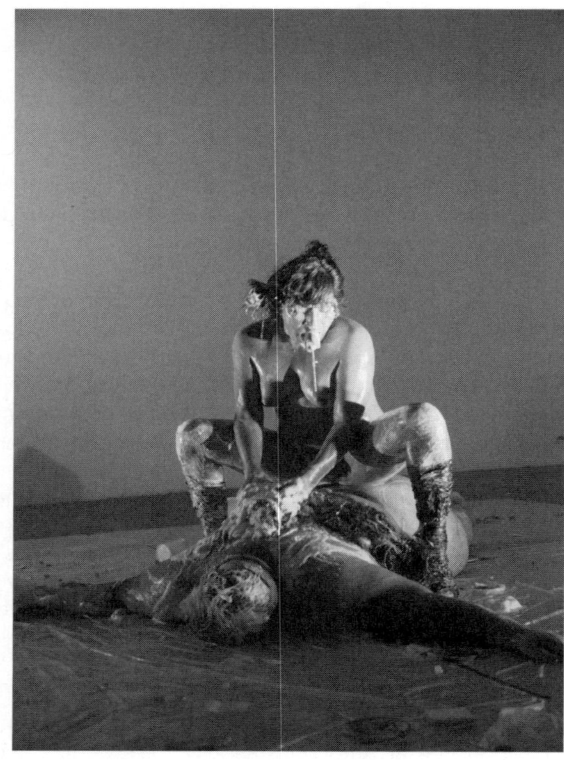

KAKE, KAKE, KAKE
first performed on January 25, 2014
Defibrillator Performance Art Gallery, Chicago, IL
performed five times in 2014

SOFIA MORENO
Jose Hernandez

Chicago, IL
s_moreno02@yahoo.com
sofimoreno.com

KAKE, KAKE, KAKE
SOFIA MORENO

By working with food, I examine questions of she-male porn, fetish and the value of the female TransBody as an artistic medium. "Kake, Kake, Kake" is a performance that takes place within an immersive installation that presents the body and food as sculpture, blurring the lines between what is physical, art and fetish. Like food, the aesthetic of the body is subjective, and the performance seeks to take back control of the perception of the TransBody as seen through popular culture and pornography and re-present it in an unapologetic, aggressive way.

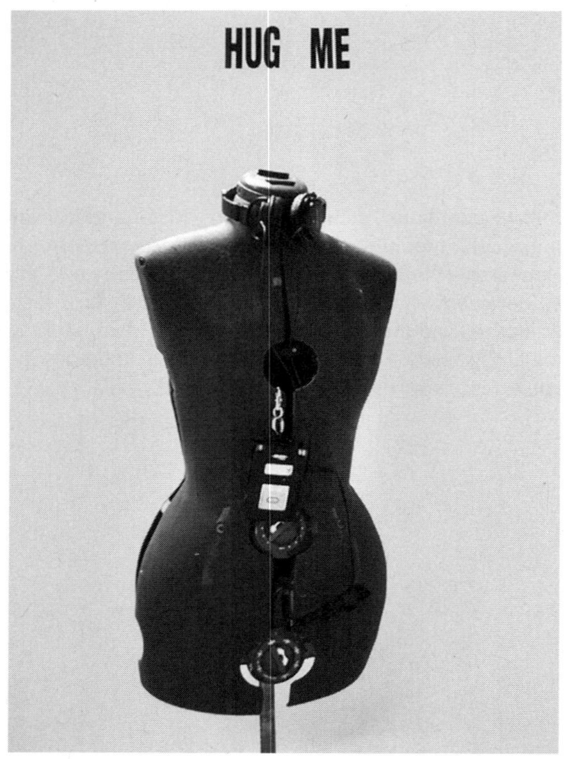

Rebekak Vargas

HARLOW'S MOTHER

first performed on January 25, 2014
Massachusetts College of Art and Design, Boston, MA
performed twice in 2014

ELAINE THAP

Boston, MA
esthap@gmail.com
elainethap.com

HARLOW'S MOTHER
ELAINE THAP

Revisiting Harry Harlow's experiments on infant monkeys in the 50s, I created a delegated performance inviting participants to reflect on their experience with their maternal parent, guardian, or lack thereof.

Through found materials, vinyl stickers, and the sterile gallery space, the situation became an experimental incubator for intimacy as well as isolation. The simple text "HUG ME" on a found mannequin and the accessibility of technology prompted participants to either witness or to engage in embracing the mannequin while listening to a song by My Brightest Diamond entitled "I Have Never Loved Another."

While Harlow experimented on rhesus monkeys and challenged the ethics of animal testing, I subverted this form in the context of the art world. I created a vulnerable situation for an audience of fellow artists within the confines of an academic institution. The participant embraces plastic, metal, and synthetic cloth. The sentimental song conjures a sense of longing for a mother figure in the profoundly lonely context of the art world. Some seek the art gallery or museum in hopes of a spiritual connection or admiration of a beautiful object. The voyeur also creates feelings of curiosity, envy, or embarrassment for the performer while the voyeur becomes implicated as the Harlow-like observer.

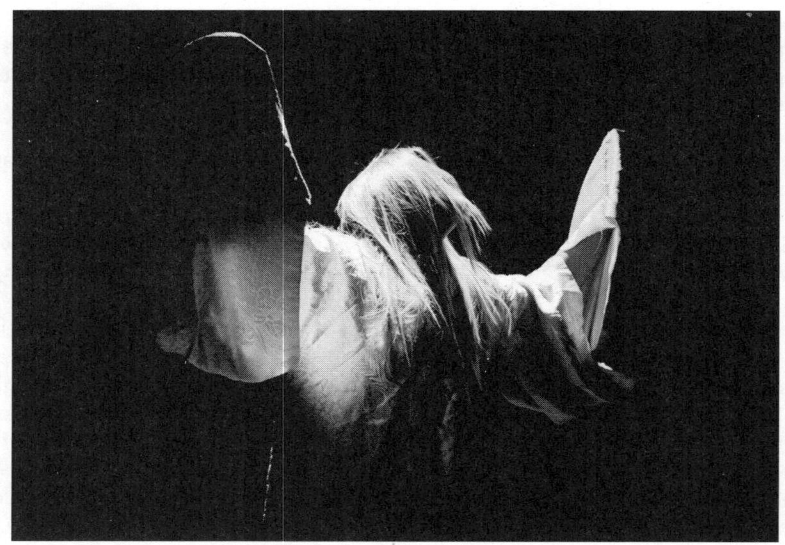

EGAO

first performed on January 25, 2014
GROKNATT at English Kills Gallery, Brooklyn, NY
performed twice in 2014

MARIA FERNANDA HUBEAUT

Brooklyn, NY
ferinusa@hotmail.com
mariafernandahubeaut.com

EGAO
MARIA FERNANDA HUBEAUT

"Egao" is an intensively expressive performance art piece where I bring and put into action sensible elements of Butoh accompanied by live rhythmic percussion. The piece addresses and questions the impossibility to smile in a natural, open way experienced specially among Asian women; which is mostly caused by the repression imposed by the cultural education, that eventually leads them to deal and struggle with social and emotional limitations. With reference to that reality, the title of this piece is also a direct allusion to it, since *egao* in Japanese means "smile."

I originally felt the need to create and express this idea based on the concept of *ochobo*, or "small and modest mouth," which is a centuries-old tradition and legacy regarded as an attractive trait for women in Asian culture. Clearly, these are perceptions and aspects that are culturally and socially dependent, which deny, ignore and deprive authentic individual subjective preferences. While it is openly known that beauty and attractiveness are subjective to the eye of the beholder, what happens when the beholders don't have the freedom to express their genuine personal choices? This is the main reverberating question that prevails and flows through "Egao."

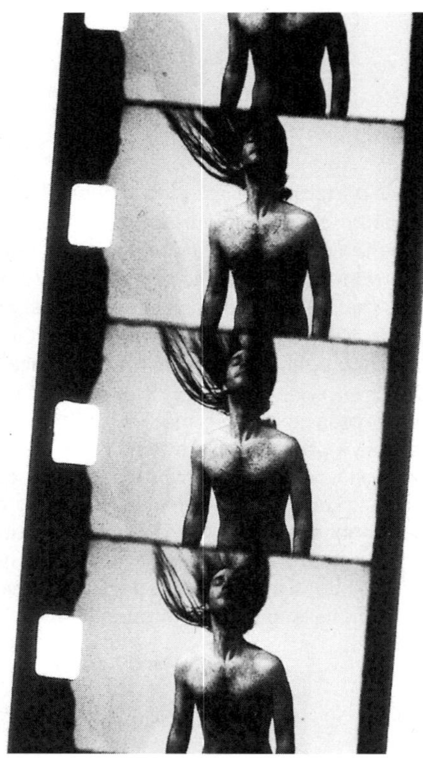

Nung-Hsin Hu

SAUDADE

first performed on January 31, 2014
Queens Museum, New York, NY
performed several times in 2014

ETHAN SHOSHAN

New York, NY
disiterate@gmail.com
disiterate.com

SAUDADE
ETHAN SHOSHAN

A film performance which through each showing I manipulate the film as it is being viewed on a manual film editor. It is then re-recorded digitally as it is being projected. The piece originated as a performance ritual act in which I try to control my body through a single repetitive motion and document it in Super 8mm film. The performance lasts a half hour in which I whip myself with wet hair until I get nauseous, dizzy and pass out. The performance purges my own insecurities as my internal balance shifts as I try to control the motion of my hair in the air; unwieldy, chaotic and undulating like a dance.

I was entranced by the process of capturing this performance on film. I wanted to keep the spirit and energy of the way light forms the image. In presenting this film as a live manipulation, "Saudade" becomes a hypnotic trance of the moving body as I vocalize an internal dialogue of my intentions, desires and experiences. When I show this film as a live film performance, I become a puppet master, manipulating my body as I watch it in film. The beginning and end are set but how I move through the film changes with each viewing.

Excerpts of Performance Script:
"…at times we often don't consider every action's consequences and most times we find ways of reconfiguring our own actions as complicated ways of self love or self hate...
we find ways to heal the imprints of others

I've never gotten into a hair fetish but because I have unruly long hair, I've invariably ended up in strange circumstances and try things I'm not even attached to emotionally. It's like people see what they want from you and when you hide something from them, they tend to want to see it…

I want to create a simple repetitive motion
One that affects me
One that forces itself on me
One that tests me
One that I'm failing at
One that unravels me
One that leaves its mark on me…"

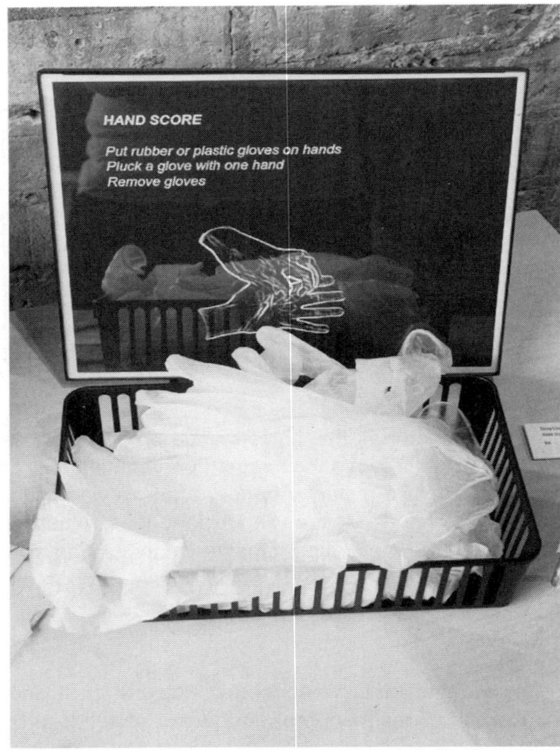

Curt Lund

HAND SCORE

first performed on February 7, 2014
Minnesota Center for Book Arts, Minneapolis, Minnesota
performed over 149 days in 2014

GINNY LLOYD

Jupiter, FL
ginnylloyd@ginnyonline.com
ginnyonline.com

HAND SCORE
GINNY LLOYD

Several Fluxus scores were performed at the Fluxjob: Purging the World of Bourgeoisie Sickness Since 1963 exhibition. The score, titled "Hand Score," was performed by multiple visitors to the exhibit:

> Put rubber or plastic gloves on hands
> Pluck a glove with one hand
> Remove gloves

I wrote this score as an exploration of interactive performance whereas the performers are the audience. They interact with the installation rather than with another performer or audience. I chose to include objects and instructions that held no inherent meaning except for in the imagination or experience of the performer. This provided room for personalized interpretation of the instructions and room to add their own actions.

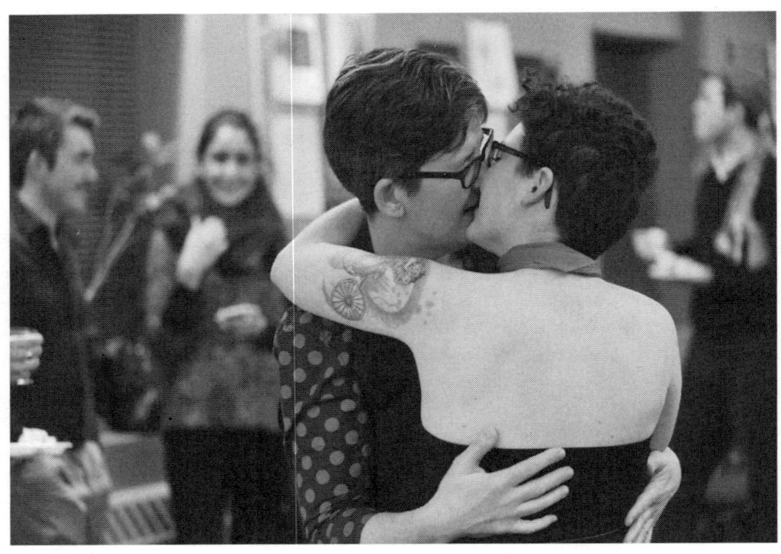

IS SHE YOUR MOTHER?

first performed on February 7, 2014
Festival of Original Theatre, Toronto, Canada
performed twice in 2014

ADRIANA DISMAN

Kate Klein

Toronto, CANADA
adriana.disman@gmail.com
adrianadisman.com

IS SHE YOUR MOTHER?
ADRIANA DISMAN

I've had it.

I refuse to surrender to the idea that my relationship can only be read as a non-sexual, familial one. This is the way we are made legible when we walk into a room.

"Is she your mother?"

No. She's not my mother.

<u>MANIFESTO:</u>

This performance gives thanks to Emily Roysdon for her "Ecstatic Resistance essay" and steals her words to say: We are expressing a DETERMINATION to undo the limits of what it is possible to be! This piece CELEBRATES the impossible, REFUSES the set limits of the intelligible, EMBRACES contradiction, BELIEVES in the transformative possibility of sharing and the NECESSITY of communicability, and wants to SPEAK PLEASURE TO POWER!

<u>PERFORMANCE SCORE:</u>

Pairs of self-identified queer women with an age difference of 20-35 years kiss for one hour.

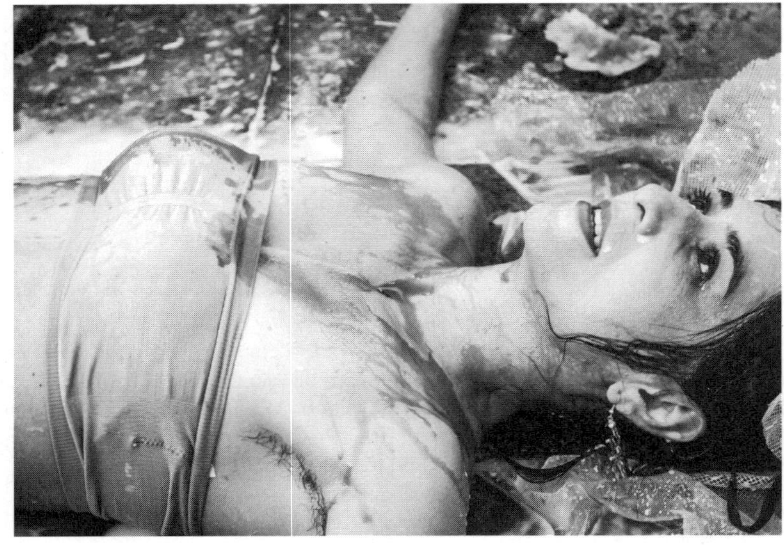

Mariana González Díaz

VIVA LA VIDA

first performed on February 7, 2014
Plaza of the Church of Santo Domingo de Guzmán, Oaxaca, Mexico
performed once in 2014

POLINA PORRAS SIVOLOBOVA

Jesus Gonzalez, Arturo Camacho

Queens, NY
polinaporras@gmail.com
polinaporras.com

VIVA LA VIDA
POLINA PORRAS SIVOLOBOVA

The title "Viva La Vida," which translates as 'Hurray for Life', comes from Frida Kahlo's last painting, a still life with watermelons. Inspired by Kahlo's resilient and self-reinventing spirit, my work centers around a woman who reinvents herself to transcend oppressing historical and social paradigms. As a site-specific, one time performance set in the Plaza of the Church of Santo Domingo de Guzman, "Viva La Vida" addresses the weight of history, religion, and societal expectations in women's lives. It seeks to empower women by subverting traditional female icons.

The main character in "Viva La Vida" is a young woman at a Quinceañera—a Mexican Sweet-Sixteen, accompanied by 25, ten-year old children. The church of Santo Domingo acts as an omnipresent setting and character to which the young woman directs her actions. The performance lasts one hour and 30 minutes and has six scenes with no text. Its structured storyline accompanied by live music makes reference to pre-Hispanic and Catholic rituals and the Quinceañera celebration.

Scene 1—The Prayers: I enter the plaza dressed as my normal self. I kneel down to pray in front of the church using the seven prayers of Saint Dominic.
Scene 2—The Watermelon Dance: The dance takes over the entire space as the children come out from the garden, each carrying a watermelon. The watermelons are left on the floor.
Intermission: 10-minute music intermission
Scene 3—The Sacrifice and The Communion: Dressed in full Quinceañera attire: a laced corset, white fluffy dress with pink bows, I walk holding a machete as the children trail behind me. One watermelon is sliced open, its fleshy heart is scooped out with my hands to feed the audience.
Scene 4—The Passion: I kneel down to repeat the prayers; this time I drag myself on the floor. I take off my high heels and put them on one of the girls. The girl and I take a watermelon and smash it on the floor. The remaining watermelons are splashed with the help of the audience.
Scene 5—The Waltz: I waltz with a pair of concealed scissors. I cut my dress to pieces and remain in skin-tone undergarments.
Scene 6—The Baths: I bathe myself with milk, lie on the floor, the boys pour honey and the girls cover me with golden glitter.
The Finale: As I get up the children hand me flowers and we all walk away from the church.

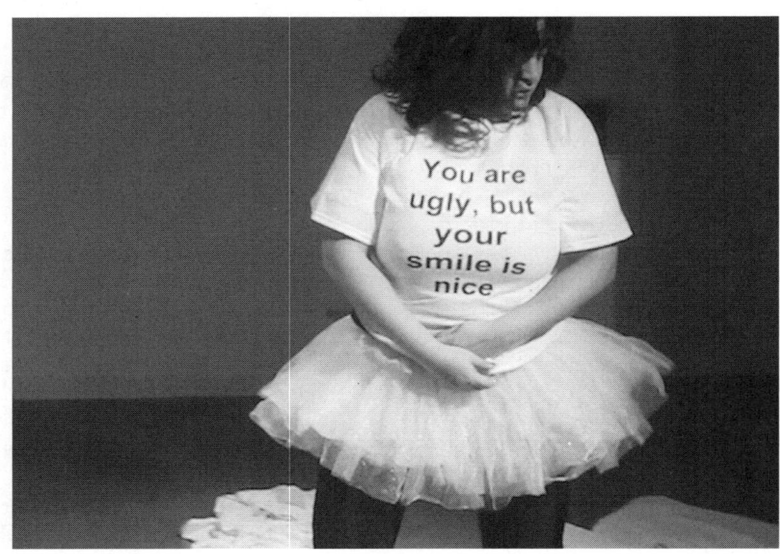

Yan Gi Cheng

ONE FINE DAY

first performed on February 12, 2014
Amelie A. Wallace Gallery SUNY College, Old Westbury, NY
performed once in 2014

KATYA GROKHOVSKY

Brooklyn, NY
katyagrokhovsky@gmail.com
katyagrokhovsky.net

ONE FINE DAY
KATYA GROKHOVSKY

"One Fine Day" is a live, 30-minute long performance, presented at the opening reception as part of "Body Conscious," a group exhibition by nine internationally acclaimed female artists curated by Dr. Emily Newman. The action addresses the issues of female body image in the culture of the scrutinizing gaze, by mining autobiographical and collected personal histories. "One Fine Day" explores the futile attempts to fit into societal ideals throughout the life of a woman, from young age well into adulthood.

Various unique insults aimed at myself were printed on thirteen T-shirts, which I wear simultaneously. I discard one by one off my body onto the floor during a sequence of choreographed gestures, generating a site-specific installation, left behind for the duration of the exhibition.

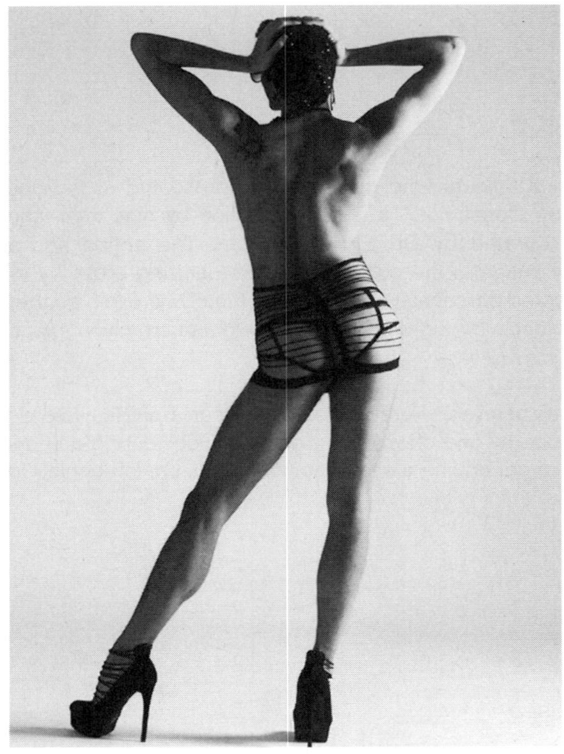

MARIA MAGDALENA

first performed on February 14, 2014
Union Square Subway Station, New York, NY
performed over six months in 2014

QWEEN AMOR

New York, NY
qweenamor@gmail.com
facebook.com/qweenamor

MARIA MAGDALENA
QWEEN AMOR

"Maria Magdalena" is a piece I took through America which establishes the image of The Madonna and brings her to life. I started the dance in Washington, DC and then took it to New York City, Philadelphia, Las Vegas and California. This was a long durational piece which took a year to complete in full effect. I danced on various street corners to an eclectic music selection that included everything from Rock 'n' Roll (Tom Petty, Queen, Aerosmith) to Pop (Lady Gaga, Madonna, Cher). All music that was chosen portrayed aspects of feminine divinity and wisdom. I relayed a message of freedom, not by speaking about freedom but by BEING FREE. The performance was a celebration of life that everyone was welcome to.

The dance was done partly naked to express the beauty of the human body. The audience experienced the performance interactively as they were moved to dance and join the celebration for a moment of bliss and freedom. Blurring the line between male and female, this performance included gender nonconformity and sought to introduce to society the Queer nature of being human. "Maria Magdalena" offers a truth that cannot be spoken, a spiritual message that must be felt and experienced in order to be understood. Without the direct experience, it is subject to misunderstanding, persecution and demonization.

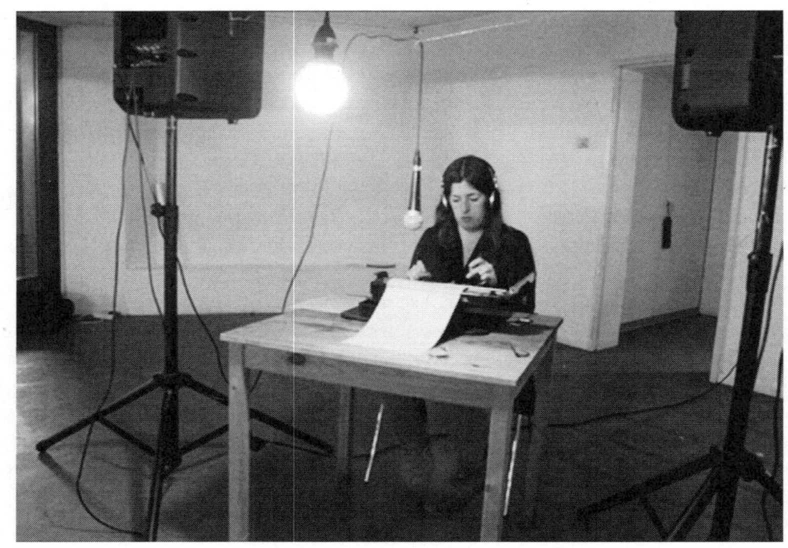

CLOCK HANDS, AN EXPERIMENT IN MAPPING (UN) EARTHLY TIME

first performed on February 14, 2014
Gold + Beton Gallery, Cologne, Germany
performed once in 2014

ELIZABETH MCTERNAN

Berlin, Germany
astheworldtilts.com

CLOCK HANDS, AN EXPERIMENT IN MAPPING (UN) EARTHLY TIME
ELIZABETH MCTERNAN

A story titled "Lonely Planet: A Moon-Crossed Romance Between Earth And Time, Told On The Full Moon On Valentine's Day" was typed on the Robotron Comfort 1981, a typewriter that was made the same year as the artist. Every line of the story took exactly 60 keystrokes to complete. After the story was typed, each individual character was read aloud at a tempo of 60 characters per minute, the speed of the second hand of a clock. This reading was recorded. During the "Clock Hands" performance, the resulting audio score was transmitted to the artist via headphones as she set to the task of retyping the story—a story whose meaning was lost in symbols disassociated by sound and slowness, while, at the same time, its new form as radio transmission was too fast for anticipating fingers. Built into the action was the inherent struggle to keep up, and the inevitability of falling out of time. Pieces of the story disappeared in the resulting textual time map. This arrhythmic clock tick generated by the act of typing was amplified by giant speakers facing west, towards the past, while the artist was oriented east, towards the future.

The falling out of time in "Clock Hands" was mirrored in a sound installation in an adjacent room. Visitors could listen to Beethoven's "Moonlight Sonata" for piano as it played over headphones at a beat a bit slower than 60 BPM. (It has been said that much of Beethoven's music was composed to be played faster than humanly possible meaning we never hear it in its ideal form.) Across the way, a radio-controlled clock was visible. The tick of its second hand was dictated by Germany's main atomic clock, located south of Frankfurt, which provides the time regime for all the so-called 'slave clocks' throughout the country. The lovelorn "Moonlight Sonata" could not keep up.

(The next possible date for this performance is 14 February 2033, the next time the full moon falls on Valentine's Day.)

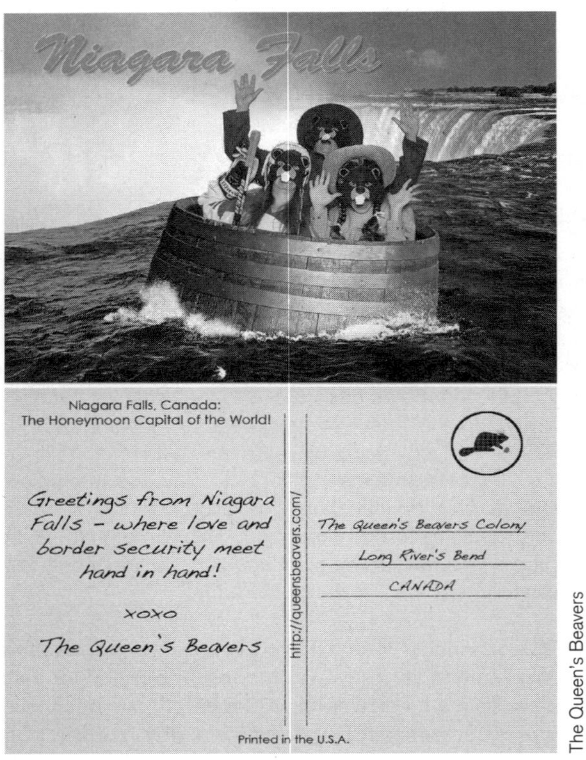

Niagara Falls, Canada:
The Honeymoon Capital of the World!

Greetings from Niagara Falls – where love and border security meet hand in hand!

xoxo
The Queen's Beavers

http://queensbeavers.com/

The Queen's Beavers Colony
Long River's Bend
CANADA

Printed in the U.S.A.

The Queen's Beavers

HOMELAND SECURITY, THAT'S AN AMERICAN THING?

first performed on February 14, 2014
Niagara Falls, Canada
performed once in 2014

THE QUEEN'S BEAVERS

Toronto, Canada
queensbeavers@gmail.com
queensbeavers.com

HOMELAND SECURITY, THAT'S AN AMERICAN THING?
THE QUEEN'S BEAVERS

What's purer than snow, sweeter than maple syrup, more wholesome that the ever-earnest beaver? Canada of course! If the United States positions itself as the world's geopolitical center and self-appointed police (backed up by righteous military might), the spin of Canadian nationalism can be seen as one of moral exceptionalism (backed up by a more reluctant and benevolent militarism). Under the menacing shadow of the U.S.'s belligerently imperialist nationalism, the light of Canada's constructed sense of national innocence glows ever so bravely and brightly. Delivered through an expanding and dazzling array of national and international public relations performances, Canada's dominant white-settler mythology requires the near-wholesale denial of Canada as a nation founded in colonial violence.

A cross between Canadian First Nation's artist, Kent Monkman's beseeching "King's Beavers" and a gender-neutral and gender-queer version of the feminist activist collective the Guerrilla Girls, the Queen's Beavers are a Canadian activist-performance collective who use embodied irony to comment on a range of idealized tropes of Canadian nationalism. With "Homeland Security, That's an American Thing?" the Queen's Beavers take a vacation from their otherwise industrious lives to explore Canada's playground, Niagara Falls. Tourism, patriotism, gambling, border security, giant dams—what more could a beaver ask for? Follow the beavers as they explore Canada's answer to both friendly tourism and border security!

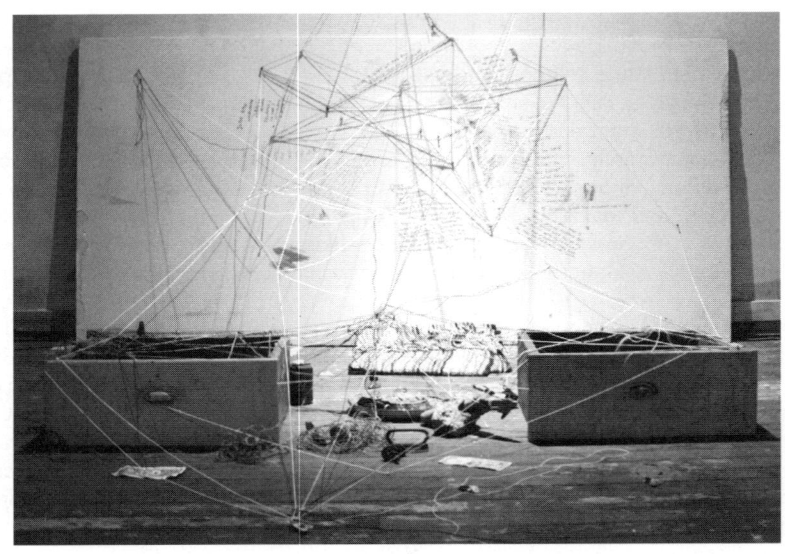

ENOUGH/\NOT/\ENOUGH
first performed on February 20, 2014
Detroit Contemporary, Detroit, MI
performed once in 2014

CHRISTINA DEROOS

Detroit, MI
chris@christinaderoos.com
christinaderoos.com

ENOUGH/\NOT/\ENOUGH
CHRISTINA DEROOS

never enough but enough but not all i have but all i give and yet it really isn't enough and yet it really is all i do while my heroes did/do/will do more this is all i do and i know it is really both not enough and enough and the most selfish thing is the most selfless thing and yet i'm sure it really is never enough unless i'm wrong and later i find out it was/is/will be just right

"enough/\not/\enough" was a performative, stream-of-consciousness meditation on the physical, emotional and mental experiences of self-doubt, failure and letting go. The work specifically explored the repercussions of partial to full disconnects between personal values and lived experience.

In an otherwise empty space, over the course of approximately two hours, I responded to sights and sounds from other performers as well as audience members while creating an increasingly complicated structure around myself. The start of the performance involved unpacking two drawers placed on the floor which contained string, twine, scissors, markers, a hammer and push pins. The bulk of the performance alternated between building a protective/restrictive home of string and twine, using overheard phrases as prompts to explore the performance theme in writing on the wall behind me, folding dollar bills into hearts and giving them away, cutting dollar bills into confetti and doing nothing.

"enough/\not/\enough" was presented as part of the Creative [performance art] Incubator, in which multiple artists presented durational work simultaneously throughout an art space.

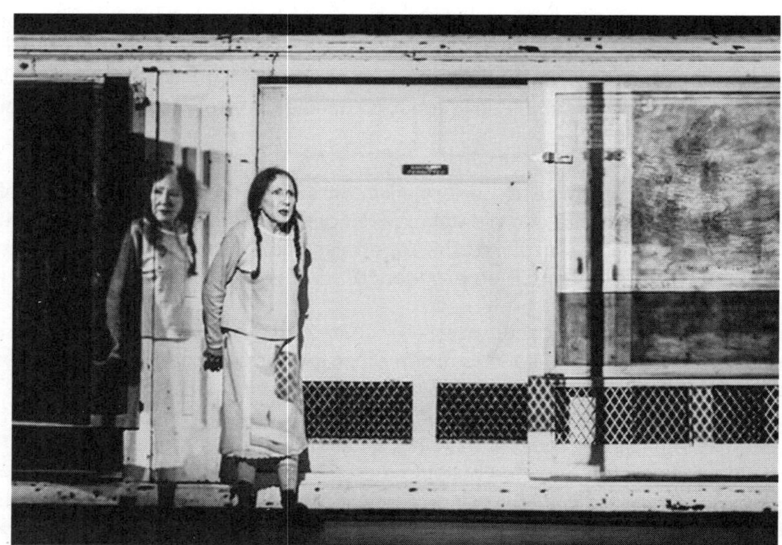

THIS WAS THE END
first performed on February 21, 2014
Chocolate Factory, Queens, NY
performed ten times in 2014

MALLORY CATLETT / RESTLESS NYC
G Lucas Crane, Keith Skretch, Peter Ksander

New York City, NY
mallory@mallorycatlett.net
mallorycatlett.net

THIS WAS THE END
MALLORY CATLETT / RESTLESS NYC

"This Was The End," a performance in which four actors in their sixties and seventies attempt each night to get to the end of "Uncle Vanya"—in a last ditch effort to alter the outcome. In Chekhov's play, Vanya asks, "What if I live to be 60?" "This Was The End" performs an answer. It uses the play to pose questions about how memory functions in the formation of the future. Having the roles played by older actors makes visible the physical manifestations of time suggesting that there might be something haunting and surprising in "Uncle Vanya" that only this older group of performers can uncover. The cast featured veteran downtown luminaries Black-Eyed Susan, Paul Zimet, Jim Himelsbach and Rae C Wright.

The set design by Peter Ksander features the actual wall from the Mabou Mines studio, which was salvaged from the PS 122 before it closed for renovation. The sound and video design features an improvisational score of voice and image that converge with the live performers. The video, which projects the wall onto itself, creates a temporal blur out of which the past can emerge and recede. The sound includes fragments of Chekhov's text mixed live onstage by sound artist G. Lucas Crane, a DJ of analog tape machines, to trigger memory and to create new configurations in the present. Like the aging characters, the physical cassette tape he records onto is a perpetually degrading medium that is breaking while it is playing.

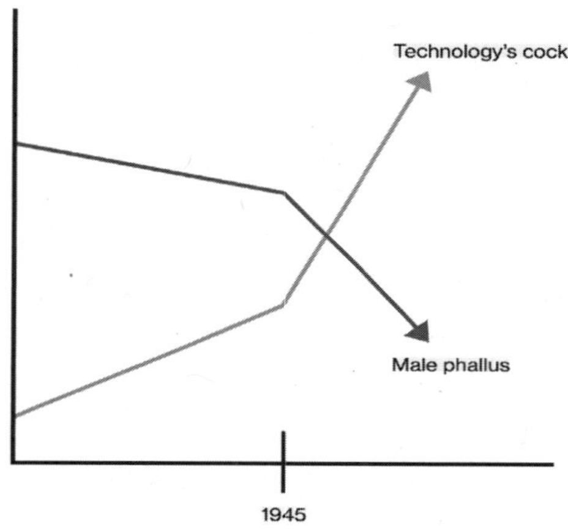

Tomáš Hodbo

THIS IS THE ENDD
first performed on February 22, 2014
The New Museum, New York, NY
performed three times in 2014

TRACY JEANNE ROSENTHAL

Los Angeles, CA
tracyjeannerosenthal@gmail.com
tracyjeannerosenthal.com

THIS IS THE ENDD
TRACY JEANNE ROSENTHAL

"This Is The ENDD" is a lecture-performance and PowerPoint presentation commissioned for Rhizome's symposium on e-cigarettes: This is The Electronic Nicotine Delivery Device. The performance delves into the factual past of cigarette advertising, in which cigarettes were linked to male power and the phallus, and offers a speculative campaign strategy for VUSE Digital Vapor cigarettes, recommending that VUSE be marketed to consumers as granting access to technology's cock.

In 1929, Edward Bernays, founder of Public Relations, used Sigmund Freud (his uncle)'s theories to develop a campaign for women's Lucky Strike. The slogan, "Torches of Freedom," merged smoking and phallic empowerment. Contemporary e-cigarette advertisements fail to depart from this theme: VIP E-Cigs asks the viewer to "Whip it out," through spokesman Stephen Dorff, blu commands "Take back your freedom," and NJOY Kings claim, "Feels like the first time."

The performance traverses this history to predict its sinister technological evolution. Since 1945, it argues, the shape of the cock in the minds of the consumer is no longer the cylindrical masculine object, but the chode-ish mushroom of technology— epitomized by the mushroom cloud of the atomic bomb. Think of the word we use to describe what e-cigs allow us to do: "vaporize." Think of the technology embedded in them that allows us to transform liquid into vapor: it's the "atomizer." Think of the singular sensation these e-cigarettes simulate: it's the "hit."

Using as evidence the maternal namesake of the airplane that dropped the first atomic bomb, Enola Gay, the atomic cannon named after Betty Grable, and more, the performance re-evaluates America's atomic history to pinpoint current consumer weaknesses: the vast chasm erupting between human emotional capacity and our destructive potential, the gender confusion emerging as technology replaces humans as objects of desire, and the settling shame that technology, rather than humans, are the agents of history. How can e-cigarettes help us "Rise Above the Flames?" "Namaste," the ad begins…

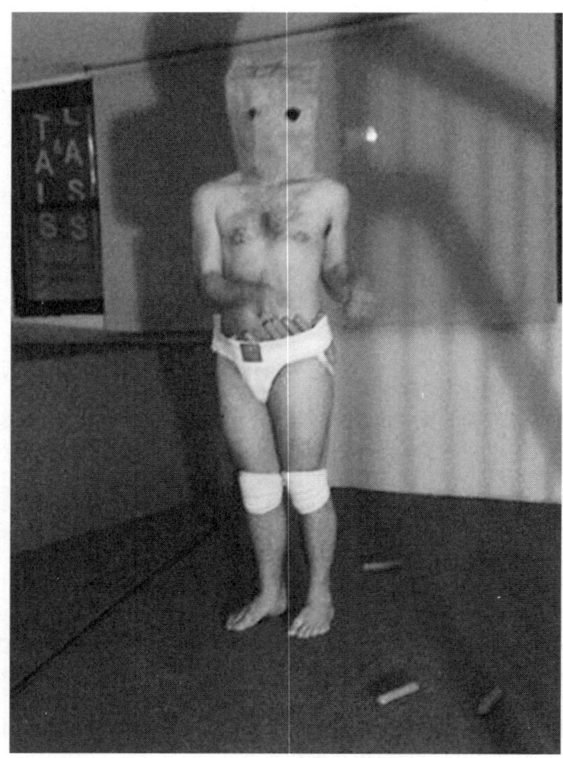

Sophia Cleary

TOFUHOTDOG
first performed on February 23, 2014
Headlong Studios, Philadelphia, PA
performed seven times in 2014

ALEX ROMANIA
Zöe Bennett, Sarah McSherry, Jonathan Wood Vincent

New York, NY
alexjromania@gmail.com
cargocollective.com/alexromania

TOFUHOTDOG
ALEX ROMANIA

"A teen-angst masturbatory love poem, a clowning drag king punk show, 'tofuhotdog' critiques the failures in masculinity through actions of shallow rage, notions of an iconic American 'Man' through food processed poetry, and the limitations of a body bound and desireful. In a phallic duet, this 'notdog' is shaken, eaten, stomped on, sung about—a choreography to digest and transform the excess. Perhaps never achieving this, 'tofuhotdog' is a beautifully humiliating mess."

"tofuhotdog" was created over a year and a half of solo research, sometimes in collaboration with friends visiting my process as 'outside-eyes'. I first showed a sketch of this piece at a work-in-progress event called REHEARSAL run by Sophia Cleary. I created "tofuhotdog" after a four year relationship ended that left me deeply insecure about my body, hating myself, my genitals, and intensely at odds with where I met gender, it would be hyperbolic to say I made it to survive that period, but it felt like that. The messy relationship did give me a greater awareness of gendered action which I am happy for, but more so it gave me a paranoia of it. 'tofuhotdog' deals with desire for something outside of, and a paranoia of, the performance that male bodies put on to survive each other, and the destruction that patriarchal masculinity causes, through the lens of my own body. It's necessary (if not already a given) to say that my pain is nothing in comparison with the violence women are dealt by men every single day. Much of this piece is me asking what is useful that I can do in relationship to feminist performance work, so I created this piece to process the anger and resentment that I felt towards my own cisgendered white male body, the odds at which I was and am with masculinity and gender at large, in hopes to be able to make space for something else. I think of the piece as an presence exploration of "feminist masculinity," a term used by bell hooks. I use absurdity to perform aspects of masculinity to the degree to which men lose their power, asking what am I left with? These are moments where I hope vulnerability allows a transformation to occur.

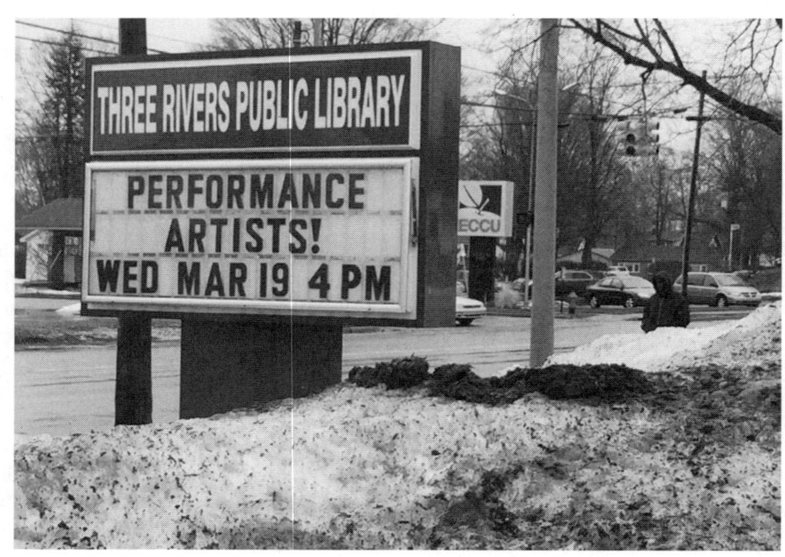

TALK OF THE TOWN: RELATIONAL MARCH

first performed on February 28, 2014
Hole in the Sky, Washington D.C.
performed 33 times in 2014

PANOPLY PERFORMANCE LABORATORY / ESTHER NEFF, BRIAN MCCORKLE // FUTURE DEATH TOLL / EDWARD G SHARP, DAVID IAN GRIESS

Brooklyn, NY / Portland, OR
panoplylab@gmail.com / info@futuredeathtoll.com
panoplylab.org / f-dt.com

TALK OF THE TOWN: RELATIONAL MARCH
ESTHER NEFF, BRIAN MCCORKLE / EDWARD G SHARP, DAVID IAN GRIESS

Panoply Performance Laboratory traveled with Future Death Toll across 23 cities, making individual relational acts of performance and acting out processes of touring. People were met, interviews performed, BBQ eaten, McDonalds visited, bowling balls taped to feet, snow melted, frozen lakes trespassed, participations conducted, songs written and sung, relational aesthetics problematized, all interspersed with much driving in a rental car.

ZOMG / it's important to consider the aesthetics of the cablez. / im w/ u on this. i'm with you on that. I am with you on this thing which you have indicated to be important and which I agree with. D'accord. / taco the town / / it's important. to consider the aesthetics of the bags. / / whyexittherealisitbentperfectly ? / / imtaking an INformal poll—/ should there be nudity in this performance? / im taking an informal poll- / should there be nudity in this performance? / *it's something important to consider / / i placed the black bag on top of brian's head and then he put the mic up to the instrument (a simple osc that he built) and it had a lot of feedback. i kind of wish we had given out ear plugz to everyone before we started. sorry. / playing a role / or is it like / / roll of the dice as / someone here says / \ / / then / them / / see / sight o for / sight / site / or / / suture / or situate / / w / what / w/ / w/. / w/ / w/ what / left to their / own / dices / / what does the / / roller player / doe? / / is it just a deer thing / / a dear / a dear / why cant you do / / what you planned / why cant / / you plan it / / out / / plan it out / before / you try it / / ok? / / it's just common sense / its fucking ranciere ok? / / why can't you fucking take on the situation / / as something sacred? / / ok? / / it is > / greater than you / you have no agency here / your mess / now / lay in it / / ok / / ok? / this is the award ceremony part / / are you smoking? / / what is your name? / / is this real? / it is very nice out today. / david turned the distorto pedal on and off.

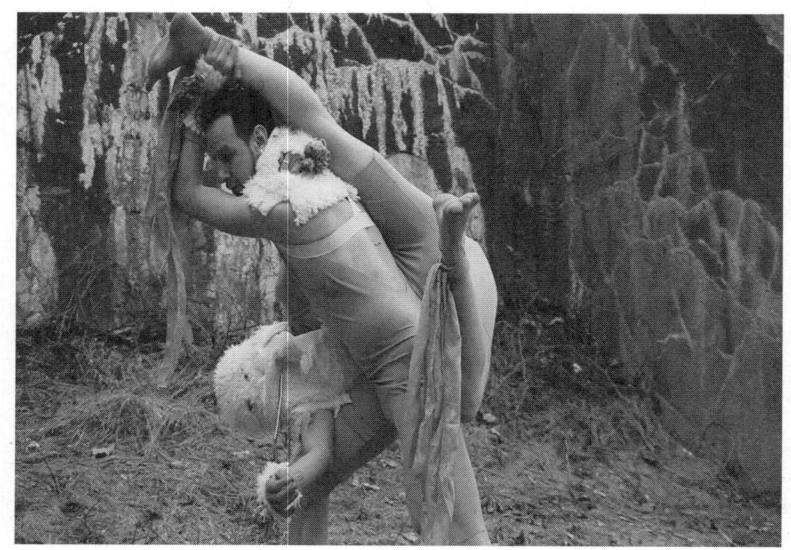

A BRIGHT HAND IN DARKNESS

first performed on March 1, 2014
The Black Rock Forest, Beacon, NY
performed once in 2014

ELIZA SWANN / THE BRIDE OF FIRE DANCE TROUPE

Kevin Bachman, Jennifer Banks, Ryan Ingersol

New York, NY
elizaswann@gmail.com
elizaswann.com

A BRIGHT HAND IN DARKNESS
ELIZA SWANN / THE BRIDE OF FIRE DANCE TROUPE

"A Bright Hand in Darkness" is an improvisational dance piece with an open ended duration. The narrative structure of the work is derived from Ursula K. Le Guin's *The Left Hand of Darkness*—a 1969 science fiction novel that is considered to be one of the first major feminist works in the genre. The text is fraught with problems, none of which are resolved. What is gender? What defines our sexuality? What is love? What is war? Le Guin herself described her inquiries as "messy, dubious, and uncertain" in her most recent introduction to the book. This uncertainty is the pivotal point of focus for both the performance choreography and cinematography, which is based entirely on chapter sixteen of "The Left Hand of Darkness." This chapter sees the two main characters (Estraven and Gently) grow closer as they are trapped in a blizzard together. Here, Estraven quotes a Winterish poem that reveals the nature of the title: "Light is the left hand of darkness and darkness the left hand of light. Two are one, life and death, lying together like lovers, like hands joined together, like the end and the way." Using this as a jumping off point, "A Bright Hand in Darkness" explores Le Guin's unique portrayal of gender and sexuality. The piece was first performed in the Black Rock Forest for an audience of five.

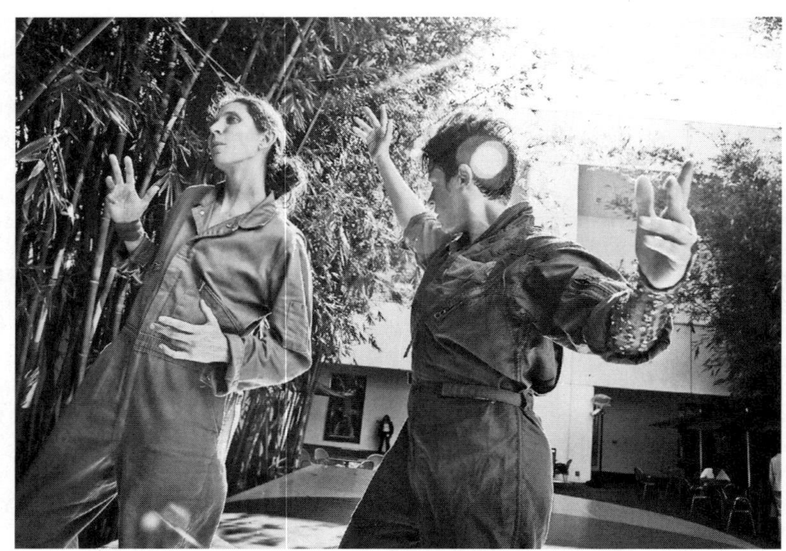

Lisa Wahlander

THE OTHER SIDE OF STILLNESS
first performed on March 10, 2014
Pieter, Los Angeles, CA
performed four times in 2014

ALEXX SHILLING / ALEXX MAKES DANCES
Barry Brannum, Alison D'Amato, Sarah Leddy, Ian Isles, Samantha Mohr, Madison Page, Taso
Papadakis, Gwynn Shanks, Laurel Tentindo, Devika Wickremesinghe

Los Angeles, CA
mail@alexxmakesdances.com
AlexxMakesDances.com

THE OTHER SIDE OF STILLNESS
ALEXX SHILLING / ALEXX MAKES DANCES

the way dances don't exist
until the dancers dance them
A REVIVAL
a ritual of revival

"the dance goes on," Rainbow said when we danced on the Hammer Museum's
Gold Stage.
Does it?
the dance goes on.
sometimes we stop. we rest.

this piece is my attempt at making it go on.

"The Other Side of Stillness" is a collaboratively created, site-specific, durational duet for five or more dancers that never stops moving. In brightly colored jumpsuits and Power accessories, one member of a duet is replaced after fifteen minutes of continuous dancing. At fifteen minute intervals, a new dancer enacts the ritual of replacement, and the dance goes on. This highly physical score utilizes and celebrates the performers' collective history while exploring endurance, replacement and constancy amidst an ever-shifting environment of spectator, site and time.

"The Other Side of Stillness" is performed for two hours (at its maximum duration). Audience may come and go, may stay. We have performed in public spaces, private studio and theatrical spaces, for the camera, and in intermediate spaces where performance and spectatorship mingle loosely. Each adaptation thoughtfully engages with each context, its challenges, limitations and wonders. With each adaptation, the piece sprouts new layers and plays with loosening or tightening the fifteen minute replacement / two hour durational framework.

We call ourselves the Modern Dancers of America. We recognize the roots of our collective movement material: Lucinda Childs, Trisha Brown, Michael Jackson, Bob Fosse, Bill T. Jones, surface through our dancing, reminding us that we are cellularly engaged with a folk form that our bodies pay regular homage to, while simultaneously innovating.

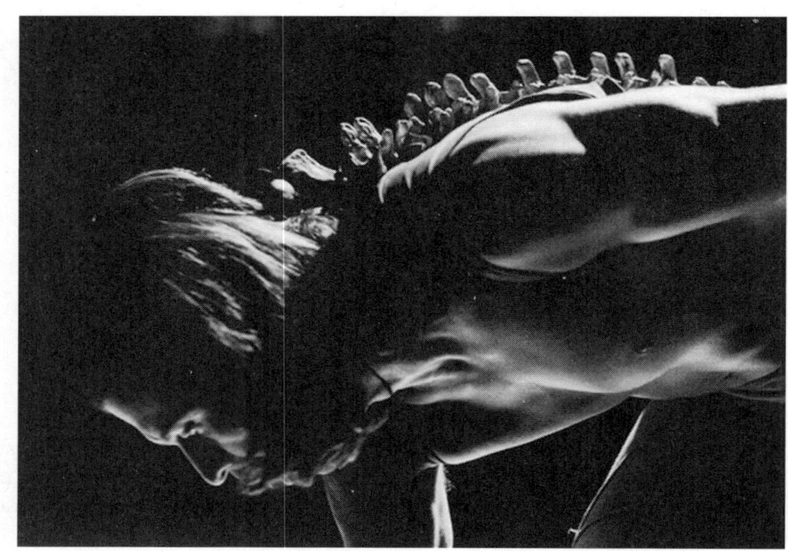

DEE(A)R SPINE
first performed on March 12, 2014
University of California, San Diego Encinitas Library, San Diego, CA
performed five times in 2014

SAM MITCHELL
Janet O'Neil

San Diego, CA
mitchellsammy.com

DEE(A)R SPINE
SAM MITCHELL

"Dee(a)r Spine" explores the connection between heritage, genetics, ancestry and culture. "Dee(a)r Spine" was the result of a lifelong, tenuous relationship with my Native American culture. In creating this work, I wanted to experience going within a ritualized ceremony, as a portal to gain insight into my heritage and cultural history. "Dee(a)r Spine" chronicles the journey of the ancient, timeless Deer Dancer, within a contemporary framework, which allows the audience to access a shared experience. The Trickster figure plays an important role, as a constant presence of lightness and darkness. He plays with the audience, coaxing them to laugh at his foolishness, and then quickly holds up a mirror to expose the real source of laughter. The ancient medicine wheel becomes an access point, a point of departure, a doorway into a threshold and a foundation for the score.

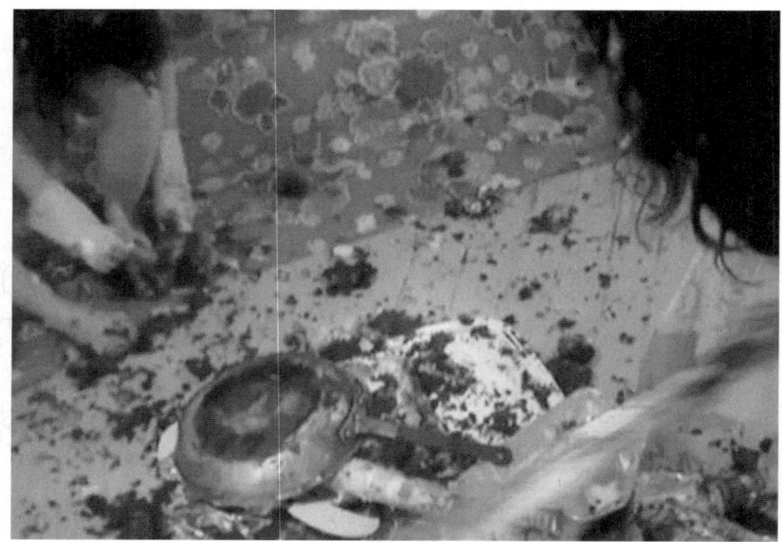

Miles Pflanz

DOMESTICIDAD
first performed on March 15, 2014
Grace Exhibition Space, Brooklyn, NY
performed once in 2014

LAURA BLÜER / HILARY SAND
Miles Pflanz, Jonathan Mittiga

Brooklyn, NY
lauraxbluer@gmail.com
laurabluer.com / hilarysand.com

DOMESTICIDAD
LAURA BLÜER / HILARY SAND

Two women bake dozens of cakes. They destroy them. They use tools like rakes, knives and hands to attack symbols of a deranged femininity. Messes without maids. Enjoy iconoclasm at home.

In "DOMESTICIDAD" we burn tampons like birthday candles and smash cakes on Lena Dunham's *Rolling Stone Magazine* cover. Wearing yellow rubber gloves we jack off Jesus candles and squirt heavy whipping cream to extinguish their flames. We do these and other actions to insult oppressive symbols and critique trends in feminism and domesticity.

Video as the final product of the performance is important to note. I wanted to experiment with video-performance as an objective of the live piece. I've seen many artists and institutions that are obsessed with the cleanest, most conventional means of documenting and archiving a performance—which is to stick a camera or two on a tripod and catch wide angle shots for a final, all but unedited video document. If the purpose of archiving performance is to preserve what it meant in front of an audience, the most effective way of doing so is to manipulate time, perspective, and sound in the documentation. "DOMESTICIDAD" was performed for over ten hours in two locations to produce a ten minute video-performance.

The piece was inspired by Fluxus event scores, the writings of Julieta Paredes and the Mujeres Creando Comunidad collective, and interviews with Camila Vallejo about being a Communist female politician in Chile.

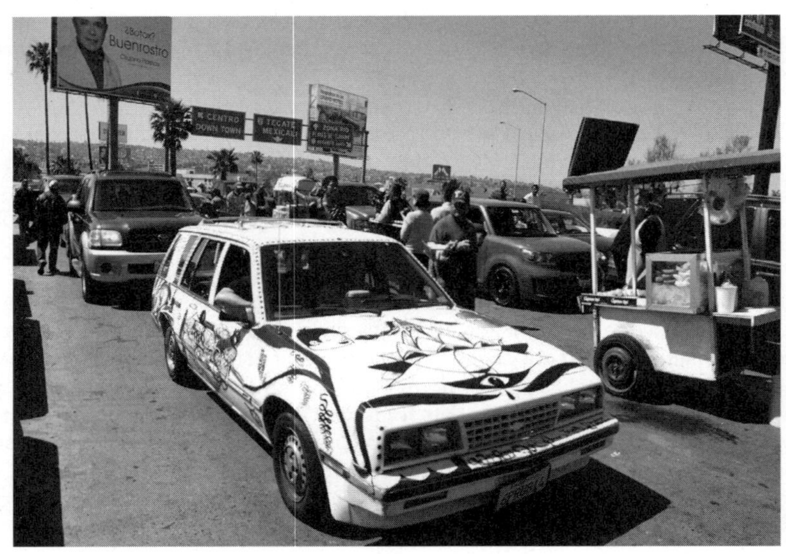

Cog•nate Collective

DIALOGUE IN TRANSIT: EVOLUTION OF A LINE // DIALOGO EN TRANSITO: EVOLUCION DE UNA LINEA

first performed on March 15, 2014
San Ysidro Port of Entry, Tijuana, Mexico
performed once in 2014

COG•NATE COLLECTIVE

Tijuana, Mexico / Santa Ana, CA / Los Angeles, CA
cognate.collective@gmail.com
cognatecollective.com / dialogintransit.com

DIALOGUE IN TRANSIT: EVOLUTION OF A LINE // DIALOGO EN TRANSITO: EVOLUCION DE UNA LINEA
COG•NATE COLLECTIVE

There are inherent connections and separations made when drawing a line across a plane. A line, after all is a link between two isolated points. But, if the distance between the points is large enough, the line drawn causes a separation in the plane, dividing it into two parts: a "this side" and "the other."

Connection and separation often occur simultaneously. On Saturday March 15, Cog•nate Collective organized a mobile conference to reflect on one such line: the U.S./Mexico border.

"Dialogue in Transit: Evolution of a Line // Diálogo en Tránsito: Evolución de una Línea" brought together researchers and artists from San Diego and Tijuana, to reflect on the evolution of the border's ideological and physical manifestations 20 years since the implementation of NAFTA (the North American Free Trade Agreement) and three years after redevelopment began at the San Ysidro Port of Entry. Unlike other conferences held to "celebrate" the anniversary of NAFTA, this conversation critically reflected on the ramifications of its implementation at both the national and local level. The conversation traced intersections across the different scales represented by these milestones, engaging both the abstract dimension of borders on a macro scale and their palpable experience in micro-sites like the San Ysidro Port of Entry—the busiest land entry in the world—with over 50 thousand cars, 54 thousand pedestrians and $1 billion dollars in commerce crossing every day.

The conference took place in a caravan of vehicles as they waited in line to cross the border from Tijuana to San Diego, and was live-broadcast on a pirate radio frequency (87.9 FM) at the Port of Entry from inside of the "Cognate Cruiser," a station wagon painted as part of a previous intervention at the border by Peru Dyer of En Masse (Montreal), Eric Wixon (San Diego) and HEM Crew (Tijuana). Speakers included Professor Norma Iglesias-Prieto, Professor Victor Clark Alfaro, Tijuana artist and poet Omar Pimienta, and long-time border shop-owner and vendor Juan Manuel Torres. As part of the intervention, Sonidero Travesura played a live musical set from the roof of the Mercado de Artesanías de La Línea as well.

The final phase of the "Dialogue in Transit" project was the publication of a workbook featuring bilingual transcripts of the conversation, distributed to pedestrians waiting in line at the San Ysidro Port of Entry in September.

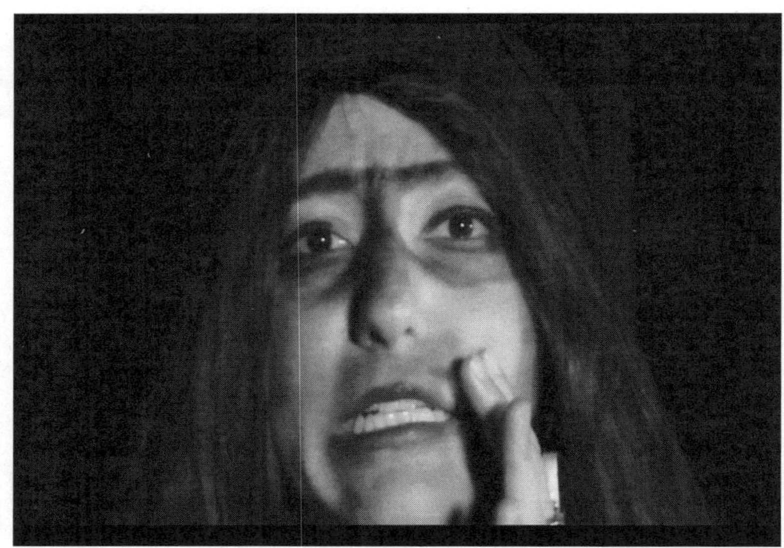

CRYING BLOOD
first performed on March 15, 2014
University of California, San Diego, San Diego, CA
performed six times in 2014

ELMIRA MOHEBALI

San Diego, CA

CRYING BLOOD
ELMIRA MOHEBALI

"Crying Blood" is a performance created for the camera. Staring into the camera, I paint my face with lipstick while impassionedly reciting a self-written, true story based on my personal experience as an Iranian woman. The story is recited in Persian (Farsi) and subtitled in English.

I was born and raised in Tehran, Iran. During my twenties, when I was an art student at Art College of Tehran, my integrity was challenged by multiple betrayals. Later on, I found similarities between my Iranian life experiences and Mesopotamian mythology. In the Mesopotamian "Epic of Gilgamesh" the goddess Ishtar is outraged by Gilgamesh's whimsical behavior. These whimsical behaviors take the form of social and judiciary law in contemporary Muslim societies. In some societies men can legally obtain up to four wives. Such social norms and laws for centuries have left women powerless and frustrated with agony and jealousy.

In "Crying Blood" I refer to this socially controversial issue common among Iranians and attempt to address them by representing Ishtar and raising her revengeful voice. By staring into the camera in a close up, I escalate the intensity and sensitivity of the issue discussed. The title of the performance also directs the reaction of the female community to the issue of polygamy.

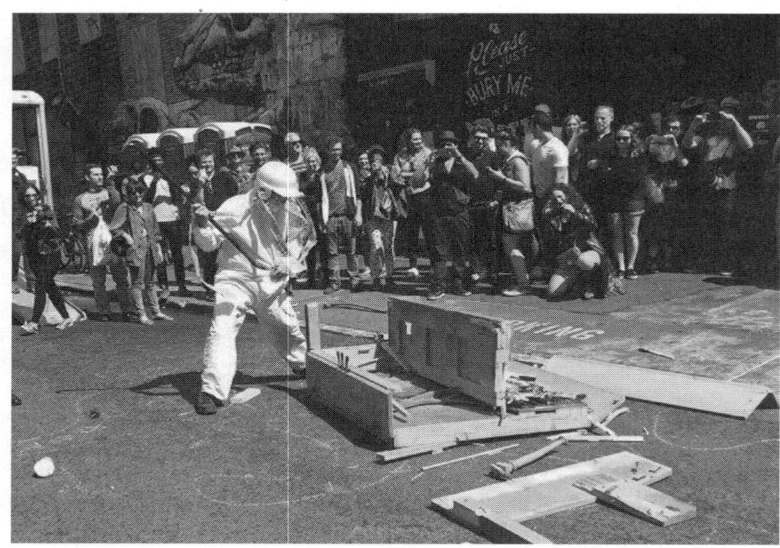

Jeffery Young

PIANO SONATA #...

first performed on March 20, 2014
Spread Art @detroit Contemporary, Detroit, MI
performed three times in 2014

THOMAS BELL

Detroit, MI
thomas@spreadart.org / info@spreadart.org
twin72.com / spreadart.org

PIANO SONATA #...
THOMAS BELL

"Piano Sonata #..." is an ongoing performance work that explores the relationship between the artist and the instrument through the simultaneous destruction of one instrument (the piano) and the creation of a new sound sculpture (piano soundboard). Having taken piano lessons for one year at age 16 but never continuing after and therefore not really "knowing" how to "play" the piano, I became frustrated with the lack of follow through with the piano lessons and practice. Although I studied Jazz Performance at Berklee College of Music (bass) and then Ethnomusicology at Florida State University as well as playing music professionally throughout my 20s, I still cannot "play" the piano as I would like to. Turning my practice towards visual art in my 30s and then performance art in my late 30s, I began to experiment with creating sound sculptures through performance and performance art.

"Piano Sonata #..." combines performance, music and art by creating a new sculpture through the performance act of completely destroying the piano and breaking it down to just the sound board which is then recreated into a sound sculpture. The frustrations of never learning how to "play" the piano are expressed through the physical destruction of the piano, sometimes violent and sometimes precise and methodical. The satisfaction of creating a new sound sculpture more than makes up for not knowing how to "play" the piano.

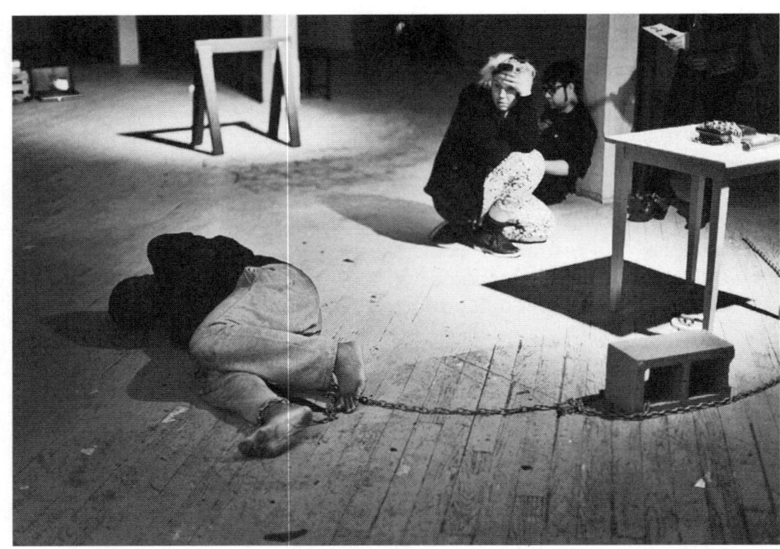

CHRYSALIS [CRY-SOLACE]
first performed on March 21, 2014
Grace Exhibition Space, Brooklyn, NY
performed once in 2014

PREACH R SUN

Kansas City, MO / New York, NY
preachrsun@gmail.com
iamfugitive.com

CHRYSALIS [CRY-SOLACE]
PREACH R SUN

How does one liberate himself in a society of sleeping slaves? This is my life's mission and praxis. "CHRYSALIS [CRY-SOLACE]" marks my evolution.

FOUR ACTIONS…

I) I sat in front of a television watching a video reflecting the enslavement of society through capitalism while drinking a gallon of red Kool-Aid. I vomited the Kool-Aid into a large bucket, extracted the red liquid with a turkey baster, squirted it into a jar and sold it to a man for $1.00.

II) A Chain, master lock, black chalk and two cassette recorders sat on a table. I wrote, "FREE SPEECH," on the table and wrapped one recorder in chains and locked it. I then pressed play on that recorder and Charlie Brown's, incoherently babbling, teacher blared out, "WAH-WAH." With the other recorder, I walked around the space recording the comments of the audience. I then returned to the table, rewound the tape and pressed play. As they all gathered to listen I took a hammer and commenced to smash the recorder until the voices were silenced.

III) There was a station set up with a straitjacket and a large cinder block attached to a long truck chain with two large padlocks. There on the floor I wrote, "American Dream Action Playset." I was strapped into the straitjacket (by an audience member). I took the chain and wrapped it around both of my ankles securing it with the padlocks. Lying on the floor I proceeded to crawl through the space while dragging the cinder block and repeatedly crying out, "RUN NIGGER!" After about an hour of this, audience members intervened in a desperate attempt to free me. One participant took a hammer and smashed the concrete block; others followed, trying to break the chains.

VI) Naked, I entered a large box. I stayed in the box for about an hour before emerging. Sliding (headlong) between the lips of my own gaping mouth, I was reborn covered in blood. There was an umbilical cord attached to my penis filled with Juju seeds. I bit through the cord to free myself and then I walked through the crowd spreading my seeds along the way. I arrived at a white wall. Kneeling before it, I lit four white candles and placed a crown of thorns, made of white light, upon my bloody head. Then, I stood and scribbled in blood, upon that white wall, the words, "I AM FUGITIVE."

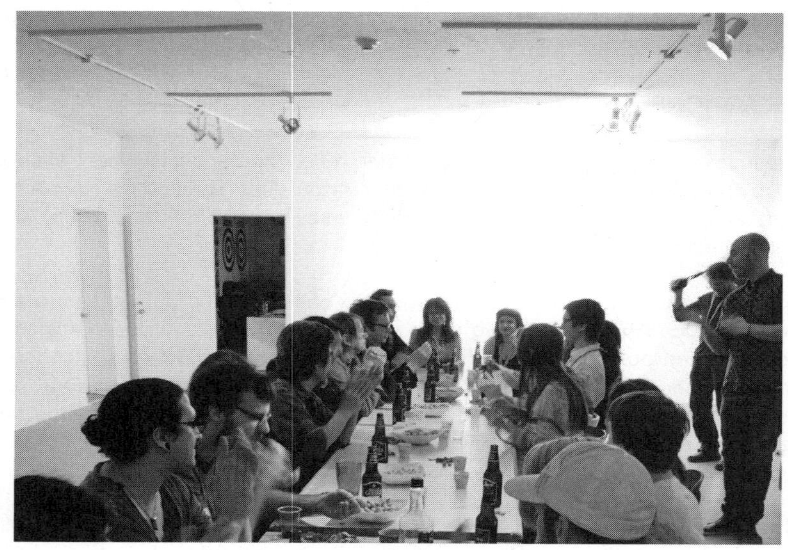

ANTI ACTION AS ANTIMATTER
first performed on March 21, 2014
Le Lieu Art Center, Quebec City, Canada
performed once in 2014

MICHEL COLLET

Besançon / Paris, France
montagne.froide@wanadoo.fr
michelcolletcopy.com / blagobung.org

ANTI ACTION AS ANTIMATTER
MICHEL COLLET

this is a piece of art action that he named anti action he uses the word art action because the word performance doesn't really exist in his mother tongue he asks us to note that this nonexistence has a direct consequence on the situation in his mother tongue performance means "exploit" anti action isn't an "exploit" anti action is special it's a mirror action that is taking place he calls it anti like antimatter anti doesn't mean "against" we speak about antimatter when it has to do with space particles stars a special void that separates them that brings them together spin around in the same space unless that space is different disunited anti action is the negative the symmetry or almost the symmetry of the action as the antimatter is the opposite of the matter the opposite spins it isn't an "anticoncept" it's about the presence and the action spin anti action is present anti action is a low key presence it's a potential that is charged and discharged anti action isn't a hole it isn't an interval anti action as antimatter isn't an absence it's a negative action that happened the presence in anti action needs a real effort we are completely involved we are not attending anti action because it isn't a show it doesn't have a surface nor volume nor limits nor greatness neither beginning nor end nor edge nor highness nor foundation spin nor gestures spin nor movement nor entry nor exit nor exactly a place but the combination of all those when the far is the close spin no time no actor no spectator no witness no beauty spin no force no peace no meaning spin anti action is a symmetry of images it's an experience aroused anti action is neither present nor absent it continues from here or a little bit before with some luck

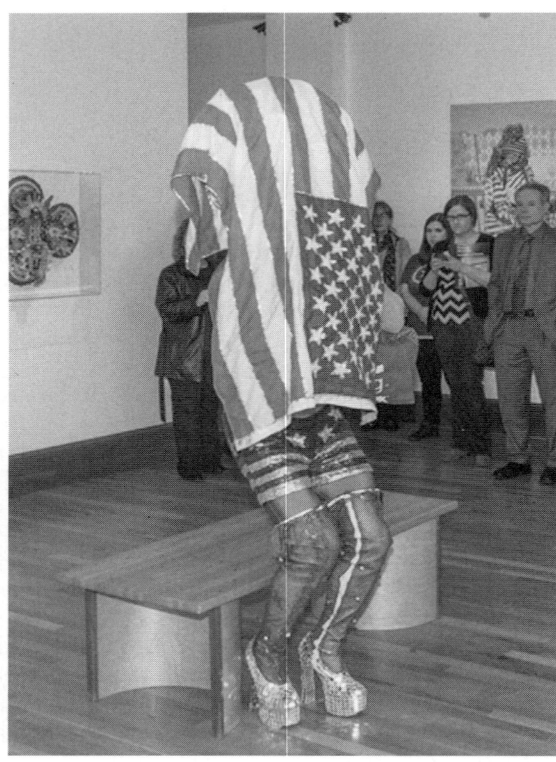

BE EXCESSIVE!

first performed on April 3, 2014
Northern Illinois University Art Museum, DeKalb, IL
performed once in 2014

ROBERT REED

Honolulu, HI / New York, NY
bertie2lulu@gmail.com
fabulousrobertreed.com

BE EXCESSIVE!
ROBERT REED

"BE EXCESSIVE!" was performed for the reception of the exhibition Hoarding, Amassing and Excess. It addressed our battle to reverse the destruction of land, air, water, health and culture in the United States due to excessive consumption and product promotion. I sat in the middle of the room with a sequined American flag over my head while people viewed the artwork. I was wearing a green body suit underneath a pair of sequined American flag shorts and matching bustier. I also had on go-go boots covered in disco ball mirrors and a pair of glasses shaped like dollar signs. I loudly moaned and threw litter about the room and sang a parody of "Bein' Green" followed by parodies of iconic American songs. For example, "If I Had a Hammer" became: "If I had a baby, I'd buy him a happy meal. I'd supersize his cola all over Disneyland. I'd ring out danger and give him a handgun. I'd tweet out hate between my brothers and my sisters and be too busy to give a damn."

This led into the song "America The Beautiful," ending with the verse "from sea to shining"…"Gimme a C! Gimme an O! Gimme an N! Gimme an S! Gimme a U! Gimme an M! Gimme an E! What does it spell? CONSUME! Go CONSUME! Go HOARDING! GO AMASSING!"

I then reached into my bustier to grab pompoms made from fast food wrappers and cheered, "E-X-C-E-S-S-I-V-E! BE EXCESSIVE, BE, BE EXCESSIVE! What do we want? EVERYTHING! When do we want it? NOW! What do we waste? EVERYTHING! When do we regret it? NOW!"

I ended by dancing around singing the 70's disco hit, "More, More, More, how do you like it, how do you like it?"

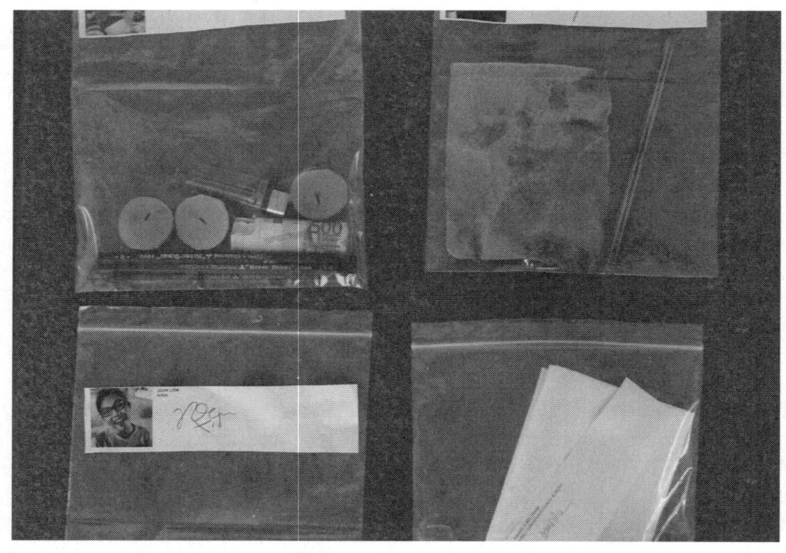

PENCIL SHARPENER

first performed on April 6, 2014
Earshot Café The The Arts House at The Old Parliament, Singapore
performed once in 2014

CHEE WEI TECK

Daniela Beltrani, Kenneth Lee, Willis Turner Henry, Joan Low

Singapore
weiteckc@gmail.com
facebook.com/cheeweiteck

PENCIL SHARPENER
CHEE WEI TECK

An interactive performance art piece, which questions our identity as the World changes. Our social identities are not as clearly defined as before.

If I hand you a Pencil Sharpener:
Can I label your job as a Pencil Sharpener, due to the tool in your possession?
While the Pencil is used for the creation of something, it dies; but it lives on via what was created.

Four artists are invited to be part of this performance, each with a different way to sharpen their pencil. As they do this, they share with the audience their story or memory about pencils.

This experimental performance was created with multiple presentation options:
(1) Monologue; (2) Audience Participation; (3) Artists Participation

The piece was designed to be a platform for an artist that is not of a performance background to engage and explore. For the performance on April 6 2014, two participating artists had performance experience while two other are new to the performance art genre. This performance was structured so that the outcome would differ with different participants.

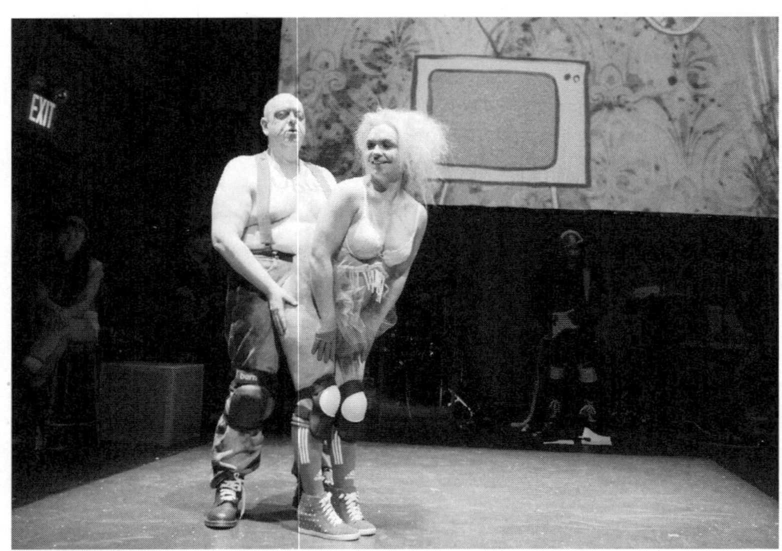

Max Basch

UBU SINGS UBU
first performed on April 9, 2014
Abrons Arts Center, New York, NY
performed fifteen times in 2014

TONY TORN / DAN SAFER / JULIE ATLAS MUZ
Vera Beren, Emmitt Joe George, Matt Butterfield, Patrick Conlon, Freddie Katz, Kaz PS, Deb O,
Jay Ryan, Katie Ingram, Sarah Ramen, Ed-den Perlove

New York, NY
ubu.sings.ubu@gmail.com
ubu-sings-ubu.com

UBU SINGS UBU
TONY TORN / DAN SAFER / JULIE ATLAS MUZ

"Ubu Sings Ubu" was a merging of Alfred Jarry's classic comic french play "Ubu Roi" with the songs of cult band Pere Ubu. Tony Torn and Julie Atlas Muz played Pa and Ma Ubu, backed by a live band (Vera Beren, Emmitt Joe George, Matt Butterfield and Patrick Conlon) who also played supporting roles. Torn adapted the original text using Google Translate. He co-directed the play with Dan Safer, who also choreographed and wore a bear suit in order to wrestle Pa Ubu to death at every performance. Katie Ingram and Sarah Ramen played dancing "Ubettes" while Stephen Boyer and Kelvin Daly alternated as bartenders. Video design was by Kaz PS, set and costumes by Deb O, lights by Jay Ryan and live sound mixing by Freddie Katz.

The piece for me was all about alchemy. The play has often been dismissed as a historical curiosity and the band as simply a commercial nonentity with a small cult following. By combining these two forces in a very collaborative working environment, we created something with a great deal of vitality. We brought a sense of danger to the New York theater scene that has been somewhat missing since the days of Reza Abdoh and Ethyl Eichelberger. I also believe "Ubu Sings Ubu" is the only time that "Ubu Roi" has ever worked as a love story.

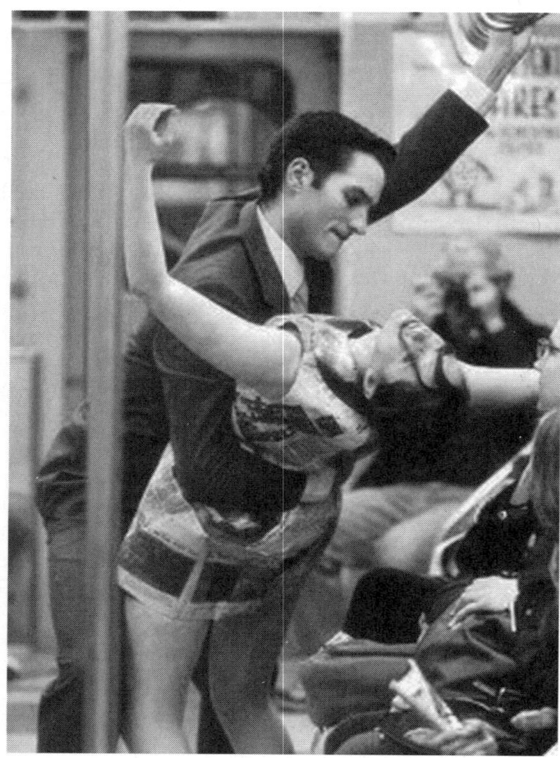

NEIL

first performed on April 10, 2014
New York Transit Museum, Brooklyn, NY
performed once in 2014

CARTE BLANCHE PERFORMANCE / SHANDOAH GOLDMAN

Julien Delbasse Leflon, Asa B. Thornton, Christopher North

Brooklyn, NY
shandoahg@gmail.com
carteblancheperformance.com

NEIL

CARTE BLANCHE PERFORMANCE / SHANDOAH GOLDMAN

"Neil"—an immersive, surreal, evocative and historical dance theater piece—takes place in a 1963 subway car at the New York Transit Museum.

As if reading the news on his daily commute, a gentlemen 'reads' a woman costumed in a paper period dress made of newspaper from the day Neil Armstrong walked on the moon. A duet unfolds exploring private space, public space and outer space.

The piece explores the private act of reading the newspaper while in transit as a metaphor for "going somewhere," the idea of collectively gaining information through private contemplative moments and the juxtaposition of transportation to near and far space via a moment in history when everyone was watching in awe.

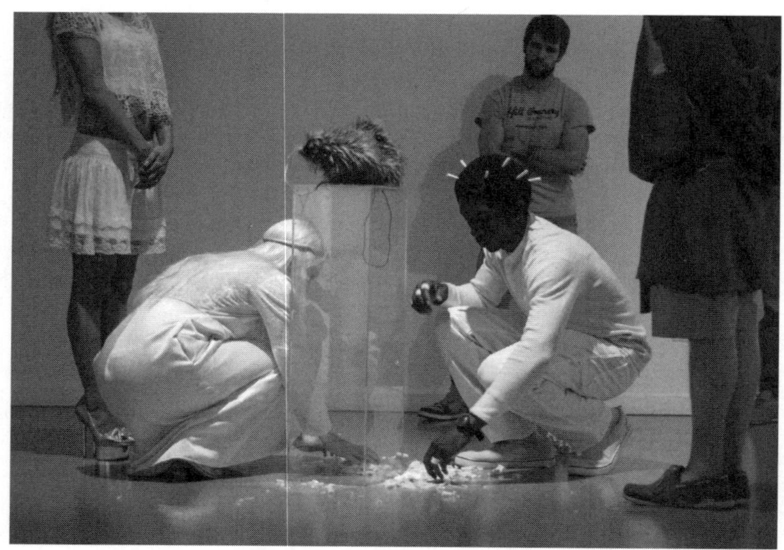

ACTION 27 / ELIXIR
first performed on April 11, 2014
The Gallery at UTA, Arlington, TX
performed once in 2014

ALISON STARR
Wesley Salazar, Uzoma Attah, Lita Bush, Paula Tabares, Lindsay Lookingbill, Matt Clark, Ezra Thomas

Dallas, TX
alison@alisonstarr.org
astarrstudios.wordpress.com

ACTION 27 / ELIXIR
ALISON STARR

Foucault mentioned in one of his texts that the wondrous cabbage often appears in paintings. Why the cabbage? Many write that its mystical powers have the potential to aid us in times of intense desire and need. Thus this interesting yet absurd idea inspires this equally absurd performance that looks at the mystical powers of the cabbage.

An acrylic pedestal is set in a gallery room. Because there is no "set stage" viewers simply gather around. An entourage enters the room: a barefoot King Ezra wearing a red silk bathrobe, white tank-top and hair awry is followed by attendant one (carrying a white cabbage head atop a velvet pillow) and attendant two (carrying a large antique cleaver). The king stands behind the acrylic pedestal and the attendants flank to the right and left of him. Atop a 13 ft ladder is the jester who chooses lovers for the king. First choice is a lovely lady with long brown hair. But the king is not interested and she is banished from the space. Second choice is a handsome man dressed in fine attire. Yet alas, he too is banished from the room. Finally the jester chooses a blond, long legged young woman wearing a dull sweater. Once presented to the king the jester flings off her sweater to reveal a svelte body. Pleased the king gives her a thumbs-up and the ritual begins. Attendant one brings the cabbage and attendant two brings the cleaver. The king—while watching the blonde bombshell—chops the head of cabbage before her eyes, nearly missing his finger. The king then slowly and calculatingly slices smaller pieces of cabbage on the pedestal. Once the entire head is cut into very small portions, the attendants are directed to pick up every single slice and place them in a fur pouch that resembles a vagina. The vagina bag is given to the blond who must stand there for several minutes while the king and attendants leave the room. Five minutes later the king returns, flinging off his silk robe and escorts the bombshell out.

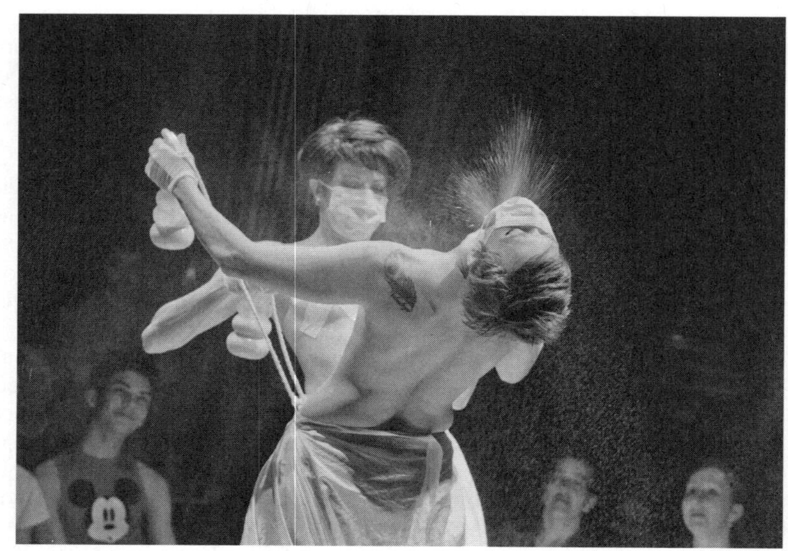

MILK AKA WHITENESS REVISED PART 4

first performed on April 11, 2014
The Englert Theatre Ten Tiny Performances, Iowa City, IA
performed three times in 2014

BAKER & TARPAGA DANCE PROJECT / ESTHER BAKER-TARPAGA

Lindsay Fisher, Sali Kobre

Philadelphia & Pittsburgh, PA / Ouagadougou, Burkina Faso
bakertarpagadance@gmail.com
btdanceproject.com

MILK AKA WHITENESS REVISED PART 4
BAKER & TARPAGA DANCE PROJECT / ESTHER BAKER-TARPAGA

Purpose:
Female bodies, motherhood, sexuality, race, Ebola, white privilege

Description:
Short performance piece with twin personas, milk bottles, a large white skirt, x tape over the breasts, flowers, white plastic gloves and surgical masks.

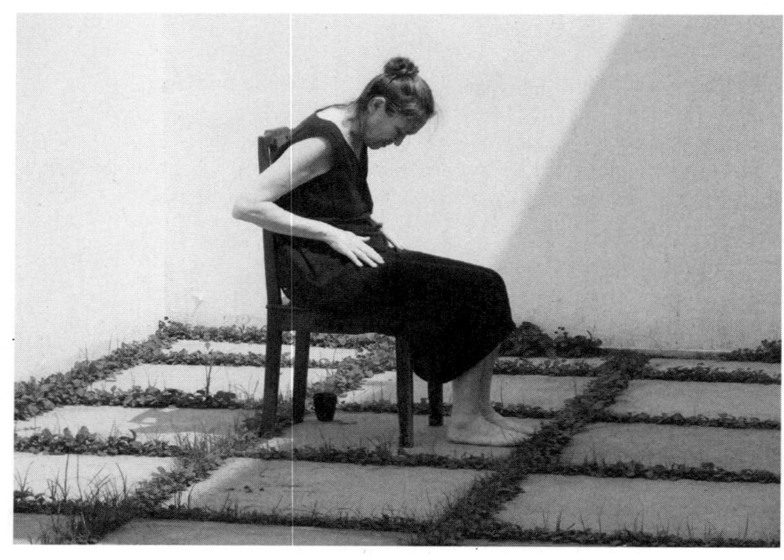

MARKED TIME: TRACING SHADOWS
first performed on April 12, 2014
Jockey Club Creative Arts Centre, Hong Kong, China
performed once in 2014

MARILYN ARSEM

Boston, MA
contact@marilynarsem.net
marilynarsem.net

MARKED TIME: TRACING SHADOWS
MARILYN ARSEM

I generally create long durational performances, but for the Festival of Performance Art in Hong Kong I was asked to make a 30-minute performance. The festival was the culmination of the week long Performance Art Laboratory Project that included 25 international artists.

In keeping with my practice, I didn't arrive in Hong Kong with a plan for what I would do. Instead I intended to create a performance in response to the site. Throughout the week we had been meeting in a converted factory building, home to a number of art related businesses and studios, so I had several days to consider the different locations that were possible to use for my performance. The place that intrigued me the most (and that I chose to use for my performance) was on the eighth floor with a space open to the sky and a covered area at one side. The floor was made of cement squares, outlined in vibrant green grass.

My initial visit to the space was in the pouring rain, but then the weather cleared and I began to consider it differently. The light of the space was nearly blinding when the sun shone on the white painted walls and I was struck by the shadows cast by the structural elements of the space.

I discovered that if I set my chair on a certain square in the space I would be fully lit in bright sunlight at 2 pm before a shadow would move from my toes, rise up my legs, up my body and pass over my head so that I was completely covered in darkness by exactly 2:30 pm.

The audience entered at 2 pm, sitting under the covered area, looking at me sitting in a chair in the glaring light, waiting for the performance to begin. In time they noticed that the performance had, in fact, already started.

With the tips of my fingers I traced the line of darkness that slowly moved up my body.

The sun performed.

At 2:30 pm, when I was fully engulfed in the shadow, I left.

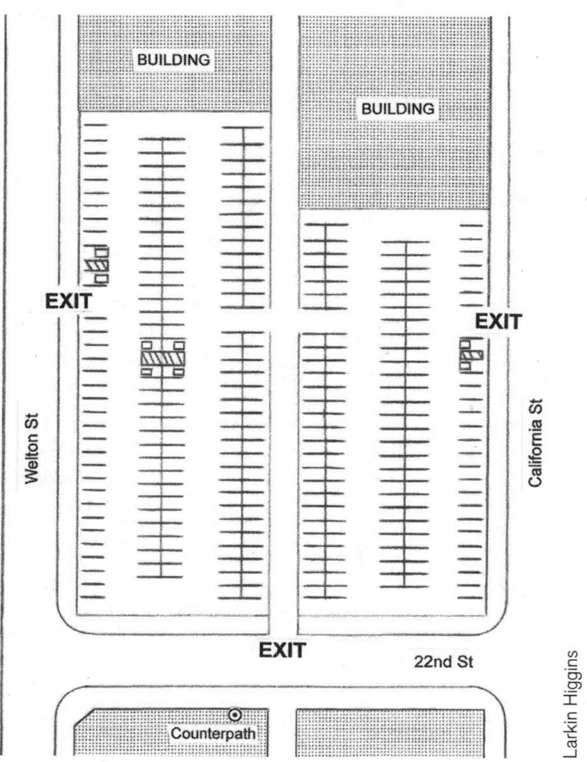

PARKING LOT LINES

first performed on April 14, 2014
A parking lot across the street from Counterpath Press, Denver, CO
performed once in 2014

LARKIN HIGGINS

Los Angeles, CA
wordimage2@gmail.com
counterpathpress.blogspot.com/2014/05/larking-higginss-parking-lot-lines.html

PARKING LOT LINES
LARKIN HIGGINS

The original instructions for "Parking Lot Lines" were hand-lettered onto architecture title block vellum and a paper blueprint was created—a "plan" for space and language. This blueprint, outlining the durational performance, was exhibited as a "wall artwork" first (1994), but never performed. Twenty years later the blueprint was displayed in my exhibit at Counterpath Press. A parking lot located directly across the street—and an invitation to fully engage the performance:

1. Select a parking lot, preferably one fully occupied at least part of the day.
2. Select a written story, original or previously published.
3. Photocopy the story as many times as there are spaces in the parking lot.
4. On the first photocopy, draw a line through all the sentences except the first one. On the second photocopy, line through all but the second sentence. Continue this sequential process until the last line. If more "unlined" photocopies remain, repeat until every sheet of paper is "lined."
5. Place one "lined" photocopy on each car windshield in the parking lot.
6. During a 24 hour period (or other time frame of choice), collect these photocopies in the same sequence as cars depart from the lot.
7. Record each "unlined" sentence in chronological order to form a revised story.

A dilemma—the parking lot had three exits. A Denver writer, Eric Siegel, volunteered to oversee one. After "essay-flyers" were placed on car windshields, smartphone stopwatches were synchronized. With pen in hand, we waited to gather story pages, then wrote down each receiving time in minutes/seconds. I managed two exits, running/walking back and forth between them. Collection duration time: 4-6:30 pm on a Monday. The purpose was not to assault people after their nine to five work day, tired and ready to go home. "PLEASE …This is an artwork you are helping to complete" was handwritten on top. As an observer, this became a sociological study with respect for entering people's private time in a public space, which then merged into a temporary social space. Coincidentally, the re-ordered text began, "The public gathers in two kinds of spaces."

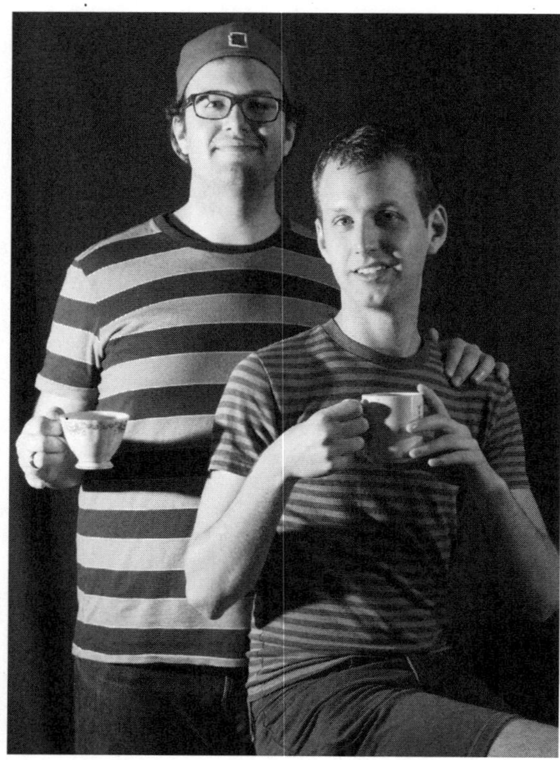

THE FAMILY ROOM
first performed on April 14, 2014
UCSD Conrad Prebys Music Center Experimental Theatre, San Diego, CA
performed once in 2014

TODD MOELLENBERG
Nicolee Kuester, Brett Moellenberg, Matthew Savitsky

San Diego, CA
tmm884@gmail.com
toddpiano.com

THE FAMILY ROOM
TODD MOELLENBERG

As a concert pianist specializing in avant-garde music, I have become increasingly active in questioning my role as an interpreter as well as the framework of the performances I offer. "The Family Room" juxtaposed memorized solo piano music that I performed (pieces by Rozalie Hirs and Katharina Rosenberger) with text pieces performed from memory by Savitsky, Kuester, and my brother Brett, written by both Kuester and myself. We removed all of the seating from the black box theatre and installed moveable set pieces built by Savitsky. Each of us wore a costume and adopted a static persona for these performances. While retaining the act of memorization and compartmentalization of each different piece on the "program," this performance critiqued music recital conventions by not only beckoning the audience to move around the space during the performance, but also by involving text, theatricality and exploring the idea of a family formed by this improbable group of characters.

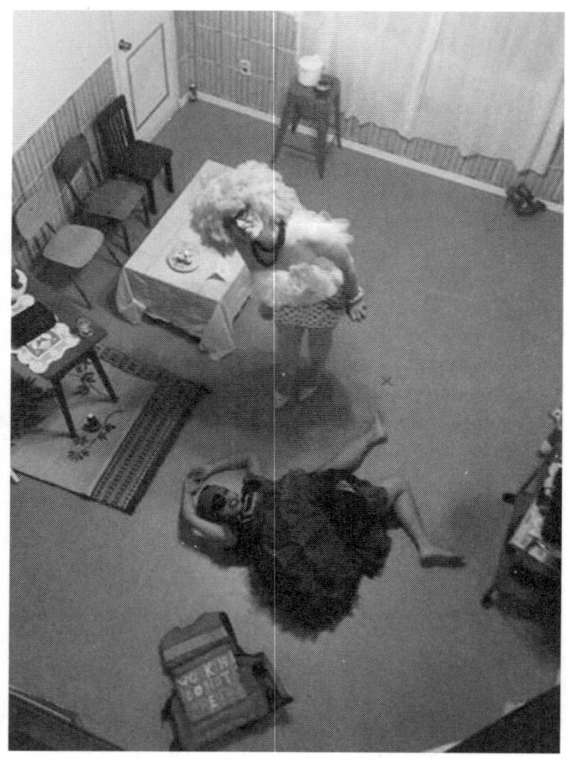

Ani Taj Niemann

YOU MAY MEET HER

first performed on April 18, 2014
Abrons Arts Center, New York, NY
performed 56 times in seven days in 2014

ZHENESSE HEINEMANN

New York, NY
me@zhenesse.com
zhenesse.com

YOU MAY MEET HER
ZHENESSE HEINEMANN

"You May Meet Her" is an IRL RPG centered on a blind playdate with a socially anxious extrovert, her house and her hired help. An entirely immersive and interactive installation "You May Meet Her" is set with 60-plus action items that, once triggered, activate a response that may delight the (singular) guest and voyeurs on the lawn. "You May Meet Her" is in an experiment in embodied encounters in a progressively digital social age, choice, if/then scenarios, social contract, etiquette, danger and safety in unfamiliar situations and surprises.

Ms. Connections, a non-verbal clown who suffers from loneliness and papers her walls with Yellow Pages pages to comfort herself, is reading *The Seven Habits of Highly Effective People* and practicing pro-activity; so she has moved her entire house to the Abrons Underground, hired entertainment, procured snacks, and engaged staff in order to properly, and safely, receive unknown guests.

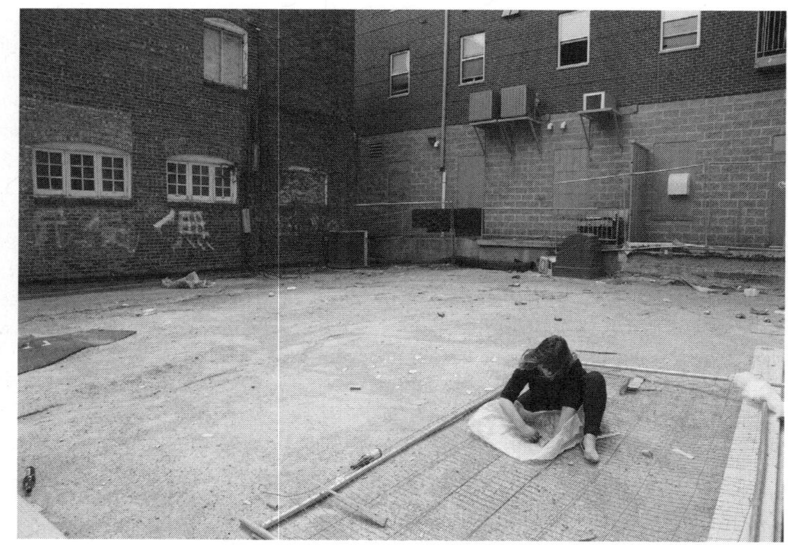

RESIDUE

first performed on April 19, 2014
Vacant Lot, 9 S Linn St, Iowa City, IA
performed once in 2014

AMY LENERS

Chicago, IL
amy@amyleners.com
amyleners.com

RESIDUE
AMY LENERS

The Van Patten House, a longstanding architectural icon of downtown Iowa City, burned down in the fall of 2011 consuming all of my possessions and entire body of work. "Residue" is a site-specific performance that examines my autobiographical experience and the effect of architecture and space on our psyche. The eight-hour performance took place in the vacant lot where my home use to stand and the only audience members were passersby.

"Residue" began as I filled the space with sheets of handmade abaca paper. I chose to use abaca for its strength, translucency and sound. The sheets emitted a low constant crackle as I began to take rubbings of the objects that were left in the space. I recorded the residue of what was left of the historic structure, my belongings, and what had been carelessly tossed over the chain link fence. After many hours I had compiled what was effectively a grave rubbing of the entire footprint of the house.

After completing the rubbings I began to clean the vacant lot. I sorted the trash and recycling, pulled weeds and piled bricks. My movements were methodical, meditative and ritualistic. I felt the need to attempt to heal the space, to bring it back from invisibility and neglect, and to be with its pain, as well as my own. The detritus that was collected was eventually transformed into handmade paper and used in subsequent performances and artworks.

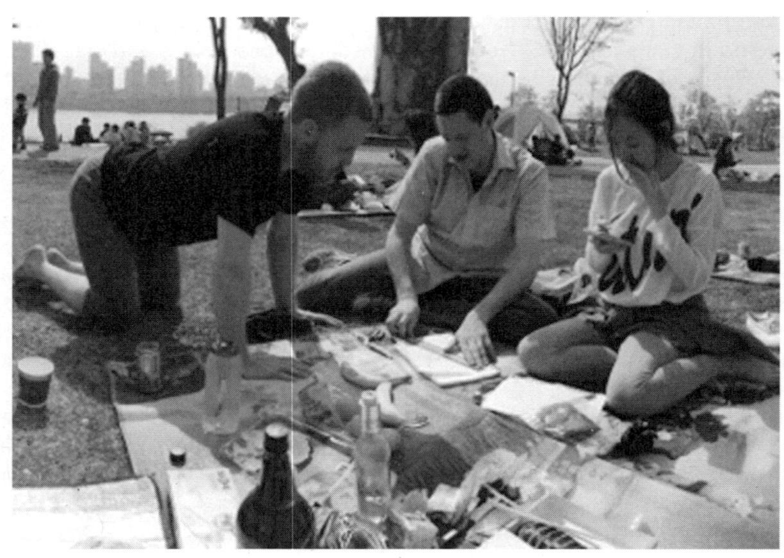

EVERYTHING HAPPENS IN A PICNIC
first performed on April 20, 2014
Han River, Seoul, South Korea
performed once in 2014

ERIC SCOT NELSON / YOKO ISHIGURO

Korea / USA / UK / Japan
yoko_jimmysparty@yahoo.co.jp
ishiguroyoko.info/iroiro/Everything_Happens_In_a_Picnic.html

EVERYTHING HAPPENS IN A PICNIC
ERIC SCOT NELSON / YOKO ISHIGURO

"Everything Happens in a Picnic" is an outdoor performance event which happens precisely in the format of a picnic—we go to a park, choose a nice spot, wait for the late comers, get bored of waiting for them, open a bottle, drink, open a basket, eat sandwiches, open plastic bags you grabbed from a corner shop, eat the unhealthiest snacks, start Frisbee and badminton, notice the text message from the late comers who has got lost totally and hopelessly, some strangers come and ask where their dog is gone, someone starts to play the guitar, people sings to the guitar but nobody remembers the lyrics of the song properly, but nobody cares about it, some people gets bitten by a mosquito and scratch all the parts of their bodies restlessly, someone spills an amount of beer on the picnic mat and make a pool of beer on it and someone unaware sits down on it and scream, a dog barks to it, a couple kiss while their bikes are being stolen, the sun is setting and the temperature goes down and we go home. "Everything Happens in a Picnic" is a picnic-specific performance event in which each individual performer will be installed in a section of the picnic events to show the picnic-specific performances. The performances are very small-scaled. The audience join the picnic on a whenever-they-can basis with a bottle or food, and leave in the same way. The duration of the pieces depends on the artists but the picnic itself is in the afternoon, only while the picnickers can have the nice sun and heat.

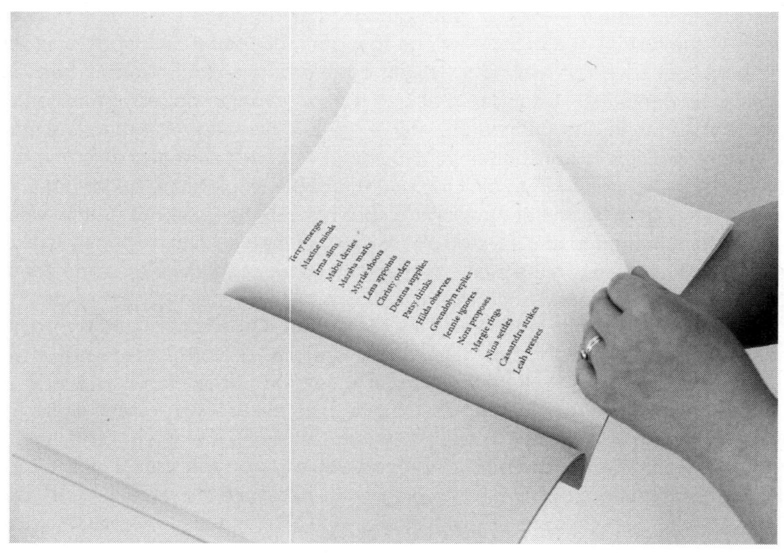

Greg Lookerse

JAYNE TELEPHONES

first performed on April 20, 2014
Presenting at 17, New York, NY
performed twice in 2014

SARAH RUSHFORD

Boston, MA
sarah@sarahrushford.com
sarahrushford.com / presenting-at-17.tumblr.com

JAYNE TELEPHONES
SARAH RUSHFORD

"Jayne telephones" is a list of six-hundred most commonly used women's names (derived from the 1990 US census) paired with the six-hundred most commonly used verbs. The pairs are listed in order of their ranking beginning first with the most common. The list begins with "Mary is" and ends with "Christi devotes." The list is bound in a newsprint book that resembles a catalog or telephone book and is passed among a group of participants who read it aloud.

"Jayne telephones" is both one of the pairs in the list and the title of the performance. The odd specificity of this alternative spelling points to the destined-seeming quality of every name in the list, alternative spelling or not. It also points towards the historic emergence of women into professional work as organizers and vehicles of information (such as librarians, typists, archivists, secretaries and telephone operators) who are discouraged from outward comment, yet wield the power of subverting meaning through subtextual or extratextual means.

The performances to date have been contemplative and charged with the genuine emotional and intellectual engagement of the participants and punctuated by moments of humor. (For example, "Dawn breaks" and "Crystal watches" are coincidental pairs.)

The work presents a defined framework of meaning and is an invitation to use this framework to cast associative lines of meaning that lead to deeply personal, nuanced feeling.

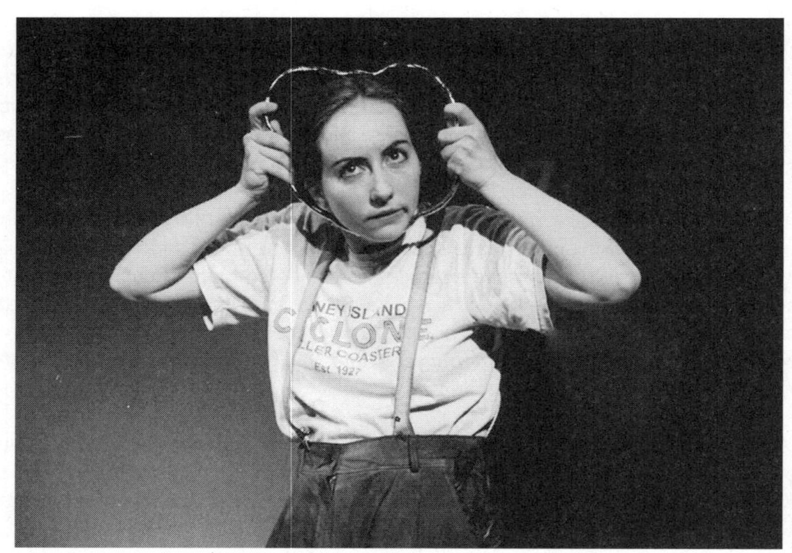

Max Lakner

SIGN FELT! (A SHOW ABOUT NOTHINGNESS)

first performed on April 22, 2014
La Mama E.T.C., New York, NY
performed eight times in 2014

ALEXANDRA TATARSKY

David Lansdowne

New York, NY
show.about.nothing.ness@gmail.com
tar-tar.biz

SIGN FELT! (A SHOW ABOUT NOTHINGNESS)
ALEXANDRA TATARSKY

The piece began from a very bad pun. If Seinfeld is a show about nothing, then "SIGN FELT!" is a show about nothingness. And the possibility that jokes might save us from the banality of existence.

The play opens with me in a bathrobe, pacing back and forth, having worked very hard to prepare nothing. The audience is led in a rousing round of screaming. From this abyss, I begin my "adaptation" of Goethe's *Wilhelm Meister's Apprenticeship*, in which young Wilhelm is obsessed with the theater but not particularly good at it. He stays in his room making little shows with a clown (which he kills), a sock (who is depressed) and a necklace (on which he hangs himself). As Wilhelm takes to the streets to rant and ramble, words and worlds disintegrate all around him into letters, characters and fragments of plays.

I wanted to think about the *bildungsroman*; what it means to tell the story of the self, who gets to tell it and what it means to grow up and do something worthwhile on this earth.

The context was: I had been asked to perform a new full-length work for a festival of female solo performances during a moment when I was feeling great doubt in the value of my female solo performance. The play would address this problematic and it was truly a problem attic, a creaky roof brain in which I began to lose my wits. But if they were witty on the way out, then what's the problem? The context was a con artist text. Words seduced me and then ran off. Trying to make it (mmm-ache-it) and share it (sshhh-air-it). Shit! (Look, the air has gone out).

Through song, movement, puppetry, monologue and associative language improvisation, the piece follows: Wilhelm's mad logic as he loses his mind, seeking meaning on a planet that feels at once glorious, absurd and doomed. It is a verbal and physical reckoning with the paralyzing quality of a world as confusing and at times horrific as ours. I hope that it is liberating and energizing, for audience and performer, to go deeply into this place of uncertainty, to give it a tune and a texture, to make ecstatic fun of it. Not only to exorcise but to exercise our demons, to allow them space to work themselves out.

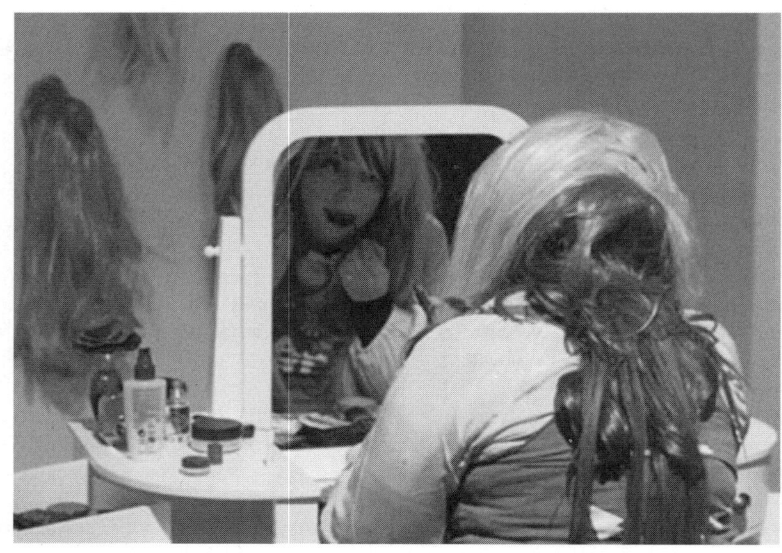

WRITING THE BODY
first performed on April 25, 2014
Des Lee Gallery, St. Louis, MO
performed once in 2014

KELLIE SPANO

San Francisco, CA / Dallas, TX
Kelliespano@gmail.com
kelliespano.com

WRITING THE BODY
KELLIE SPANO

I created this performance work as the culmination of a year long body of work which explored ideas of person vs persona, specifically when the camera lens was present. "WRITING THE BODY" is a three-hour-long performance piece meant to be performed live and for the public in an institutional setting. The first performance of "WRITING THE BODY" occurred the night of April. 25, 2014. I turned the camera on myself and my own personas by performing the act of getting dressed with all of the accompanying accessories for different personas that I possess; artist, partner, receptionist, yogi, etc. I layered each outfit (complete with different types of makeup, wigs and jewelry) on top of each other. The set was the entire contents of my bedroom from my actual bed to the paintings that hang on my bedroom walls. The piece, which began as humorous and light hearted, evolved into the struggle of a woman, trapped and disfigured by her own personas. The viewer saw an intimate moment in the performance of everyday life inside the private and vulnerable space of the bedroom.

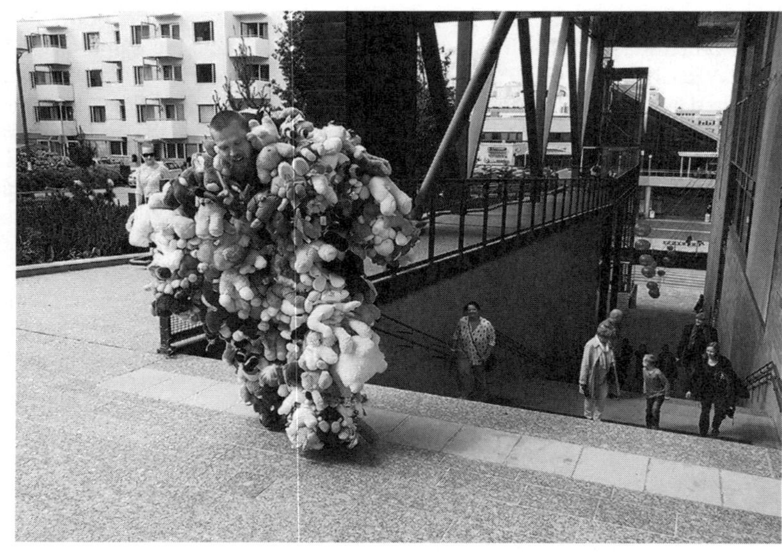

BODYCOUNT
first performed on April 26, 2014
Media Centre Lume, Helsinki, Finland
performed twice in 2014

HARRI PIISPANEN

Helsinki, Finland
harri.piispanen@gmail.com
harripiispanen.eu

BODYCOUNT
HARRI PIISPANEN

"Bodycount" was the first performance in a triptych of works. Each consisted of an object specifically made for each performance. The performances explored ways of presenting selfhood and identity in relation to death and the inevitable in three segments: as a consumer, in a time of crisis and within a funeral ceremony.

"Bodycount" is a performance that situates itself within a giant suit. Meticulously sewn by hand from hundreds of discarded cuddly toys, the suit resembles a cute, soft and colorful fur coat. However it weighs over 45 kilos and is uncomfortable, hot, rigid and next to impossible to wear, let alone to move in. Because only headless toys were used to make the suit, when worn the only head that appears is that of the performer.

In each of the two performances I attempted to wear the suit. It was initially performed inside the gallery of Lume Center in Helsinki. During it I managed to squirm inside the suit and a struggle to stand up ensued. Once finally standing I realized that getting out of it would be another struggle.

The second time it was performed outdoors in Espoon Keskus as a part of OBJECT, a contemporary sculpture, installation and environmental art exhibition. There I first dragged the suit inside the shopping mall Espoontori. After descending from the escalators to the plaza of the mall I squeezed myself into the suit, this time with the intention to actually walk while wearing it. From the plaza I managed to make my way through an adjacent shopping mall ending up inside the local community center where I finally allowed myself to peel the suit off.

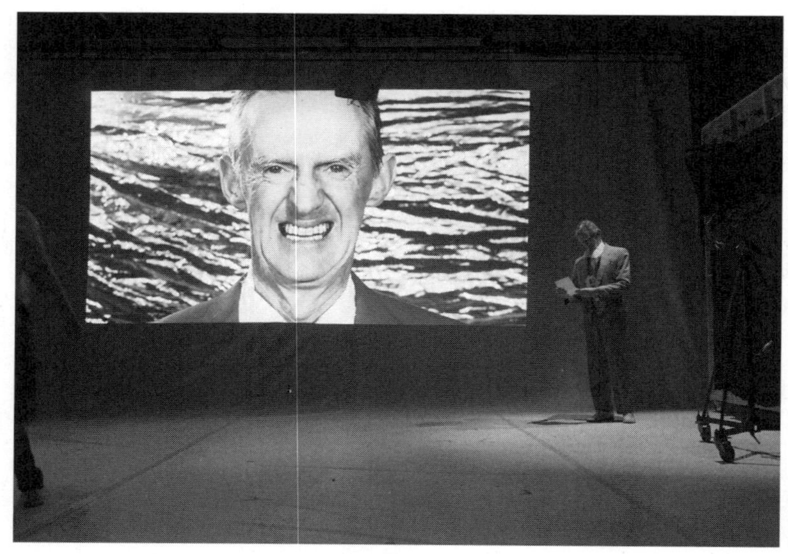

HELLO THERE, WE'VE BEEN WAITING FOR YOU

first performed on April 30, 2014
Australian Centre for the Moving Image Part of Next Wave Festival, Melbourne, Australia
performed twelve times in 2014

LOURIS VAN DE GEER

Samara Hersch, Aaron Orzech, Genevieve Giuffre, Susie Dee, Don Bridges, Amelia Lever-Davidson, Lucy Thornett, Eugyeene Teh, Justin Batchelor, James Paul, Ariadne Sgorous, Caitlyn Barclay, Sam Eddy

l.vandegeer@gmail.com

HELLO THERE, WE'VE BEEN WAITING FOR YOU
LOURIS VAN DE GEER

"Hello there, we've been waiting for you! It's time to play Truth or Consequences!"

A small town in the New Mexico desert changes its name to the name of a television game show called Truth or Consequences in the 1950s. Sixty years later, someone in a library in Australia tells me about the town and I book a plane ticket from Melbourne to attend the annual Truth or Consequences Fiesta. "Hello There, We've Been Waiting For You" is the play I wrote about this town. It's a play about wanting to be on the map, and staying there, about having a dream of something bigger and finding a way to get it, about transformation and remembering the past. The renaming of Truth or Consequences taps into a collective desire for immortality.

"Hello There, We've Been Waiting For You" pieces together the fragmented narratives of a town in New Mexico and a dated TV show to tell a new local narrative for Australians. The story of the town represents the fragility of identity, as well as the complexities that come when one tries to reinvent history and the disconnectedness that comes with the individualistic pursuit of being 'seen.'

In the play, worlds are erected and discarded, a room is only half a room and the laughter is only a recording. Unrelated scenes happen in and around each other to knit together the narrative of a society doing its best to be noticed. A young girl practices for the annual Truth or Consequences Beauty Pageant, an aging game show host fails to recognise himself in a mirror, people audition for their fifteen minutes of fame, stories are re-worked for the ratings and images appear on screens only to be replaced in the next frame.

The performance took place in a television studio in the Australian Centre for the Moving Image and consisted of live on-stage action as well as live and pre-recorded video footage. In creating and documenting this performance I continue the quest, like the residents of Truth or Consequences, to being remembered.

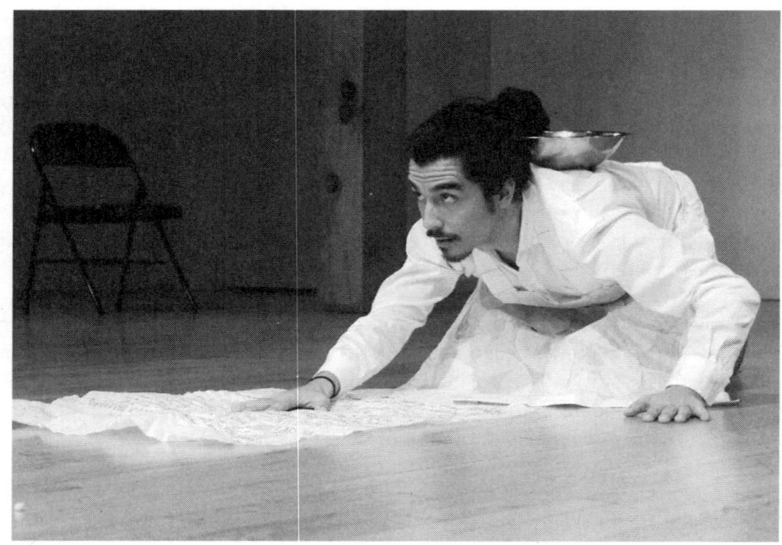

HOLD/RELEASE
first performed on May 1, 2014
Villa Victoria Center for the Arts, Boston, MA
performed twice in 2014

BENJAMIN LUNDBERG

New York City, NY / Providence, RI
benjofaman@gmail.com
jointhebenjam.org

HOLD/RELEASE
BENJAMIN LUNDBERG

"Hold/Release" was originally created for TODO BAJO CONTROL: MAY DAY, a performance extravaganza curated by Anabel Vázquez Rodríguez to commemorate International Workers' Day through the exploration of art as a "labor of love" ("por amor al arte") and the reframing of cultural production as a site of labor, struggle, wages and organization.

The piece embodies my relationship to two mothers: the woman who gave birth to me and the woman who adopted and raïsed me; to their labors; to mother countries: Colombia and The United States; to the bonds of debt that link me to each. In "Hold/Release" I ask, to what do we owe our making? And to what do owe our makers?

A silver bowl with two brown eggs rests in the middle of the space.

I enter pushing a custodial mop and bucket. I am wearing all white, including an apron sewn out of coffee filters, repurposed from my performance "Lundberg/Torres-Sanchez." I dip my mop in the water from the bucket and trace a large circle around the bowl, while humming "Mother" by John Lennon and the Plastic Ono Band. I then stand behind the bowl and look at the audience while a third brown egg is slowly birthed from my mouth and lands in my cupped hands.

I speak text while holding the egg: I ask the audience to remember the day they were born, I speak of longing, of the story of my mother(s) and of "too much and not enough." I speak of debt. I then juggle the three eggs while running backwards and forwards. When two eggs are broken, I release the other towards the audience in a soft toss.

I fill the silver bowl with water using the mop and bucket. I get on all fours and ask a member of the audience to place the bowl on my back, revealing a poetic text scribed on another coffee filter surface. I crawl towards the broken eggs, using the poetic surface to clean them, inevitably obscuring the words I am attempting to read. Once the eggs have been scooped up, I use the mop to clean the entire floor of the space while speaking about the rebel mothers of the FARC, and a poetic version of my own adoption story.

I finish by singing Harry Nilsson's "Everbody's Talkin'" as I exit the space, pushing mop and bucket.

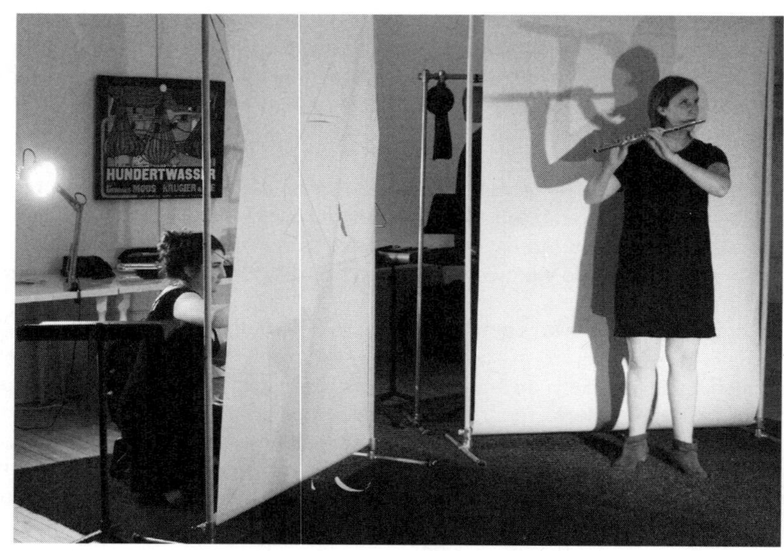

Flux Aeterna

SCRIPT-RESCRIPT

first performed on May 2, 2014
preFAB Space, San Diego, CA
performed once in 2014

NICHOLE SPECIALE / RACHEL BEETZ

San Diego, CA
nichole.speciale@gmail.com / rachelbeetz@gmail.com
nicholelizspeciale.com / rachelbeetzflute.com

SCRIPT-RESCRIPT
NICHOLE SPECIALE / RACHEL BEETZ

"Script-Rescript" was a performance between flutist Rachel Beetz and myself in which lines drawn on a paper surface were translated or interpreted into musical notation for the flute and vice versa. As I made a mark on the paper, Rachel began to play a tone. When she saw a change in my hand, she initiated a musical change with her instrument. I heard her progression and translated that movement back into a visual form. We fed off of each others lines working to create an overall musical composition and a drawing that acted as a remnant of the performance. This performance is the most recent iteration of an ongoing project of the same title, in which sound and drawing are translated back and forth in a game of telephone.

In February of 2013, I made a set of drawings as a response to a solo flute concert that Rachel curated and performed. With these drawings, I performed gestures of iteration: one mark tries to follow a musical line in each of the pieces on the concert and any following marks attempt to repeat the first, but ultimately gets translated into a new form that echos the preceding. Rachel made fixed audio pieces based on my drawings by assigning a sound to each of the linear gestures. Those were then measured within the proportions of the page and put into a two minute framework. The translation of the Script-Rescript drawings into flute pieces (some with sine tones and white noise) created a completely new sonic landscape for the flute. By working separately, we realized that there were elements that leant themselves to a live realization of the project, which was performed in May 2014. We are looking to push the ear-to-eye-to-ear translation into a developed way of composing both visually and musically.

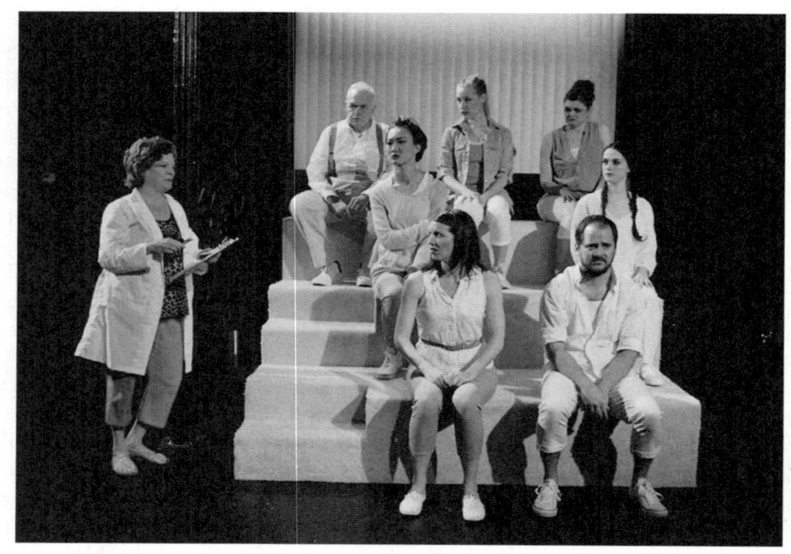

MAGIC BULLETS

first performed on May 3, 2014
Incubator Arts Project, New York, NY
performed eight times in 2014

ADAM R. BURNETT, JUD KNUDSEN , NICHOLAS KOSTNER, JENNIFER STIMPLE KAMEI , CASEY MRAZ

Caitlin Bebb, Abigail Blueher, Catrin Lloyd-Bollard, Donna Jewell, Jud Knudsen, Erin Mallon, Michael McKim, Kate Schroeder, Mari Yamamoto

New York City, NY / Minneapolis, MN / Albuquerque, NM / Lawrence, KS
burantheatre@gmail.com / adamrburnett@yahoo.com
burantheatre.com / adamrburnett.com

MAGIC BULLETS
ADAM R. BURNETT, JUD KNUDSEN, NICHOLAS KOSTNER, JENNIFER STIMPLE KAMEI, CASEY MRAZ

"MAGIC BULLETS" was an evening-length comedic performance work that entertained a trip through mental health and "wellness." How do you know you are unwell? How do you know you are better? Is wellness a journey to a new place? Or a return to where you've already been? Can you save yourself by coupling with an other? What are you doing and how did you get here? With a cast of nine performers. "MAGIC BULLETS" was an overwhelming, sensory experience dance/theater/music/fruit smoothie explosion that utilized Buran Theatre's rambunctious and immersive performance style

Opening on a hapless doctor (Donna Jewell) in the midst of an existential crisis with her fruit blender, a chorus of patients enter, singing a spritely spiritual tune, taking their place in a purgatorial waiting room. Throughout the course of their waiting-stay they are given a range of (mis)diagnoses and (mis)prognoses and attempt to couple with anyone(!) who will make it all better. Near the end of the performance they all dance to "rumspringa" and die.

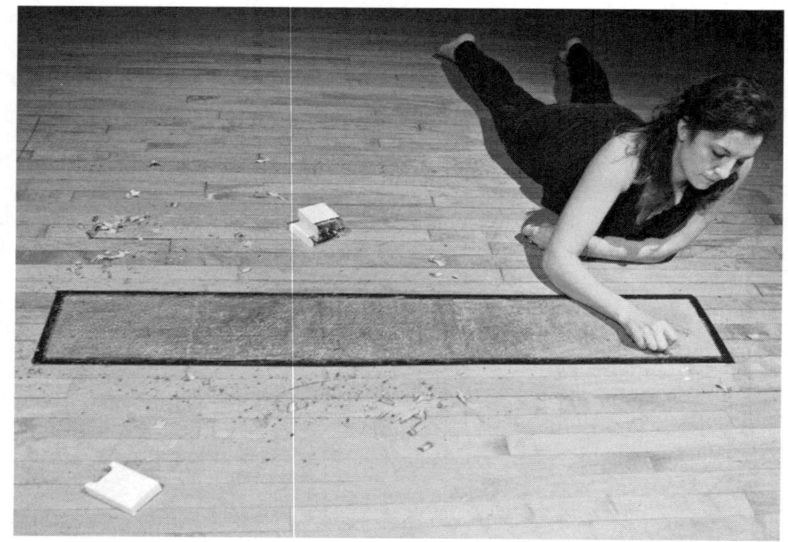

SPENDING TIME

first performed on May 5, 2014
Pozen Center for Interrelated Media, Boston, MA
performed once in 2014

NICOLE CARIMA DUBE

Boston, MA

SPENDING TIME
NICOLE CARIMA DUBE

"Spending Time" evaluates the physiological effects of aging and the intensity of the daily spectrum of life occurrences. This performance reflected directly on the last half-decade of my career, pondering my time as an emerging artist and simultaneously braiding together my knowledge of the past and the markers of personal importance. In many ways this was an introspective self-portrait.

Durationally this performance spanned three consecutive hours, focusing on my connection to what normally would be the simple act of coloring. Materially I used sandpaper as my coloring surface with the absolute rule that I could only use one color at a time. As a boundary, I didn't allow myself to choose a new color until I managed to fully retire the crayon—meaning I had to dull the wax down until it had completely dissolved itself into the rough surface of the sandpaper. I used sandpaper and a box of crayons—as light visually wrapped around me—to metaphorically symbolize the poignancy of memory and how we physically relate to current time.

I focused on the difference between natural movement and repetitive movement. Over the course of my performance, my actions—while above all wildly meditative—ranged from relaxing to aggravating to intensely fast and boring to almost painfully slow. The sound was encapsulating and from time to time sounded like white noise.

Aside from photographic documentation, the state of the sandpaper at the end of my performance existed as its own kind of visual performance documentation. It became easy to get lost doing something so repetitive, so in the end having something physical to show was comforting—only leaving behind the ephemera of crayons completely dissolved into the sandpaper, a muddy but beautiful visualization of color and texture.

Ultimately leaving things unanswered, I gave viewers the ability to formulate their own questions and find resolution for themselves.

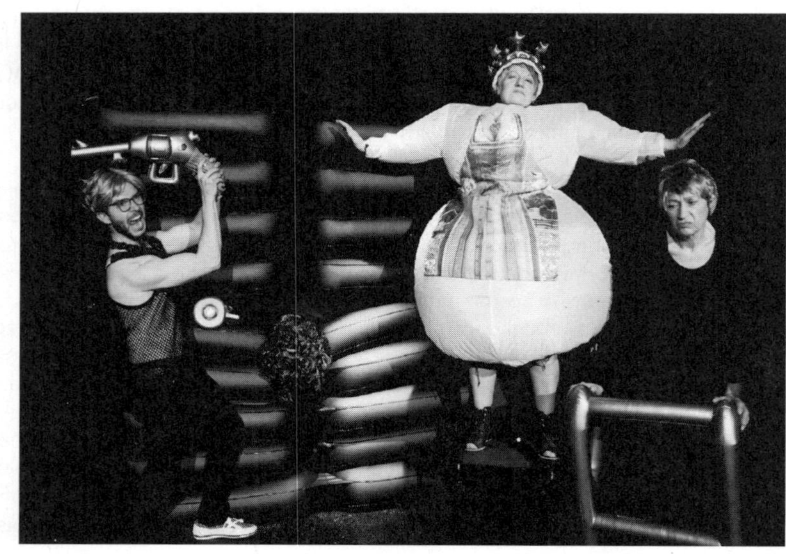

DEAD AT LAST, AT LAST NO MORE AIR
first performed on May 6, 2014
Camden People's Theatre, London, UK
performed thirteen times in 2014

JUST A MUST / VANDA BUTKOVIC
Simon Donger, Meredith Oakes, Diana Damian Martin, Ana Vilar, Berislav Juraic, Denise Heinrich-Lane, Niall Murray, Andrew McKenzie, Ingrid Evans, Jeremy Hancock, Delia Remy, Tom Jacobs

London, United Kingdom
info@justamust.com
justamust.com/vimeo/justamustco

DEAD AT LAST, AT LAST NO MORE AIR
JUST A MUST / VANDA BUTKOVIC

Werner Schwab's final work, "Dead At Last, At Last No More Air" is a brutal, irreverent and bizarrely comical piece about what happens when an emerging stage production is sabotaged by outsiders.

Following our last production of Elfriede Jelinek's Sports Play, our priority remains in understanding the ways in which *postdramatic theater*, particularly iconic continental plays that have not yet been translated or adapted here, might be able to construct a more situated practice. For us, staging Schwab is not merely an exercise in adaptation or interpretation. The play itself, in its humorous, sharp and nuanced critique of the stifling theatrical institution and the dangers of conservatism and nationalism, echoes clearly with the current political and cultural context, bringing forth productive situations and conceptualisations that hold the ability to contribute to a wide range of conversations.

In discussing the play, Director Vanda Butkovic asserts, "Amongst many themes that Schwab is proposing in his final text, the most prominent for me is the death of theater. Schwab is suggesting that the theater space is abused by pointless texts and 'make believe', used as political mouthpieces. I feel as a theater community we are in a situation where the very purpose of theater as a tool for commentary and dialogue is not only threatened, but totally undermined. I am not hopeful about this—I am afraid. I think death of theater will have the same consequences for the society as the extinction of bees will have for the earth."

Simon Donger's scenography takes its cue from the play's key operating metaphor, air, and consists of inflatable mattresses arranged as a progressively changing and deflating structure. This acts, particularly at the onset, as an interpretation of the 'theater stage on the stage,' engaging with a neo-Brechtian register that destabilises both the real and the representational.

Air thus becomes a discursive material onstage, rather than an operative metaphor. Actors have to respond to the spatial dynamics imposed by such a malleable set. Thus, the set is not merely an aesthetic container for the text but rather it enables a more embedded, embodied and intertextual conversation with the dialogue itself. Similarly, we wanted to invite the audience into the unfolding performance, playing between dichotomies and homogenisation, order and chaos. After all, dirt remains a powerful material and image in the neoliberal era.

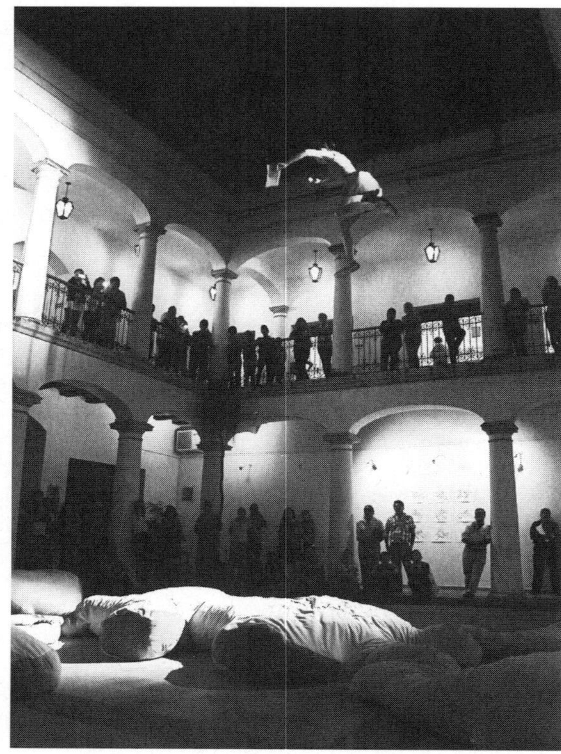

LA MUJER

first performed on May 8, 2014
GOETHE Center, Santa Cruz de la Sierra, Bolivia
performed once in 2014

NADJA VERENA MARCIN

Brooklyn, NY / Nordrhine-Westfalia, Germany
nvmstudio@gmail.com
nadjamarcin.com

LA MUJER
NADJA VERENA MARCIN

On a road trip through the Chapare region, I witnessed a sad situation: A dead woman, victim of a violent crime, lays on the rocks under the bridge Coni, surrounded by a group of police officers and excited locals. In "La Mujer" I devote a performance to the image of the fallen woman. An oversized, pale doll lays in the courtyard of the Goethe Centre outstretched, serving as both a seat and jumping pillow. During the performance I stand on a 16ft (5m) high and 13ft (4m) long board, looking into the deep courtyard and citing abstractions from Jelinek's *Sleeping Beauty*. The text tells of the turmoil of the emotional life, its intensity, depth and risk of dependence. The central image is the sleeping princess who wakes kissed by the living prince. Due to my unexpected and sudden jump on the doll in the courtyard, the risk disappears. The caricature of the *Übermother* becomes a symbol of ambiguity: the potential violence connected to emotional scenarios, the creeping indifference, the loss within their entertaining qualities.

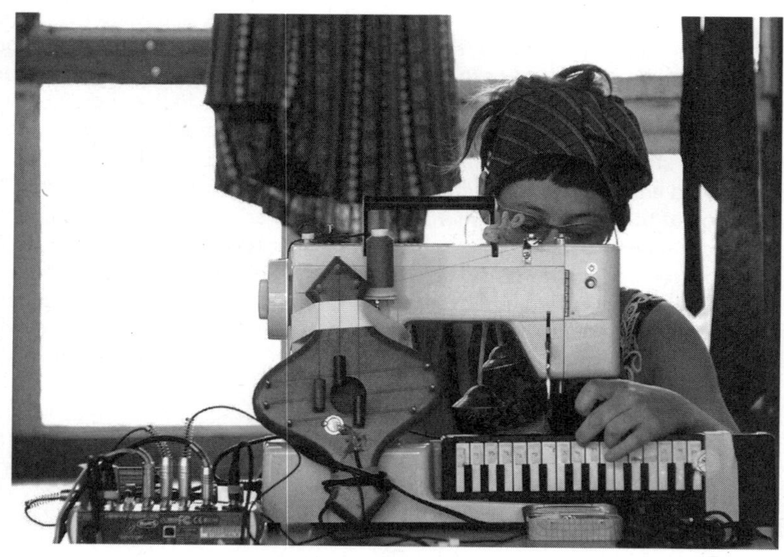

AGENTE COSTURA

first performed on May 11, 2014
Month of Performance Art – Berlin, Berlin, Germany
performed four times in 2014

LISA SIMPSON

Berlin, Germany
agentecostura@gmail.com
musicalsewing.blogspot.com

AGENTE COSTURA
LISA SIMPSON

Lisa Simpson is armed with scissors, needle, thread and a musical sewing machine ready to mend and redefine your wearables, creating a melody of change. Watch as garments are instantly stitched into unique sculptural works, following the rhythm of a prepared sewing machine. The performance is interactive and encourages the participation and activation of a constructed sewing space. It explores improvisation and spontaneity, turning skirts into dresses and viewers into performers, making music out of making clothes.

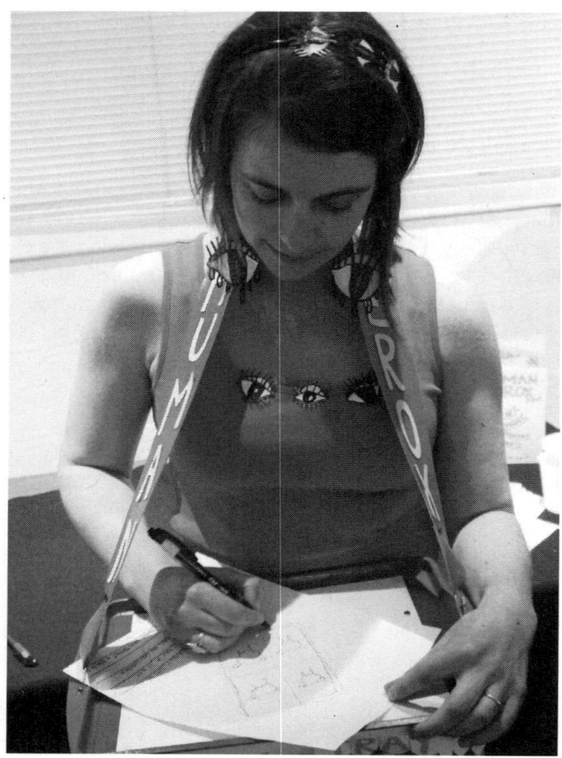

Jena Seiler

THE HUMAN XEROX PROJECT
first performed on May 16, 2014
The Dairy Barn Arts Center, Athens, OH
performed once in 2014

CAYLA SKILLIN-BRAUCHLE

Walla Walla, WA
skillinb@gmail.com
caylaskillin-brauchle.com

THE HUMAN XEROX PROJECT
CAYLA SKILLIN-BRAUCHLE

In this performance I functioned as a human xerox machine, recording and duplicating the material landscape of Athens, Ohio in May 2014. Starting with the simple question, "Can you describe your favorite thing?," "The Human Xerox Project" illustrated favorite objects as described by Athens' citizens. The drawings were then compiled into a collaborative zine which was distributed to participants. The zines are archived by "The Human Xerox Project" to keep a real-time, ongoing catalog of American ownership.

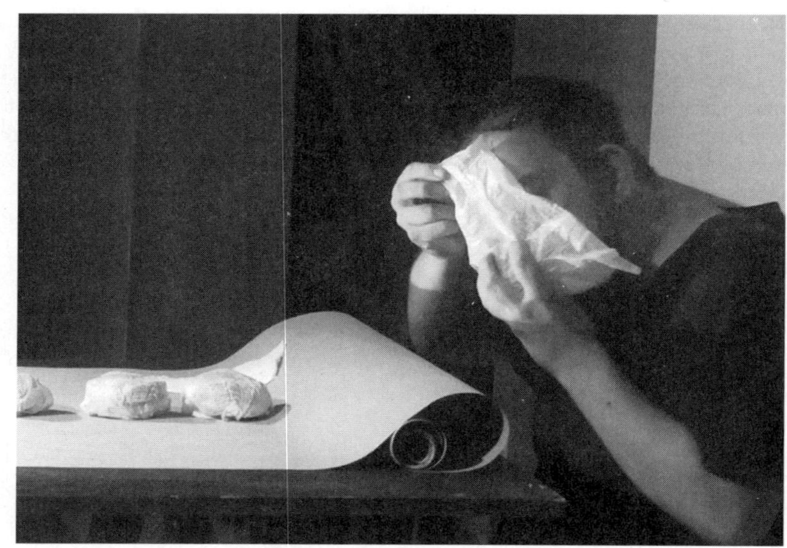

BURGERTIME

first performed on May 16, 2014
Grace Exhibition Space, New York City, NY
performed once in 2014

PANCHO LÓPEZ

Mexico City, Mexico
performance001@hotmail.com

BURGERTIME
PANCHO LOPEZ

My work regularly surrounds the day-to-day: rituals established around food, love, despair and the politics of desire. In particular I am interested in manifestations of love (and the processes that come as a result of diverse intrapersonal relationships) and generating pieces that point out and question the ways in which these relationships develop and possibly rupture.

Within the frame of the MEXTRA 2! Festival, I presented "Burgertime," a performative action where I ate ten cheeseburgers against the clock (in a race against myself) to not only demonstrate the ways in which I can simultaneously win and lose but also to explore the ways in which my food disorders, conflicts and behaviors shape who I am.

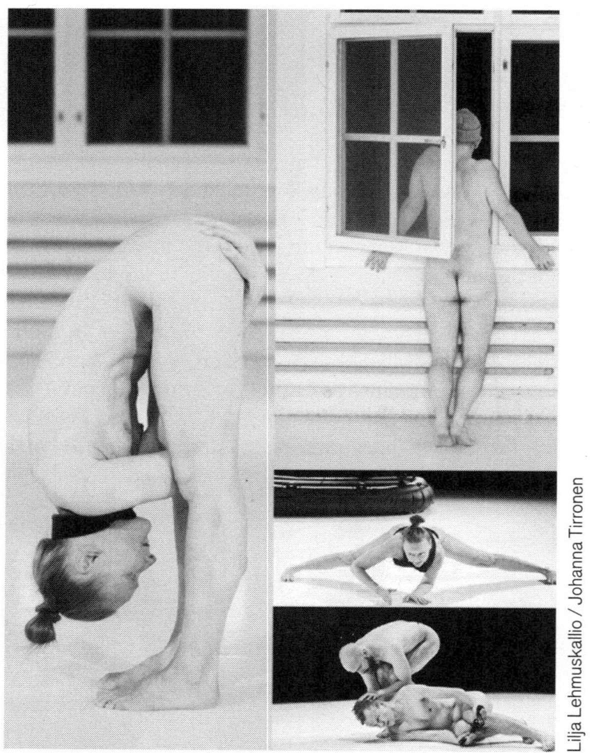

THE PRIVATE-PROJECT
first performed on May 17, 2014
Pannuhalli, Cable Factory, Helsinki, Finland
performed twelve times in 2014

K&C KEKÄLÄINEN & COMPANY / SANNA KEKÄLÄINEN

Helsinki, Finland
kc@kekalainencompany.net
kekalainencompany.net

THE PRIVATE-PROJECT
K&C KEKÄLÄINEN & COMPANY / SANNA KEKÄLÄINEN

Choreographer-dancer Sanna Kekäläinen:
"Private is a political choice. This is about making space, body, text and existence private in this world ruled by the spectacle. I mirror the narcissistic madness of our time and reach for a humane, shared reality. I bring on stage alternative means of communication as a counterforce for rejection and narrow mindedness, which symptomizes as infinite self-imposing. A few concepts, through which I think about representing gender on stage: The locus: where does the stage exist? How does the context affect performance and its reception? Right now the stage is in Finland, a familiar culture. The resources: what are the resources for realizing the performance? In what framework does the performance take place? What is its relationship to money and societal power? Private or common discourse: meanings are formed and received differently depending on whether the performance on stage is private or spectacular. That is why I divide art into two separate discourses, private and spectacle. The question is: how does the private combine meanings and how does the spectacle combine meanings? My stage is private. The work consists of two parts (1. SPEECH & SPECTACLE, 2. PRIVATE—Narcissism Remix) and continues as their anarchic dialogue. This is a proposal for a representation of gender on stage. This is about searching for an existence free of control—a place, where the norms of the spectacle will not reach."

Performer Janne Saarakkala:
"Sanna directs me: like my ass would be speaking. Like my jerking leg would be speaking. Never let your forehead speak like a character in theater, though. It makes your body mute and you become public instead of private. The journey is an "impossible" task in my body, during which I start to express something so private that I'm only vaguely aware of it. It's longing, it's sensual, it's emotional."

The performers in Part 1 (SPEECH & SPECTACLE) were Sanna Kekäläinen, Janne Marja-aho, Panu Varstala, with lighting design by Heikki Paasonen, music by Niko Likainen and produced by K&C Kekäläinen & Company / Zodiak – Center for New Dance. In Part 2 (PRIVATE—Narcissism remix), performers were Sanna Kekäläinen and Janne Saarakkala, music by Debussy and text by Kari Hukkila. Script, choreography and direction for both parts were by Sanna Kekäläinen.

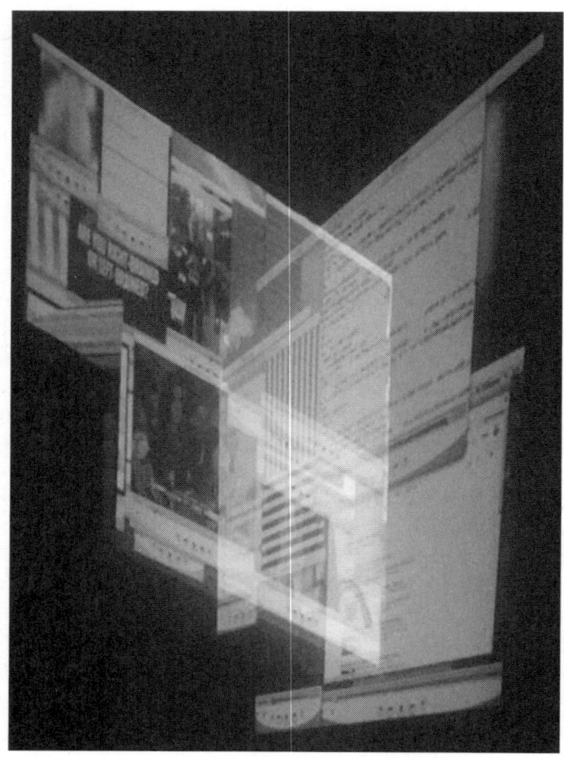

SHINY HAPPY PEOPLE
first performed on May 17, 2014
LaunchPad, Brooklyn, NY
performed twice in 2014

R.A.M.
Jesse George, Julie Rossman

Brooklyn, NY
peoplefortheautomatic@gmail.com

SHINY HAPPY PEOPLE
R.A.M.

"Shiny Happy People" is a direct reaction to the everyday experience of digital media and information overload.

We sit hooded at two laptop computers, each projecting fresh desktop spaces that overlap on a wall. Using a cache of audio/video clips downloaded from the internet (some deliberate, others random), we open files one at a time in default (Quicktime) media player windows, adjusting the size and placement of each window in relation to both of our previous selections. From here, we allow two types of physical manipulation: 1) rapid, back-and-forth touchpad pressure movements that scramble the linear advance of the clip's position in the timeline, and 2) repeated keyboard shortcuts that loop, reverse or isolate certain portions of the clip. Eventually both of our desktop spaces are filled with overlapping media player windows. After roughly thirty or forty windows, each computer's active memory begins demonstrating difficulty sustaining the data load: our cursor movement begins to slow and the clips glitch or stop entirely. At this point, we begin closing windows one by one—maintaining the same physical manipulations—until the last window is closed and the performance is complete.

R.A.M.'s frantic, finger-based improvisational technique exaggerates (barely) the universal daily use of the computer keyboard and touchpad. The spectacle and cacophony unleashed throughout "Shiny Happy People" violently challenges the traditional temporal and spatial authority of the source media, ultimately demonstrating physical restraint out of respect for the communicating machine.

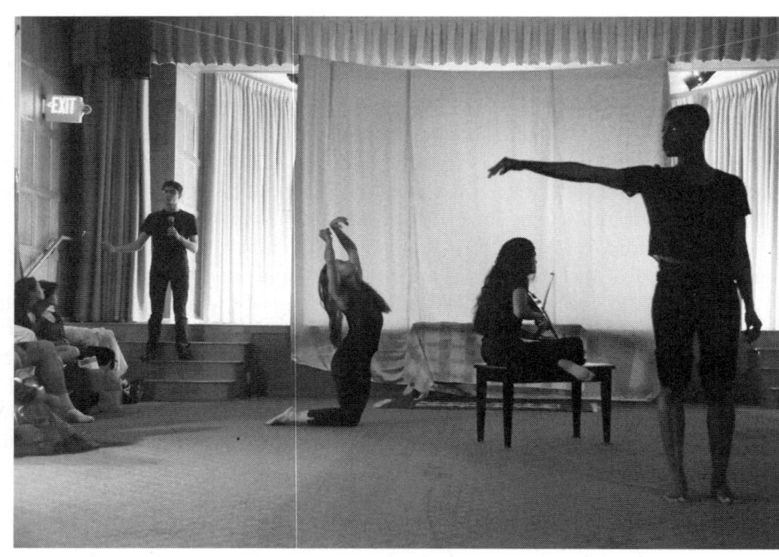

Sharon Chen

ALMOST...HOME...

first performed on May 18, 2014
Roble Hall Theater, Stanford, CA
performed three times in 2014

SUKANYA CHAKRABARTI / VINITH MISRA / ANDREA HALE / KUNAL SANGANI / SRUTI SARATHY / YVETTE DICKSON-TETTEH

Myrton Wesley Running Wolf, So-Rim Lee, Michael Vang, Anneka Kumli, Linda Hess

Palo Alto, CA
sukanyac@stanford.edu

ALMOST...HOME...

SUKANYA CHAKRABARTI / VINITH MISRA / ANDREA HALE / KUNAL SANGANI / SRUTI SARATHY / YVETTE DICKSON-TETTEH

A musician sits in the middle of a room and plays Carnatic classical music on her violin. There are seating arrangements on either side of the room—curtains, pillows, rugs and sofas make the room look like the drawing room of a house. Audience members walk in and take their places as my voice narrates stories about the Partition of Bengal, the formation of Bangladesh and of grandmother remembering the violence of such a divorce, with families separated and friends lost.

There is no formal division or marked border between the spectators and the performers in this piece. We are all witnessing the (his)tories of our 'homes' together, our liveness intermittently interrupted by some faces and voices on the screen—a white curtain that flows down from the ceiling of the room. At one point, two of the performers take us through a tour of their *imagined* homes.

Through the recreation of memories as performance, a musician, a dancer, a movement artist and a spoken-word artist explore how our bodies remind us of our homes and the ways that *home* gets mapped onto bodies. "Almost...home..." explores ideas of home (or homelessness) articulated by different bodies across races, ages, genders, professions and communities.

The conversations are generated through the recreation of memories by people we interviewed prior to the performance. The idea of travel is juxtaposed against the idea of rest, and thus, this performance reiterates, reaffirms and rearticulates the definitions of 'rest,' 'travel,' 'body,' 'memory' and 'home.' In having the theme define the format, the entire performance exists in a type of 'flow' or perpetual travel-state, one story intermingling with another through reminiscence and shared consciousness. The audience is invited to participate in a ritual-like chant. The performers reiterate 'I come from...' going round and round a circle, while the audience members, who join in, fill in the gaps.

How are people forming ideas of home when cultures and races are always in flux, in a mix and in travel? What does home mean to people with mixed heritage, multiple identities and jobs that entail travel and migration?

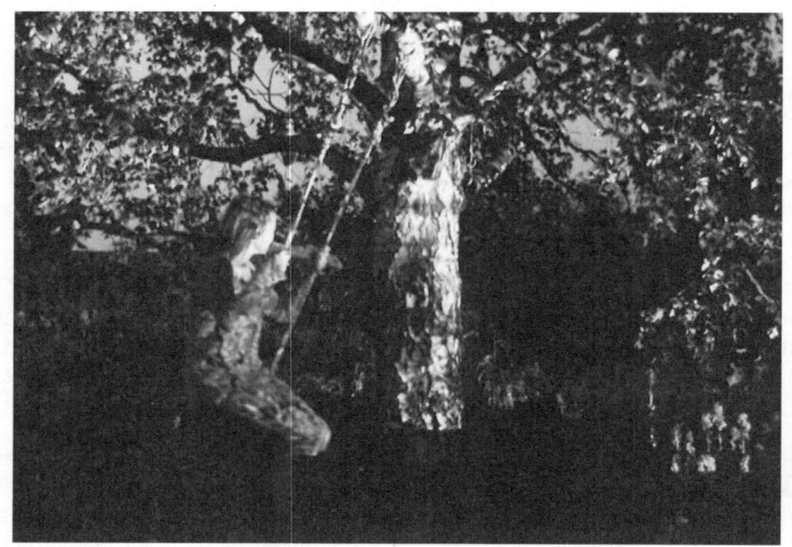

SWINGING TONIGHT / SWINGING BY THE MOON

first performed on May 23, 2014
Gallery Augusta at Suomenlinna, Helsinki, Finland
performed twice in 2014

ANNETTE ARLANDER

Helsinki, Finland
annettearlander.com

SWINGING TONIGHT / SWINGING BY THE MOON
ANNETTE ARLANDER

"Swinging Tonight" in Suomenlinna and "Swinging by the Moon" on Harakka Island were performances with projections created in the same places. I fastened the blue swing from my 2013 performance "Year of the Snake Swinging" on a tree, invited the public to swing and documented their swinging on video. In the actual performance the edited video was projected onto the same site, while I tried to swing synchronized with the swinging in the image. I have combined live action with the projected image of that action before, but have never before projected a video onto the site of its making. Marianne Hirsch's description of Lorie Novak's projections on vegetation at night in *Interfaces* (Smith & Watson 2002) was an inspiration for my outdoor projections.

The first participatory pre-performance took place at the tONiGHt event in Suomenlinna (May 23-24). I invited those present to swing in a tree next to gallery Augusta just before sunrise. For the actual performance at the next tONiGHt event (July 25-26) the edited video was projected on the roof next to the tree, while I tried to swing synchronized with it for approximately 90 minutes.

The second participatory pre-performance took place at the opening of the exhibition "Water Images" on Harakka Island (May 29) with the swing fastened to an old birch tree in the yard. The actual performance took place at the Moonlight Party (August 9) on the same site. At night the projection was visible against the white trunk of the birch. Part of the performance was recorded (vimeo.com/103242549).

Performing with the projection of an image on the site of its making is something I plan to experiment with further.

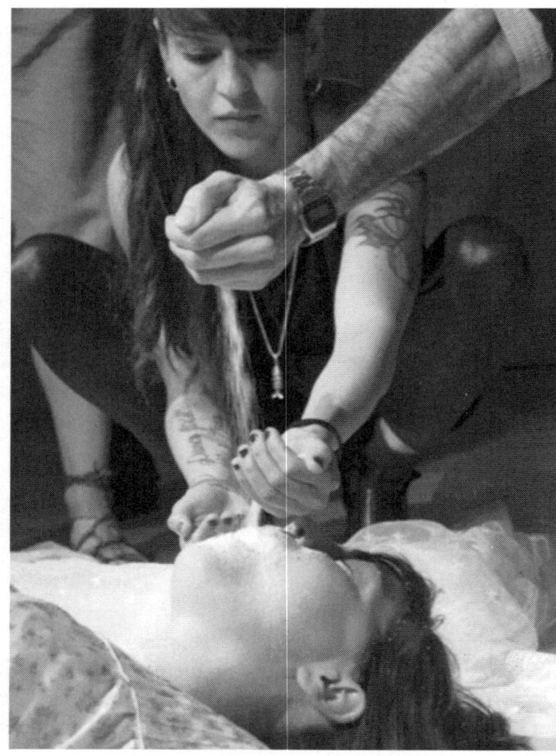

CALLING ANCESTRAL
first performed on May 23, 2014
Artpotheek at Sign 6, Brussels, Belgium
performed three times in 2014

RAE GOODWIN

Lexington, KY
goodwinrae@gmail.com
www.raegoodwin.com

CALLING ANCESTRAL
RAE GOODWIN

"calling ancestral" was a 30 minute participatory performance in three parts exploring ritual practices of ancestor worship and maternal ancestry. In the first part, the audience gathered around me on a sheet or around a door. I began reading a poem as a chant and handed out pages so the audience could read along with me. Written on large paper, like a storybook, this first part of the piece alluded to a mother reading to a child.

I was
I just
she who
where how
ring ring ring
libations, serpents, birth, tree
ring, ring, ring

They continued to chant until I slammed my fist and yelled "*ecoute moi!*" (listen to me!). I then poured sugar into a salt container and mixed it while humming a gospel refrain. The audience picked up on the melody and began to hum with me as I handed out teacups of sugar. While laying down, on top of the book pages, I gestured for them to fill my mouth with the sugar. The sugar filled my mouth, nose and ears. We hummed together until everyone had offered their sugar to me.

I arose as if from the dead, spit out the sugar and began the third part of the performance with the idea in mind that grandmothers are women who have much to offer and need help along the way. Through the action of stepping or walking on objects, I exposed the vulnerability of the body. By risking physical harm I asked the audience to empathize and ultimately help me move forward. I attempted to walk on teacups, saucers, a box, a soup touraine filled with water and roses. After offering the audience chocolates, I walked on what was left behind. After the performance I was greeted by audience members, some who had been laughing (at the ironic humor of the work) and others who had been crying (in empathic response to the risks I took).

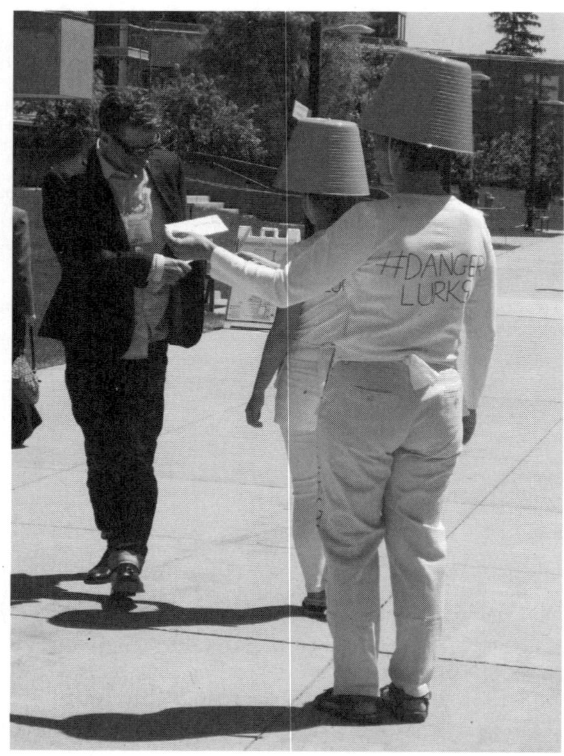

Adriana Disman

STATE THE NATURE OF YOUR EMERGENCY
first performed on May 25, 2014
Brock University, St. Catharines, Canada
performed twice in 2014

KIMBERLEY MCLEOD / HELENE VOSTERS

Toronto, Canada

STATE THE NATURE OF YOUR EMERGENCY
KIMBERLEY MCLEOD / HELENE VOSTERS

"State the Nature of Your Emergency" was a participatory performance that explored safety and surveillance on university campuses. The blue glow of emergency poles and phone boxes figures prominently as a physical presence on campuses across North America and is proudly displayed as a signifier of safety consciousness in student handbooks and on university websites. In our day-to-day movements, these objects generally recede into the background—a figure of the imminent but rarely present emergency. Bodies—student bodies, women's bodies etc.—are at the center of this implied emergency and, as such, we explored these questions through embodied activism. We considered what it means to embody the role of these emergency beacons—to meet in the blurry zone between the calming and silencing effect of the blue glow and the surveilling gaze.

Score:
Dressed as embodiments of blue light emergency poles, we wandered a university campus and engaged passersby in considering the role these sites play in the life of scholarly communities.

Participants were given one of the following questions:
What's the emergency?
What are we afraid of?
What keeps us safe?
Who keeps us safe?
What is safety?
What dangers lurk?
What don't we do when we're watched?
Who is watching us?
Who are the cameras for?
Does blue mean we're safe?
When will we be secure/safe enough?
What is safety worth?

Participants were then invited to engage with the question in one of four ways:
1) Inscribing a response on our bodies with a pen.
2) Recording a response on-site with a camera.
3) Using the hashtag #dangerlurks to respond via social media.
4) Discussing the question with someone else.

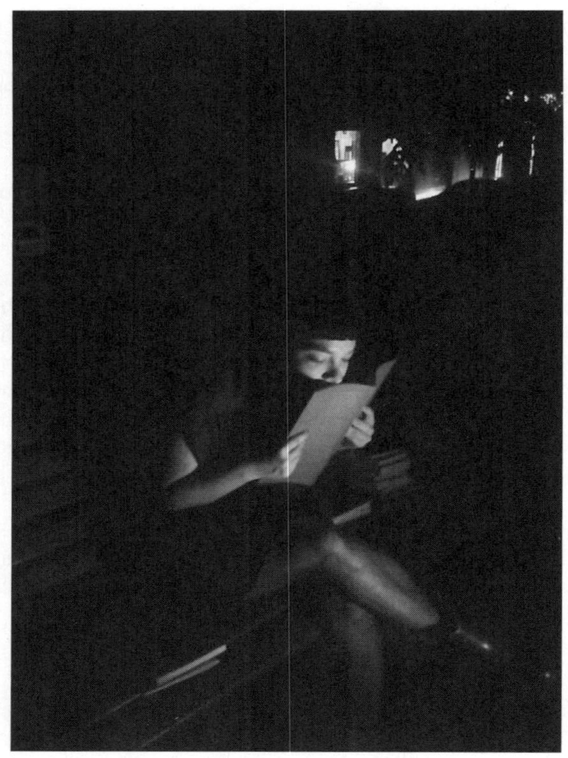

THEORETICAL FETISHES
first performed on May 25, 2014
El Hatillo Square, Caracas, Venezuela
performed twice in 2014

DEBORAH CASTILLO

Brooklyn, NY / Caracas, Venezuela
deborahcastillo@gmail.com
deborahcastillo.com

THEORETICAL FETISHES
DEBORAH CASTILLO

In "Theoretical Fetishes" I wanted to address the subtle way in which society is controlled by others' discourse. Knowledge is a way of power, and its influence through discourse creates a net of control over the individual body and its desires.

This is a performance where I decided to make a corporal interaction with books on power and sex. The action consists of turning the pages and licking them, underlining with my tongue, every word, every page and every sentence. The time is passing and my tongue is taking over the complete book. With this gesture, orality tries to survive the discourse. In this way I would like to accentuate this oral action as the ephemeral experience that wants to survive beyond the moment, reiterating a desire for permanence and sensuality.

The action is performed in the street; I sit on a bench in the square with a pile of books beside me and I slowly lick them one by one until the last page. I selected books by authors whose works are about power in different fields, such as: Michel Foucault, Judith Butler, Giorgio Agamben, Julia Kristeva, Antonin Artaud, Elias Canetti, Karl Marx, among other important authors.

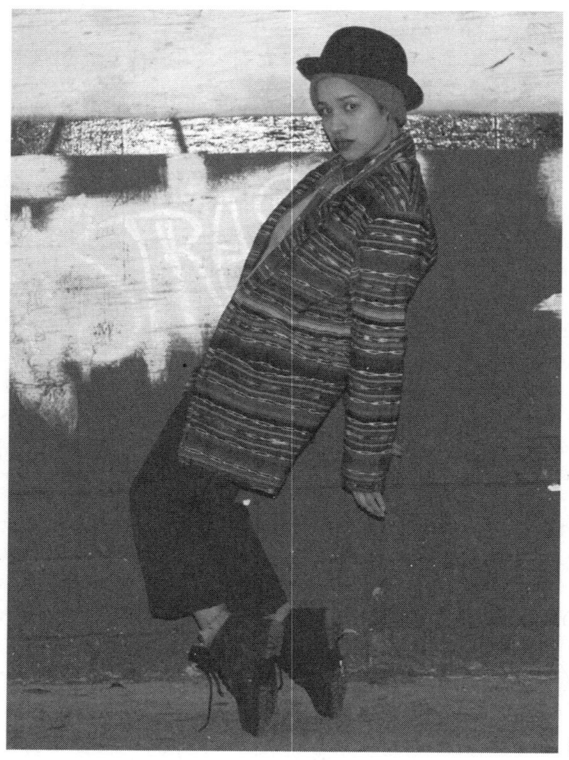

Kiara Jade

ONLY YOUNG EMO FEMMES ALLOWED
first performed on May 25, 2014
Mana Contemporary, Chicago, IL
performed twice in 2014

CHRISTIAN CRUZ

Mexico
ms.christian@gmail.com
c-cruz.tumblr.com

ONLY YOUNG EMO FEMMES ALLOWED
CHRISTIAN CRUZ

I perform a ten minute poem while incorporating street battle dance styles, such as juking and krumping. The aggressive *mafioso* poem addresses the complex nature of a bisexual, traumatized, gangster woman and her inability to smile on command. This narrative is told in a feminine, rogue character created with the use of costume and props.

"Only Young Emo Femmes Allowed" expands the medium of performance poetry by adding an element of dance to transcend the idea of internal frustration. This performance was created to address street harassment through the lens of queer identity with a particular emphasis on bisexual femmes. I wanted to give a face to bisexual femmes who are often unrepresented in the queer community.

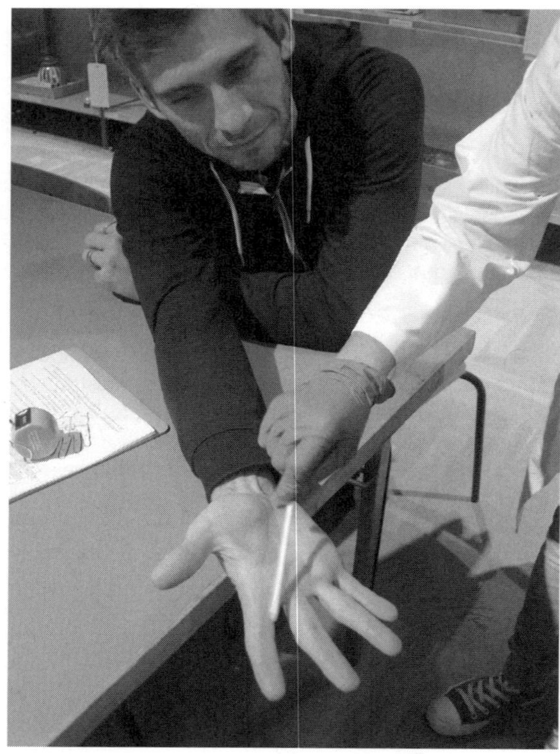

1000 HANDSHAKES
first performed on May 28, 2014
Panum Institute, The University of Copenhagen, Copenhagen, Denmark
performed twice in 2014

FRANÇOIS-JOSEPH LAPOINTE
Adam Bencard, Louise Whiteley

Montréal, Canada
francois-joseph.lapointe@umontreal.ca

1000 HANDSHAKES
FRANÇOIS-JOSEPH LAPOINTE

The microbes that live on and in our bodies weigh over 1 kg; they outnumber us on a cellular level by 10:1. There is increasing scientific interest in regard to the impact of the microbiome on everything from autoimmune diseases and body weight, to our cognitive and emotional states. Still, relatively little is known about this hidden universe of cohabitors.

My practice revolves around the revolution that human microbiome research has brought with respect to our definition of Homo sapiens and to multiple concepts of self. I address these important questions by transforming the bacterial communities on my body (collecting the microbiome before and after the experiment) and generating a series of microbiome selfies, so to speak, to illustrate the metamorphosis of my bacterial self. Sometimes, my wife joins me to investigate how two people affect each other at the bacterial level on a daily basis. In my research and creation, I use art and science as a way of engaging with the public on important societal issues. As such, my experiments are both scientific hypotheses and artistic performances.

"1000 Handshakes" is part of a long series of such performance/experiments I have been doing to keep track of the changes in my microbiome through various types of activities. At the Panum Institute, University of Copenhagen, I shook hands with 1066 people, including students, staff, patients and members of the public passing through the building, attending lectures and eating their lunch. Periodically, assistants took a swab sample from the palm of my hand, and the DNA of my skin microbiome was analyzed to reveal how our contact with others shapes the microbes between us and how it changes who we are, one handshake at a time. On Friday October 10th, the same performance was repeated at the University of Copenhagen's Medical Museion during Culture Night. For this second experiment, I shook hands with 1218 people who gradually changed the invisible microbial community in the palm of my hand. If it is true that 'you are what you touch,' I will never be the same again.

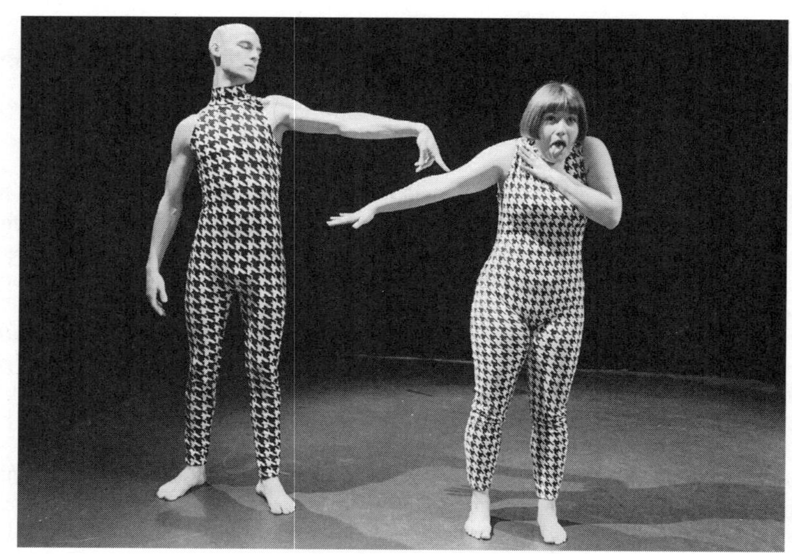

TIME HAD A JOB
first performed on May 28, 2014
Red Eye Theater, Minneapolis, MN
performed eight times in 2014

FIRE DRILL / EMILY GASTINEAU, BILLY MULLANEY

Minneapolis, MN
emily.gastineau@gmail.com / billymullaney@gmail.com
fire-drill.org

TIME HAD A JOB
FIRE DRILL / EMILY GASTINEAU, BILLY MULLANEY

"Time Had a Job" is a 15 minute contemporary performance duet comprised of 150 discrete six second segments, each with its own choreographic logic, performance quality and sound design. We borrow the structural principle of the Vine compilation and perform the six-second segments sequentially without interruption or repetition. A quick blackout forms the visual transition between each six second section, while the sound score jump-cuts between corresponding six second clips of music, noise, special effects, television, etc. The movement in the individual segments spans a wide range of choreographic intentions—the recognizably "dance"-like, the gestural, the mimetic, the theatrical and varying qualities of stillness—requiring lightning shifts in performance quality throughout. A key conceptual text we applied to the piece was Sianne Ngai's *Our Aesthetic Categories: Cute, Zany Interesting*. Between the shortness (cuteness) of the individual dances, and the durational and serial nature (zany and interesting, respectively), Ngai's text informed the range of contemporary aesthetics in the work.

Both we as performers as well as the audience are asked to juggle multiple senses of timing—clock time, rhythmic time, body/felt time and durational time—and sense the congruence and disjunctures between them. The repetitive structure presents an alternative to the classic sense of choreographic development and builds a sense of audience expectation in the overall duration of the piece. "Time Had a Job" challenges the viewer to process large amounts of information very quickly, to decide whether and how to draw connections between individual pieces and to test their expectations for change over time.

The pieces in our body of work focus on modes of contemporary spectatorship, often creating a particular tension for the viewer. The tension we create in "Time Had a Job" pulls between the audience's engagement and investment, and a state of boredom and burnout over time. Viewers oscillate between these two states as the piece presents an incessant barrage of new information within a rigid choreographic structure. This tactic references the sense of timing in today's media landscape and instant-share culture: How many news reports of shootings and injustices does it take before a viewer feels apathetic towards them? How long can we sustain a genuine interest in pictures of cats? "Time Had a Job" similarly saturates the audience and encourages a wide range of qualities of attention as the piece progresses—warning that no piece will last more than six seconds and promising that something new is always six seconds away.

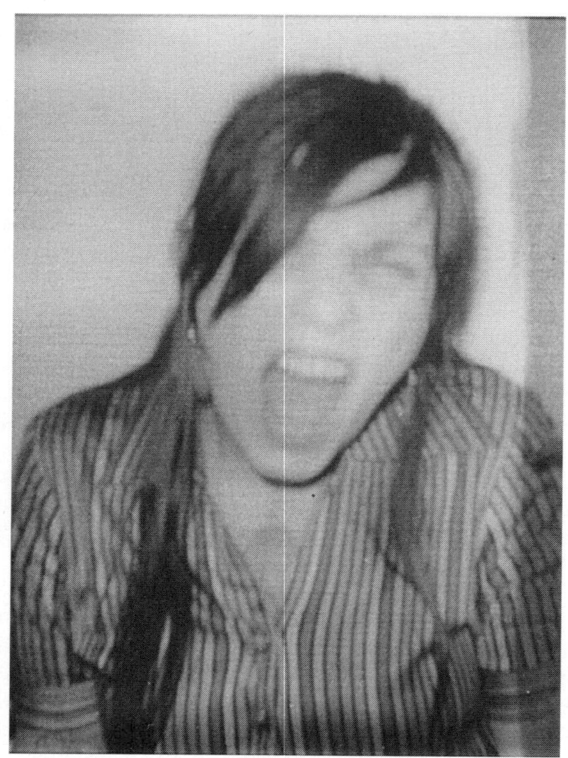

Jason Cerrato

THE BALL

first performed on May 28, 2014
The Buzzard's Banquet at Soda Bar, Brooklyn, NY
performed four times in 2014

JESSICA ROGERS

Brooklyn, NY
rogers.jessicalee@gmail.com

THE BALL
JESSICA ROGERS

When I began "the ball," I thought I was writing a book-length serial poem, but as the piece expanded, the work evolved into something else: a massive performance script. Though I may have composed the words, "the ball" had seized control of the lexicon.

"the ball" represents something intangible I wanted to make tangible, to touch. Desire, ego, our collective ego: for sale. The spectacle of modern culture, the weight we carry within and without internalized capitalism. The surveillance state. The commodification of self. I rent my insecurities as advertising space. As Debord states in *Society of the Spectacle*, "All that was once directly lived has become mere representation." I wanted to take this overwhelming spectacle into my hands and toss it around. I learned it's hard to hold, but even harder to let go.

Each performance begins with an invocation of "the ball" as a tactile and audible object, as a concrete memory. An attempt to choke the air with seemingly safe and docile nostalgia. I ask the audience: think of the image of a ball, any ball, perhaps from childhood, kids at play. Hear it bouncing around: the sound of tennis balls being hit—that pop, a baseball cracking off the bat, scores of bouncing basketballs in a high school gym, a handball court, the satisfying ring of a kickball off the inside of a foot. For me, it is always a red rubber ball: sometimes it fits in my hand, a choking hazard; sometimes its dimensions are larger than I can calculate. Imagine playing with *the ball* outside, a lovely afternoon, a park, a playground.

Then, the audience is asked to imagine that ball being taken away. Someone snatching it. Holding it above your head. Close enough to see but not touch. You remember what it feels like, but memory is now suspect. It is in this atmosphere that the performance emerges, sections of the work delivered in animated gestures and tones from valley girl to predator under the bed, "the ball" allowing itself to be held only briefly before resuming its position as an object of desire. "the ball" as trickster working itself outward into the audience, challenging those present, as well as myself, to take responsibility for the spectacle, culminating in a line which attempts definition, but provides no comfort: "The ball is empire, the Marxists say, but the ball is the empire in you."

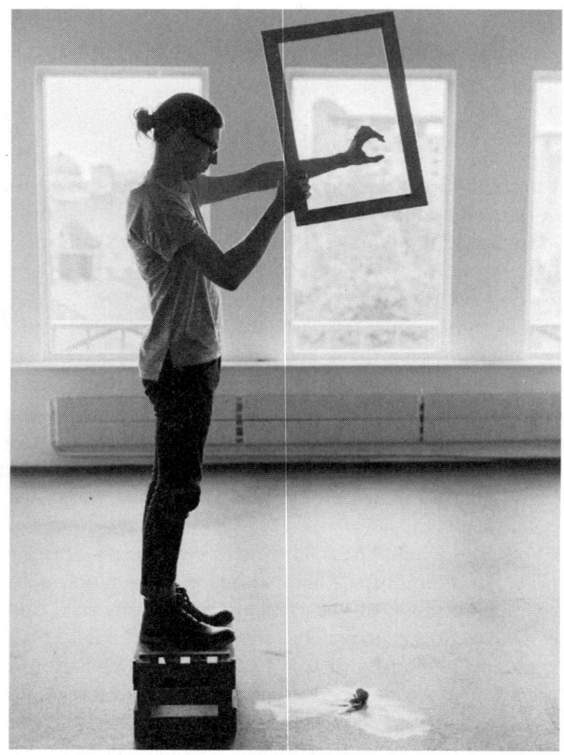

Monika Sobczak

SUNSET OVER THE RUINS OF THE PLASTER HOTEL
first performed on May 30, 2014
POST galerija, Kaunas, Lithuania
performed once in 2014

DAVID FRANKOVICH

Helsinki, Finland / Toronto, Canada
contact@davidfrankovich.com
davidfrankovich.com

SUNSET OVER THE RUINS OF THE PLASTER HOTEL
DAVID FRANKOVICH

I stand on a wooden box wearing a gold t-shirt, my arms outstretched in front of me. In my right hand I hold a wooden picture frame. In my left hand I hold an egg. A chair is positioned to my right so that if someone sits in it their perspective will line up the picture frame and egg with the window of the gallery and an unfinished hotel in the distance (which has been abandoned since the end of Soviet rule in Lithuania). I hold this position as long as possible, until the egg slips from my hand. When the egg hits the floor, it breaks and gold glitter spills out. I carefully balance the picture frame on the floor so that it frames the broken egg.

This piece was created during the PAS # 35 I Resistance workshop, at the CREATurE Live Art Festival in Kaunas, Lithuania. During my time there, I was fascinated by the Soviet architecture throughout the city. One building in particular stood out, unfinished and abandoned, looming over the Kaunas skyline. This building was clearly visible from around the city, including from the windows of POST galerija, where the workshop was taking place. So the architecture of that building, with large circular holes running up the side became the inspiration for my piece.

The gallery's architecture, with regular rectangular windows evenly spaced along one wall also inspired me as it reminded me of a film strip and my background as an experimental filmmaker. I began to think of how my film work might influence my performance work. In particular, I thought of how Jack Smith's work in film and performance had influenced me, and how I might be able to evoke a camp sensibility using only the materials I had available to me. The piece became about using minimal action and material to hint at some sort of queer possibility lying beyond the concrete ruins that served as its backdrop.

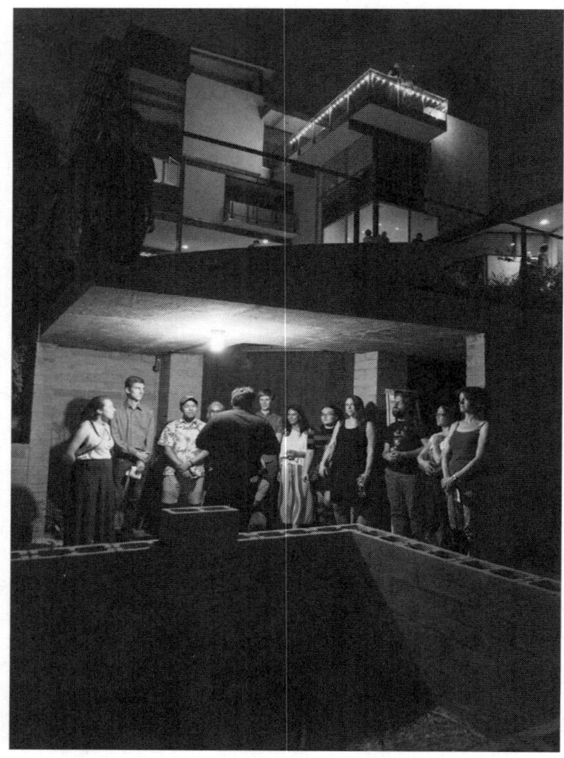

ENTER>TEXT

first performed on May 30, 2014
Human Resources, Los Angeles, CA
performed twice in 2014

HENRY HOKE / MARCO FRANCO DI DOMENICO

Los Angeles, CA
entertext.eds@gmail.com
enter-text.com

ENTER>TEXT
HENRY HOKE / MARCO FRANCO DI DOMENICO

"Enter>text" is a living literary journal, an immersive series of events where the audience is activated to seek out their own unique encounters with writers. There is no stage or podium. As a divergence from traditional reading series, we fill large public and private spaces with literary pieces, both installed and performed, and allow audiences to roam freely. We strive to explore the textual nature of our surroundings, always searching for new voices, histories and fictions. We have created seasonal performances since fall of 2011, mounted in galleries and private residences all over Los Angeles, and featuring an ever-evolving lineup of, on average, 15-20 writer-performers, whose contributions seek to enliven original literary work through interaction, intimacy and theatricality.

On May 30th, at Human Resources, we staged "Rumors." Audiences were welcomed via a side alley, where, in an enclosed doorway, in groups of 1-3, they were told that if they had to speak, to whisper, as there was something inside that we were trying not to wake. Each literary work inside was presented through whispers, passed notes, and silent installation. Guests participated in a variety of encounters, exchanging secrets and gossip, designing abstracted restaurant menus and speaking last words into a blindfolded person's ear. To conclude the evening, all performers began reading aloud at once, breaking the hush and ushering all attendees out to the street.

On September 7th we staged "In the Air" at an expansive private home in Mount Washington. Attendees ate popsicles and found fragments of a short story on the stripped sticks. A mermaid read from her book in the outdoor hot tub while guests dipped their toes and leaned in to listen. Bathrooms, closets, bedrooms and balconies were populated by press conferences, rituals and secret one-on-one readings. A drone hovered over the property. The moon replaced the sun.

"Rumors" and "In the Air" featured contributions by Karen Adelman, Diana Arterian, Sam Bloch & Mark Gerard & Ilya Malinsky, Andrew Choate, Meriwether Clarke & Claire Cronin, Sam Cohen & Stephen Van Dyke, Stacy Elaine Dacheux & Danielle Sommer, Kate Durbin, Emma Zakes Green, Dan Hockenson, Jen Hofer & Yelena Gluzman, Jen Hutton, Nicholas Katzban, Emily Kiernan, Janice Lee & Laura Vena, Joseph Mosconi, Beau Rice, John Rossiter, Sylvie Spencer, UNFO (with Harold Abramowitz, Amanda Ackerman & Andrea Quaid), Matias Viegener, Writ Large Press, Emerson Whitney and Yelena Zhelezov.

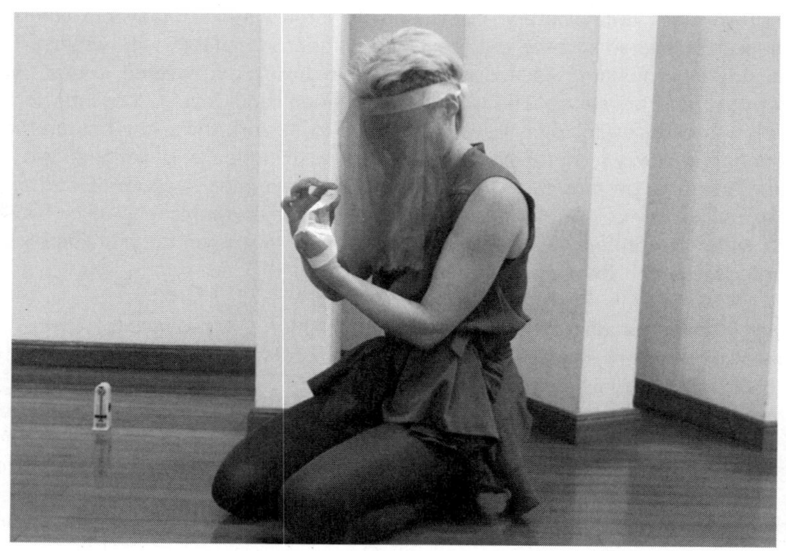

CARRIED BY THE SOLES OF YOUR FEET
first performed on May 31, 2014
Peras de Olmo, Buenos Aires, Argentina
performed once in 2014

AGNES NEDREGARD

Paris, France / Bergen, Norway
agnesnedregard.com

CARRIED BY THE SOLES OF YOUR FEET
AGNES NEDREGARD

"Carried by the soles of your feet" is a solo performance, derived from a tradition of visual performance art, making use of bodily actions, sound, costume and other materials, and audience interaction. The work responded to the specific context of the event, the space and the public present, addressing cultural and personal perceptions and baggage.

The performance started as I marched through the public and around the space, banging two solid wooden rackets together. I wore brown shorts, a shirt and neon, pink shoes. I came to a halt by the wall where I set up a metronome. I picked up a brown dress and held it up in front of me, then let it fall on the floor. The action was repeated several times before I resolved to tie the dress around my waist. I picked up an elastic band and a piece of see-through fabric and made it into a veil covering my face with it. Using an adhesive bandage I tied my left hand up into a fist. I walked over to the back door leading to the garden, pointing the way out with my bandaged fist while blowing repeatedly on the veil. When all members of the public had moved out into the garden, I lay down on my back and pushed my way out on the lawn, continuing to blow on the veil. On the lawn, I began picking up pink petals that had fallen from a tree, collecting them in my blouse. Meanwhile, the public was seated on a row of chairs which I had set up on a wooden platform in the garden. I walked over to the person sitting at one end of the row and took off her left shoe. I tried the shoe on and threw it over my shoulder into the garden. I proceeded to try on the shoes of about ten people, before choosing to keep a sneaker on, exchanging it for my own shoe. I went back inside, and poured the flower petals out on the floor. I arranged them neatly on one of my wooden rackets. When finished, I put the dress on back to front. I picked up both rackets and slowly ground the flower petals between them, until they were crushed. I went over to the owner of the sneaker I was wearing and we swapped the shoes back. I took my dress off and put it on the right way. I stopped the metronome and thanked the audience for their attention.

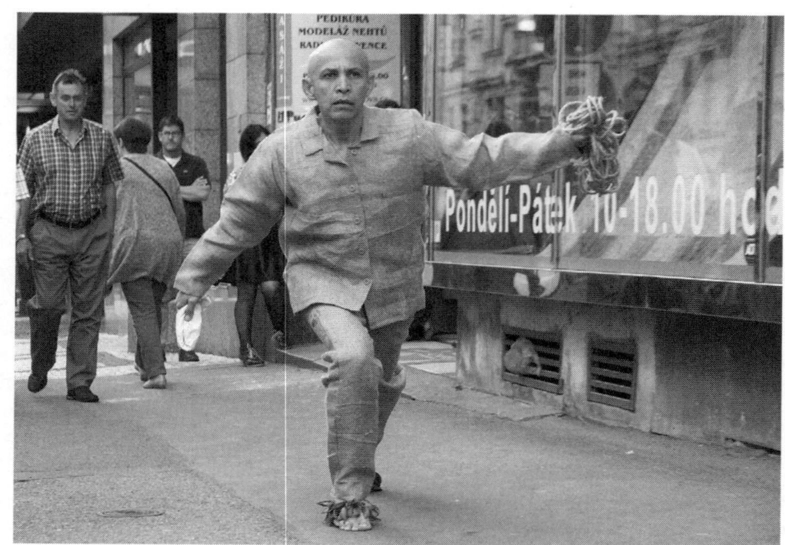

Tomas Hodbod

KŘEČE (CONVULSIONS)

first performed on May 31, 2014
Fourth Festival of Performance: Online / Offline, Prague, Czech Republic
performed once in 2014

HECTOR CANONGE

New York City, US / Buenos Aires, Argentina / Santa Cruz de la Sierra, Bolivia
hector@hectorcanonge.net
hectorcanonge.net

KŘEČE (CONVULSIONS)
HECTOR CANONGE

"Křeče (convulsions)" is a performance that explores the appropriation of public spheres, the exclusion of individuals from society and the socio-economic forces that change urban landscapes. As I travelled through Eastern Europe in the summer of 2014, I found myself in places that reminded me of the crisis that afflicted Latin America when my family left in the eighties. Moving from Poland to Hungary and later to the Czech Republic served as an inspiration to revisit my own family history and to reflect on common issues that make human experiences universal. The actions that constitute "Křeče (convulsions)" led the observers to follow me from an open space to a crowded city street in Prague and ultimately to the empty hallways of a commercial gallery that had been left almost abandoned due to the European economic crisis of 2014. The performance took place during the peak hours when people were returning home from their work. Wearing a rustic suit made of "yute" (natural South American yarn), I lay inert on the floor for almost an hour. People went from indifferent pedestrians to worried citizens as they stopped to check what was going on or to observe the strange presence on the sidewalk. After an hour, I began to activate my body with slow butoh-like movements and proceeded to walk wearing a bunch of small goat hooves brought with me from Bolivia, that had been attached to my ankles as heels. The walk was hard because I had to make sure not to crush and cut myself with the sharp hooves. Once inside the hallway, I managed to undress and burst several black balloons while inviting people to inflate white ones with colored confetti inside of them. The balloons burst on my body leaving their impact marks on me; the colored confetti started to melt and dye my skin. I blew and burst balloons until I could no longer breathe. End of the performance.

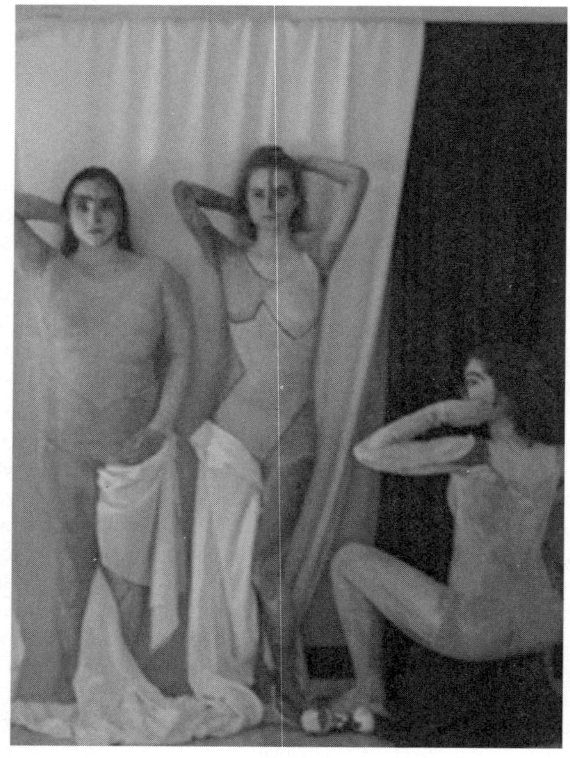

A SERIOUS BANQUET

first performed on June 1, 2014
Judson Church / New York Theatre Workshop, NYC, NY
performed eleven times in 2014

THIS IS NOT A THEATRE COMPANY / ERIN B MEE, JESSIE BEAR

New York City / Singapore
thisisnotatheatrecompany@gmail.com
thisisnotatheatrecompany.com

A SERIOUS BANQUET
THIS IS NOT A THEATRE COMPANY / ERIN B MEE, JESSIE BEAR

This Is Not A Theatre Company's "A Serious Banquet" (Judson Church, June 2014) was a theater-dance-dinner structured around the party Pablo Picasso threw for the painter Henri Rousseau in 1908 as recorded by Gertrude Stein in *The Autobiography of Alice B. Toklas*. If cubism is the opportunity to see something from multiple angles and perspectives at once, then this piece asked: what would a cubist experience be? "A Serious Banquet" challenged singular perspectives in many ways, the most obvious being that we repeated key scenes from different emotional and visual perspectives so audiences could experience the same scene from many "angles"—a theatrical version of cubism.

Partakers were welcomed into the world of the play by Picasso's mistress Fernande Olivier, and then invited to talk with a guitar programmed to respond to sound with music; to answer the phone, which recited Apollinaire poems; to listen to a still life (a bottle and vase that spoke); to view Picasso's *Les Demoiselles D'Avignon* recreated with live bodies; and to introduce Apollinaire (played by an absinthe glass with speaker) to other guests. After everyone had arrived, guests had an opportunity to experience *salon* moments—one-on-one interactions with various characters: Georges Braque took a single audience member to the corner bodega to get more water while discussing art and cubism; Max Jacob enlisted an audience member's help in creating a poem; Picasso invited three audience members to paint on miniature canvases with nail polish and to discuss art. After the *salon* moments, everyone sat down to dinner. They drew their dinner plates on a paper tablecloth, and three-dimensional food was served on their two-dimensional plates. During dinner, characters offered their birthday gifts to Rousseau in the form of toasts: a sculpture made up of audience members (Picasso); a silent dance by Ida Rubenstein; poetry by Max Jacob, Andre Salmon and Gertrude Stein; and a cabaret song by the Demoiselles D'Avignon.

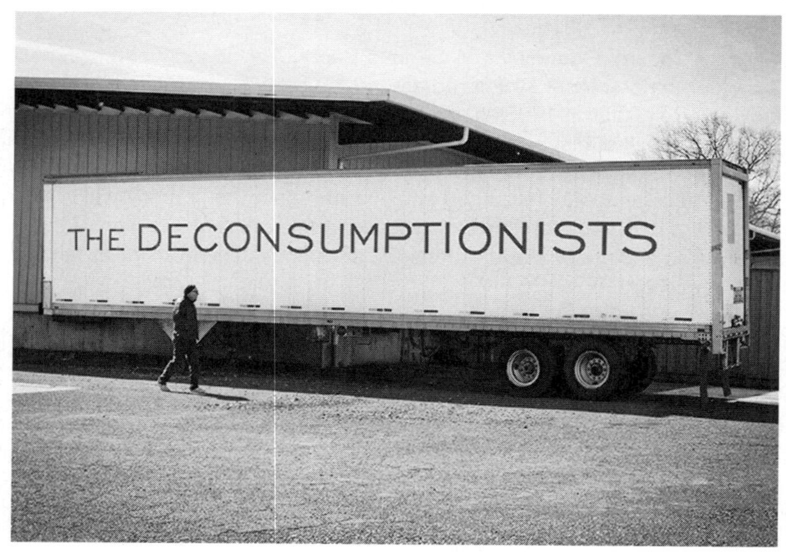

THE DECONSUMPTIONISTS ART AS ARCHIVE
first performed on June 6, 2014
Museum of Contemporary Art Detroit, Detroit, MI
performed nineteen times in 2014

EIDIA / MELISSA P. WOLF, PAUL LAMARRE

New York City, NY
eidiahouse@earthlink.net
eidia.com

THE DECONSUMPTIONISTS ART AS ARCHIVE
EIDIA / MELISSA P. WOLF, PAUL LAMARRE

EIDIA, our collaborative identity (Melissa P. Wolf and Paul Lamarre), performed in Detroit, June 6-29, 2014 during a month long DEPE Space residency at MOCAD, the Museum of Contemporary Art Detroit.

"The Deconsumptionists: Art As Archive" disseminates knowledge of the archiving of our life's production through exhibitions, performance and lectures. Inside a 48 foot semi-trailer, 50% of the interior is exhibition space with the remainder housing 171 boxes of previously created artworks spanning our 30 year collaboration. A photographic record has been made of the contents of each box. Performances by us or with other artists are a significant aspect of "The Deconsumptionists: Art As Archive" trailer—nomadic hybrid art archive and exhibition space with a solar panel array roof.

This performance took place within the trailer over a nineteen-day period coinciding with MOCAD's museum hours. We personally engaged with over 300 visitors, disseminating knowledge through performance and discussion, incorporating photographs, text and video (single channel) as well as staging collaborative exhibitions inside the trailer and museum—organizing and moderating a panel discussion on "artist run spaces" (June 20) with representatives from five Detroit galleries and one based in Toledo.

Our performance raised tough questions about sustainable life practices for the artist and non-artist alike. What art are you making now or do you plan to make and what is your strategy for all the "physical" objects you plan to generate throughout your art career? With potentially hundreds of accumulated paintings or sculptures, what "future" will all that you create have?

Our practice posits the modality of reassembling, repositioning and reshaping the found object, as well as previously created artworks, to provoke a differing (counter) conversation about production and consumption. By questioning what our responsibility is as "cultural producers," we present the struggles and contradictions of the production of art within the capitalist economic model—questioning the current model of production and consumption, with a particular focus on the environment. By example, we propagate the possibilities that recycling can bring to an art practice, as well as to design and progressive architecture.

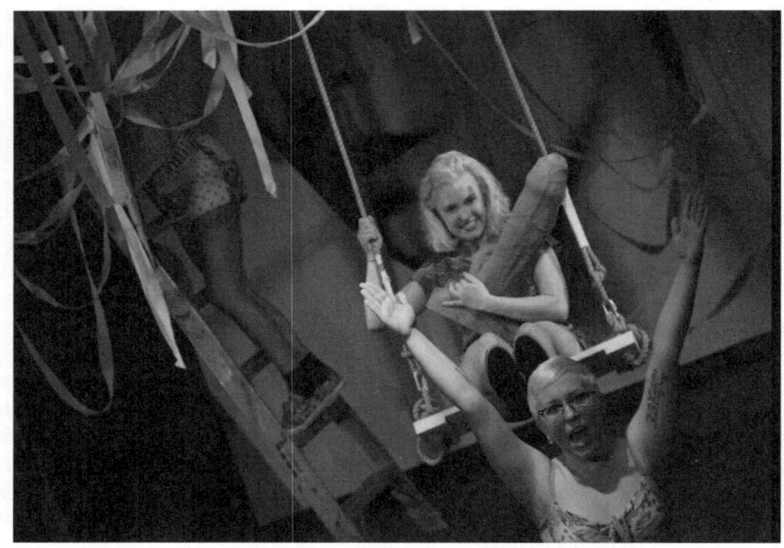

TOO MANY LENAS 3

first performed on June 12, 2014
Ars Nova, New York, NY
performed five times in 2014

CARROLL SIMMONS / JAIME WRIGHT, DAVID BERNSTEIN

Tessa Skara, Sam Corbin, Haley Traub, Elizabeth Trieu, Peter Mills Weiss, Chris Tyler, Mike McGee, Blake Palmer, Stephanie Levin

Brooklyn, NY / Toronto, ON
jaimeawright@gmail.com / todavidbernstein@gmail.com
carrollsimmons.tumblr.com

TOO MANY LENAS 3
CARROLL SIMMONS / JAIME WRIGHT, DAVID BERNSTEIN

"Too Many Lenas 3" is a performance piece which uses camp, presentational dance and institutional intervention to excavate and problematize notions of artistic success through the deceptive form of theater. As a collective of writer-performers emerging from an overcrowded education and entering an overcrowded downtown scene, the piece was our coded *cri de coeur*, cloaked in aesthetic excess, that was designed to directly confront our place in the current moment of performance making.

In the tradition of freeform feminist character study, our code took the form of a well-known figure as surrogate. Our figure, Lena Dunham, was chosen for her public persona; a fictionalized self crafted around the perceived anxieties of her generation. Throughout the piece, her name and a constellation of referential paraphernalia are obsessively invoked, leaving a rubble of language and character piled up sculpturally by the play's end. Divorced from context, these shards of meaning can only be attributed back to the attitudes of the performers themselves.

The narrative imagines a coven of Lena Dunhams living together, enacting the mundane rituals of their daily life through extremes of self-dramatization. The Lenas play make-believe, they prepare for job interviews, they soliloquize. Using found and original texts, we fashioned a mashup that queered expectations of structural cohesion and the separation of character and creator. It was a theatrical culture jam responding to the absurdity of the earnest creative impulse and the pipe dream of economic stability.

Built into the piece's structure was a false ending that gave way to an incongruous, site-specific appendix. An unidentified speaker enters unexplained and launches into a digressive monologue, jarringly disrupting what was left of the narrative. For each engagement we had, we created a new surreal awards ceremony for this speaker to conduct, supposedly at the behest of the programming institution. Invoking the real names of the institutions' administration—and in one case, using an actual administrator as an onstage body performing call-and-response choreography—we gave ourselves a vague but triumphant accolade for "winning" the festival into which we had been programmed. Then, we celebrated with a Broadway song-and-dance. We aimed to turn our attention to the framework we were being presented in, and the problematic hierarchies within it. However, in mocking ourselves in equal measure, our fashionably-meta deconstruction refused the easy catharsis of moral clarity and succumbed to the temptation of unapologetic spectacle. It is still a *show* after all.

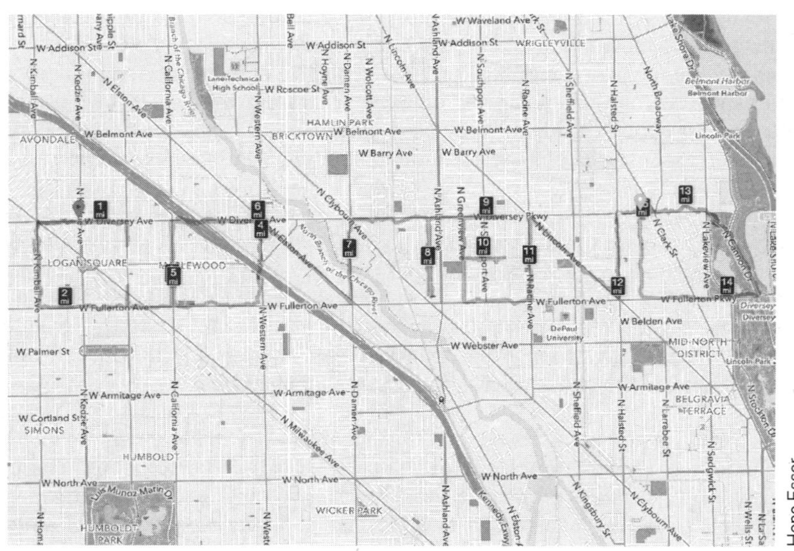

CONTEND

first performed on June 13, 2014
15 mile route beginning at artist's house and ending at Lake Michigan, Chicago, IL
performed once in 2014

HOPE ESSER

Chicago, IL
hope.esser@gmail.com
hopeesser.com

CONTEND
HOPE ESSER

On June 13, 2014, I completed a 15 mile run in honor of Stamata Revithi, a 30 year old woman who ran the marathon in the 1896 Olympic Games (the first modern Olympics), even though women were not allowed to compete. It was also reported that another woman named Melpomene ran the course, but since nothing else is known of her, many believe that these two women were actually the same person.

Melpomene is the name of the Greek Muse of Tragedy, and thus could be Revithi's pseudonym, referring to the denial of her achievement. The records of the run(s) were not recognized by the Hellenic Olympic Committee, and very little is known about the women, even whether or not they actually existed. Instead of Revithi/Melpomene being remembered for her run, she was excluded from history.

For this work, I traversed a section of Chicago beginning at my home and ending at Lake Michigan. I tracked myself with GPS and spelled out the word "CONTEND" as a small gesture towards the forgotten woman/en. This dismissed piece of history that should have been well recorded suggests that even not so long ago, a legend worthy of a Greek myth was witnessed.

I was inspired to make this work while training for my first half marathon and investigating the history of women's running. The tragic story of Revithi and the mystery behind her life compelled me to make a work that honors her achievement in a small way. Working with GPS also speaks to the ephemerality of running as a writing tool, and even the authenticity of images and stories that cannot be verified.

Women were not granted their own Olympic Marathon until 88 years later, at the 1984 Games (the year of my birth). I have done this run as a gesture towards the first female Olympic competitor and the first Olympic protester. I chose the word "CONTEND" because it means both "to compete" and also "to assert a right."

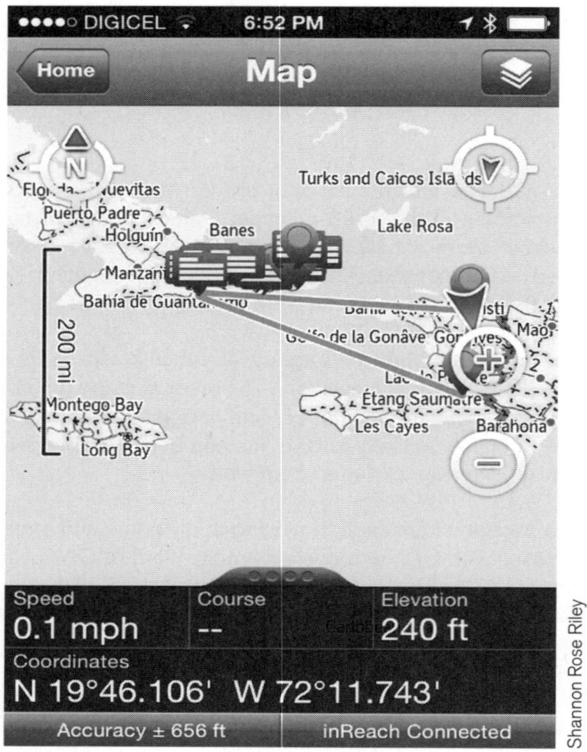

Shannon Rose Riley

CROSSING THE WINDWARD PASSAGE

first performed on June 19, 2014
Punta de Maisí, Cuba; the Windward Passage between Cuba and Haiti; Cap Haitien, Haiti
performed once in 2014

SHANNON ROSE RILEY

San José, CA
misstranslation@gmail.com / shannonrose.riley@sjsu.edu

CROSSING THE WINDWARD PASSAGE
SHANNON ROSE RILEY

In the context of the Panama Canal centennial, I performed a kind of "black ops" crossing of the Windward Passage, the 50-mile-wide strait between Cuba and Haiti and the only deep sea-lane from the eastern US seaboard to the Canal. Crucial to US interests by the 20th century, the US commanded the Passage from its military base at Guantánamo (GTMO) and via occupations of Cuba and Haiti (1898-1934). The aim was to control the route to the Canal and monitor the countries, which were perceived as unruly sites of black resistance. The Passage is the very reason GTMO is located where it is and US patrol of the waterway continues today.

My question was "who can cross the passage, in which directions, and in what manner?" I had proposed to sail across the Passage and theorized that regardless of the outcome the attempt would reveal information about the geopolitical zone. But crossing by water was only possible by illegal or risky craft. No US-based or licensed boat rental company sails into Cuban waters because of the US embargo and Cuban maritime border regulations. No commercial boat from the DR crosses because they uphold the embargo. No Cuban tourist rentals leave national waters without breaching their own maritime laws. Cuban border guards vigilantly patrol Cuban coasts and the easternmost point of Cuba closest to Haiti, the Punta de Maisí, is highly patrolled because of increased drug and human trafficking as well as regular illegal Haitian immigration. While some Cubans legally travel abroad since 2013, they do so primarily by commercial air travel because airspace crossings by documented subjects who pay the price of a ticket are more easily monitored than water crossings. Thus, I also crossed by air.

I flew from Miami to Santiago de Cuba. From there I took a bus to Baracoa to find a way to the restricted and well-patrolled Punta. Wearing my black-case GoPro, I rode in a 1953 Jeep to the Passage and nearby cemetery where they bury Haitians who die crossing. Accompanied by a Cuban friend of Haitian descent, we paused under the watchful eye of border patrol while he said a prayer at the edge of the water. Several days later I flew to Haiti carrying at his request objects to float in the water on the Haitian side.

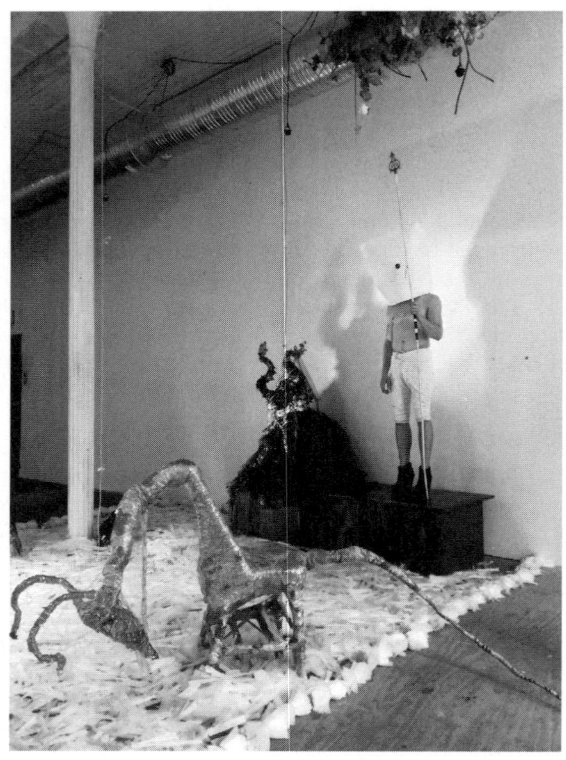

Carly J. Bales

CITYSCAPE(GOATS) WITH NORTH AMERICAN SHEPHERD

first performed on June 19, 2014
EMP Collective, Baltimore City, MD
performed once in 2014

HOESY CORONA

Baltimore, MD
Hoesycorona@gmail.com
hoesycorona.com / labbodies.com

CITYSCAPE(GOATS) WITH NORTH AMERICAN SHEPHERD
HOESY CORONA

For this performance I called upon the archetype of the Scapegoat and the Shepherd in an effort to have us imagine a deliberate manipulation of individuals by skillful strategists who understand the mechanisms of victimization and who knowingly sacrifice innocent victims with ease for their own gain.

Guests entered the gallery looking up to a large horned white creature hanging from the ceiling while tripping over a long wiry pink tail that took up most of the lobby floor. The tail led to a shiny pink scapegoat chair structure with a long flowery neck tied down to the floor covered in mesh netting bits. In order to enter the rest of the gallery viewers had to pass through my installation (in this way doubling as a border).

On the floor I wrote, imploring the viewer to, "enter me softly." The installation was populated by two scapegoat thrones, three scapegoat idols and two performers including myself (Scapegoat) and movement artist Alexander D'Agostino (Shepherd). The two of us enjoyed the vista against a white wall and I was pleasantly surprised by how many people naturally felt compelled to touch us throughout the performance. The thrones in the installation were created in my living room using the wrapping technique of visionary/outsider/untrained artist Judith Scott. I began with a pre-existing contemporary chair frame and carefully wrapped silk flowers, bones and other recycled materials before sealing them with resin.

The Shepherd stood on a brown platform against the white wall while I laid inside a similar but inverted platform. We were lit by a strong changing multi-color LED light. I wore a large horned black headdress that covered my entire body while the Shepherd, a white man, held a staff and wore a large white square hood that covered his entire face except for a peep-hole in the middle. For three hours I created slow and repetitive gestures as though bound in place while next to me the Shepherd surveyed the installation for the duration of the performance.

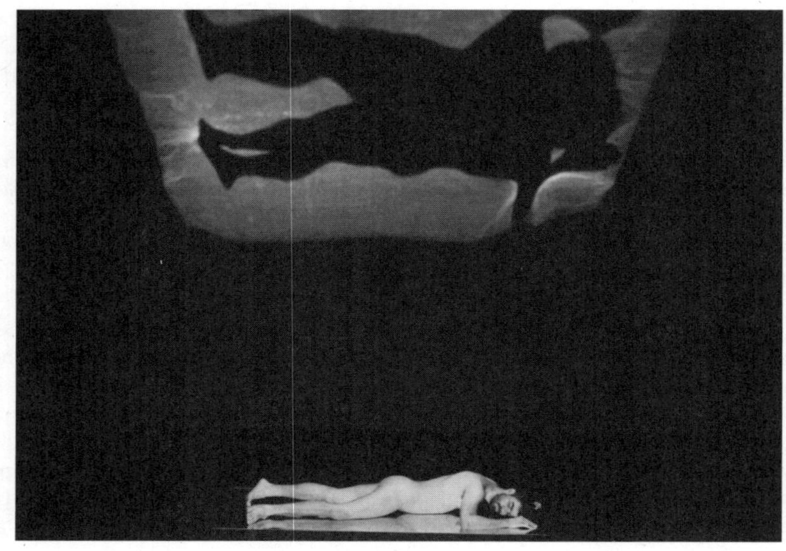

Paulo Aureliano da Mata

REVERSE
first performed on June 20, 2014
CAAA – Centro para os Assuntos da Arte e Arquitectura, Porto, Portugal
performed once in 2014

CIA. EXCESSOS / TALES FREY

Porto, Portugal
ciaexcessos@ciaexcessos.com.br
ciaexcessos.com.br

REVERSE
CIA. EXCESSOS / TALES FREY

On June 20, 2013, I presented the first work in my series of performances that make a commitment to convert the rite of passage of my birthday into an artistic procedure that alludes to what we know as *memento mori*.

"Reverse," the second creation from this series, is a kind of regression to my origin; it is the reverse of the chronological sense as an alternative to refuse the inevitable death of my story. In this performance, with the help of my mother, I trigger a recall of all my past birthdays, through a game that takes the concept of Lacan's "mirror stage," until I reach the moment I left the comfort of the womb.

I lay down on a mirror (two feet by one) and remain (for 32 minutes) contemplating every part of my body that I can see through the mirror while I am listening to a recording of a reversed conversation that I had with my mother to remember and learn the details occurring on the day of my birth and all birthday parties until the last before this one.

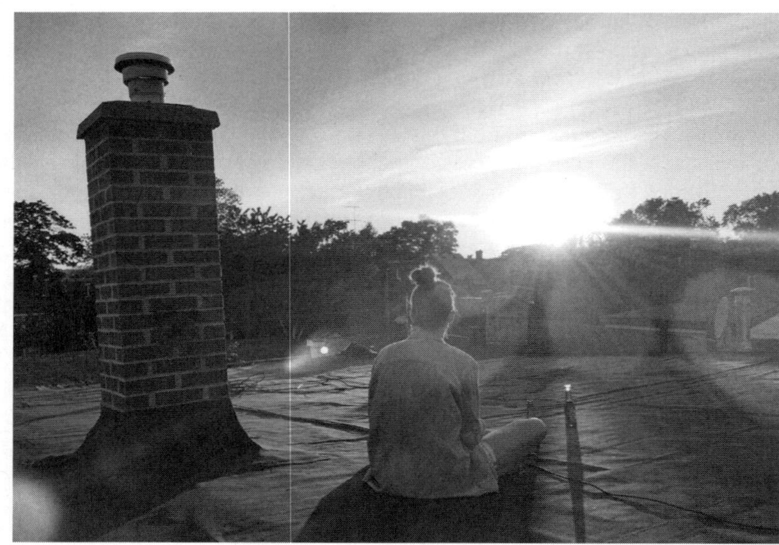

SET TOGETHER

first performed on June 21, 2014
Top of CN Tower, Toronto, Canada
performed once in 2014

EMILY DICARLO

Toronto, Canada
emilydicarlo@gmail.com
emilydicarlo.com / set-together.com

SET TOGETHER
EMILY DICARLO

"Set Together" is a globally collaborative project that asked participants to share in witnessing and documenting the setting sun on the longest day of the year in the northern hemisphere and shortest day in the southern hemisphere—Saturday, June 21st, 2014.

The project explores the interplay between simultaneity and displacement by attempting to render collectively lived experiences into one compounded time and space. Through the simple gesture of watching a sun set, the project intuitively explores the intensifying post-modern need for connection and communal interaction.

Co-ordinated with The International Society for the Study of Time's conference at the Beijing Normal University over 90 participants from 50+ cities in sixteen countries submitted documentation of their experiences, which now lives as an online testament at set-together.com.

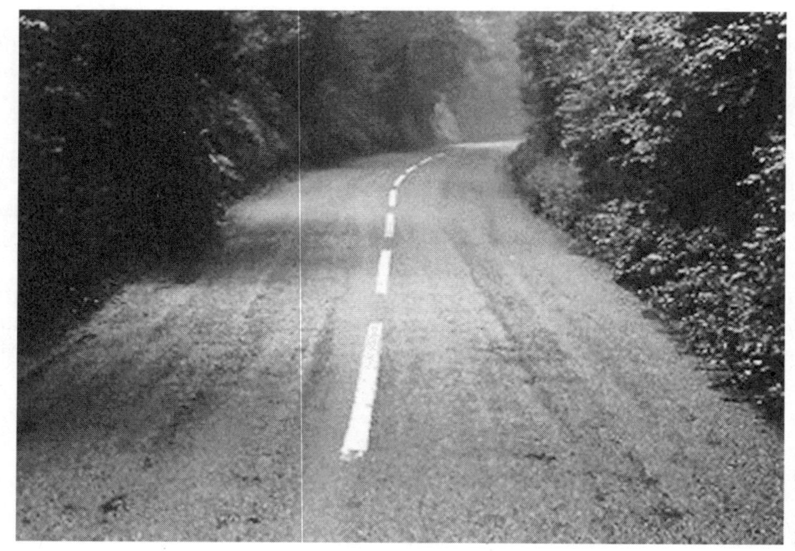

NO FOREIGN ROADS
first performed on June 21, 2014
a country road, Somerset, England
performed once in 2014

MICHAEL BRAMWELL

Cary, North Carolina
MichaelBrmwell493@gmail.com

NO FOREIGN ROADS
MICHAEL BRAMWELL

"One recognizes one's course by discovering the paths that stray from it." —Albert Camus

Whether exemplified by Paul the Apostle's conversion on the road to Damascus or Dorothy's experiences on her way to Oz, roads consistently function as metaphors for encounter and self-realization; dynamic chronotopes collapsing time and space of our present circumstances into the potential future of where we hope to be. "No Foreign Roads" is, among other things, a durational performance work requiring the artist to travel to a random, solitary country road in Somerset, England and over a course of seven days, hand-sift three hundred and fifty-two white traffic lines, in powdered chalk, down the center of the road for a distance of one mile.

Each line as it was drawn, was an existential meditation for me on the modes of spiritual progress, namely, self-discovery and self-making. Each mode possesses a distinctive mood as it were. Even if people happen to stray into unfamiliar territory and despite what may happen during this diversion, it is never unchangeable. Each individual possesses creative ability, as Joseph Beuys the post-war German artist liked to say, to restore the lines of continuity, and re-discover their original path. In this mode of spiritual progress human failure is seen as a condition in which the person has fallen off their "true" path in life and followed divergent roads; many of which consistently lead to death and destruction.

The second mode is more existential and emphasizes breaks and novelty and focuses less on the Plotinian theme of returning to original sources. It is what Camus is referring to in the epigraph. It is punctuated by crises of loss of the familiar and encounter with the unexpected. Artists often call this effect an accident i.e., what was intended to be in the work but never made it in, or what made it in that was never intended. In the spirituality of self-discovery, I am what I was in my origins; for the spirituality of self-making, I am what I may hope for.

This work utilizes aesthetic methodology to explore ontological issues of being in the world. It also uses text in addition to photography as a form of performance art documentation. An entire seven days of work was washed away by an afternoon thunder shower.

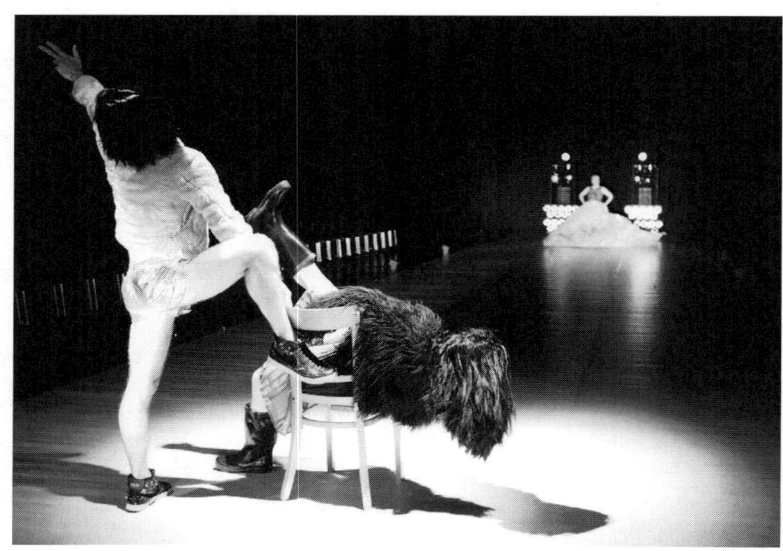

CREATING MY OWN TOMORROW
first performed on June 21, 2014
Mousonturm LAB, Frankfurt, Germany
performed three times in 2014

2+ / PHILIP BUSSMANN, CÉLESTINE HENNERMANN
Marek Lamprecht, Janice Perry, Kristina Veit, Alfredo Zinola

Frankfurt, Germany / Cologne. Germany / Hamburg, Germany / Ferrisburgh, Vermont
philip@2plusco.com
2plusco.com/work/creating-my-own-tomorrow

CREATING MY OWN TOMORROW
2+ / PHILIP BUSSMANN, CÉLESTINE HENNERMANN

Success is a fragile construct that can manifest and collapse in a fleeting moment. "Creating My Own Tomorrow" addresses the polarity of success and failure in artistic creation. Fame and the desire for artistic success has repeatedly emerged as a theme in pop culture (whether encapsulated by Andy Warhol or popularized by David Bowie and Lady Gaga). In "Creating My Own Tomorrow" 2+ seeks to illuminate the passion and inner drive that sanctions the exploitation of those who may one day experience fame and/or eventually be destroyed by that which they most desire.

Philip Bussmann and Célestine Hennermann, in collaboration with performance artist Janice Perry and dancers Kristina Veit and Alfredo Zinola, have scavenged personal history and news media to establish a performance landscape of creative vagabonds drifting between the pursuit of fame and fear of failure. Bussmann's blinding white floor is divided by a white polythene curtain (4 m x 30 m), with audience members on either side. The curtain's height and length allows it to respond to movement and thus exists as a fluid, reacting backdrop to the dancers' movements. Marek Lamprecht's lighting transforms the curtain from a cold, opaque white background to a warm translucent veil that offers a view of the dancer on the opposite side. Perry crosses around and through the curtain, linking the sides, and eventually tears it down, allowing the audience a full view of the performers and each other. The piece ends with a series of questions about fame and its pitfalls, as Veit and Zinola gradually escalate a pas-de-deux from melancholy to frenzy.

2+ is a platform for collaboration with artists from all disciplines, based in Frankfurt, Germany. Bussmann and dramaturg Célestine Hennermann are its core members.

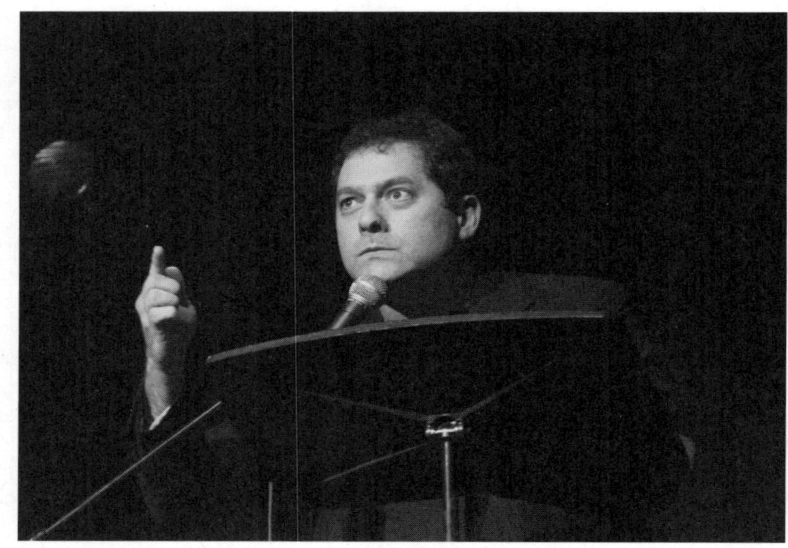

GGPS: THE GUILLERMO GÓMEZ-PEÑA GLOBAL POSITIONING SYSTEM

first performed on June 22, 2014
Sala Rossa, Montreal, Canada
performed once in 2014

L.M. BOGAD
Guillermo Gómez-Peña

Berkeley, CA / San Francisco, CA
lmbogad@gmail.com
lmbogad.com

GGPS: THE GUILLERMO GÓMEZ-PEÑA GLOBAL POSITIONING SYSTEM

L.M. BOGAD

I am alone, directionless and disoriented. I turn on my "GPS" system. The recorded voice of my colleague Guillermo Gómez-Peña (known as GGP) booms in the darkness. At first I just use the "GGP-GPS" to move through space geographically, but quickly the directions become existential, absurd, embarrassing. The GGPS system and I argue hotly, ludicrously—in Nahuatl, Basque, and *gringoñol*—about choosing ethical directions as artist-activists, body fascism, our contrasting aesthetics and borders of privilege.

It is strange, creating a performance in which you are writing rather harsh lines with which a treasured friend mocks, provokes and berates you. But this is the relationship that I have with Guillermo Gómez-Peña. We smile and jest at each other across porous, fluid, but substantial and significant borders of identity, ethnicity, sensibility, privilege and profession. In our rehearsal process Gómez-Peña adapted and improvised his lines so that they were sharper, stronger and fit his style.

GGP and I both played cartoonish versions of ourselves; he using a mock-robo-chicano voice and I as a haughty academic with pretensions of egalitarianism. But soon enough the unseen "robot" is subverting and overturning the power relationship— misdirecting me so I miss a faculty meeting and lose my job (to provide a slot, finally for a scholar of color in my ossified department), pushing me to Mexercise™ onstage while quoting Marx in Esperanto, sending me on confrontational missions out into the audience—to exchange bodily fluids, confessions, or legally-binding pledges of solidarity. It is darkly fun to use the premise of El Maestro GGP's "commands," which I have written, to push myself.

Gómez-Peña's directives become more challenging and ridiculous. I fight back. Our differences in agenda and style become starker. However, as we approach a border checkpoint that must be crossed, we reach a synthesis or at least a syncretic truce, in tentative coalition if not in alliance.

Meanwhile, the unfolding performance is a provocation I deliver to myself—a chance to raise the personal stakes in my own aesthetic, to take more personal risk, not just physically on the street but emotionally in terms of self-exposure, and ethical self-critique and implication. Inspired by GGP's actual lived example, and prodded by this cyborg-fabulous version of him, I intend to cross this border. The piece avoids, I hope, narcissism or solipsism as it uses the "vehicle" of the GGPS to engage with larger issues of racism, scholarship and dissent.

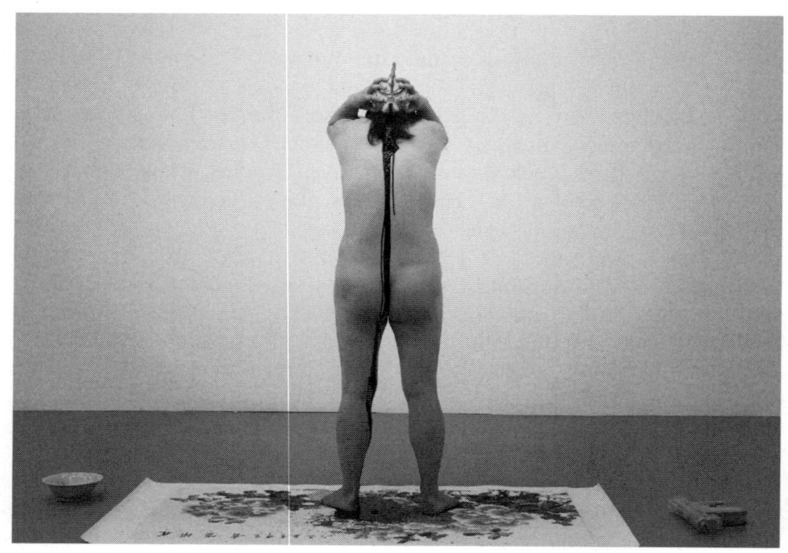

THE LOST TWELVE YEARS
first performed on June 24, 2014
ENCUENTRO 2014 at Centre Phi, Montreal, Canada
performed twice in 2014

CHUN HUA CATHERINE DONG

Canada

THE LOST TWELVE YEARS
CHUN HUA CATHERINE DONG

Performance steps:

step 1. I slightly bend my head to the right, pinching my forehead with water until a dark red dot appears.

step 2. I continue pinching my forehead while bending my body with tension.

step 3. I pick a porcelain spoon in the bowl and scratch my neck firmly with the spoon until a dark red line appears from my lower chin to upper chest.

step 4. I posit the teapot on my head, pouring ink from the teapot to my arched back to create a line. After the ink is gone, I straighten my back and stand still. I suddenly shake my head; the teapot smashes to pieces.

step 5. I kneel on the painting, lift the water gun and point to my head and shoot, and then I point to my heart and shoot. The shooting is gentle in the beginning but becomes gradually faster and faster. I repeat the action of shooting my head and heart until the ink in the water gun runs out.

This work examines the relationships between where I live, what I have lost and what I have gained as a racial minority. The piece is a ritual meditation, as the ink traditionally used as an artistic tool is used as a weapon upon myself. The gestures are political gestures. It is not only an apology for my twelve year absence but also a manifestation that reveals my urgent need to renew my lost tradition and culture. In this work, I baptize myself with Chinese ink to preserve my identity from self-transformation and self-assimilation, and to capture my stray soul in a foreign land.

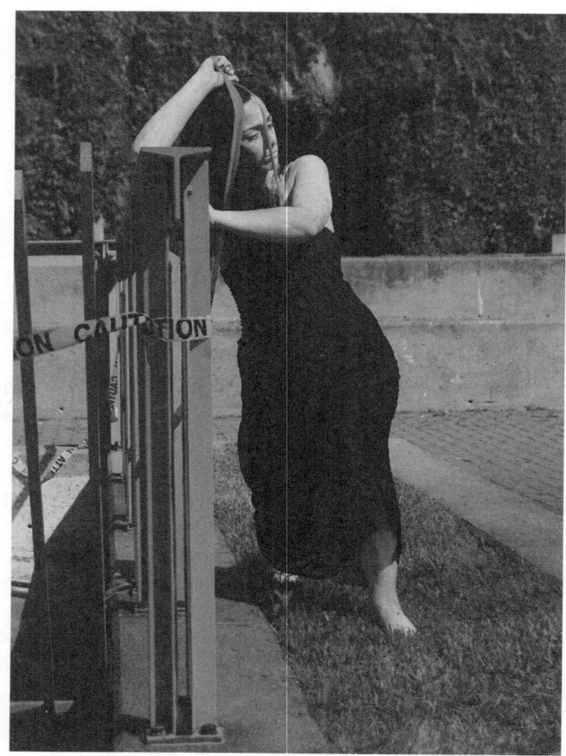

Shane Miersch

MOURNINGFESTO: I GRIEVE (EU LUTO)
first performed on June 27, 2014
Square Viger, Montreal, Canada
performed once in 2014

CARLA MELO

Toronto, Canada
carlabeamelo@gmail.com
hemisphericinstitute.org/hemi/en/enc14-urban-interventions/item/2366-enc14-ui-melo-mourningfesto

MOURNINGFESTO: I GRIEVE (EU LUTO)
CARLA MELO

Just as the translation of the noun "grief" (a private feeling) from English to Portuguese offers us "luto" (mourning), the public manifestation of grief, it also evokes the act of "lutar" (to struggle). Inspired by my native language, butoh aesthetics, mourning practices, structured improvisation, modernist manifestos, the Situationists and Afro-Brazilian cosmologies, I created an itinerant solo-performance/urban intervention—a self-invented mourning ritual that took place in a public park in Montreal and lasted for about 45-minutes.

As I moved out of a fetal position and began to slowly move across the urban space my goal was to find a place where I could *mourningfest*, that is: to publicly manifest the pain over the loss of my mother and my gratitude to her spirit for the gift of my life. I also wanted to express that the struggle of the grieving subject is twofold: she must struggle with loss itself and with normative notions of proper grieving. A powerful component of the piece was the unpredictability that is always at play when a performance directly interacts with spectators in an intimate manner and also the use of ritualistic objects and clothes whose meanings transformed throughout the pieces. For instance, a tunic printed with self-help and psychological texts on the "stages of grieving" served as shelter, wall and a restrictive garment that is eventually torn up, while a number of transparent water filled balloons that I carried across the park conjured images of the womb, tears and containment.

In this sense, "Mouriningfesto" sought to embody and purge the ways in which the grieving process has been repressed, homogenized and regulated, particularly for women. By challenging the limits between private grieving and public mourning, the piece foregrounded the near absence of mourning rituals within contemporary urban spaces.

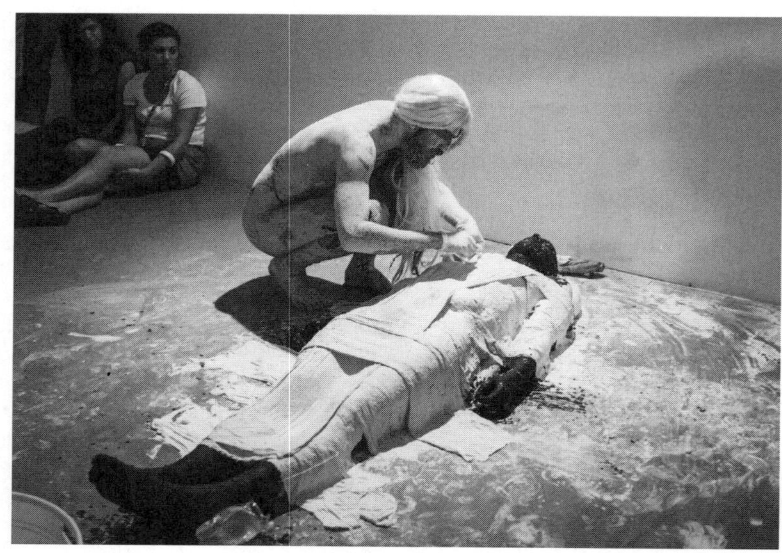

THE MESSIAH COMPLEX 1.0
first performed on June 28, 2014
Ortega Y Gasset Projects, New York City, NY
performed three times in 2014

MICHAEL DUDECK
Daniel Houdin

New York / Toronto / Rome
witchdoctor@michaeldudeck.com
michaeldudeck.com / museumofartificialhistories.com

THE MESSIAH COMPLEX 1.0
MICHAEL DUDECK

"The Messiah Complex 1.0" is the first of a series of performances that explore the construction of the Messianic figure in both ancient religion and pop culture as a ritualized transition of an individual from subject to object. For the past seven years my work has explored the invention of a queer religion and prehistory, and disseminated that fiction through a range of media, including: ritual performance, museological installation, authoritative publications, fictive documentaries, the construction of artifacts and the drafting of sacred texts. For this new series, I wanted to undergo a ritual wherein the body of a fictional prophet is performatively mummified and transformed into physical materiality, exposing and exploring the narrative and mediatic procedures that construct icons out of pulsing, bleeding flesh.

Central to my religious prehistory was a Messianic figure who was characteristically bald, painted white, with an orange marking below his lips. For years I worked with the same performer, in a series of images and publications that explored his placement directly within my invented cosmogony. For this performance, I collaborated with a new performer: one who fit the visual description and had a similarity to the earlier 'version.' I was interested in how messianic figures, particularly Christ, have maintained characteristic and recognizable features over centuries of image-making, and yet utilize entirely different 'models' to produce.

It was the closing performance of "The Body as Omen," curated by Sheilah Wilson at Ortega Y Gasset Projects, one of the last performances to take place in the mythic 1717 Troutman Street which housed a plurality of galleries in Queens, New York. It was alarmingly fitting that I was mummifying and in effect, performing a death ritual for such a meaningful place in the New York art world.

The performance began with the fictional prophet, painted white, sprawled naked on the concrete floor. Over the course of approximately one hour, I coated the prophets' body with black heated wax, hockey tape, rope and thick plaster bandages, while moving in and out of ritual trance. I had intended to use the wax and plaster to make molds afterwards, to produce the prophet as commodity, however the mold refused to stay. In the end I released the prophet from its mummification shortly after it had been encased, revealing, in the way that only performance can, the persistence of the temporal despite the yearning to make it material.

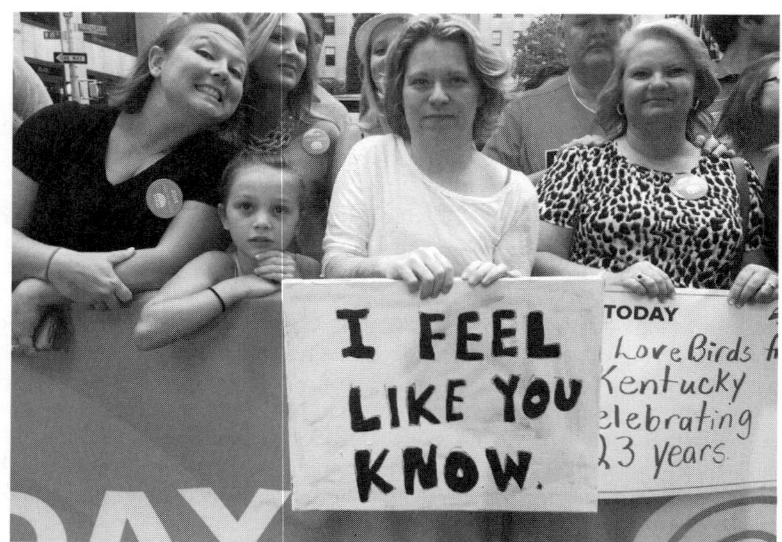

I FEEL LIKE YOU KNOW

first performed on June 28, 2014
Rockefeller Center, New York, NY
performed five times in 2014

CHRISTIE BLIZARD

San Antonio, TX
christieblizard.com

I FEEL LIKE YOU KNOW
CHRISTIE BLIZARD

"I feel like you know" started in June 2014 and consists of poetic signs that I hold up in the audience of "The Today Show" for national TV. By transforming the original filming of a television show into a place of artistic exhibition and performance, I am trying to disrupt the narrative of conventional television media. I want to reveal the hidden structures of the medium while also creating interventionist moments for a mass audience and testing what I can get away with within the structure of the show. The only rules for the signs for "The Today Show," as stated on its website, is that they cannot be vulgar or political. I view mine as statements on freedom of expression.

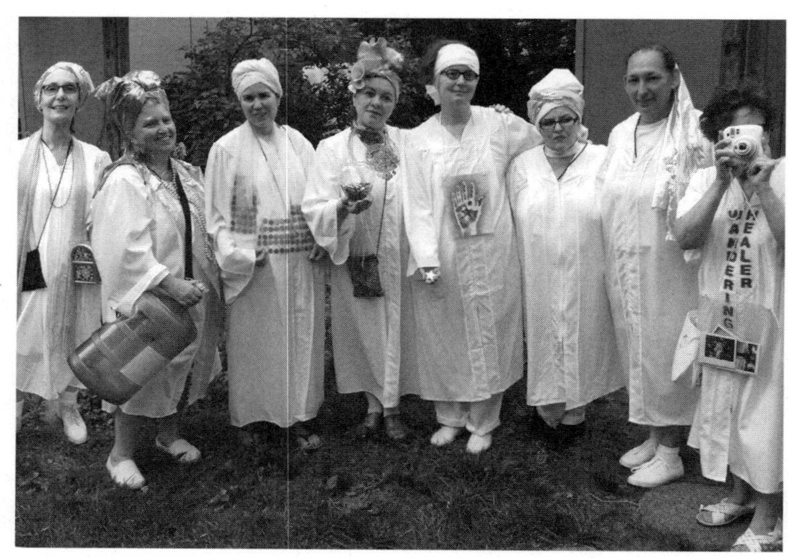

Taylor Moore

WHAT DO YOU WISH FOR?
first performed on June 28, 2014
Lumen 2014 Video and Performance Art Festival, Staten Island, NY
performed once in 2014

DAY DE DADA PERFORMANCE ART COLLECTIVE

Staten Island, NY
daydedada@yahoo.com
DayDeDada.com

WHAT DO YOU WISH FOR?
DAY DE DADA PERFORMANCE ART COLLECTIVE

The Day de Dada Wish Sisters collected wishes from the Lumen festival attendees from 7-9 pm and then released the wishes into the world in a ceremony at 10 pm. Each Wish Sister collected wishes in a different way. Milenka Berengolc took instant photos which she later performed reiki on, Mary Campbell supplied a fountain for coins to be tossed into, Margaret Chase supplied beads to be attached to a string, Viv de Dada had people whisper in her ear and then she transferred the wish to her bottle, Leslie Lowe gave people fans to write on, Barbara Lubliner with her magic wand and box, Tamara Wyndham had participants write on stars and Lydia Grey had seeds to plant. Some approached festival attendees while others waited for curious attendees to approach them. All were dressed in white robes with gold accessories. A sticker with the saying "Be careful what you wish" was given to participants. At the release ceremony we circled a fire in a cauldron that had been created for us and one at a time dispersed the wishes.

The Lumen performance inspired participants to consider a wish that is important to them and then reveal it. We believe there is great power in a disclosed wish as it begins an energy movement. Thinking, writing and revealing a wish helps one to recognize themselves and prioritize their actions. Related to hope, wishes become a constant reminder of how life can be better. Our performance intended to encourage contemplation of goals and desires. Many people took the action very seriously as they closed their eyes, concentrated and took a deep breath before making their wish. Our performance highlighted an action that people may often do in a time of stress or pessimism but we gave them an opportunity in this scenario to take a moment for themselves and acknowledge their dreams. We are interested in creating these kinds of positive moments in our performances.

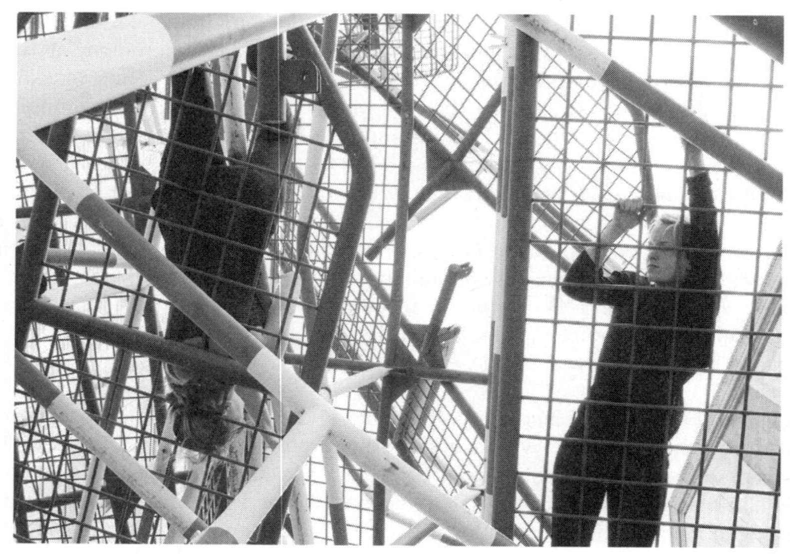

ACCESS EXIT
first performed on June 29, 2014
On the Mediaspree at "13.4.1981" by Olaf Metzel, Berlin, Germany
performed four times in 2014

TANJA KNAUS
Raegan Truax

Berlin, Germany / San Francisco, CA
tanja-knaus.com / raegantruax.com

ACCESS EXIT
TANJA KNAUS

"Access Exit" is a series of ten embodied interventions taking place at, on and around public sculptures from June 2014 to June 2015. The work questions how we access and exit public spaces, dialogues, historical context, memory, time, artistic practices, relationships, authorship and notions of monumentality.

"Access Exit I/X" was performed June 29, 2014 for 90 minutes by myself and my collaborator, Raegan Truax, in Berlin at "13.4.1981" by Olaf Metzel (1987).

"Access Exit II/X" was performed August 1, 2014 for three hours by myself at "Two concrete Cadillacs in form of the naked Maja" by Wolf Vostell (1987).

"Access Exit III/X" was performed September 3, 2014 for three hours by Raegan in San Francisco at "Vaillancourt Fountain" by Armand Vaillancourt (1971).

"Access Exit IV/X was performed October 26, 2014 for 90 minutes by myself at "Large Divided Oval: Butterfly" by Henry Moore (1987).

I continue alternating performances with Raegan until we reunite (physically) to create and perform the final six hour piece, "Access Exit X/X," in June 2015.

By exchanging nine minute films and other physical materials from each three hour performance instead of verbally describing our performances to one another, we explicitly engage the gap between live performance and documentation and between our physical bodies as we collaborate to realize each layer of "Access Exit."

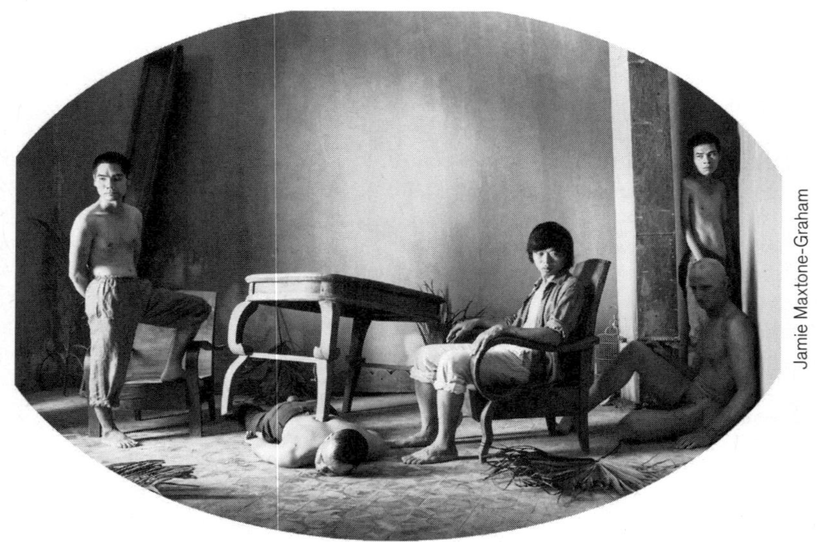

THAT LITTLE DISTANCE
first performed on July 2, 2014
In the artist's studio, Hanoi, Vietnam
performed once in 2014

JAMIE MAXTONE-GRAHAM

Hanoi, Vietnam
jamie@jamiemaxtonegraham.com
jamiemaxtonegraham.com

THAT LITTLE DISTANCE
JAMIE MAXTONE-GRAHAM

The performance of "That Little Distance," as a series of photographs, was backed into somewhat accidentally. The images themselves were produced in a daylight studio in a former state-owned factory in Hanoi, Vietnam. The photographer appears with the subjects in the portraits. The images, made through long exposures of around 20 seconds each, ultimately became documents of performances of stillness produced by the subject and the photographer sitting silently together in front of the open shutter.

The purpose of the work was to engage by means of the photographic image the temporality of place and to create a conversation with history, art and mortality. The work attempted to engage in a dialogue with 19th century neoclassical art and a period of time when photography, then in its infancy, embraced the aesthetic of painters who were also in conversation with an earlier period of classical Greek art.

The initial impulse of the work was to produce a series of portraits utilizing long exposure photography in a daylight-only illuminated, interior space. The second impulse of the work was, as the producer of the work, to reside within the photographic space—alongside the principle subject of the works—nude. By occupying a part of the framework of the image and simultaneously performing the roles of producer, subject and object, the intent of the work and its result became somehow secondary to the act of sitting silently and motionless many times over in conjunction with other people in the act of producing a single image.

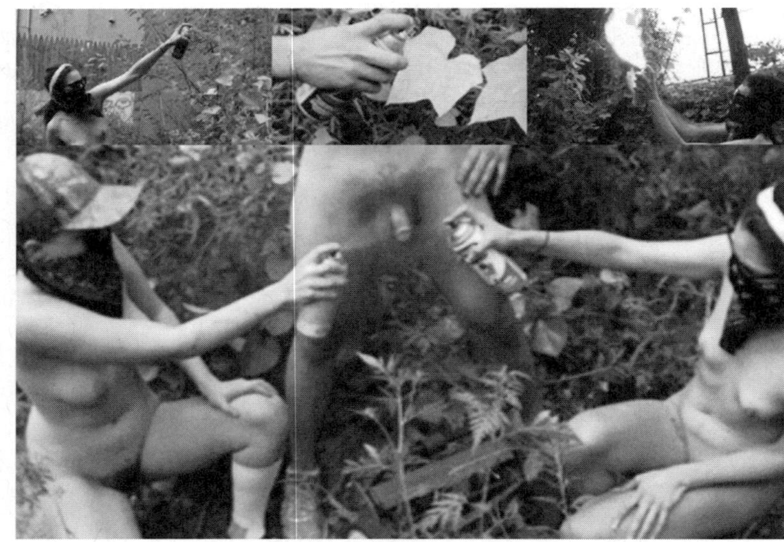

MASS ARCADIA
first performed on July 4, 2014
Outdoors, New York, NY
performed once in 2014

MILES PFLANZ
Sean Connery, Nick Broujos, RVL, Zoe Wardlaw

New York, NY
milespflanz@gmail.com
youtube.com/user/milespflanz

MASS ARCADIA
MILES PFLANZ

Four naked youth spraypaint flora. The ground is already toxic, so why not demand explosive color of greenery? In their exuberance, they spraypaint their genitals.

Nature must be appropriated for both subsistence and aesthetics. Paradise is vandalism. A conspiracy to insert oneself into the big picture that leaves Krylon dripping from every surface. Make anywhere Eden, a reprieve from storm and survival.

We notice an old IRAK tag and post the video on PornHub later.

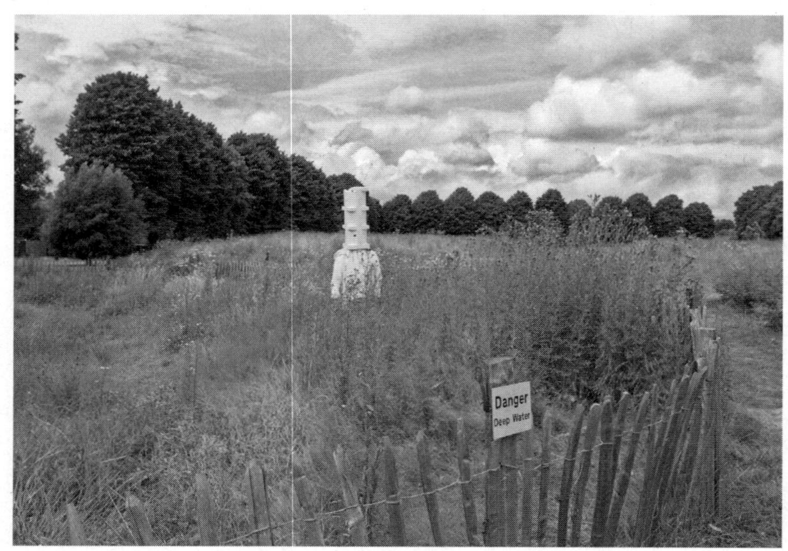

Shahin Shahablou

DANGER DEEP WATER

first performed on July 5, 2014
Lloyd Park, London, UK
performed once in 2014

ED WOODHAM

Brooklyn, NY
artinoddplaces@gmail.com
edwoodham.com

DANGER DEEP WATER
ED WOODHAM

Developed in the drawingshed residency IdeasFromElse[w]here, this performance was initially intended as a visual presentation in Lloyd Park in East London. In the gallery/work area that the curators established, I found large polystyrene packing materials and created a mask. Then I walked through the park and discovered what was left of a pond. There was no water and it was overgrown. Officials had fenced it in and put up a sign that read,"Danger: Deep Water."

Wearing the mask and dressed in all white, I climbed over the fence and stood on a stool in the middle of the pond. I stood as a statue where no one had stood for years to interrupt an ordinary day in the park.

The first people to notice me were a couple of unruly boys. They gathered round the fence and throwing sticks and stones in my direction yelled at me to "GET OUT!" The newly gathered crowd felt angry. Slowly though, as I stood there, I felt the mood shift from concern to curiosity.

Suddenly, out of nowhere, a little boy yelled, "Are you ok? Do you need help?" I spontaneously responded with hand gestures and body movement. Then more questions: "What's your job? Are you getting paid? What's your favorite shape? Are you lonely? Are you in love?" And then, "Is this art?" He was the voice of the crowd that connected everyone. For two and a half hours, I heard various streams of conversations around me. I kept hearing people asking, "Is this art?"

For those visiting the park that day, they saw more than individuals looking at a human statue in a waterless pond. They saw a community connecting and energizing public space.

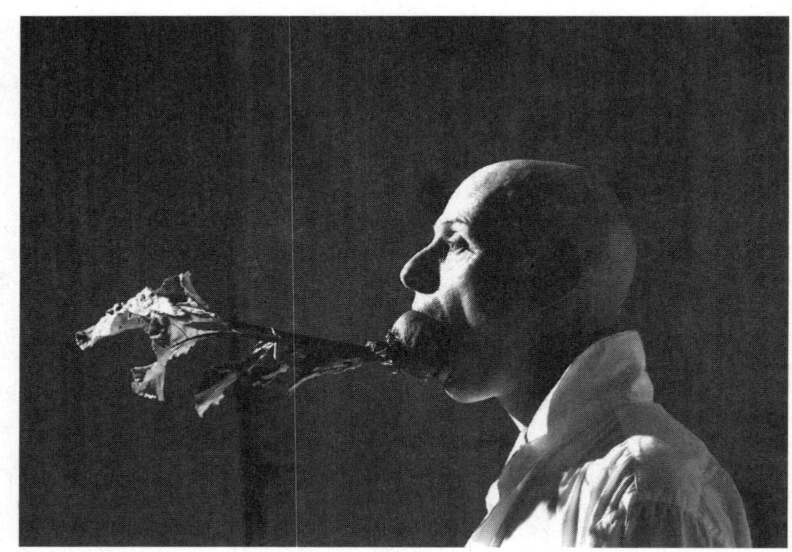

BEETROOT
first performed on July 7, 2014
DEFIBRILLATOR Gallery, Chicago, IL
performed once in 2014

JOSEPH RAVENS

Chicago, IL
joseph@josephravens.com
josephravens.com

BEETROOT
JOSEPH RAVENS

"BEETROOT" is part of a series of works where I combine imagery and actions from past performances as a sort of physical archive or personal retrospective. I've been indexing my visual vocabulary and assembling an action lexicon in order to create remixes or mashups of my work. This approach is relatively new for me. The beet itself is one of many root vegetables I have held in my mouth and eventually chewed into pulp to conclude a performance. Changing from white to black, large silver bowls, paper airplanes, black circles and roots are all elements from previous performances that embrace reoccurring ideas of transformation, alienation, insatiability and an oxymoronic desire for escape while longing for home.

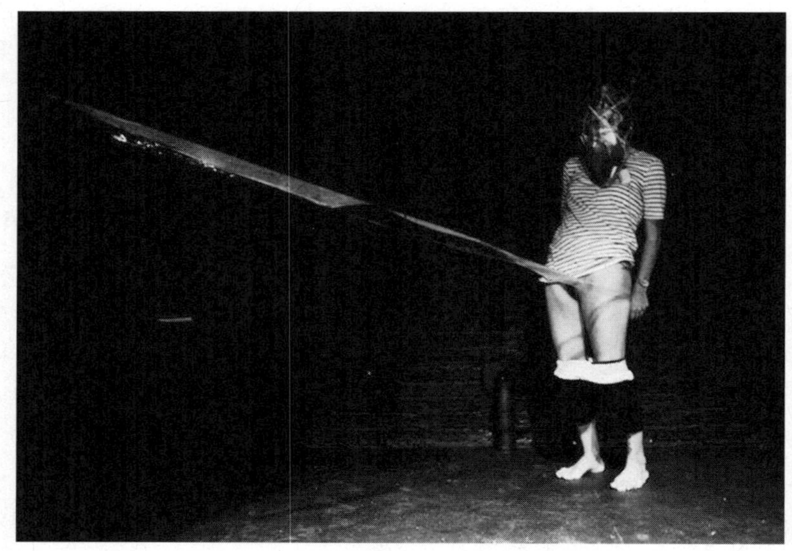 Matt Dunn

HEAVENLY BROWN BODY
first performed on July 11, 2014
Department of Columbia Arts Center, Washington DC, USA
performed four times in 2014

ANAZE IZQUIERDO
Marc Mosteirin

Lima, Peru
anaze.izquierdo.azorin@gmail.com
cargocollective.com/anazeizqvierdo

HEAVENLY BROWN BODY
ANAZE IZQUIERDO

I show up, spill oil in the floor, take out my shoes and start having conversations with people about police brutality, queer community and POC. While I'm telling the audience my personal experiences in regards to these topics, I start slipping on the floor, interrupting the conversations by multiple falls while getting wet with the oil. After this I tell people I want to share a prayer from "the deepest part of herself." I take off my pants, pull a paper out of my vagina and start reading it, getting louder and louder:

Litanies to my heavenly brown body
Blessed are the sissies
Blessed are the boi dykes
Blessed are the people of color my beloved kith and kin
Blessed are the trans
Blessed are the high femmes
Blessed are the sex workers
Blessed are the authentic
Blessed are the dis-identifiers
Blessed are the gender illusionists
Blessed are the non-normative
Blessed are the gender queers
Blessed are the disabled
Blessed are the hot fat girls
Blessed are the weirdo-queers
Blessed is the spectrum
Blessed is consent
Blessed is respect
Blessed are the beloved who I didn't describe, I couldn't describe, will learn to describe and respect and love
Amen

After people answer Amen, I leave the space.

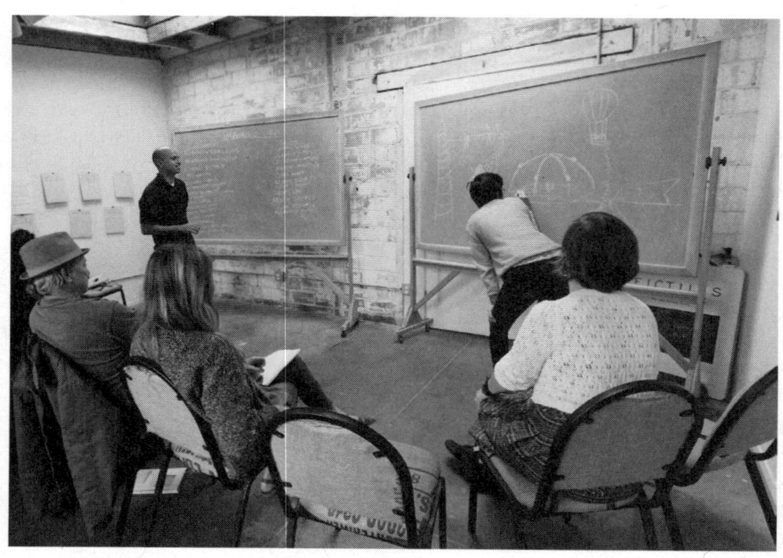

VAGUE NOTIONS

first performed on July 16, 2014
Interface Gallery, Oakland, CA
performed seventeen times in 2014

FICTILIS

Oakland, CA
info@fictilis.com
fictilis.com

VAGUE NOTIONS
FICTILIS

From July 16th to August 10th 2014, FICTILIS performed "Vague Notions," a series of low-pressure, open-ended "brainstorming sessions," at Interface Gallery in Oakland, California. Each session was free and open to the public. "Topics" for the sessions were submitted by gallery visitors and artists from Oakland and beyond, and ranged from broad themes or subjects to specific issues, questions, problems or single-word prompts—anything that could feasibly be discussed for approximately one hour in a small group setting.

Topics included: What to Brainstorm; Art and the Mundane (from Felicity Fenton); anticipatory haiku (from Missa Coffman); the problem of the ORIGINAL in new media arts (from Omer Golan, facilitated by Jennifer Parker); Vague Notations, or Please Befigulate: The League of Imaginary Scientists in conversation with FICTILIS and friends; Vagina-Centered Artworks: a discussion (from Allison Kotzig, facilitated by Sabrina Habel); Imagined Cities (with Justin Mata); entertainment for disability in public places (with Sanaz Sarabi); Prolepsis and Creativity (with Alan Hopkins); earliest childhood dream or memory (with Den Zolo); childhood language games; Prowling The Deep; and What's the Point?

Some sessions were scheduled, some were impromptu. Some were facilitated by the submitters of the session topic while others were led by special guest facilitators. All sessions were conducted using large rolling chalkboards, with FICTILIS and other participants assisting with transcription. After each session, these chalkboards were systematically photographed, then left in the space un-erased until the next scheduled brainstorm, to be experienced as artifacts containing the traces of conversations which took place there. Visitors to the gallery could add to the boards or erase them and perform their own brainstorming sessions.

The purpose of this performance series was to force ourselves into some uncomfortable situations, to see how a diverse set of prompts could be translated into spoken and written form by a small group of participants, and to attempt to fashion a performance out of the very process of coming up with an idea for a performance in the first place. The project was a response to increasing consideration of ethics in socially engaged art and the already-widespread privileging of "ideation" and other "creative" practices in Bay Area tech culture.

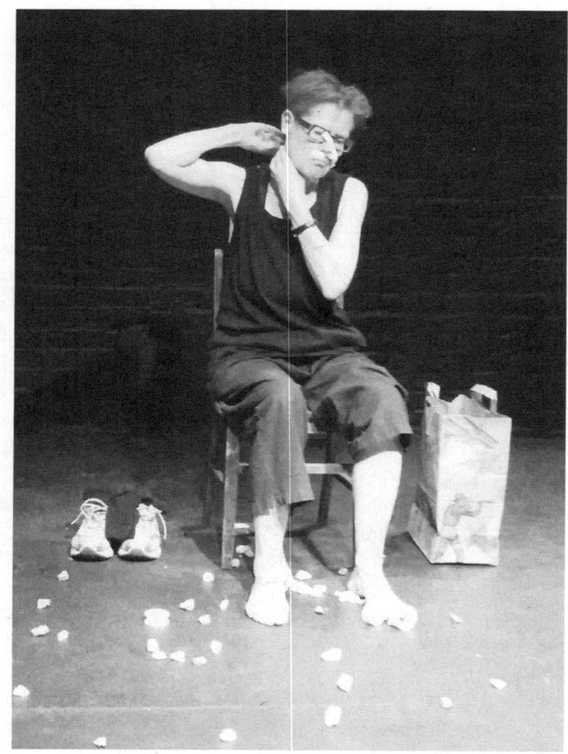

SCAR TISSUE

first performed on July 19, 2014
District of Columbia Arts Center, Washington, District of Columbia
performed twice in 2014

LEENA RAUDVEE

Toronto, Canada

SCAR TISSUE
LEENA RAUDVEE

"Scar Tissue" was a one woman performance art piece, part of the 25 hours of performance festival at the DCAC in Washington D.C. on July 19, 2014. I was addressing issues of memory and loss, through the metaphor of a wound, physical and/or emotional, which may heal but leaves a scar, a trace, a residue. It may be invisible but there is a scarring that remains present in the tissue and in the memory.

In "Scar Tissue" I sat in a chair facing the audience, my shoes and socks removed, and a large paper bag in my lap. Suddenly, I picked up the bag and turned it upside down. With a loud clatter, rough black stones and rolls of surgical tape spilled out onto the floor.

I picked up a stone and searched for the memory on my body. I taped the stones to my body, marking old wounds, invisible aches, losses and painful memories. Large white X's of white tape held the irregular excrescences in place, disfiguring the body and making visible a history of past and present scars. I pulled socks and shoes over my transformed feet and adjusted glasses on my reformed face.

Standing up, painfully, I pulled clear latex gloves out of a pocket and carefully put them on. Slowly kneeling down on the floor I started gathering up the stones and rolls of tape with my gloved hands and threw them back into the bag. I was cleaning up. But my body still held the remnants of the remembering, the honoring and the mourning.

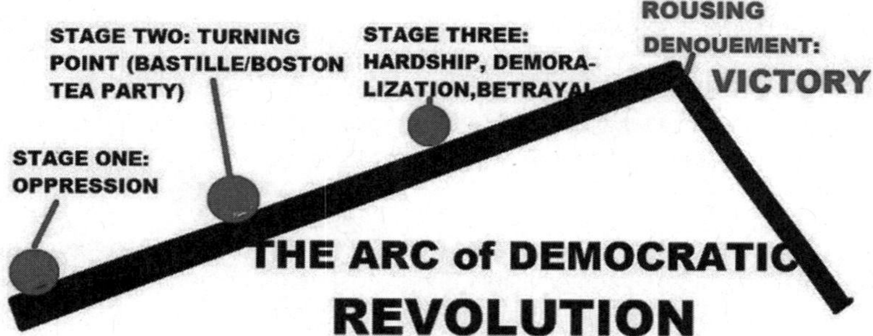

Andrea Liu

INSTITUTE FOR POLITICAL HYPOCRISY
first performed on July 24, 2014
ACUD Kunsthaus Gallery, Berlin, Germany
performed once in 2014

ANDREA LIU

New York, NY
naxalbelt@gmail.com
replaceandrea.blogspot.com / jvea.org/institute-for-political-hypocrisy

INSTITUTE FOR POLITICAL HYPOCRISY
ANDREA LIU

"The Institute for Political Hypocrisy" is a satirical lecture-as-performance by me as a representative of a fictional organization whose stated mission is to "help hegemons fabricate the rhetoric, the image and the aura necessary to maintain the illusion that they are democratic societies while they act in ways that are antithetical to democracy." The mission statement says, "If you are a fledgling nation or polity who wants to develop into a full blown democratic hegemon, we will help you create a shimmering 'creation myth' with any parts of your nation's history that contradict this myth (slavery, genocide, colonialism) expunged."

Much of the performance is spent selling "democratic creation myths" with overtones of scientology or "self-help cults," only this organization is to help whole countries benefit from the hegemony of "liberal democracy."

> For $27.99 one can purchase the colorful tale of revolutionary heroes overthrowing an autocratic regime and starting a republic.

> For $19.99 we help you construct a national anthem that tells the narrative of how your republic was born and reaches a climactic denouement.

> For $7.99 we can help you choose your national colors and design a flag that involves a convoluted esoteric story about how these colors are related to the birth of your republic.

My performance elucidates four stages of training that every democratic hegemon goes through:

> 1.) ERASURE (erasure of history of indigenous people exterminated or other factors that don't fit one's democratic "creation myth")

> 2.) HISTORICAL AMNESIA ("forgetfulness" of assassinations of foreign leaders, invasions, and overthrows of democratic regimes all over the world)

> 3.) MYSTIFICATION (create a smokescreen or fog that obfuscates one's imperialist intentions)

> 4.) DEMONIZATION OF THE "OTHER" (demonize world leaders of countries who threaten Western hegemony: Khomeni, Gadaffi, Noriega, Castro, Arafat, Milosevic, Saddam Hussein, Osama and Putin)

Much of the challenge of the performance is about inhabiting the language of advertising while simultaneously collapsing that language unto itself and causing that language to betray itself. The performance also deals with Barthes' notion of mythology: ways of thinking and doing that masquerade as nature emptied of their historical specificity, imbued with a patina of inevitability and timelessness (in this case, of democracy). Myth is an airless vacuum, things that seem already fully formed, assumptions so internalized they don't need to assert themselves as something distinct from what would already be taken for granted as true.

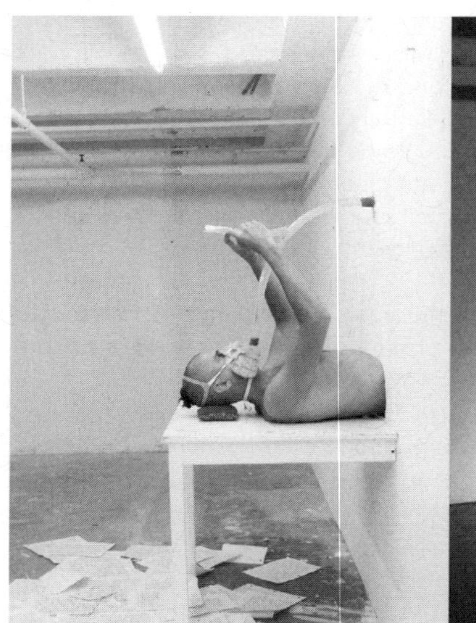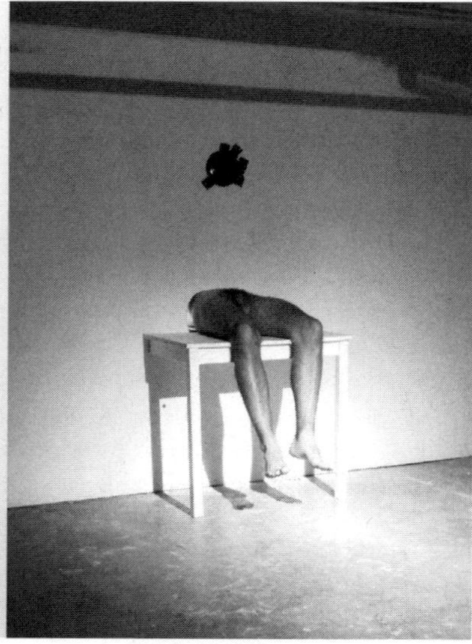

Matt Savitsky

THE MORNING PAGES
first performed on July 26, 2014
Perform Chinatown 2014:CHAOS REIGNS!, Los Angeles, CA
performed once in 2014

MATT SAVITSKY

Los Angeles, CA
mpsavitsky@gmail.com
mattsavitsky.com

THE MORNING PAGES
MATT SAVITSKY

I was invited to create a performance for an annual festival held in Chinatown organized by Paige Wery, Lee Lynch and Doug Harvey. I was given a basement to use as my performance space that was bisected into two rooms by a wall. To activate both areas, I sawed a kitchen table in half and placed either end in each room under a waist-sized hole. During the performance, I inserted my naked body through the hole so that, from the waist down, I was in one room while my top half occupied the other. During the performance, I spoke into a muzzle attached to a funnel mounted above my torso, projecting my voice over my lower half and into the opposite room. Over seven hours, I read from approximately 200 pages I had written as part of a daily writing devotional. I had not reread these writings before the performance. Without my knowledge, art-goers could first inspect my genitals and listen to my writing before entering the second room to view my top half.

In this performance, I embedded my body in the walls of the space. As in my installation work, I was interested in exploiting garden-variety orientation of built spaces, in particular here, the distinct front and back of a wall. More than practical, choices we make while moving through a space can reflect and communicate codes of conduct, especially when the space is used to host social events. I strategically positioned myself in the basement according to a set of choices I imaged the audience having to make. Do I look at him? And for how long? How do I hide my reaction? How do I communicate my reaction? Do I look on the other side?

Most visitors were very cautious, confused and or mocking. One particularly daring guest, breathed onto my penis and licked it several times, but very quickly. I am interested in the range of responses to the situation I created, but to the extent of needing proof that what I did meant something. Overall, the gesture reflected the physical and psychic distance I feel between my head and my sex. In this work, rather than imagining a would-be agent, bridging the gap, I chose to eroticize distance to illustrate a conflicted presence.

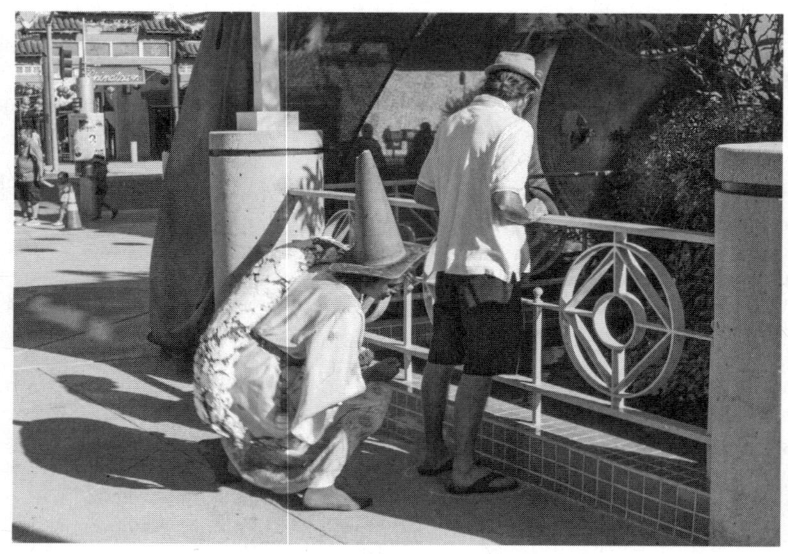

Lindsay Bloom

DUNCE EXTENDED + SERVITUDE!

first performed on July 26, 2014
Chinatown, Los Angeles, CA
performed once in 2014

ANGIE JENNINGS

San Diego, CA
angelamichellejennings@gmail.com
angelajennings.tumblr.com

DUNCE EXTENDED + SERVITUDE!
ANGIE JENNINGS

During Perform Chinatown: Chaos REIGNS! LA's annual gathering of performances, I decided to extend a previous "Dunce Performance" addressing issues of hierarchy, the phallus, gender constructs, race (I am mixed, black and white), knowledge and labor. For Chinatown there was an added addition of servitude and dress!

I roamed the pedestrian walkways of Chinatown wearing an oriental pink floral robe, red tights on my legs, a diamond ring napkin holder tied around my forehead with a pink shoelace, a pink construction cone worn as my cap and a 25 lb hay-net barrier covered in plaster, which I carried throughout the four-hour duration. During my promenade I used white chalk to trace onto the concrete bodies of pedestrians and showgoers along with fixtures and objects, all the while holding the barrier crumbling and leaving its trail. I bowed and kneeled politely at times with the accompaniment of *Twinkle Twinkle Little Star* playing through a toy microphone that was attached to my hip.

Towards the end of the performance I began simply outlining the crevasses in the cement with chalk. While outlining, a male musician played pop music next to me and a small crowd enjoying the music stood to the right. I ended the performance by planting the barrier next to my styrofoam bust of the Roman emperor Caligula and used a broom to sweep away the debris left behind including plaster bits and hay. I used a bucket of water and a yellow sponge to wash the chalk off the cement. The feet of my red tights were torn by the concrete. And my right ankle gave out during the last hour of the performance due to the added weight of the barrier combined with the act of kneeling.

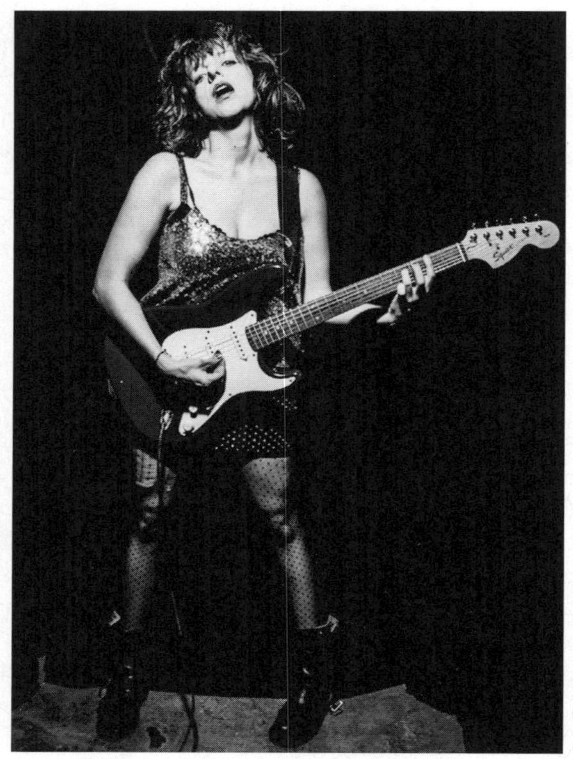

POSTCARDS FROM NEVERMORE
first performed on July 31, 2014
Dixon Place, New York, NY
performed four times in 2014

SABRINA CHAP
Anna Hovhannessian

New York, NY
mail@sabrinachap.com
sabrinachap.com

POSTCARDS FROM NEVERMORE
SABRINA CHAP

"Postcards from Nevermore" is a one-woman electric guitar radio musical with live performance. Combining original songs, theatrical monologues and abstract projections, it tells the story of two queers who escape a life of violence for Hollywood and heartbreak. The purpose of the work is to create a story-driven musical that is accessible to an audience of any income. Although performed live, it also will be slated for an album release in 2015, which will allow listeners across the world to access this story of the violence, survival and desperation that occurs in young queer love.

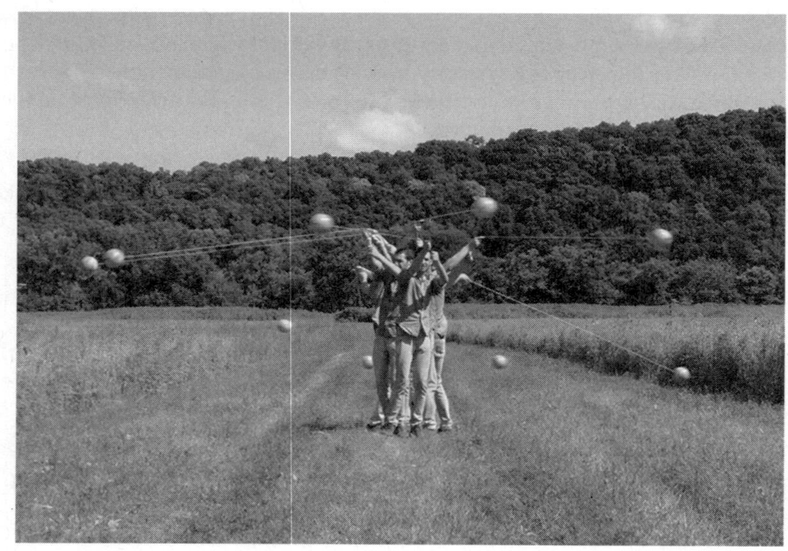

ORBIT 2
first performed on August 1, 2014
ACRE Residency, Steuben, WI
performed three times in 2014

BRADLEY TSALYUK

Los Angeles, CA
bradley.tsalyuk@gmail.com
cargocollective.com/tsalyuk

ORBIT 2
BRADLEY TSALYUK

The moon orbits the earth. Both of those simultaneously orbit the sun. Our sun orbits the center of the Milky Way Galaxy. All of these orbits happen without consideration for or knowledge of our daily movements and interactions. It's easy to forget these celestial bodies are constantly moving while we are constantly moving, thinking, breathing and consuming.

The idea of scale brings all of these actions together. I wanted to add to this spectrum of scale with this orbit. I wanted to create a small moment with some rope, an outdated lunar globe, and me spinning. I affixed the globes at the end of a 15 ft long rope and found an open field that could handle the diameter of the orbit. I began to spin, letting the centrifugal and centripetal forces lift the globe into the air to begin the orbit. The globe spun around me in wild and inconsistent circles. Every few moments I would get dizzy, let the globe drop and then begin again. The action was repeated until I could no longer stand.

I also want to include the words that inspired this work. This excerpt of text is from a 1980's children's book titled *Earth: Our Planet in Space* by Seymour Simon:

> "You live on Earth. You may live in a city or in the country. You may live where snow often falls or where it never snows at all. But wherever you call home, you live on Earth. We all live on Earth."

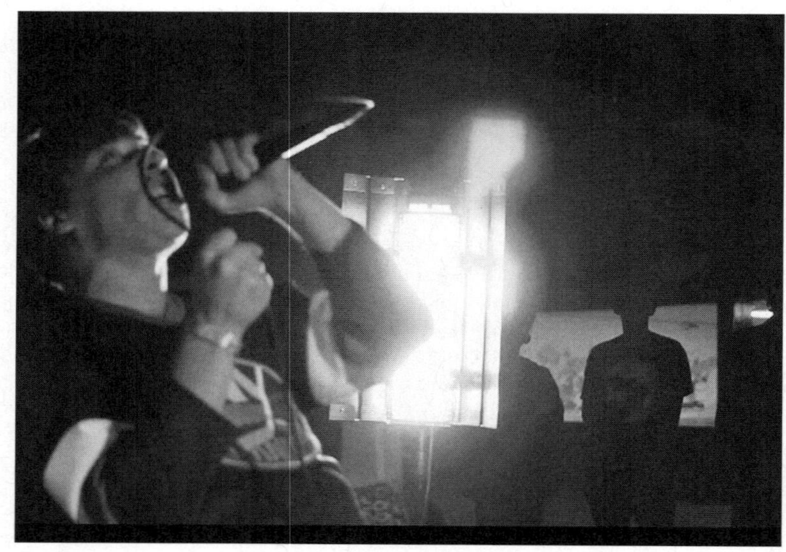

MY BROTHER, THE PUNK SINGER
first performed on August 1, 2014
Just For Fun Roller Rink, McHenry, IL
performed twice in 2014

CAITLIN RYAN
Patrick Ryan

Chicago, IL
ryan.e.caitlin@gmail.com
caitlinryan.com

MY BROTHER, THE PUNK SINGER
CAITLIN RYAN

"My Brother, the Punk Singer," is a cappella punk show inspired by Jean-Luc Godard's *Sympathy for the Devil*, and Ian Svenonius's *The Psychic Soviet*. In *The Psychic Soviet*, Svenonius points out in an essay entitled "Beatles VS. Stones" that in Godard's film "...the Rolling Stones are trying out endless approaches for their new song, "Sympathy for the Devil." As all manner of instruments are auditioned, the one constant is Mick Jagger's vocals..." The performance spotlights the singer, my youngest brother. Despite having been in numerous punk bands, my brother has never truly learned to play an instrument. Like Jagger, the one constant in his performance has been his vocals, and his role as the punk singer.

"My Brother, the Punk Singer," first took place in our hometown, at Just For Fun Roller Rink, which also doubles as a music venue. My brother approaches the improvised stage and audience, where he performs the show. Once he has taken the stage, without musical accompaniment, he stampedes into his role as The Singer.

"My Brother, the Punk Singer" was aimed to illuminate the absurdity of punk postures, but also their resonance.

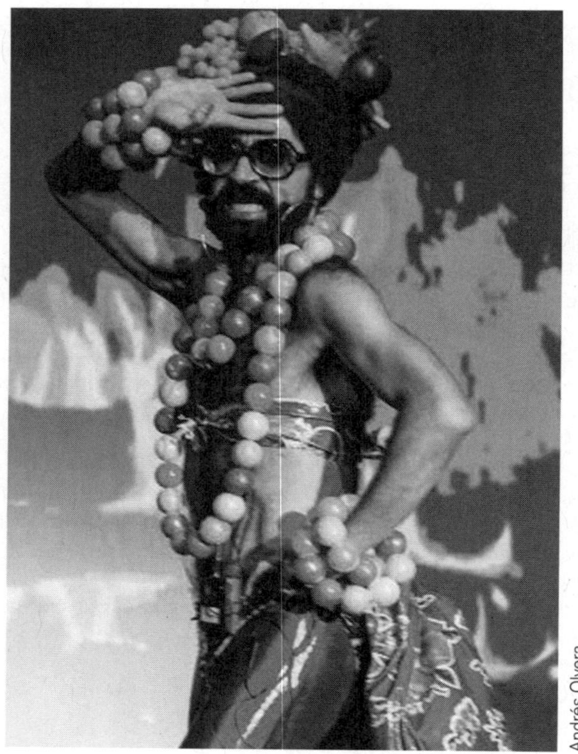

Andrés Olvera

CARNE Y PARRANDA, REVISITANDO A CARMEN MIRANDA
first performed on August 2, 2014
Foro Roma, Universidad de la Comunicación, Mexico City, Mexico
performed once in 2014

YECID CALDERÓN RODELO

Mexico City, Mexico
yecid.rodelo@gmail.com / pierandello@gmail.com
deviniendoloca.wordpress.com / pininaflandes.webnode.mx

CARNE Y PARRANDA, REVISITANDO A CARMEN MIRANDA
YECID CALDERÓN RODELO

The intention of playing with the figure of Carmen Miranda—a cliché repeated *ad nauseam*—arises from twisting the figure of the Diva to become a transvestite, a "bizarre" character. Pinina Flandes plays "Carne y Parranda" ("Flesh and Clubbing") as a kind of imitation referring to the singer and dancer Carmen Miranda, while emphasizing the sissy transvestite. I take the name "Carne" (flesh), instead of "Carmen," because Pinina fits most southern feelings: Latin American flesh is tender, very sensitive and is crossed by multiple stories to the rending of pleasure and pain, as it is released into the pathetic act of his condition. This is a conscious flesh that makes fun of his own suffering. Yecid Calderón, as Pinina Flandes, brings to the stage the pathos of Latin flesh and sinks into that feeling without shame of his drama.

With this Caribbean character from the Banana Republic of Colombia, I aim to demonstrate that the body of fags in the South is a body marked by pathos. The South is characterized by mad passion, or living passionately. Yecid has a text that says: "We live life *carnesimente* (crimson-ly)," referring to the intensity of crimson. The "sureados" bodies are flesh, raw and sentient. Not surprisingly, folklore gives us the platitudes of suffering through music, in Mexican rancheras, or in Caribbean music: son, bolero, vallenato (last one the music most listened to in Colombia). "Men, women and queers suffer Latin American infatuations, love hard, we fell in love and enjoyed great happiness, though love was perishable and fragile. Then comes disappointment, spite, the open wound of the passionate heart," Pinina says while her headdress is retouched, after the fruits have fallen from it.

Therefore, the performance of "Carne y Parranda" starts with a passionate love song. And then, as a set of images of fags and transvestites from the South with the charm of their poverty and their bizarre beauty unfolds, this "Carne" tells of his love and failures. The easy sentimentalization of suffering and poverty in the South is undercut by the fleshy, hairy Pinina. Educated by the culture of the soap opera, all altruistic love is a trick—it is just selfishness. The faces and naked bodies of some of her lovers appear while the fag "Carne" narrates the excesses of his sufferings with each of them. For all its critique, finally, this performance evokes love through sharing the fleshy memory of passions and failures.

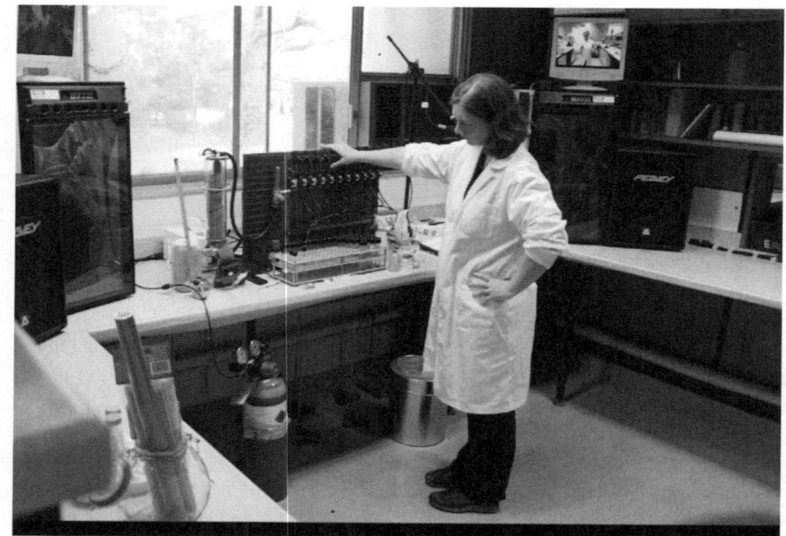

LAB FOR APOLOGIES AND FORGIVENESS V5
first performed on August 2, 2014
SymbioticA Centre for Excellence in the Biological Arts Laboratory, Perth, Australia
performed once in 2014

MEGHAN MOE BEITIKS
Christopher Cobilis

Chicago, IL
mobeitiks@gmail.com
meghanmoebeitiks.com

LAB FOR APOLOGIES AND FORGIVENESS V5
MEGHAN MOE BEITIKS

"A Lab for Apologies and Forgiveness" is an ongoing work in which I perform within a multimedia workspace, creating dialogues between disparate entities in order to gain greater understanding of our relationships to each other, land and pollution.

In Version 5, I build a gassing station for the cultivation of anaerobic bacteria. Specifically, this gassing station is intended to cultivate *Geobacter Sulfurreducens*, a bacteria that transforms radioactive uranium through respiration into a non-water soluble form.

I modeled my gassing station after an air conditioning unit at the SymbioticA lab in Perth, Australia. With this apparatus, I inoculated a single test tube containing soil from the Montebello Islands, the site of the first British nuclear test in 1952.

In my performance with the gassing station, I used documentation of that nuclear blast to set the countdowns to my own gassing protocol, making references to advances in fusion technology and my own problematic process in building the device. Two screens above incubators screened the black-and-white historical film, along with moments of the 1997 movie *The Saint* and performances from scientists who work with *Geobacter Sulfurreducens* in Melbourne, Australia. Throughout the piece I lectured on different aspects of scientific research and history, adjusted the gassing station, and physically quoted moments from the nuclear test documentation. The piece lasted about 20 minutes, and consisted of four "Acts of Research:" bubbling the media, putting the cap on, clearing the headspace and inoculation.

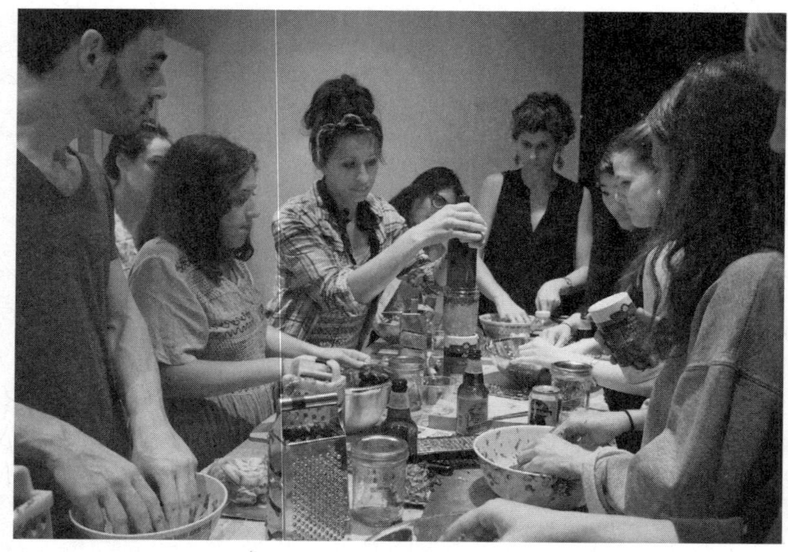

OS FERMENTATION

first performed on August 4, 2014
e-flux, New York, NY
performed twice in 2014

ECOARTTECH / LEILA CHRISTINE NADIR, CARY PEPPERMINT

New York, NY / Rochester, NY
lcnadir@gmail.com
ecoarttech.org/projects/fermentation

OS FERMENTATION
ECOARTTECH / LEILA CHRISTINE NADIR, CARY PEPPERMINT

"OS FERMENTATION" is a slow-cooking class, a healing ritual, and a spiritual revival of human-microbial collaborations. It is part of Leila Nadir and Cary Peppermint's new series of social sculptures that work collaboratively with local communities (human, bacterial and ecological) to resuscitate historic food practices and to facilitate recovery from what we call "industrial amnesia."

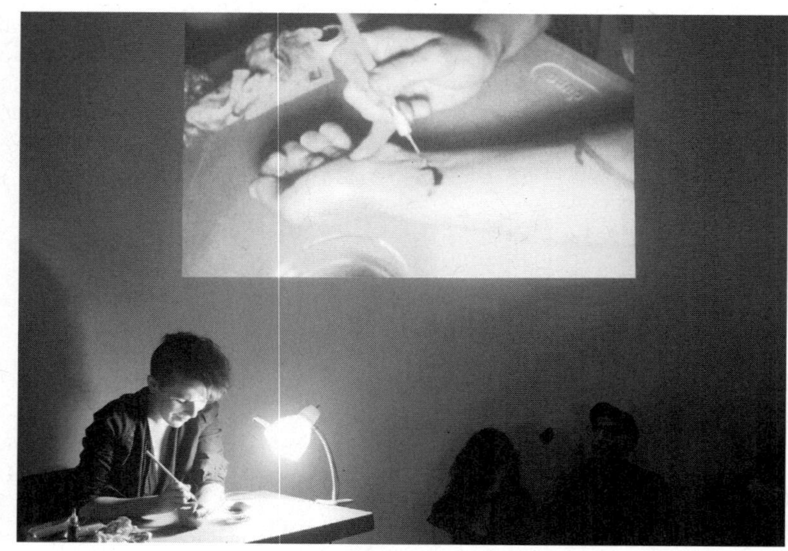

Violette Bule

ARE WE HAVING FUN YET? NO, I DON'T THINK SO.

first performed on August 8, 2014
Bikini Wax, Mexico City, Mexico
performed once in 2014

ARTEMISA CLARK

Los Angeles, CA
artemisaclark@gmail.com
artemisaclark.com

ARE WE HAVING FUN YET? NO, I DON'T THINK SO.
ARTEMISA CLARK

"Are We Having Fun Yet? No, I Don't Think So." is a performance in which I gave myself two tattoos—one happy face and one sad—comprised of one dot for, respectively, each audience member that entered the space in which the performance took place and each that left or passed by. While the act itself was very small and the room was lit solely with a lamp hanging over my forearms, a small camera was mounted on the lamp and projecting a live feed of the action on the wall behind me. Before I made each mark, I looked up, keeping track as best I could of the movements of those around me. While most of the audience was not entirely sure of what was happening, many told me later that they knew their physical presence had something to do with the marks I was making and they felt they should stay, even if watching me tattoo myself wasn't wholly enjoyable. When a face was complete, the piece was done.

This was a response to the expectation that a performance piece entertain. This is certainly an issue not exclusive to performance art, or art in general. As a teacher, I feel this often; in order to receive positive reviews from my students, I need to entertain and teach. As a woman, I have been taught to constantly practice making others comfortable even if doing so might be detrimental to what I have to say. Given these and other examples, it is no surprise that this sentiment would come up with my work as well. "Are We Having Fun Yet? No, I Don't Think So." makes physical, permanent, and bloody the effect that the audience's reception and interaction have on me. Their responses to the piece created an either happy or sad mark that will remain on my wrists forever.

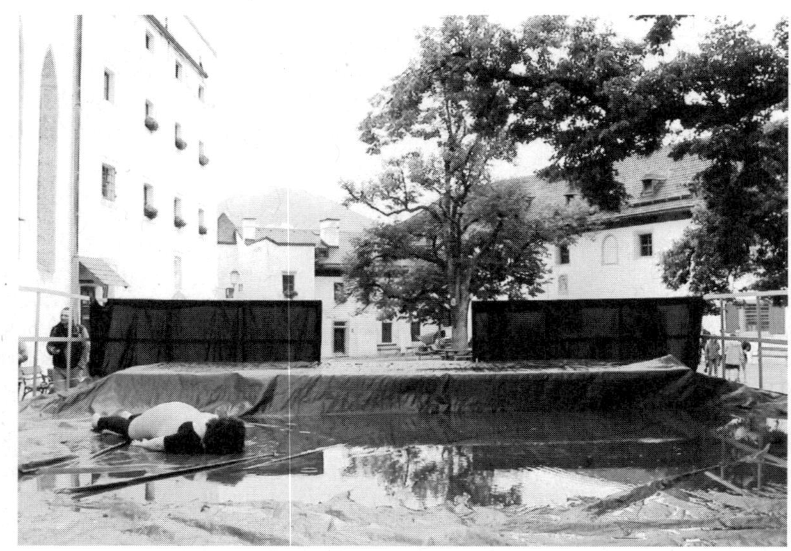

DIE GUTE BUTTER / DIE POLITIK DES BUTTER KÖRPERS (THE GOOD BUTTER / POLITIC OF THE BUTTER BODIES)

first performed on August 13, 2014
Hohensalzburg Fortress, Salzburg, Austria
performed twice in 2014

JESSICA POSNER

Syracuse, NY
posner.jessica@gmail.com
jessicaposner.com

DIE GUTE BUTTER / DIE POLITIK DES BUTTER KÖRPERS (THE GOOD BUTTER / POLITIC OF THE BUTTER BODIES)

JESSICA POSNER

"Die Gute Butter / Die Politik des Butter Körpers (The Good Butter / Politic of the Butter Bodies)" is the second performance in the ongoing series "Butter Body Politic." The BBP proposes butter as a metaphor for the body politic: feminist, queer, collective language for a body politic with a public body. The languages of butter—material, bodily, written, performative, social and political—are slippery.

The first performance in this series, "Butter Body Politic," first took place at Strange Loop Gallery in New York City, January 2014. In this performance, the artist sculpted approximately ten pounds of butter onto her head, rendering herself an unrecognizable butter monster.

"Die Gute Butter" takes a more linguistic, metaphorical approach by translating butter's material and social languages into body language. This performance took place on a borrowed stage in the courtyard of an eleventh-century castle in Salzburg, Austria. The piece combines improvisation with a written score based in the material language of butter (i.e., melt, blob, spread, mound, etc.). All of the directives within the score act both as noun and verb, allowing for significant slippage in the translation between languages surrounding this loaded substance. During the fifteen-minute performance, the artist moves around the stage finding language for her fat, female body through the material language of butter. It is important to note that the artist is a fat woman wearing compression garments/shapewear. It was performed live to unsuspecting international tourists and was video-documented.

According to Nazi Hermann Göring, "Guns will make us powerful, butter will only make us fat." A guns vs. butter macroeconomic model calls upon nation-states to balance the needs of the military (guns) against the needs of the people (butter). The New York State Fair hosts an 800-lb (360-kg) butter sculpture. In Minnesota, the winner of the Princess Kay of the Milky Way beauty pageant has her head carved in butter. Rock n' roll groupie Barbara "Butter Queen" Cope used butter as a lubricant. The Land O'Lakes butter box is an image of a Native American woman holding an infinite image of herself holding a box of butter reflecting herself. The first butter sculpture was the bust of a woman made by a bored dairy maid. The history of butter is as fraught with genocide as it is feminism.

In German, butter is referred to as "die gute butter." The good butter. There is no bad butter.

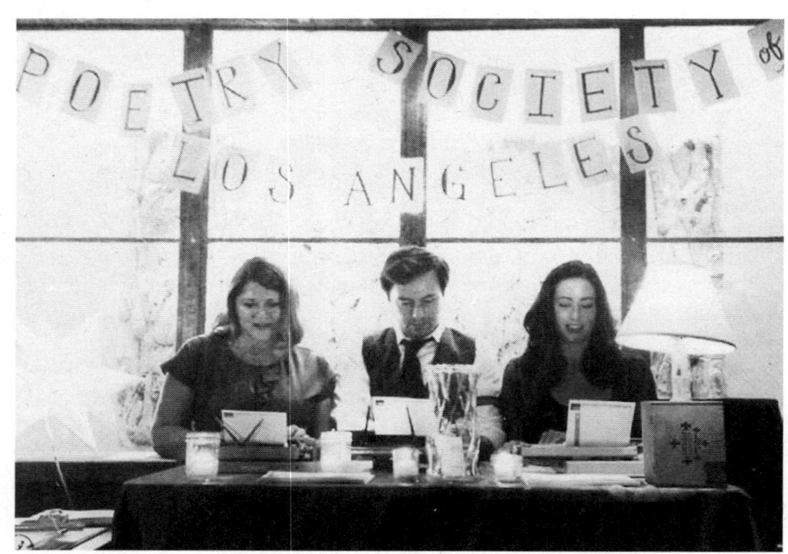

Anthony Christie

TYPEWRITERS ANONYMOUS

first performed on August 16, 2014
Wilshire Restaurant, Los Angeles, CA
performed three times in 2014

THE POETRY SOCIETY OF LOS ANGELES / PHILLIP T. NAILS, ELISABETH S. NAILS, AMANDA HOSKINSON, DEVIN MILLER

Los Angeles, CA
PoetrySocietyLA@gmail.com
PoetrySocietyLA.com

TYPEWRITERS ANONYMOUS
THE POETRY SOCIETY OF LOS ANGELES / PHILLIP T.
NAILS, ELISABETH S. NAILS, AMANDA HOSKINSON, DEVIN
MILLER

"Typewriters Anonymous" is an offline interactive poetry experience. As anonymous poets, we occupied vintage typewriters whipping up spontaneous poems inspired by short intake forms and distributed freely to audience participants. Through this performance installation we delivered private, one-on-one poetry experiences to audience members as an anodyne to the public experience of being "tagged" or "tweeted," with the added benefit of providing analogue texts that are not subject to surveillance by the United States National Security Agency. We also worked on manual typewriters because of their aesthetic beauty, kinesthetic sensation and celebration of freedom and privacy to express one's self outside the boundaries of digital surveillance.

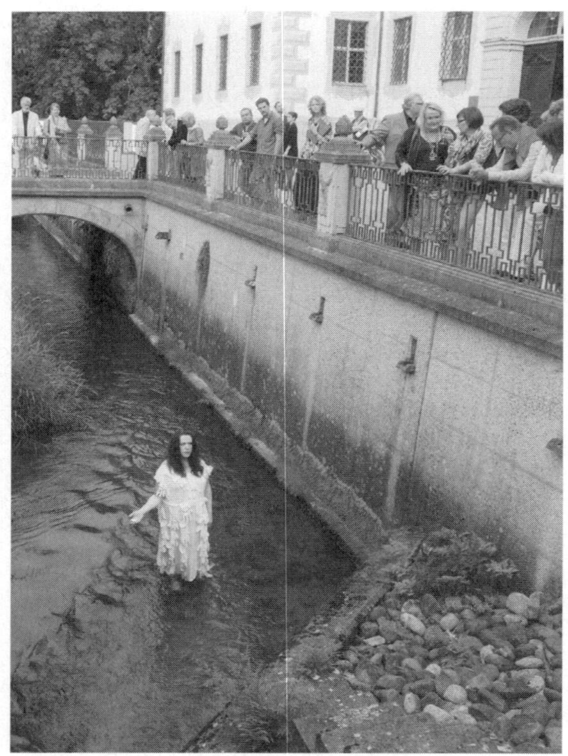

A MAIDEN STILL LESS

first performed on August 22, 2014
Schloss Salem Palace and Historic Abbey, Salem, Germany
performed once in 2014

LAUREL JAY CARPENTER

Alfred, NY
laureljay.com

A MAIDEN STILL LESS
LAUREL JAY CARPENTER

"A Maiden Still Less" is based entirely on site-specific research at Schloss Salem Palace and Historic Abbey and the Lake Constance region in Germany, and was performed for three and a half hours in the waterway in front of the palace. Down below in the moat's rushing current, a woman wears a bright white dress festooned with 40 archivist gloves. In each glove, weighing her, is a stone; thirteen of the stones are gilded gold. Walking at an indiscernible pace, the woman releases and excruciatingly slowly drops each stone in the water.

"A Maiden Still Less" conflates the artist's fascination with materiality, time and presence—fascinations historically shared by the resident Cistercian monks themselves. The monks' daily practice of devotion is the starting point for the piece. From there the artist applies a feminist perspective to reveal the darker history of early modern witch persecutions of the peroid that extended to any wise or brave, and therefore outcast, woman. The title of the piece, "A Maiden Still Less," is adopted from a record of those locally convicted and burned for witchcraft, unnamed: "… the apothecary's wife and daughter. The prettiest girl in town, aged nineteen. Four strange women found sleeping in the marketplace. A little maiden, nine years of age. A maiden still less." The title also refers to the age and experience of the woman presented here, strengthened now, able to release the burden, no longer an innocent maiden. A trail of stones—both invisible and glinting gold on the dark riverbed—remains as a marker after the woman disappears into a shadowy underground channel.

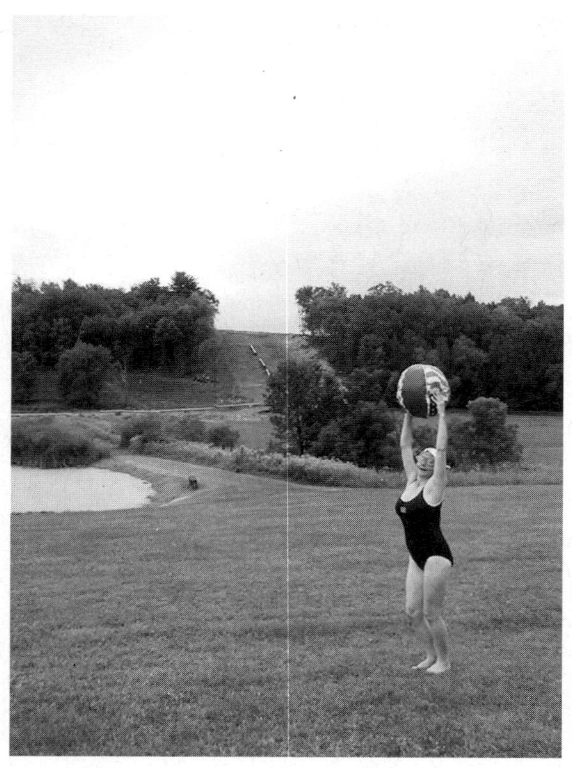

Suzanne Stroebe

DIANE THE AMERICAN SWIMMER SAYS, "DON'T WORRY, AMERICA!"

first performed on August 29, 2014
a field, Laceyville, PA
performed once in 2014

DIANE DWYER

Brooklyn, NY
diane@dianedwyer.info
dianedwyer.info

DIANE THE AMERICAN SWIMMER SAYS, "DON'T WORRY, AMERICA!"

DIANE DWYER

"DIANE THE AMERICAN SWIMMER SAYS, 'DON'T WORRY, AMERICA!'" is an ongoing performance/persona project. As Diane the American Swimmer, I am an iconic hero who can do anything because she is American. Through absurd acts and constructed scenarios, the project considers issues of nationalism and hegemony around the contentious and dire issues of water.

The performance is a response to the fracking that is devastating rural Pennsylvania. It lasted approximately ten minutes. As a photographer shot images, Diane the American Swimmer tried earnestly to pose as an exuberant athlete. She held a slightly deflated American flag blow-up ball above her head. The pose recalls the Lichtenstein painting *Girl with Ball*, which is actually based on an ad for the Mount Airy Lodge, also in Pennsylvania, not far from the site.

Recreation may seem one of the least significant issues around water, given that water resources are a global crisis. However, this act hopes to provoke concern over the cavalier disregard of fracking consequences to the wells in the area by recalling the homage to the historic beauty of the area's natural resources. A reverence and celebration of nature cannot be undervalued.

While the staging of this image is the primary performance, in my mind the performance includes and extends to the long-term experience of watching the landscape, the environment and the Earth be both transformed and cut into.

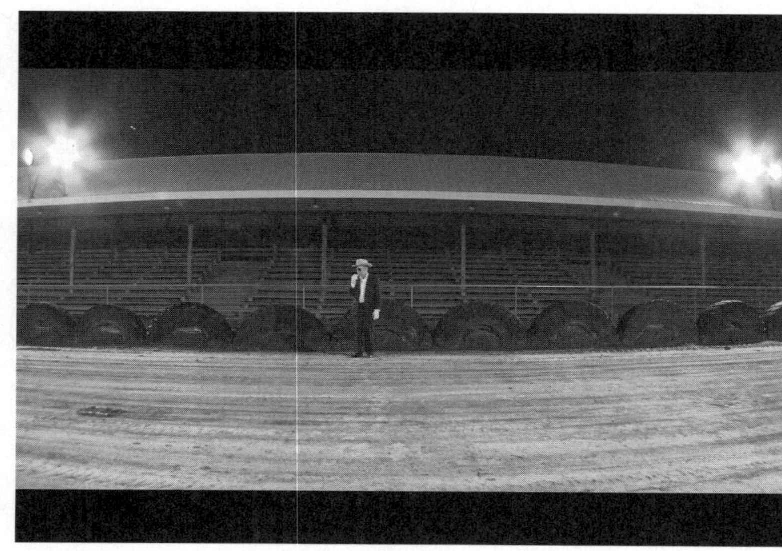

ODE TO MONTGOMERY
first performed on September 2, 2014
Ruritan Park, Grounds for the 44th Annual Turkey Trot Festival, Montgomery, IN
performed once in 2014

WILD AMERICAN DOGS / BEVERLY FRESH, GREG SCOTT
Chris Main, Chad Nicholson

Chicago, IL
beverly@beverlyfresh.com / greg_scott@me.com
beverlyfresh.com / sawbuckproductions.org / bathtubsongs.com

ODE TO MONTGOMERY

WILD AMERICAN DOGS / BEVERLY FRESH, GREG SCOTT

"Ode to Montgomery" serves to isolate archetypal figures from their customarily pronounced orientation to the communalistic ethos of rural settings. Sociologist Molly Merryman describes "Ode" as "a performance art piece that meditates on male rural isolation, freedom and peace." Each of the four segments focuses intensively on a particular figure. The four segments, while differentiated by character, adopt a common visual rhetoric and narrative grammar such that each one stands on its own but is best understood in relation to the other three segments. The emotional resonance of "Ode" derives from the script's intentional reliance upon the interplay of competing states: pathos and ecstasy, nostalgia and indifference, romanticism and pragmatism. The narrative through-line of "Ode" rests on a radical deconstruction of rural masculinity and, more generally, the nature of human subjectivity in relation to the built and natural environments of the rural Midwest.

On an empty demolition derby track, the night preceding the Annual Turkey Trot Festival, a car idles in the distance. "The Crooner" enters the track and lip-synchs to a slow, densely reverberated version of Ricky Nelson's "Lonesome Town" that plays through the track's antiquated PA system. As the last of "Lonesome Town" rattles through the empty grandstand, "The Driver" approaches the center of the track and proceeds to maneuver through a series of figure-eights at a slow speed. He suddenly accelerates. Mud flies as he tears up the track, completing several doughnuts. As "The Driver" cuts his eights into the dirt, the announcer issues a garbled list of local businesses, the names of random townspeople and catchphrases from the regional vernacular; he asks unanswerable questions, delivers inscrutable bits of wisdom, and makes poetry of boosterism. The car slowly exits. "The Player" enters the track and plugs his electric guitar into an amplifier. He plays drawn-out drones and high-pitched squeals. His playing builds into an atmospheric bastardized version of "The Star-Spangled Banner."

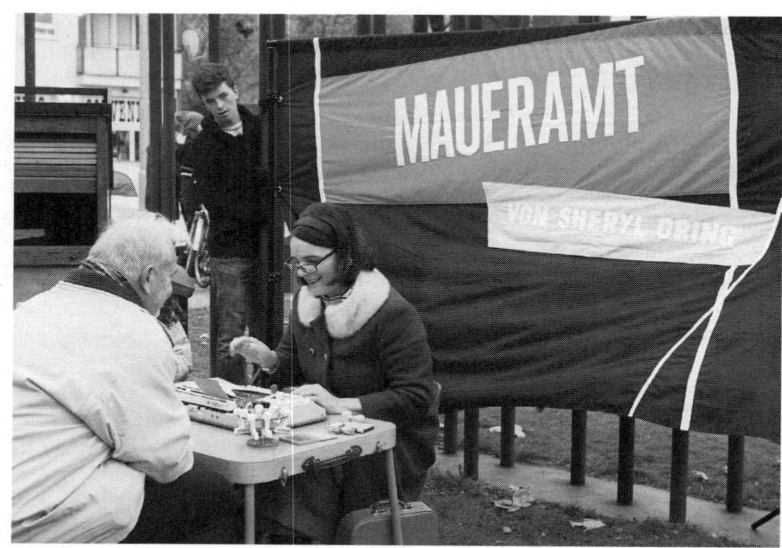

Dhanraj Emanuel

MAUERAMT

first performed on September 4, 2014
Berlin Wall Memorial, Berlin, Germany
performed twelve times in 2014

SHERYL ORING

Greensboro, NC / Berlin, Germany
oring@iwishtosay.org / saoring@uncg.edu
sheryloring.org

MAUERAMT
SHERYL ORING

November 9, 2014 was the 25th anniversary of the fall of the Berlin Wall. As I've engaged various aspects of German history with past projects, this anniversary compelled me to create a work that examined how this critical moment in history is viewed today by both Germans and non-Germans. With "Maueramt" or "Wall Department," I set up a public office along what remains of the Wall that separated East and West Berlin and asked passersby: "What do you think about when you think about the Berlin Wall?" I was dressed in 1960s era office attire; my office desk was an East German camping table that folded neatly for easy transport by an old three-wheeled bike with wooden compartments. Answers were typed on a West German Princess typewriter and these documents plus Polaroid photos of each participant were then integrated into an installation at the Museum THE KENNEDYS in Berlin.

The work engaged both young and old and served to provoke reflection on changes over the past several decades that have radically rebuilt the city. Said one Berliner: "I've lived in Berlin since 1958. In the West. Without family. Mother and brother remained in the East. It wasn't easy. Little to eat. Studies and work with no family." For young people who have grown up without this division, the project served as a provocation and often led to long conversations about the Wall and its impact on people and families. Said one German child: "When I think about the Wall, I think about the DDR and of death and war. And of escape and separation—that many people didn't see their families for a long time." For my own daughter, age six, watching the performances led to discussions on protest and democracy, and I'm certain that these lessons—enhanced by seeing remnants of the Wall—will remain vivid in her mind for years to come. Her message read in part: "Some people might ask how did they force the government to take it down—they went on the road and lots of people did it and the government went with it because they couldn't stand to hear all the shouting and see all the signs."

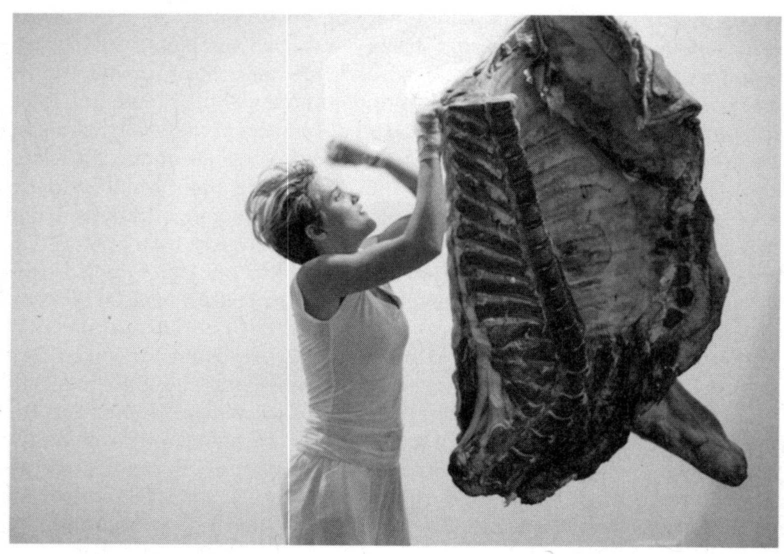

QUARTER BEEF
first performed on September 5, 2014
Mana Contemporary, Chicago, IL
performed once in 2014

EMMA SAPERSTEIN
Industry of the Ordinary

Chicago, IL
emma.saperstein@gmail.com
emmasaperstein.com

QUARTER BEEF
EMMA SAPERSTEIN

"Quarter Beef" was a performance in which I purchased the front quarter of a cow, hung it in the gallery space and boxed it for two hours. At the end of the two hours, I collaborated with a local butcher and we butchered and barbecued the quarter beef. This performance was a part of a larger study on the history of meatpacking in Chicago and meat culture in the United States at large. It spoke to the limited interaction we as consumers and carnivores have with the meat that we consume and sought to bridge that gap. Additionally, it spoke to the feminist politics of meat, and conversations surrounding meat and ethics.

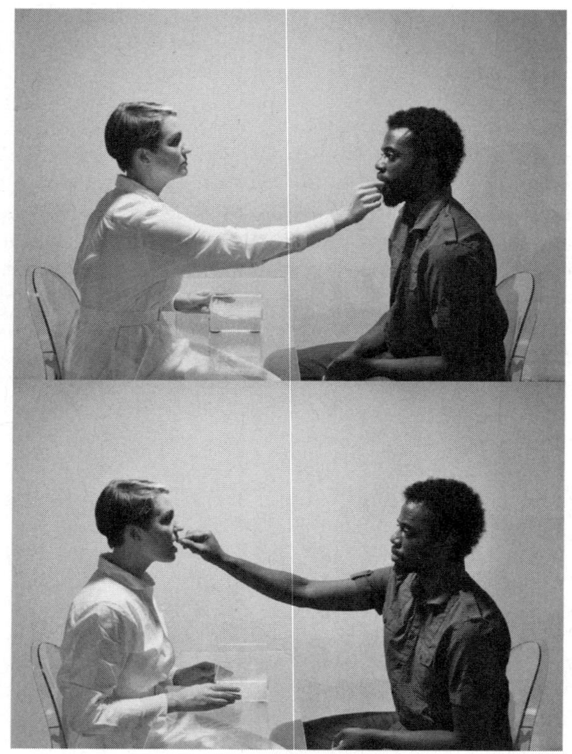

US, AN INVESTIGATION OF CONSUBSTANTIATION
first performed on September 5, 2014
Mana Contemporary, Chicago, IL
performed once in 2014

CYNTHIA POST HUNT

Chicago, IL / Fayetteville, AR
cynthialpost@gmail.com
cynthiaposthunt.com

US, AN INVESTIGATION OF CONSUBSTANTIATION
CYNTHIA POST HUNT

When I was a girl, my grandmother would take my brother and me to the library. After story hour, we would traditionally walk to the nearby diner. At the end of our meal, my grandmother would take her box of daily vitamins from her pocketbook and my brother and I would take turns feeding them to her. I can remember how my fingers felt on her lips and how she would click the vitamin in her teeth and giggle before swallowing. This became a peculiar game to us. With each vitamin I anticipated my next turn. From these memories, I created the piece "Us, an investigation of consubstantiation."

The performance begins with a transparent table and chairs positioned under a spotlight. Alone, I sit at the table, clothed in white, with a transparent box in front of me. The box is filled with translucent, moist spheres, smelling of extreme sweetness. I stare straight ahead. A participant sits down in the chair across from me. Our knees touch and our eyes lock in silence. Slowly, I open the box, pick up one of the spheres and put it to my lips. I open my mouth and place it on my tongue. As I chew, our eyes remain locked. I swallow, I close the box and I rotate it 180 degrees. I open the box facing the person in front of me. They pick up one of the spheres and eat it. Each participant reacts differently to this silent invitation and to the taste and texture of the sphere. I close the box and rotate it 45 degrees. I pick up a sphere and bring it close to the participant's lips. They accept the offer and open their mouth to consume the sphere from my fingertips. The box stays open and I wait with my mouth open as a gesture for the participant to feed me. The sounds of the gallery surround us but do not break our connection. The box remains open and the participant and I continue to take turns. The duration of the game varies from participant to participant. Sometimes I lose myself in the actions and reactions. I am intoxicated by the motions and the sweetness of the spheres. Sometimes the participant intimidates me. They are strong, beautiful, indecipherable or overtly sexual. Sometimes the participant is confident and challenges me. It feels like they want to win.

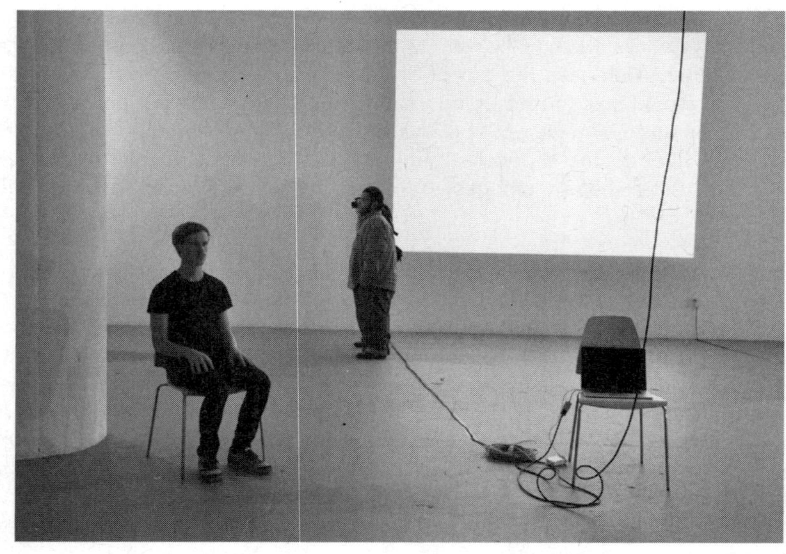

ZEN FOR DIGITAL
first performed on September 5, 2014
Mana Contemporary, Chicago, IL
performed once in 2014

EMERSON SIGMAN
Benjamin Scott

Chicago, IL
emersonsigman@gmail.com
emersonsigman.com

ZEN FOR DIGITAL
EMERSON SIGMAN

"Zen for Digital" is an investigation of silence, interaction and nothingness. A white image was projected onto a white wall. The brightness of this visual was mapped to the volume of the audience in the space for a duration of three hours.

The performance was devised as a response to the act of silencing, in which a piece of art can exist only under the condition of silence. Herein lies the complication of the impossibility of true silence, as explored by John Cage. The piece's title is a reference to Nam June Paik's work *Zen for Film*, in which the medium is stripped down to its most bare, formalistic elements. In my digital rendition, minimalism and boredom manifest themselves as a call and response from the audience, a gratification of our existence through technology.

I was unable to be present for the performance and had a proxy body in the space. Much of the generation of the work was in consideration of my body's absence. This further pushes the focus on zen and the absence that fills, realized by the projection of a white image onto a white surface.

The flickering image was also recorded, serving as an abstract, silent video documentation of volume for a space during a specific time, without any of the actual content of that volume.

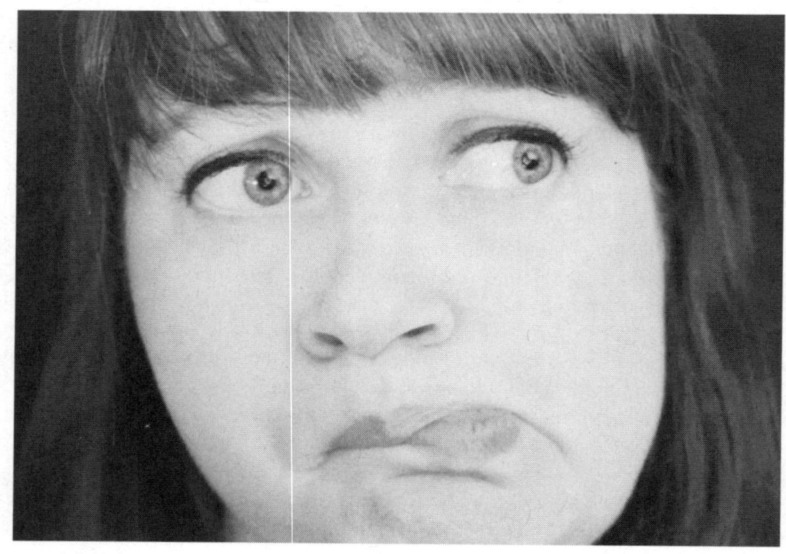

A VERY SOMETHING OR OTHER
first performed on September 6, 2014
New Museum, New York, NY
performed twice in 2014

ANYA LIFTIG

Brooklyn, NY
aliftig@gmail.com
anyaliftig.com

A VERY SOMETHING OR OTHER
ANYA LIFTIG

In "A Very Something or Other," I explore the potential of the face as a terrain for choreography. My initial inspiration for this work came from an impulse to work on a smaller rather than larger scale. Since my youngest years, I have always been fascinated by the world of miniatures and practically obsessed with any cultural exploration of tiny. (I wrote my senior thesis on Jonathan Swift, and my master's thesis dealt in part with the miniature object as facsimile.) Part of my inspiration to make "micro" works came simply out of a very New York problem. I cannot afford studio space and therefore, much of this work has been created in the bathroom of the 375 square foot apartment I share with my husband and my dog. At first I was skeptical that I would be able to create any type of "dance" using only my face, but after viewing the Charles and Ray Eames film *Powers of Ten*, I resolved that my understanding of movement and space was only limited by my imagination and not by my physical surroundings. As in my live performance work, I set out to animate inanimate miniature objects. I birth a baby out of my mouth; a tampon erupts from my bloody nose; a pizza pie is randomly ejected; a tiny turkey takes flight. On stage, such minute movements are unable to reach the viewer. Via the camera, the viewer is able to engage with a micro-world that challenges the boundaries of proportion and, most ambitiously, perception. The central question of the work is: Can the face be a compelling and complete material for choreographic exploration? What are its boundaries and what is its potential for extending a collective notion of choreographic space?

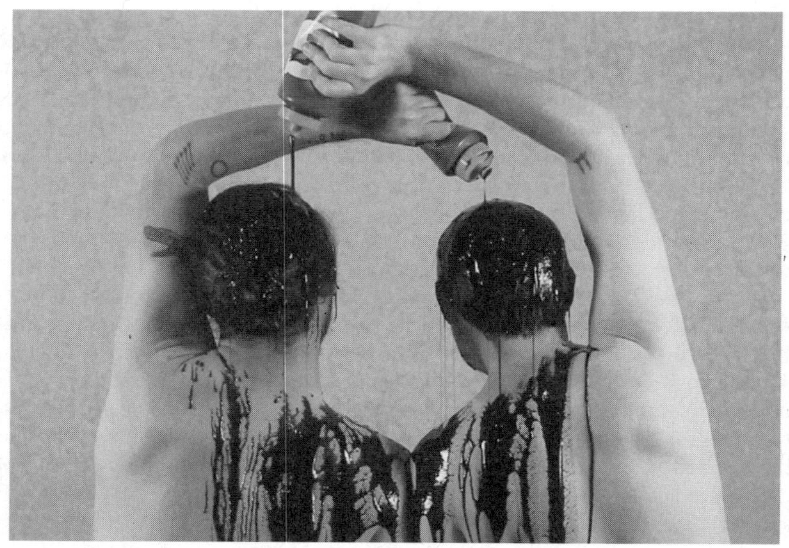

SHOULDER2SHOULDER
first performed on September 6, 2014
Crane Arts, Philadelphia, PA
performed once in 2014

KRIS HARZINSKI / WILL HAUGHERY

Philadelphia, PA
krisnwill.com

SHOULDER2SHOULDER
KRIS HARZINSKI / WILL HAUGHERY

In "Shoulder2Shoulder," we continue our exploration of friendship and homosocial intimacy between men. We question male camaraderie, taking aim, in particular, at the pop-culture construct of the bromance and *esprit de corps* within sports-related activity. By eliminating the need to end our jokes with an acknowledgement of the hetero, we search for a re-imagined future form of a relationship, one that involves a more inclusive form of queer embodiment.

This dissolve, a spinning relief, the chaos made one, two remain two, but together they say one.

The bell tolls. I walk to you and kneel on your butt. I lift your shirt and pour black liquid into the small of your back. I lower my mouth to it, my lips pressed against the sweet, sticky, viscous liquid, and then I blow. I pull your shirt down, and we stand up. I kick my feet while spinning in a circle, clockwise. Catch my foot with your hands. Spit black liquid onto my shoe, smearing it around with your face. Release my foot. Now we'll embrace, hands on shoulders, bending to our knees. We crouch down to the floor, as we lower our faces to sponges. Wipe left, wipe right, left, right, left. We stand up, biting the sponges with our teeth, then grab them and wipe each other's faces. We pull each other's pants down. We reach and dip into Nutella, then back to each other, smearing and lathering our inner thighs. Look forward and up. Step away and pick up a Gatorade bottle, then step back toward me. I crouch down a bit. Now lean into me. I'll lift you up on my shoulders, your legs apart. Keep one hand on me. With the other, squeeze the bottle, expelling its contents in a circle on the canvas below. We spin counterclockwise. I put you down, and we stand side by side. We reach into each other's pants, pulling athletic cups from inside our underwear. We cross arms and each crack open a beer, then lift them to our faces, pouring the beer through the other's cup and into our mouths. We walk off as the bell tolls.

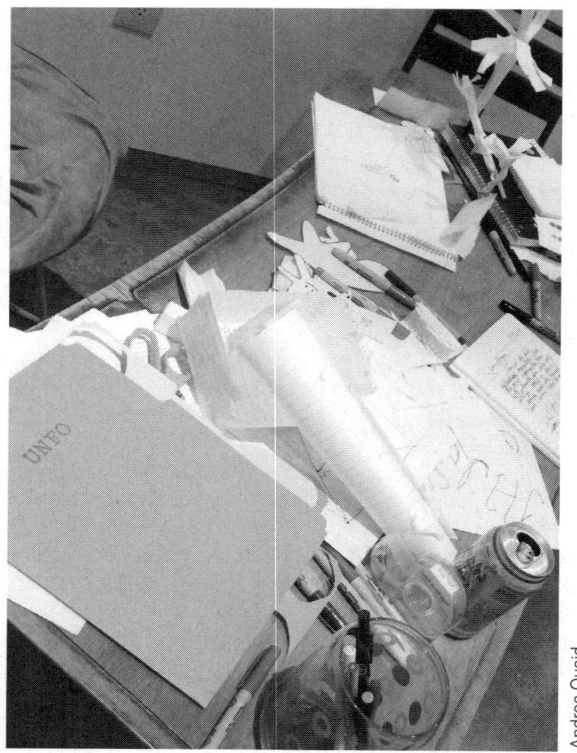

Andrea Quaid

UNFO LEAVES THE WORLD ALONE
first performed on September 7, 2014
ENTER>text: in the Air, Los Angeles, CA
performed once in 2014

UNFO (UNAUTHORIZED NARRATIVE FREEDOM ORGANIZATION) / HAROLD ABRAMOWITZ, AMANDA ACKERMAN, ANDREA QUAID

Los Angeles, CA

UNFO LEAVES THE WORLD ALONE
UNFO (UNAUTHORIZED NARRATIVE FREEDOM ORGANIZATION) / HAROLD ABRAMOWITZ, AMANDA ACKERMAN, ANDREA QUAID

How does the compromised body relate? Relate to itself, to others, to the living world, or to the relics and remnants of the past? And, also, when should this body leave the world alone? Can it leave the world alone?

These were questions that Harold Abramowitz, Andrea Quaid and Amanda Ackerman (UNFO) were asking while creating a performance in which we would leave the world entirely alone. We called it "UNFO Leaves the World Alone."

We decided to create a text-based performance in which the following would happen: a random number of people would be brought into a room. Then we would say something like the following: "Hello. We are UNFO (the Unauthorized Narrative Freedom Organization), and for the next five minutes, you are the world." We would offer them a set of index cards, of which they could choose three. On each card would be a set of instructions. We would tell the world, "You may execute these instructions in any manner you see fit. This includes the option of not executing any of these instructions at all. Good luck. We will come back to get you soon." Then we would walk away, close the door behind us and leave the world alone.

The room would also have some basic materials like blank notebooks, lined yellow paper, pens, pencils, tape and one pair of scissors.

The room where the performance took place was inside a small guesthouse. It had a bathroom, a sink, a bed, some cupboards, a desk, a chair and some art on the walls. It had large sliding-glass doors so we could actually look in and view the world if we wanted to take a glance.

Throughout the course of the night, several worlds were built and then replaced by new worlds. Each world existed as the world for about five to seven minutes. The smallest world consisted of one person and the largest of about twelve people.

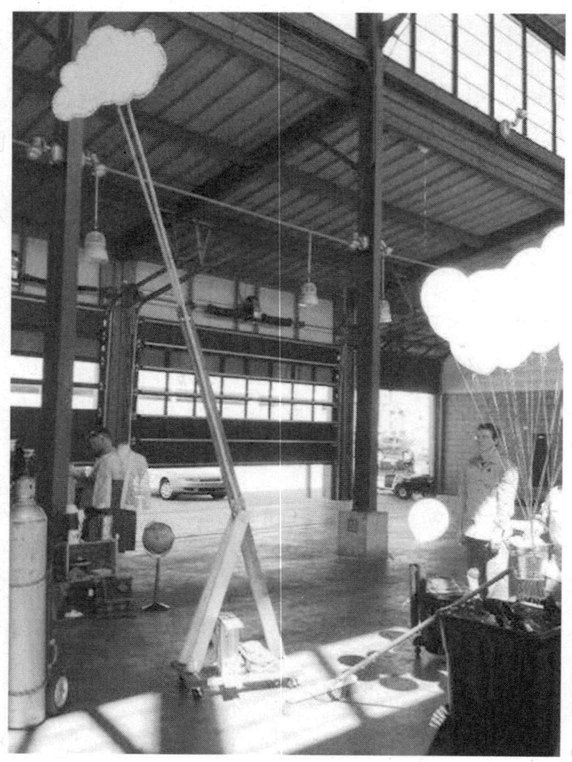

TO HOPE MEANS ATTEMPTING TO CAPTURE CLOUDS LL
first performed on September 7, 2014
Eastern Market, Shed #3, Detroit, MI
performed twice in 2014

UPENDED TEACUPS

Ann Arbor / Detroit, MI
stefaniemovingstories@gmail.com / coreygearhart69@gmail.com
facebook.com/pages/Upended-Teacups/135193736552398

TO HOPE MEANS ATTEMPTING TO CAPTURE CLOUDS LL
UPENDED TEACUPS

Two custodians named Grace from the Cloud Maintenance Department tend the ongoing operations of cloud formation and rainfall. A nod to Sigmar Polke and the anonymous author of *The Cloud of Unknowing...*

Before:
We are commissioned to create an interactive performance piece for The Eastern Market Sidewalk Jamboree in Detroit. We endeavor to create a simple set of repeated actions to present as an intervention in the market. In response to the vaulted architecture of the indoor market we build a tall, comically cumbersome structure to support a small cardboard cloud. We buy janitorial uniforms and a collection of cleaning equipment to pull along with us as we traverse the market, quietly migrating around other performers, the audience and vendors. We will make it rain inside the market by using the leaf blower attachment to a Shop-Vac to shoot blue confetti and glitter into the air. This spectacle will last for only fifteen seconds. We will laboriously and contemplatively sweep up the remnants. Each hour we will repeat the explosion.

Our planned interactions include inflating a second "cloud' of helium balloons which, one by one, we will give to spectators. Before distributing the balloons we must paint a silver-lined cloud on each one. We stand on a step stool, apply glue and glitter and only then hand the balloon over, enforcing on its recipient our extended time-sense. One after another, small clouds will float off into the market.

During:
People mistake us for actual janitors; our own friends do not always recognize us. Adolescent boys look dubiously at Corey covered with glitter from the "rainstorms" we have created. They wonder aloud why a man would want to look all sparkly like that. Later, they wait for us to perform each explosion on the hour and deliberately stand underneath to absorb all they can.

A man gazes upon the pile of confetti and glitter which we sweep up to reuse, commenting, "This seems very labor intensive. You just do this over and over again?" Stefanie replies, "That's the thing about the water cycle. It's the same water again and again since the beginning of time..."

After:
We become concerned with invisibility.

We become interested in the terms of the agreements we make around fantasy— everyone seems to understand that glitter and blue confetti equal rain.

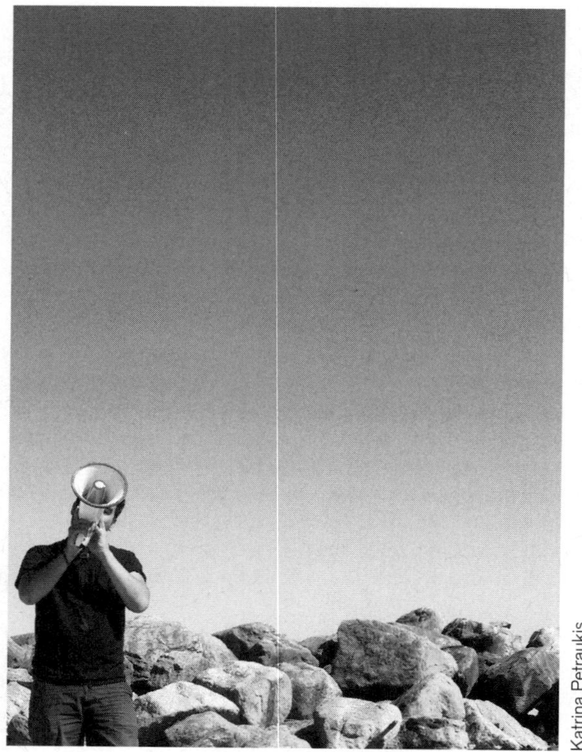

CAVITIES (5)

first performed on September 7, 2014
Ven6018North / Hollywood Beach, Chicago IL
performed twice in 2014

ALEJANDRO T. ACIERTO

Chicago, IL
info@alejandroacierto.net
alejandroacierto.com

CAVITIES (5)
ALEJANDRO T. ACIERTO

"Cavities (5)" is a work first performed on a North Side Chicago beach for the musical and performative works exhibition Water Music. Continuing my work around the voice that was previously focused on language, identification and the stutter, this project turned to the breath and inhalation (occasionally mediated by spit inside of my mouth) as primary sources of bodily expression and presence. Engaging in a durational performance in which a continuous inhalation is amplified through the horn of a megaphone held close to my mouth, I use a technique of reverse circular breathing to maintain continuous sound combined with changes in the vocal cavity. By amplifying these inhalations, I highlight the complexities of the breath as part of a paradox of power inherent in expressions of the voice. Positioning the performer in a state of continuous inhalation is to proclaim (via megaphone) one's constant state of presence (for the breaths and pauses we take during speech signal a psychological state of thinking, becoming or about-to-ness). Unlike an exhalation that is mediated through the mouth by the tongue (as in speaking or singing), a constant inhalation obscures the sound emanating from the body, dislocating the signifiers that would otherwise proclaim its identification. With the megaphone positioned closely to my mouth as I manipulate the shape of my oral cavity, the audience was unable to see or anticipate how sounds come out from the megaphone. An important feature of the work, this positioning allows me the ability to conceal the techniques I employ during performance while also suggesting a tenuous relationship between the body and the technologies that mediate it.

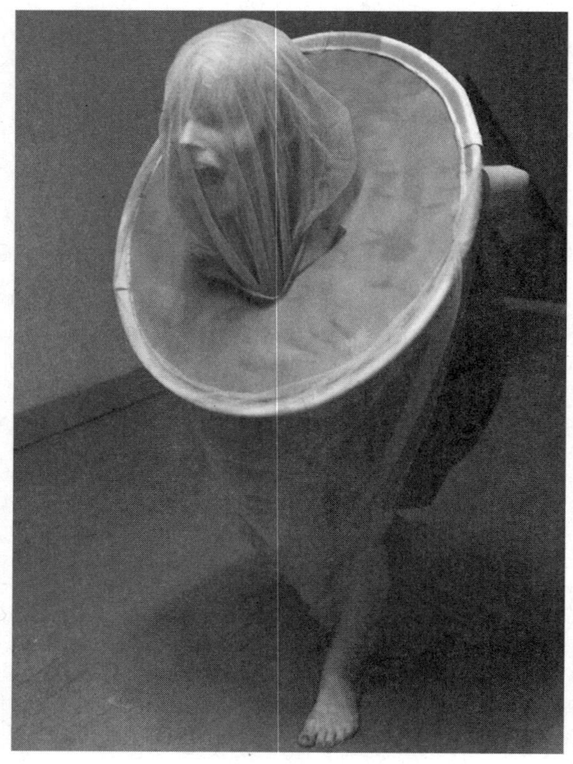

Robert Zott

ANY SIZE MIRROR IS A DICTATOR
first performed on September 12, 2014
Momenta Art, Brooklyn, NY
performed 27 times in 2014

PANOPLY PERFORMANCE LABORATORY / ESTHER NEFF, BRIAN MCCORKLE // DREARY SOMEBODY / LINDSEY DRURY

Jessica Bathurst, Lorene Bouboushian, Matthew Gantt, Kaia Gilje, Paige Fredlund, René Kladzyk, Thea Little, Ellen O'Meara, Sarah McSherry, Butch Merigoni, Matthew Stephen Smith

Brooklyn, NY
lindsey@drearysomebody.com / panoplylab@gmail.com
panoplylab.org

ANY SIZE MIRROR IS A DICTATOR
PANOPLY PERFORMANCE LABORATORY / ESTHER NEFF, BRIAN MCCORKLE // DREARY SOMEBODY / LINDSEY DRURY

"Any Size Mirror is a Dictator" was a process-based dance-opera that problematized reflective methodologies for analyzing, experiencing, constructing and learning "culture." Dominant throughout contemporary Western anthropology, philosophy of mind and other fields, reflective theories construct "culture" using formal processes toward understanding, diagramming, containing, reflecting, modelling and mirroring. Within Euro-centric hegemony, these processes, derived from Platonian paradigms for the interpretation of reality, project and produce our very selves. "Any Size Mirror is a Dictator" (ASMiaD) exploited language forms, scoring systems, dramaturgy and symbolic interactionism as bridges between performance and reflective theories, translating theory directly into performative processes via the artistic methodologies developed in context with them:

1.) attempts in opera and dance to construct Total Art (*Gesamtkunstwerk*) as analogy for colonialist conceptions of culture(s) and

2.) attempts of relational aesthetics and anthropology to model social interactions.

These two aesthetic attempts shared with reflective theory a reliance on fundamental models for how culture can be understood, including *theatrum mundi* (world-as-theater and vice versa), production-based cultural ecology/economy models, biology and total reductions of meaning-making to formal process.

Two teams of performers created functional strategies to reveal failures and problematics in methodologies and approaches, emphasizing conceptual conflicts and communication paradoxes situated within social performance. The first team, a "rehearsive" cast of performers, used the opera book, 41+ fragments of text, learned choreographic directives and tasks, objects, substances and hours of through-written music. The performance of this material failed to make itself into an auto-poetic object comprising many smaller objects and failed in its attempts to close itself aesthetically around nothing but itself. Suffering became the consequences of desires to communicate accurately, efficiently, productively or empathetically. ASMiaD also failed to become a work of "totally relational art" and the "success" of any dedicated attempts to "accurately reflect" auto-poetic cultural components, including definably cause-and-effect (Totally Relational) relationships, was "successfully" unconfirmed. The second team, a "recursive" cast, refracted the material of the first team's rehearsed opera through a lens of analysis, explication and contextualization derived from their own enculturated methodologies. The three dictators continued to reform processes and attempted to direct and define culture using their subjective systems, causing transparent and intentional collapse into dictatorial (fascistic) performance-forms.

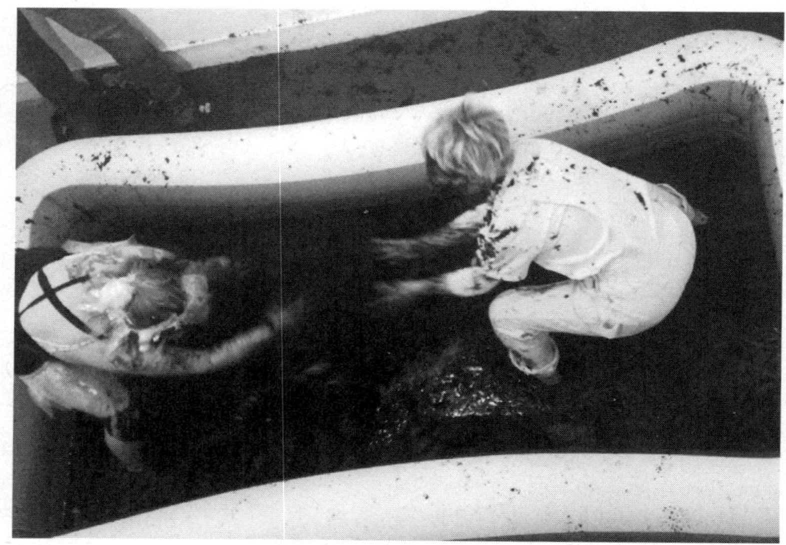

BLIZARD VS. DE KOONING
first performed on September 13, 2014
Epitome Institute, San Antonio, TX
performed once in 2014

CHRISTIE BLIZARD
Carol Cunningham, Tom Turner, Mark Watjen

San Antonio, TX
christie.blizard@utsa.edu
christieblizard.com

BLIZARD VS. DE KOONING
CHRISTIE BLIZARD

I mud wrestled Carol Cunningham who dressed as Willem de Kooning for title of Mud Greatness and the Greatest Painter of all time. I wanted to wrestle de Kooning because of the aggression he painted toward women. My intention was to battle with the aggression to show the absurdity of it. The mud represented paint and was flung all over the walls, faux de Kooning paintings and the audience. There was an announcer, two referees and two trainers. De Kooning's trainer was Death and mine was Frosty the Snowman. I won the match very clearly and trained for six months leading up to the fight.

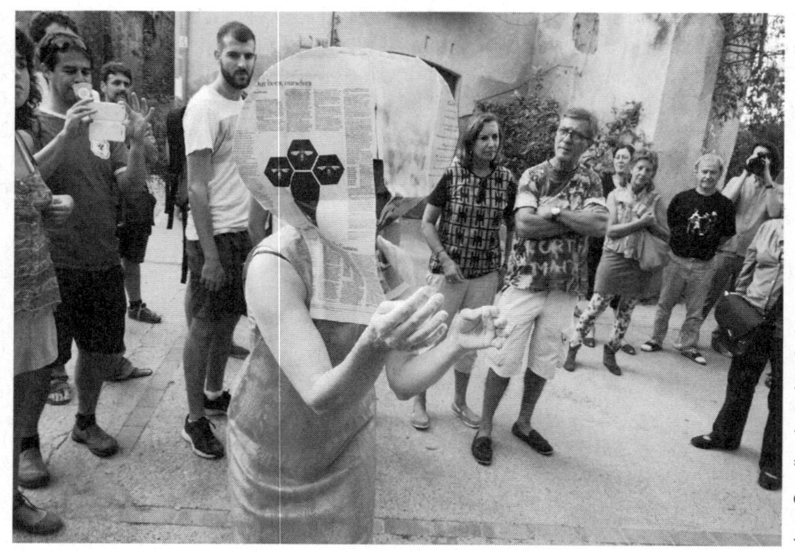

EX-VOTO, OR, SYMPTO OF POTENTIAL DEFAULT
first performed on September 13, 2014
Muga Caula International Performance Festival, Les Caules, Spain
performed once in 2014

VALENTINE VERHAEGHE

Besançon, France
montagnefroide.org / valentineverhaeghe.com

EX-VOTO, OR, SYMPTO OF POTENTIAL DEFAULT
VALENTINE VERHAEGHE

This performance took place in a small village in the north of Spain, in Catalonia, at the invitation of MUGA CAULA EVENT and produced by Catalonian artist Joan Casellas. This festival is dedicated to Marcel Duchamp in memory of his visit to the region, and more precisely of his interest in La Muga Caula waterfall. I attach importance to the context in which my action takes place: here the natural environment has a feeling of isolation; the incredible involvement of the inhabitants of this small village ensures the success of this international festival. Thus, my performance can be compared to a force field interacting with the feeling of the place, the people and personal encounters; I test out the global situation in its constant changes.

For this action, I asked two members of the audience to participate. I wanted to work on imbalance—or how to play with gravity—while I was making my way across the village's main square. I led the two spectators into a mad race forward while leaning on them to avert a fall. For the second part of the performance, I had made a sort of paper mask resembling the leather hoods used in falconry to temporarily blind the birds. This mask, placed on my head, became a sort of legible surface. It was made of newspaper and one of the articles on the page I had used was about the disappearance of bees. I was in a state of insecurity only vaguely in terms of being able to distinguish my surroundings; I was at once in communion with the audience and at their mercy.

Translated from french by Peggy Tyrode.

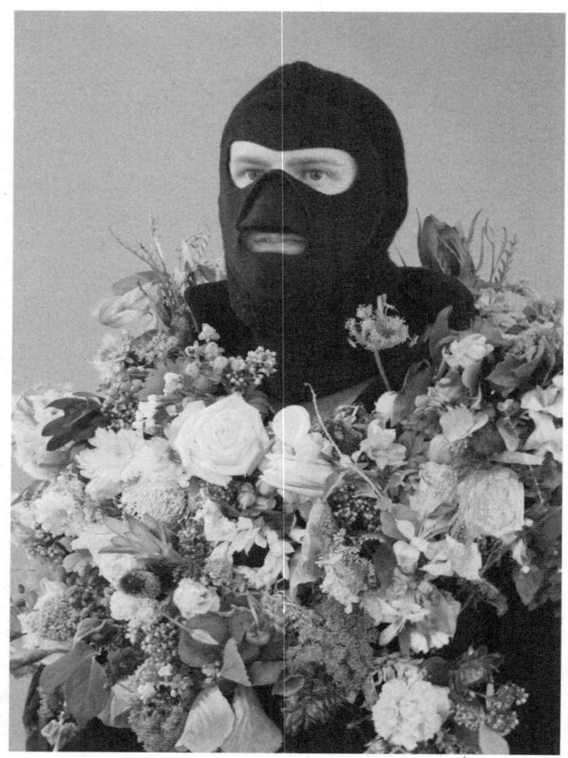

THE FLOWERS OF THE FIELD ARE FREE
first performed on September 17, 2014
Expo Chicago, Chicago, IL
performed once in 2014

JOSHUA KENT

Chicago, IL
JoshuaJJkent@hmail.com
joshuakentworksamples.tumblr.com

THE FLOWERS OF THE FIELD ARE FREE
JOSHUA KENT

"The flowers of the field are free" is a performance exploring chance encounters, generosity and the poetic within the everyday.

The work is composed of myself as a single performer completely camouflaged in living flowers. The flowers are affixed to a floor-length coat and cover the entire surface of the garment. By donning the vestment, the majority of my distinguishing features and signifiers (such as sex and age) were subtracted. Additionally my face was obscured by a black ski mask, creating an element of uncertainty regarding my intentions.

Creating a "living image," the floral figure alternates between stillness and slow movements, yet remains silent. My gestures simultaneously invited interaction with strangers, yet remained consciously internal. Though my figure positioned itself in stances of openness, the lack of verbal communication demanded the audience exercise agency in regards to how they chose to engage the spectacle before them.

Conceptually fundamental is the reality that the work was completed with no associated cost. "The flowers of the field are free" was constructed outside of any financial exchange: the coat was sourced from the homeless shelter where I both work and live full time, the ski mask was lent to me and the hundreds of flowers used to fabricate the assemblage were sourced from donations. These particular flowers were to be discarded as waste prior to my interception of them through my daily work in food/resource recovery. I was particularly interested in showing this work within the format of a large art fair. As an unpaid performer I debuted the piece alongside galleries that were conducting business transactions at an exorbitant level of financial exchange. Thus I became uninterested in creating any further matter that could be commodified, and instead exclusively employed pre-existing material. As the piece is composed entirely of items deemed "garbage," the work becomes concerned with questions of labor and privilege. "The flowers of the field are free" exists because of the waste of others, however it is only through acts of care and an application of time and conscious effort that the possibly transcendent image might emerge.

(It should be noted that due to a miscommunication between festival organizers, all materials related to "The flowers of the field are free" were destroyed as waste upon completion of the fair. While unfortunate, this reality perhaps seemed appropriate as an unintentional conclusion for both the poetics and the life cycle of the performance.)

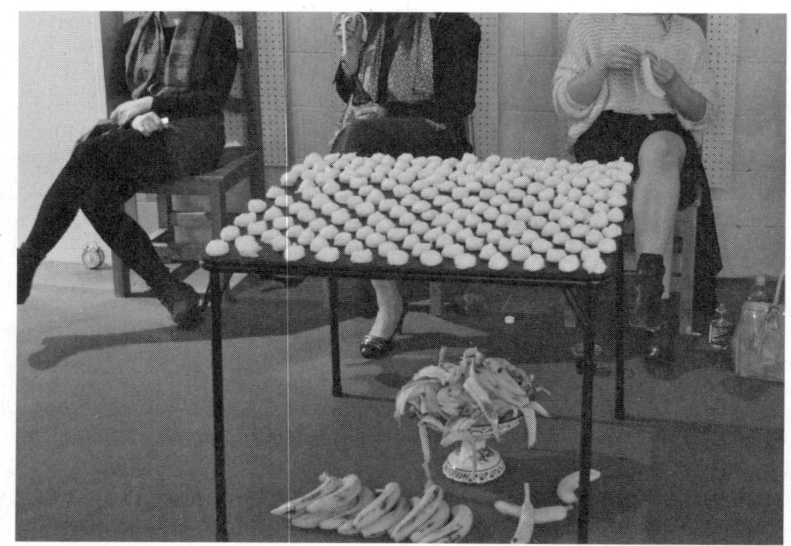

CLEAR BANANAS

first performed on September 18, 2014
Expo Chicago, Chicago, IL
performed once in 2014

ALBERTO AGUILAR / ALEX COHEN

Chicago, IL
contact@albertoaguilar.org
albertoaguilar.org / alexbradleycohen.com

CLEAR BANANAS
ALBERTO AGUILAR / ALEX COHEN

I teach painting and drawing at Harold Washington College but I use it as a way to teach other things as well. In one class a while back I had a student like no other. He had a lot of playful energy and would constantly interrupt the class, especially when I would give painting demonstrations. I liked his disruptions and played off his energy. One day he was jumping over stuff in the classroom so I thought it would be funny if he jumped over me as I gave a demo. We had to do a several takes (kicked my head a few times) but he eventually cleared me. We formed a life-long bond and still make work together. Just this past year at Expo Chicago we did a performance together where we set up a table with cotton balls on it and bananas underneath and chairs for people to rest and eat a banana. As people gathered to eat their fruit or figure out what its meaning was, we would come running out of nowhere and both jump over the table, one after the other. My relationship with him is an extraordinary exchange. It's one that you rarely come across in teaching, but when you do it's great and generates work on both ends. I taught him how to take play and interruption and make it into art and he taught me how to jump over things.

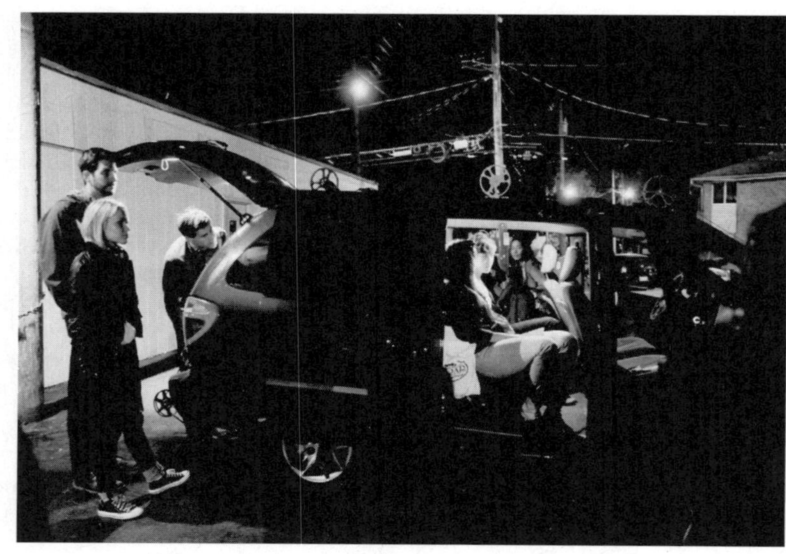

CARAVAN: DOUBLE FEATURE
first performed on September 19, 2014
Mote Gallery, Columbus, OH
performed five times in 2014

EVAN DAWSON / PAIGE PHILLIPS
Stephen Takacs, Liz Roberts

Marpha, Nepal
evn.dwsn@gmail.com
evandawson.info / movepaige.com

CARAVAN: DOUBLE FEATURE
EVAN DAWSON / PAIGE PHILLIPS

"Caravan: Double Feature" presents a traveling performance and expanded cinema event that was created to address several different problems that to us were wound up in the 2001 Dodge Caravan that we owned.

Bricks could be seen in the back of the van, where the back row of seats had been removed to hold the cargo. They were found bricks, stolen or discovered over the course of many years. In the performance they were taken out with alternate movements to build a hearth, then stacked to form low stools around a hearth, then moved to arc around the film. With other synchronized movements we opened up the doors to create an entrance to the van, and manipulated the audience space with ropes as we made several circling passes. The key to the journey was a balance of energy; the car battery was the epicenter. Two more bricks, carefully placed on the gas pedal, charged the battery, while also making the wheels spin at an uncomfortably fast speed. The closed auto-electrical system was kept in motion with a delicate balance of power, as the 16mm film projectors which now sat in place of headlights pulled about as much electricity as the AC/DC converter could supply. The film lasted as long as the circumference of the car, and looped the wanderers forward for as long as the battery would last (approximately 20 to 25 minutes).

We had found our rising dependence on the car was structured into the design of the city, and that structure weighed on our efforts to make ends meet. So there was a personal problem and a city planning problem. More importantly, it was a relationship problem—the very mechanisms that are meant to close distances produce distances. Think about how many empty seats are sitting in traffic. In our estimation much of the culture feels a need to make short-term gains to cope with their long-term losses, even though it is a self-fulfilling prophecy. We felt a need to address this object in particular but it was also a stand-in for other forms of technology.

What we had at our disposal to address this vehicle and all of its baggage was a concurrent contemplation about our long-term commitment to each other, as we had decided to marry that same year. While it presented many tempting analogies, what it led us to instead was a sentiment described by Ludwig Mies van der Rohe: "Architecture starts when you carefully put two bricks together." The thought was later picked up by Lawrence Weiner to address social structures, in which the brick becomes analogy for human relationship as material. Of course cars and cinemas can be different types of social spaces, but here they came together in a site of exchange that packed up and toured to five cities in the eastern United States.

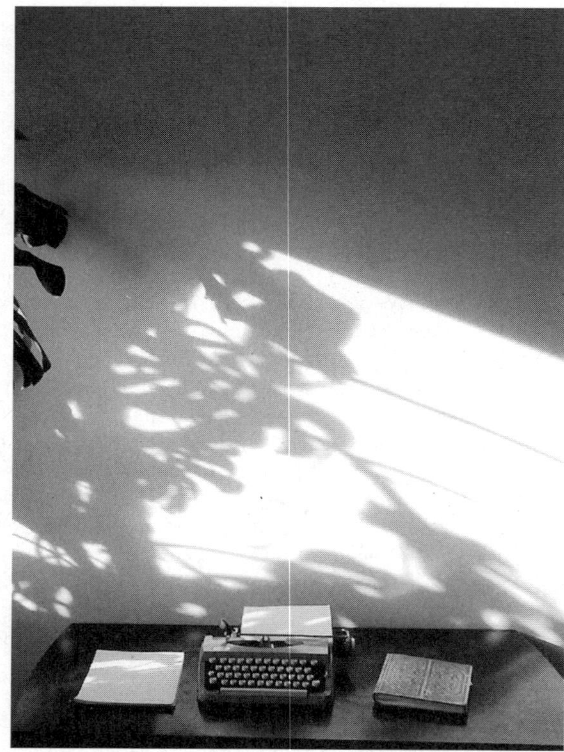

UNTITLED XX

first performed on September 21, 2014
Projekthaus on Jessnerstraße, Berlin, Germany
ongoing performance for 123 days in 2014

ISMAEL OGANDO

Berlin, Germany
ogando@savvy-contemporary.com
ismaelogando.com

UNTITLED XX
ISMAEL OGANDO

For this piece—a research project conducted using anthropological/social psychology field research tools for hypothesis validation—I infiltrated an intimate group of 47 Neo-Nazis with the intention of obtaining and stealing data through the tactics of observation and emulation, data which belongs to a particular segment of German society, a cultural context I have been studying since 2012: "Neo-Fascism."

The group covers their *modus vivendi* under a political direction proportionally inverse to their actual doctrine, concealed by political correctness. The aim of my performative research was to undermine the strong presence of racist statements, which in my opinion limited people of color and/or non-European activists and causes from having relevant presence in the political spectrum. I spent four months sharing a communal house in the heart of gentrified Friedrichshain with 47 German individuals ranging between 26 and 50 years old, neo-Nazi militants disguised as average left-wing people.

My concerns for conducting such research began with the issues related to a political movement started by African asylum seekers in October 2012, which the politically left scene of Berlin later appropriated as the only German socio-political structure with interest in solidarity and support. As a result of such a phenomenon, the "Refugee Strike" movement lost credibility and degenerated.

My intention with this piece was to study in a closer, yet suicidal approach, the behavior and intimacy of the white "supporters" who all fit in the collective profile of "German left-wing" individuals living in former squatted houses (today known as collective house projects) to expose certain flaws. I infiltrated as an activist interested in renting a room, having then the privilege to take a closer look from inside.

Once inside, I performed a silent interaction as a passive subject to experience other than impositions and shocking demands and accusations registered in a *crescendo* mode day after day. During four months, I conducted one-on-one interviews, collected trashed letters and mapped the relation between the 47 members of the house with the far-right party in Germany. At the end, I assembled and archived one single item and several pages of evaluations.

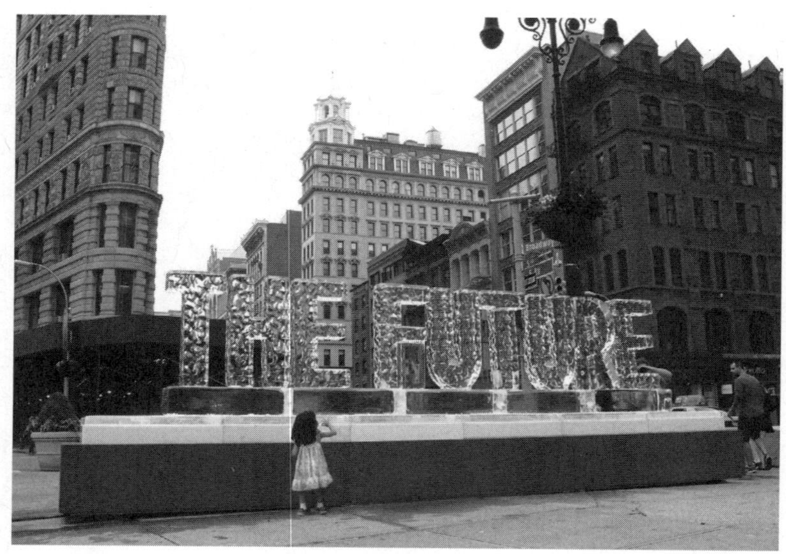

DAWN OF THE ANTHROPOCENE
LIGORANOREESE / NORA LIGORANO, MARSHALL REESE

At 10 am on Sunday, September 21, 2014, we unveiled a 3,000-pound ice sculpture of the words "The Future" at the intersection of 23rd Street and Fifth Avenue at Flatiron North Plaza in New York City. This public artwork coincided with the UN Climate Summit and the People's Climate March to underscore the necessity for immediate action to confront global warming.

This event is part sculpture, part installation, part performance and an internet media event. But most of all, we make art for social change, installing temporary public sculptures to mark important historical events. The Climate Summit is that and more. Our plan for "The Future," measuring 21 feet wide and 5 feet tall, was that it melted away. We photographed and filmed the installation's disappearance streaming it on the internet in real-time. We think of the website as an expanded documentary incorporating video, stills and written commentary. We're going to have several short-term writers' residencies happening simultaneously on site and post those writers' texts as they're written.

We call the piece "Dawn of the Anthropocene" to describe the effect of humanity on the earth's systems. The term comes from Nobel Prize-winning scientist Paul Crutzen. In his and other scientists' view, humanity has entered an age when the power and impact of humans is as great, if not greater, than nature's.

When you begin to witness the rapid changes occurring on the planet—rising temperatures, increasing droughts, the extinction of vast numbers of species—you think about loss and disappearance. Ice is the perfect material for bringing awareness of what that kind of change means.

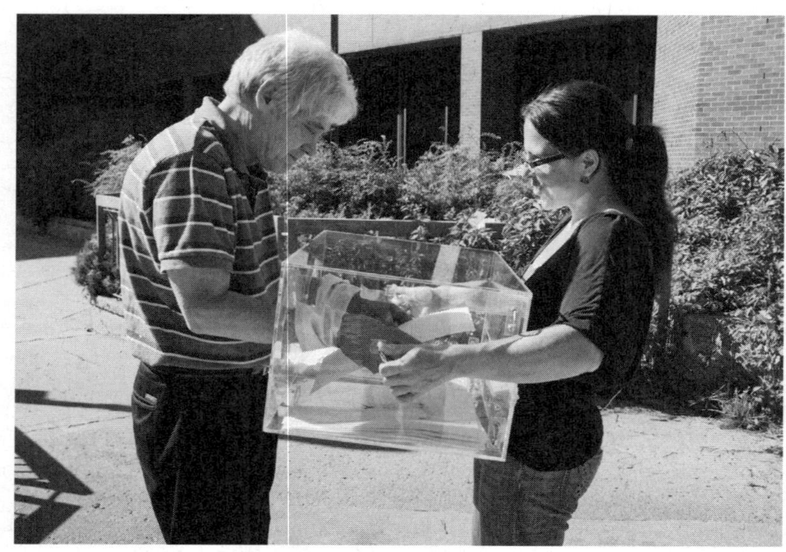

L'INCUBATEUR À TEXTES ET À DESSINS (THE DRAWING INCUBATOR)

first performed on September 25, 2014
Exterior public spaces in Saint-Roch district, Quebec City, Canada
performed twice in 2014

CAROLINE BOILEAU

Montreal, Canada
studio@carolineboileau.com
carolineboileau.com

L'INCUBATEUR À TEXTES ET À DESSINS (THE DRAWING INCUBATOR)
CAROLINE BOILEAU

Holding a clear plexiglass incubator, I invite visitors to shuffle texts and watercolors housed inside. The typed texts, poetry and short biographical narratives moving across different social roles (from domestic to medical spaces) are in English and French, since the idea of translation—the movements between languages in space and time—is central to the action. The drawings accompanying the texts show improbable bodies created by imagining what transpires beneath the surface of the skin and which is ready to surface at any moment. I love bodies that spread out and overflow, bodies whose limbs and organs proliferate and unscrupulously appropriate those of other creatures from the animal or vegetable kingdoms. Through the metamorphosis of these hybrid beings, working from a feminist perspective, I strive to re-enchant the world that surrounds me, a world that all too often leaves me at a loss for words.

In order to see and read this extended book based on personal history, passersby must do so in my presence by inserting both hands through the circular openings at the front of the box, slipping their fingers into domestic kitchen gloves. We are now intimately close. Facing each other, our hands through the transparent walls of the box seem to almost touch while the plastic walls and rubber gloves prevent any skin-to-skin contact. I am standing here as myself, both author and subject of these texts and images.

Discussing personal history, the body and embodiment in public spaces is a political gesture.

Passersby must commit to this strange ephemeral relationship by stopping and taking the time to look, read and discuss what is there. Understanding the body as a social construction, I am interested in the influence of medicine and domestic space on the understanding of what constitutes us as human beings. Through the different social roles that we toy with and come to internalize, I am fascinated by the various ways in which one can inhabit, depict and talk about the body.

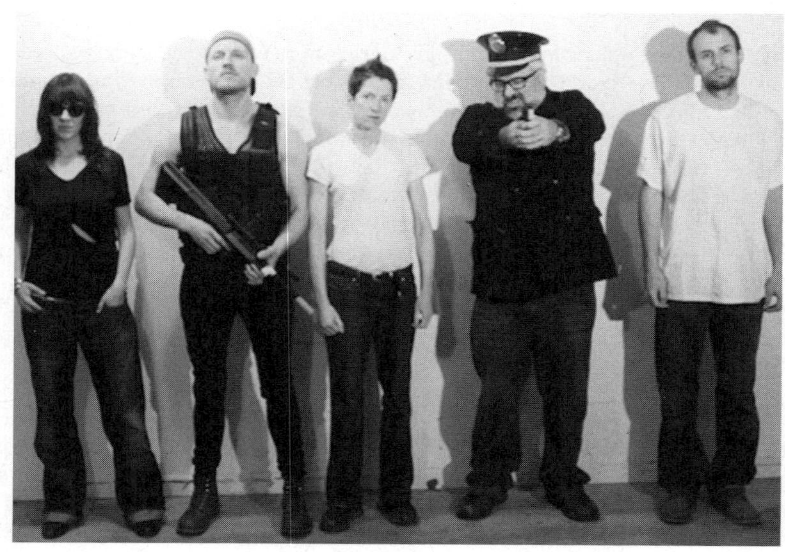

FAST FIVE

first performed on September 26, 2014
Northampton Arts Trust Building, Northampton, MA
performed twice in 2014

CRVPT (CONNECTICUT RIVER VALLEY POETS THEATRE)

Patrick Gaughan, Ish Klein

Northampton, MA
crvpt2014@gmail.com
patrickgaughan.tumblr.com

FAST FIVE
CRVPT (CONNECTICUT RIVER VALLEY POETS THEATRE)

As more and more mainstream films open on Broadway ("Rocky," "Shrek," et al.), CRVPT answers with a verbatim theater production of "FAST FIVE," the fifth installment of *The Fast and the Furious* franchise, calling attention to the gap between blockbuster and underground stage, between massive budget and zero budget. A movie about cars staged by people who don't own cars. A script engineered for mass teenage-boy appeal with Vin Diesel cast as a woman. Beefcake stars chased by ballerina cops.

"FAST FIVE" holds a mirror to the misogyny and sleek sheen of action culture. Paul Walker, Ludacris, The Rock and Tyrese played by poets and fiction writers: actors who never disappear into their roles, a simultaneity of male action-star body and female poet body. The dancing and fight sequences fail to be seamless, a conscious amateurism that highlights the underlying humanity of the movie version is concealed beneath thumping music, sheen and melodrama. CRVPT's version places equal burden on the critical apparatus surrounding Hollywood and parades a cast of critics to share their equally ludicrous opinions about the film. Action is not inherently evil. Genre is not the culprit. The show champions the lovable chase scenes and clunky dialogue while lampooning critics' condescension, prudishness and indifferent shrugs. The Hollywood system demonstrates one way to be Fast and Furious; CRVPT's performance shows another.

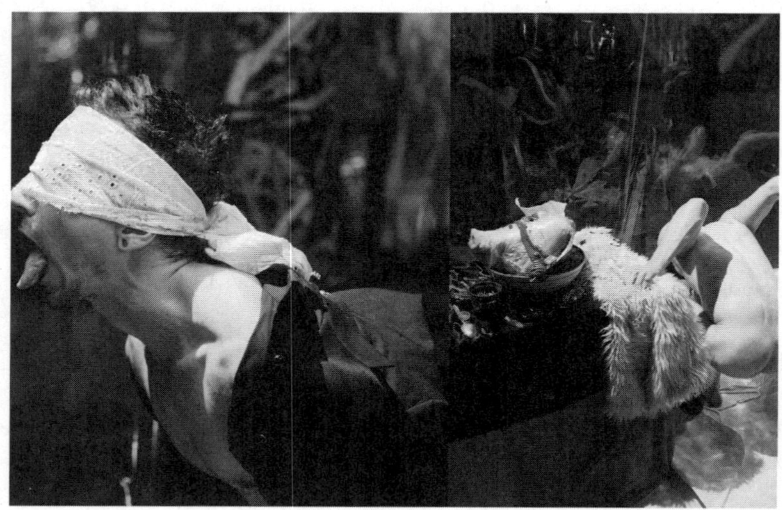

PERSEPHONE/TIFFANY

first performed on September 26, 2014
Sub Basement Art Gallery, Baltimore, MD
performed twice in 2014

ALEXANDER D'AGOSTINO

Baltimore, MD
charmcitygnome@gmail.com
alexanderdagostino.com

PERSEPHONE/TIFFANY
ALEXANDER D'AGOSTINO

"Persephone/Tiffany" was a durational performance exploring the power dynamic between Hades and Persephone as part of Over/Under Limbo Lab, a performance art event curated by Baltimore performance laboratory LABBODIES. Persephone's banishment to Hades was retold as violent argument between the two over an elegant dinner. The feast itself consisted of animal organs and a pig's head enshrined in flowers, beads, cutlery, bones and other magical objects. Thesmophoria was an ancient Greek festival honoring of the goddess Demeter and her daughter Persephone. A ritual of the ceremony involved burying a sacrificial pig into the earth by night and unburying the decaying remains of the pig sacrificed the previous year to commemorate Persephone's banishment to Hades. The rituals were exclusive and secretive. I saw the exclusive and mysterious nature of this ritual as one of the first examples of a Queer Safe Space. "Persephone/Tiffany" was the Thesmophoric ritual obfuscated into performance art. The audience witnessed me moving from one side of the dinner table to the other, climbing over the enshrined pig's head shifting personas from Hades to Persephone. Hades emerged as a strict, virile male energy in a black suit. Persephone was more wild and androgynous, performing vulgar erotic gestures wearing nothing but (at times) a faux fur coat. I began the ritual performing the dining etiquette described in *Tiffany's Table Manners for Teenagers*. Blindfolded, grabbing forks to pantomime-eat an elegant meal, the gestures would trigger a trance like state that would allow me to transform back and forth from Hades to Persephone. Persephone's role was to destroy socially expected rules of the body. Interacting erotically with the pig's head, and catching the gaze of people in the space, I became the protest and outrage of Persephone. Hades's intention was to subdue the outbursts and dominate the wild Persephone. The dinner battle between two characters allowed me to embody the tension and pain of Persephone's circumstance, and Hades's oppressive demands. Although Hades wins in the end, the residue of the ritual can resonate far beyond the initial performance. The performance empowers me, the audience and the pig with a sense of confidence regarding the critique and protest of social norms.

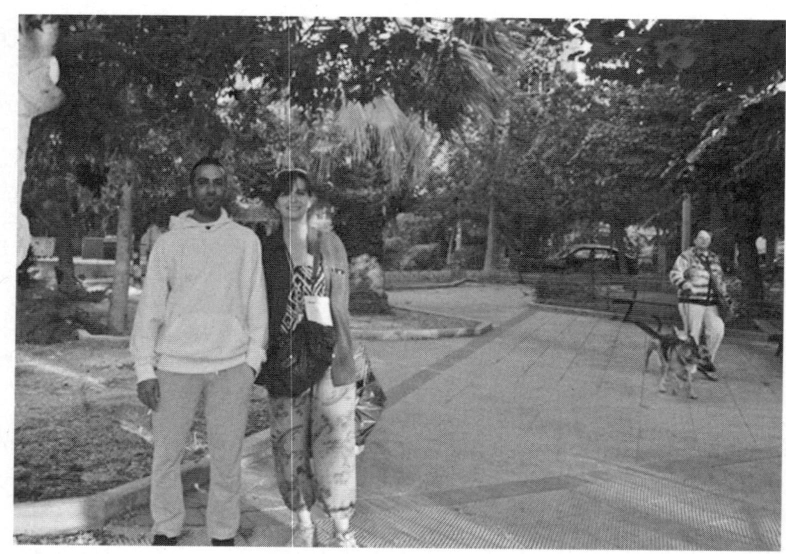

KEY-STORIES / UNKNOWN FRIENDS
first performed on September 27, 2014
Public space in the district of Neos Kosmos, Athens, Greece
performed once in 2014

KATRIN WÖLGER

Vienna, Austria
bureau@katrinamuri.net
katrinamuri.net

KEY-STORIES / UNKNOWN FRIENDS
KATRIN WÖLGER

…tough as a pirate…

Welcome to the island!

No suitcases, bathing suits, sun lotions!

What you have on your body and maybe personal belongings of emotional value.

You stay some time and then go on. It is not a comforting place.

It is lonely on the island. Inhospitable.

If there were not little escapes in the escape to comfort you, where you find some relief to breathe, you might give up. But you are tough as a pirate.

As soon as possible you want to start a new life.

Maybe away from your comrades with whom you experienced violence, aggression, escape and danger.

You have had enough adventures.

Time to arrive.

"KEY-STORIES / UNKNOWN FRIENDS" was designed for Dourgouti Island Hotel" a project about urban solitude, a neighborhood festival, which intended to bring together time and people, a two-day outdoor local creative-works festival in three adjacent places. The festival included performance art, theater, dance, exhibition, walks, music all inspired by the yesterday, today or tomorrow of the neighborhood.

"KEY-STORIES / UNKNOWN FRIENDS" is a participatory performance in two parts:
> Live in the area
> Find intangible treasures such as a remembrance, a story, a look, a glance, an encounter
> Mark the territory

"KEY-STORIES"
>keys on a pigeon-defense-skirt
>brushwood on head
>handing out keys
(what is this? this is a key. what for? to open a door. which door? a door, which is closed for you.)

"UNKNOWN FRIENDS"
>would you mind being my friend for a second?
>may my friend take a picture of us?
This intervention will be continued in several places throughout in 2015/2016.

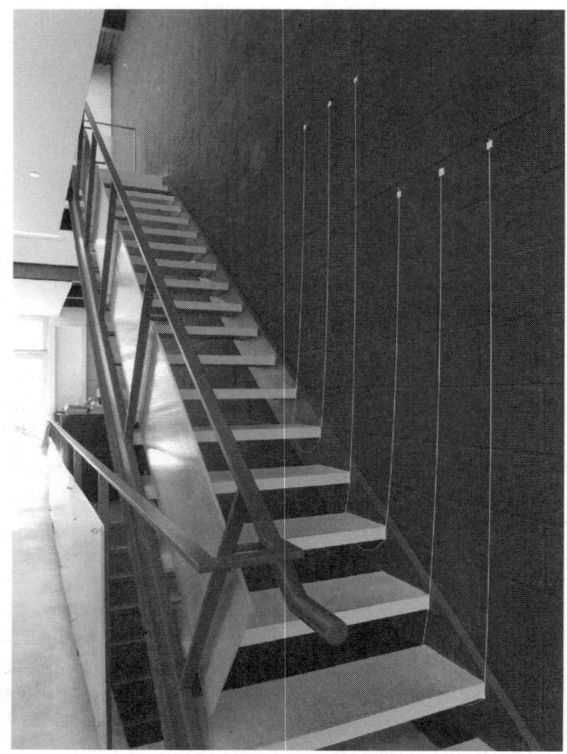

RESONANT TRACES
first performed on September 27, 2014
Union Street Studio, LLC, Brooklyn, NY
performed once in 2014

EMILY HARRIS / JONATHAN ZORN
Sam Morrison

New York, NY / Boston, MA
emily.mharris@gmail.com
emilymharris.com / jonathanzorn.net

RESONANT TRACES
EMILY HARRIS / JONATHAN ZORN

"Resonant Traces," a collaboration with sound artist Jonathan Zorn, was a series of private performances and installation aimed at exploring the sonic characteristics of the architectural/design studio. Zorn and I devised a general game-form for writing scores. Each score would include an action, object, location, relation and duration. The objects were found within the studio or they were everyday objects we had brought along. After listening and making note of different sound qualities and sources, we, together with composer Sam Morrison, generated and compiled a series of text scores on index cards: "Drop beanbags from all heights in anticipation of an airplane," "Tap all surfaces with any object in the rhythm of chirping birds," "Spread balloons throughout. First person pops a balloon, second and third people silently count to thirty and then pop balloons. Continue until there are no more balloons." Rubbing, sliding, kicking, blowing, humming, tapping, dropping, popping in different locations, we explored the building's surface materials, reverberation potentials, architectural layout and sound's permeation connecting exterior and interior sonic aspects of the space: airplane traffic, a neighbor's band saw, birdsong, contingencies between performers, sound textures, reflexes and relational distances and durations. Fashioned as a game, we anticipated that it would open up a field of play and experimentation.

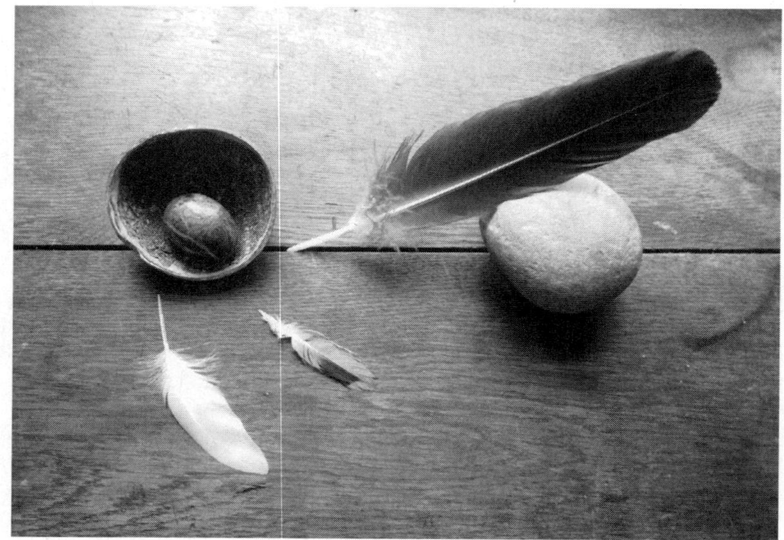

BIRD MEDICINE: A TRIO IN THREE PARTS
first performed on September 27, 2014
Triskelion Arts, Brooklyn, NY
performed once in 2014

KRISTIN HATLEBERG
Janet Aisawa, Cecilia Fontanesi, Rebeca Medina, Nadia Wallace, Ophra Wolf

Chicago, IL / Brooklyn, NY
kristinhatleberg@gmail.com
kristinhatleberg.com

BIRD MEDICINE: A TRIO IN THREE PARTS
KRISTIN HATLEBERG

"Bird Medicine: A Trio in Three Parts" is a three-layer dance: a solo, a duet and a trio. Each was created separately using the same movement score and then all three were performed simultaneously.

The braid of these dance improvisations illustrates the synchronicity that arises when people who know each other well meet and attune to what matters collectively. It was refreshing to witness how the three iterations commingled to make a unified statement. We performers also experienced how bonding can grow out of shared pasts with one another.

The score for "Bird Medicine" was crafted from memory. A year before, three of the performers (Cecilia Fontanesi, Kristin Hatleberg and Rebeca Medina) had danced a trio together called "The Eagle has landed." In 2014, six of us gathered to recall and share that dance—how could we pass it along? The choreography of "Bird Medicine" contains a shadow of the dance that came before.

"Bird Medicine" was titled in honor of and accompanied by a passage read aloud from Evan Pritchard's book *Bird Medicine*. Pritchard's reflections and observations on shorebirds articulate the dancer's own behaviors and values being enacted on the stage.

"Bird Medicine" is, in a way, a reincarnation and expansion upon "The Eagle has landed." It is a shared experience that grew from group memory. It is also a rebirth, an entirely new dance, with twice as many people interacting and creating fresh memories, inviting new cycles to begin.

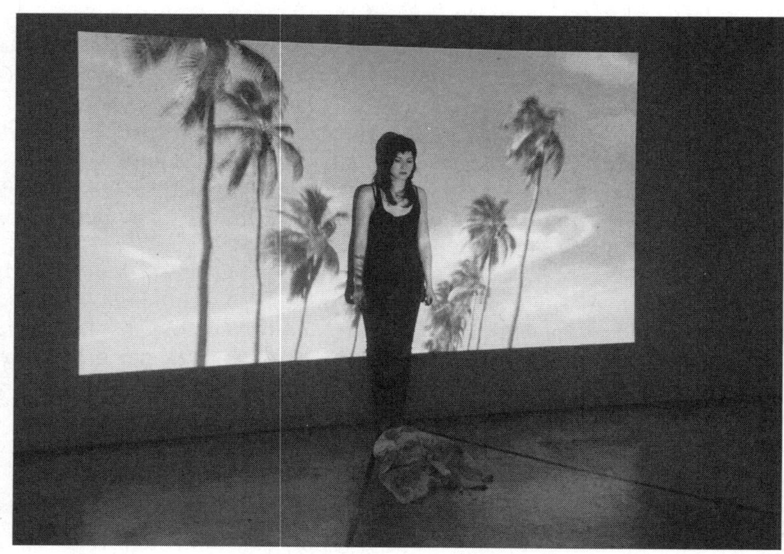

Ian Deleón

AUTO GALÁCTICA EN EL TERCER ESPACIO
first performed on September 27, 2014
ÁREA: LUGAR DE PROYECTOS, Caguas, Puerto Rico
performed once in 2014

ANABEL VÁZQUEZ RODRÍGUEZ
Ivanna Bergese

Boston, MA / San Juan, Puerto Rico
anabel@anabelvazquez.com
anabelvazquez.com

AUTO GALÁCTICA EN EL TERCER ESPACIO
ANABEL VÁZQUEZ RODRÍGUEZ

Closing my month-long residency and exhibition "AUTO GALÁCTICA EN EL TERCER ESPACIO" at ÁREA: LUGAR DE PROYECTOS in Caguas, Puerto Rico, I performed an immersive, multi-disciplinary piece that spoke about displacement, belonging and my experience as a foreign *Other* within Puerto Rico and the Northeast of the United States.

There were two murals (both painted black-on-black historical maps of New England and Puerto Rico) and a projection of my film *Visión Doble*, connected by a black triangle on the floor. Dressed in white I engaged the two murals by vigorously retouching them in black oil paint and using my shirtdress to wipe my hands, evoking the influence of both places by literally marking myself with the layers of paint. The smell of oil filled the space. After affecting both maps I blindfolded myself and walked and crawled along the triangle. When I reached the map of New England I drank maple syrup and felt my body react to the sugar, meditating on the rush and channeling the absorption to find the third space. Still blindfolded I kept walking/crawling around the edge of the triangle, encountering the maps with my whole body in an identity rumination fueled by the soundtrack of a thunderstorm. After three journeys around the triangle, I reached the projection and removed the shirtdress. As the moving image shifted my still body remained in the middle of two parallel rows of palm trees in motion. Cleansed by this tropical passage, I went beyond the third space and asserted the fourth dimension. For the final action, artist Ivanna Bergese joined me, expanding the ritual by tattooing a black triangle on my forearm. The bond between us—the ink and blood, the pain and pleasure—brought a tangible consciousness to close the performance.

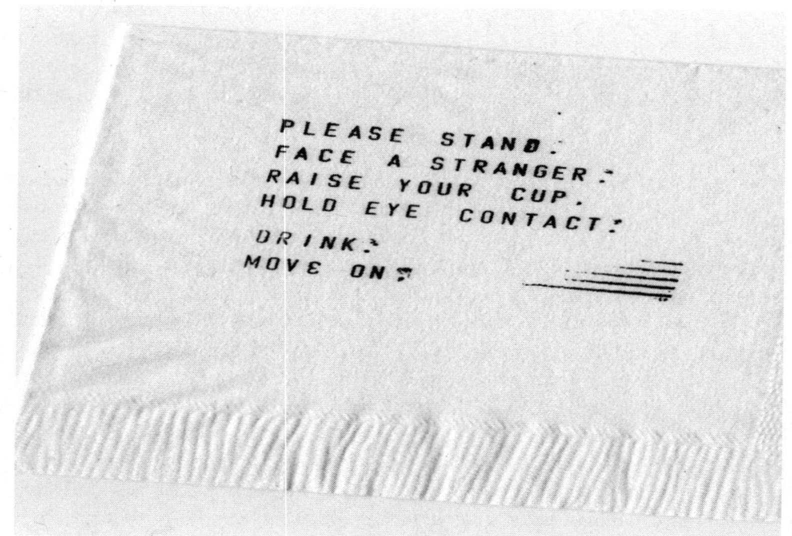

Chloë Bass

THE LINGER LONGER TOAST

first performed on September 30, 2014
The Sunview Luncheonette, Brooklyn, NY
performed once in 2014

CHLOË BASS

Brooklyn, NY
info@chloebass.com
chloebass.com

THE LINGER LONGER TOAST
CHLOË BASS

"The Linger Longer Toast" was developed for Sally Szwed's second Pairings event at the Sunview Luncheonette. Pairings is a wine and art tasting event, matching five wines with five creative works over the course of a single evening. The "Linger Longer Toast" is a simple social choreography that asks people to pair up briefly, make eye contact, and drink to one another. Each participant received a glass of red wine (flavor-paired to match the language of the toast) and a custom-stamped, custom-scented cocktail napkin with the basic choreographic instructions. The toast was read aloud by the artist, almost as music to accompany the "dance." The paired wine was Fenouillet 2013 Vin De Pays de Vaucluse: a dusty, dusky almost-autumn red.

The script of the toast is as follows:

> If I told you seven years of bad luck, if I told you bad sex, if I told you I love you, (Cheers.) (Move to the left.)

> If I looked and you looked away, if you looked and I looked away, if we found each other for just one second, what would that be? (Cheers.) (Move to the left.)

> When we drink to absent friends, what does that mean? (Cheers.) (Move to the left.)

> If I said drink to your country, how would you feel? (Cheers.)

> It's autumn, the leaves are falling, this is no time to linger. Move on.

> Warmer. We will never have been more or less than this. Hold each other tight. Move on. (Cheers.)

The "Linger Longer Toast" was designed to promote intimacies that we usually reserve for family and close friends (or even romantic partners) between strangers. The simple instructions to connect and move on highlighted both the discomfort of finding a partner, and the sense of loss accompanied when asked to disrupt a new connection. The performance also required all present in the room to participate, raising questions of who a performed act is for in a condition where no one serves as an audience. The toast is part of my ongoing series Interactions & Play. The series utilizes simple gestures, clear vocabulary and brevity of time to spur varying conditions of intimacy.

"The Linger Longer Toast" is dedicated to Naeem Mohaiemen.

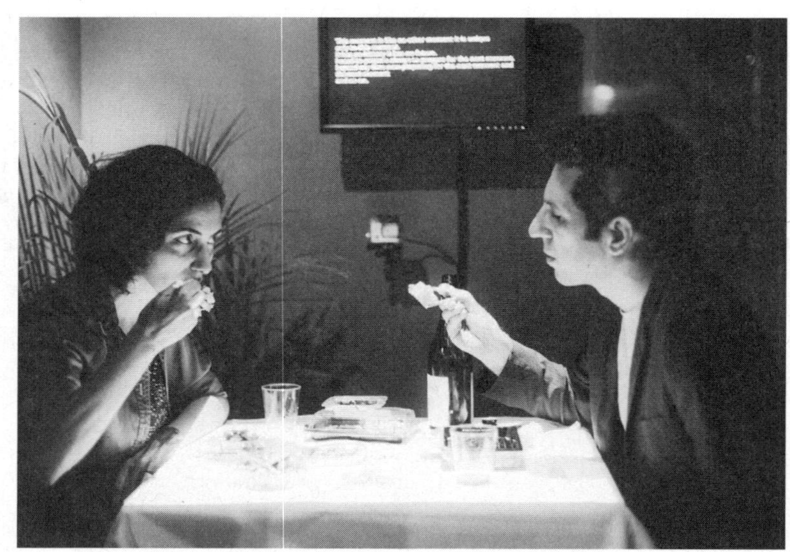

LUNCH SPECIAL

first performed on October 1, 2014
Roger Smith Hotel, New York, NY
performed once in 2014

A COUPLE OF ARTISTS / ADI SHNIDERMAN, MERAV EZER-SHNIDERMAN

Brooklyn, NY
studio@acoupleofartists.org
acoupleofartists.org

LUNCH SPECIAL
A COUPLE OF ARTISTS / ADI SHNIDERMAN, MERAV EZER-
SHNIDERMAN

The Window at 125 plays host to "Lunch Special," a work by Merav Ezer and Adi Shniderman, a married couple who create work collaboratively. For "Lunch Special," they sit across from one another and share a meal of Thai takeout.

The physical limitations of this space neatly confine the meal and its diners to their seats, their moment and their task at hand. As we watch them slowly consume, their physical interactions can be seen as a kind of choreographed dance. A few sentences repeat on a nearby screen creating a zen-like poem, reminding us that this is an ordinary occurrence, both a mirror of the one repeated by so many individuals daily and a completely special shared moment in time.

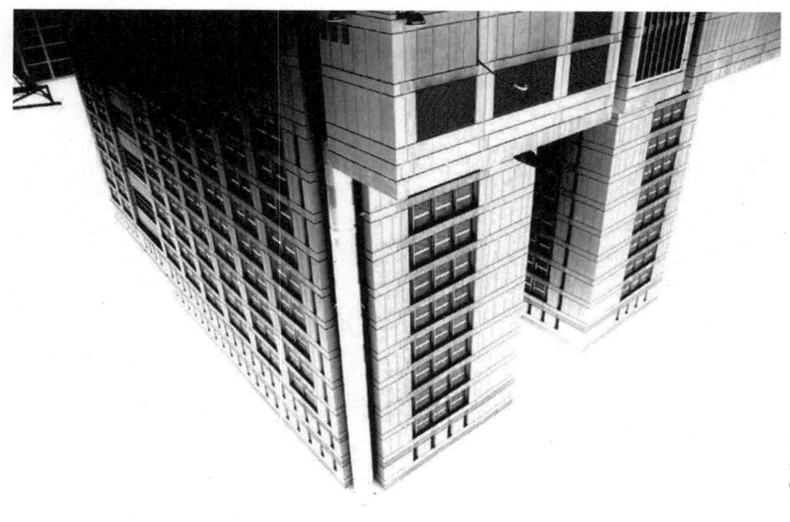

OUBLIETTES

first performed on October 1, 2014
Sunset Park, Brooklyn, NY
performed over several months in 2014

NSUMI COLLECTIVE

New York, NY / Baltimore, MD / Westchester, NY
swirls@nsumi.net
nsumi.net

OUBLIETTES
NSUMI COLLECTIVE

The first phase of "Oubliettes" took place between October and December of 2014, within and around the vicinity of the Metropolitan Detention Center in Sunset Park, Brooklyn and at Momenta Art in Brooklyn as a part of the exhibition Work it Out. "Oubliettes" was conceived as a small, temporary offshoot of the prison abolitionist movement, situated both within and beyond the art context. The goal of the prison abolitionist movement is to transform society so that prisons and carceral techniques are no longer needed—to create a world that is truly free and just out of reach of the one we currently inhabit. "Oubliettes" is a follow-up to an earlier collaboration with artist Trevor Paglen, who at the time (2005) was the Critical Resistance artist-in-residence. Critical Resistance was formed by Angela Davis, Rose Braz, Ruth Wilson Gilmore and others in the 1990s to help abolish the prison-industrial complex, which they define as "the overlapping interests of government and industry that use surveillance, policing and imprisonment as solutions to economic, social and political problems."

MDC, also known as "Brooklyn's Abu Ghraib" after coverage on Democracy Now, is significant as a site where at least 84 people were illegally rounded up, imprisoned without due process and systematically tortured—via humiliation, sleep deprivation and physical and sexual abuse—by the US federal government, shortly after 9/11, using similar methods to those used at illegal US sites around the world. MDC is situated steps away from the trendy Industry City art and design center.

Nsumi's practice involves deep analysis of social systems and grassroots movements for social change, and then carefully focusing an unexpected array of skills, labor and collective intelligence so as to bring about shifts in perception, increased capacities and catalytic growth within these movements. This process involves research and analysis of how social systems work, the study of collective intelligence and social biology, the complex nature of modern society and the history of social change.

"Oubliettes" involves an array of integrated practices including open-source intelligence analysis and production, strategic mapping, pedagogy, design, community engagement (workshops & outreach), grassroots neighborhood mobilization, an art installation, zine production and direct action. The work has two tactical goals: informing residents of Sunset Park about MDC and the abuses taking place within it and questioning—for a larger audience—the nature, consequences and trajectory of the prison-industrial complex and solitary confinement as instruments of state control.

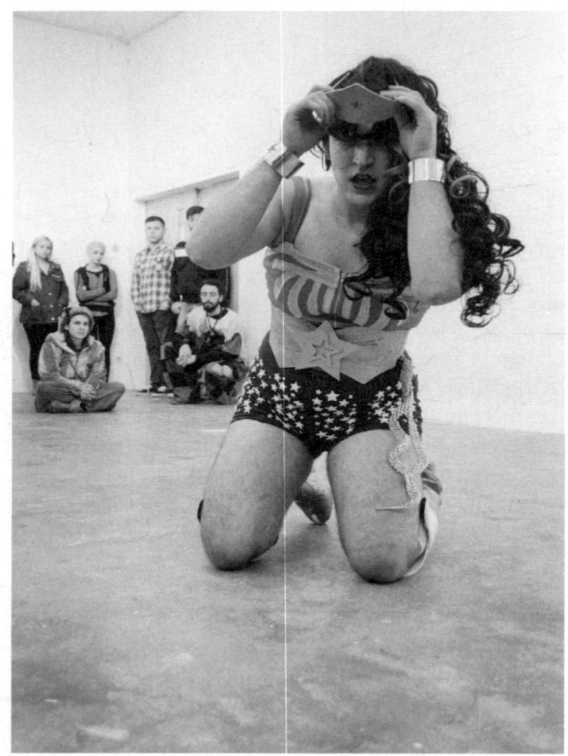

THEY WONDER
first performed on October 2, 2014
The Highest Closet, Beverly, MA
performed once in 2014

SARAH HILL

Austin, TX
sarahhill.org

THEY WONDER
SARAH HILL

By engaging in the art of queer craft aesthetic, I hand-crafted my own version of a Wonder Woman costume. During the performance "They Wonder" I repeatedly spin around and around in circles until I fall down. I am interested in the repetitive action of spinning and getting nowhere, falling down and getting back up. This specific action of spinning comes from the Dara Birnbaum piece "Technology/Transformation: Wonder Woman (1978)" in which Birnbaum has Wonder Woman spin around and around.

"They Wonder" goes against the populist template of art as a form of leisure or entertainment. I am not a blockbuster artist. Claire Bishop states in *Radical Museology* that an artist must not bend to the pressures of commodification but rather insists "that they mobilize the world of visual production to inspire the necessity of standing on the right side of history." As a queer artist I seek to create a temporal historical rupture and point backward to forms of historical queerness. Comic books have always revealed themes and characters that can be identified as queer; the majority of superheroes always live two lives, one as hero and one as civilian.

"They may not be worshipped, but they have not been forgotten, and that itself is a start."— Wonder Woman

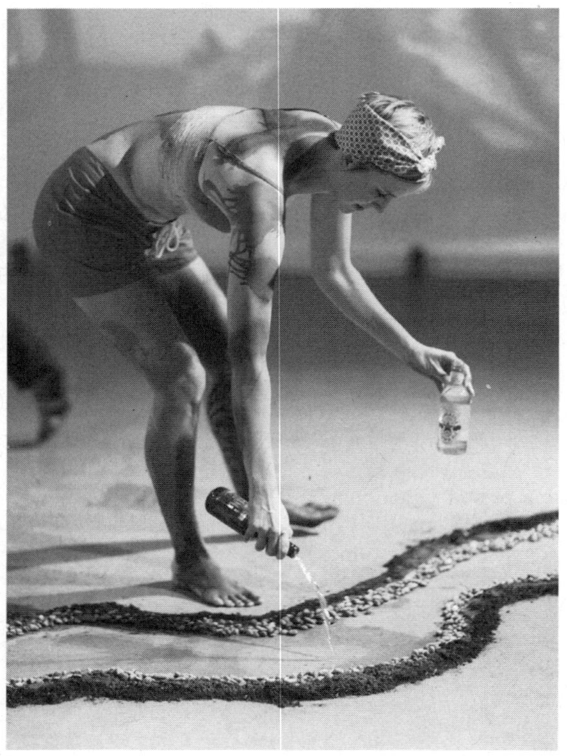

Monika Sobczak

SIBLING RIVERS
first performed on October 3, 2014
Contemporary Calgary, M:ST Festival, Calgary, Canada
performed once in 2014

ALLISON WYPER / TERRENCE HOULE / SAM FOX

Los Angeles, CA / Calgary, Canada / Perth, Australia
allisonwyper@mac.com
allisonwyper.com

SIBLING RIVERS
ALLISON WYPER / TERRENCE HOULE / SAM FOX

"Sibling Rivers" is a live intermedia performance installation that bridges three sites—Perth, Western Australia; Los Angeles, California; and Calgary, Alberta—through a dialogical exploration of the rivers that run through the heart of each city, carrying the social histories of each site. Experienced collectively, in dialogue within the defined space and time of the performance (one hour), these embedded/embodied histories call forth transnational themes of colonialism, cultural erasure and economic conflict.

For our world premiere performance at the 2014 Mountain Standard Time Performative Art Festival (M:ST 7), collaborators Allison Wyper (Los Angeles); Sam Fox (Perth); Terrance Houle (Calgary) presented live, mediated and recorded actions that critically bore witness to historical and contemporary points of contention while foregrounding the contingent subjectivities of the artists—each a resident with deep familial roots in their respective city. Motivated by the feminist ethos "the personal is political," our collective actions claim the river space as public and also deeply intimate—as home to many, living and deceased.

Large-scale projections of site-responsive video performances in and around the Swan, Los Angeles and Yukon Rivers, plus a real-time performance by Fox in his studio in Perth, were complemented by live performances by Houle and Wyper with local artists Trey Madsen and Dani Navia. The live performers created a "river" of dirt, rock and sand in the space, using their bodies to shape the river banks. Navia created a living mural on Wyper's body with spray paint. Houle bathed in dirt and communicated in Native Sign Language, evoking his indigenous Blackfoot culture.

The video element featured performance, videography and sound contributions from Chris Dirksen, Ella-Rose Trew, Aes Tchiachovsky, Sete Tele, Erika Katrina Barbosa, Rafa Esparza and Sebastian Hernandez.

Our project draws upon the practice of citizen journalism to investigate and report on specific local histories, undertaking primary research at sites and direct engagement and exchange with oppressed communities through consultation, interviews and artistic production. In an ongoing dialogical collaboration, we collectively witness, testify and draw out the social memories of our sites through performance, text and video documentation.

"Sibling Rivers" was created primarily via online collaboration, and is available for touring, with a workshop on remote collaboration that grew out of our process.

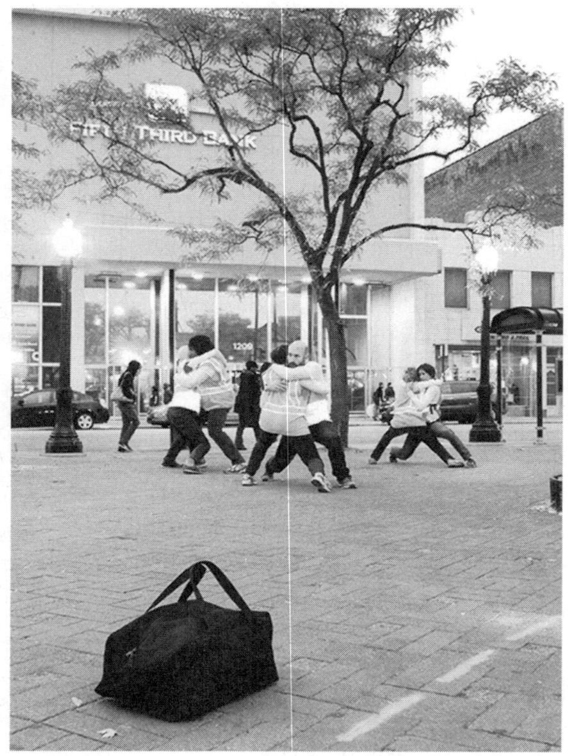

Eugene Park

EMERGENCY RESPONSE TEAM
first performed on October 3, 2014
Polish Triangle, Chicago, IL
performed once in 2014

SARA ZALEK / GINGER KREBS

Chicago, IL
sara@saratonin.com
saratonin.com

EMERGENCY RESPONSE TEAM
SARA ZALEK / GINGER KREBS

Inspired by the the Federal Emergency Management Agency's "Resolve to Be Ready" campaign, "Emergency Response Team" treated the Polish Triangle as an assembly point and training area for disaster preparation. The six ERT team members conducted a series of drill maneuvers designed to build stamina, hone communication skills and demonstrate readiness for the physical and emotional rigors of catastrophe. The coordinated team action exemplified possibilities for cooperation in public spaces, while highlighting the ways in which public anxiety is increasingly "managed" as a public relations exercise. The speed of the movement alternated between crisply official and very slowed down to appear surreal, suggesting the kind of time warp sometimes experienced during moments of trauma.

From the brochure distributed to audience and passersby on October 3, 2014, 5 pm:

> Thank you for volunteering to be a witness to our preparedness exercise. You will be role-playing the part of an onlooker at a disaster scene. All reasonable and customary safety measures will be performed during the exercise. If at any point you are asked to stop acting, please do so. For example, if the drill is called off because of a real emergency, please stop acting. If at any point the drill begins to jeopardize "really" injured people, you will be instructed to "freeze." This means you should immediately stop acting to allow professionals to appropriately care for "real" victims.

> During a disaster, you may see and hear things that will be unpleasant. Vicarious trauma, also known as compassion fatigue, is a natural reaction to exposure to a survivor's trauma. A person who identifies too strongly with a survivor may take on that survivor's feelings. Don't dwell on the worst possibilities. Doing things that you enjoy, sticking to your normal routine and being with friends and family will help make you feel better and keep you from worrying about the event.

> Emergency Response Team is committed to strengthening the security and resilience of the United States through systematic preparation for the threats that pose the greatest risk to the security of the nation. We continue to become more secure and better prepared to prevent, protect against, mitigate, respond to and recover from the full range of threats and hazards the nation faces, including aircraft emergencies, assaults, bomb threats, fire emergencies, hazardous material spills, hostage situations, medical emergencies, missing and kidnapped children, natural disasters, school disturbances, shootings, terrorism, utility failure and workplace violence.

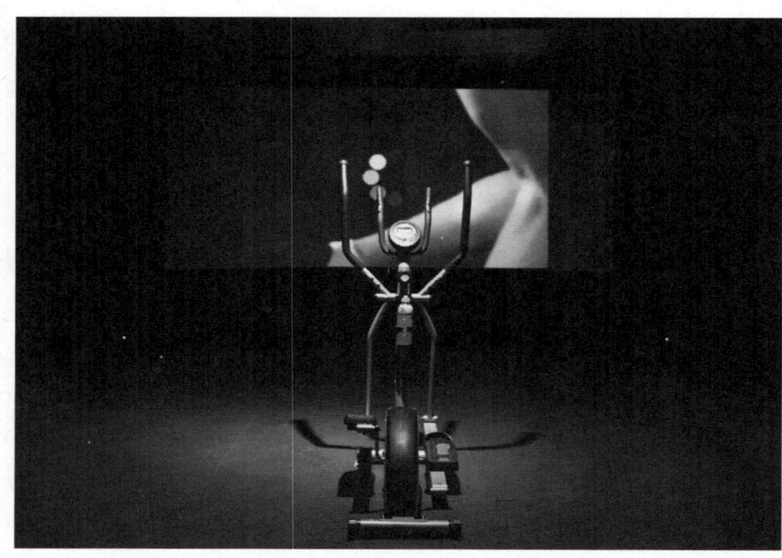

1, 2, 3
first performed on October 4, 2014
EMMEDIA, M:ST Festival, Calgary, Canada
performed once in 2014

ANDRÉS GALEANO

Berlin, Germany
andreugaleano@gmail.com
andresgaleano.eu

1, 2, 3
ANDRÉS GALEANO

Materials:

High performance running clothes and drinks, elliptical cross trainer.
Video "Loading" 2014, 16:9, 35 min. (loop), fragments of Youtube.
4 channel audio installation with 2700 tracks of 4 seconds selected randomly and played by a computer program.

Concept:

"1, 2, 3" is an installation-performance based on rotating sound, Youtube video footage and one long durational action.

A voice repeats "1, 2, 3" uninterruptedly. A collection of four-second field recordings from different parts of the world, abruptly recorded during one year. Two thousand and seven hundred soundtracks are played, randomly selected by a computer program. 1...2...3... like a martial tempo of a transitory body confused in time. 1...2...3... as a sound check for... 1... 2... 3... for a disciplined workout and high performance... 1...2...3... a blocked enumeration for a non-exhausted body suspended in loop...

The performance lasts three hours and is obsessively shredded in seconds. Perhaps a footnote to the old and arthritic Cunningham in its minimal choreography for the video installation *Stillness* by Tacita Dean. Or maybe the search of reaching a trance state through fitness. Or just the simple boredom of a repetitive voice filling the emptiness of a diary when you forgot what to say... Once and again... 1... 2...3... running in circles is running around... *uno, dos, tres...*

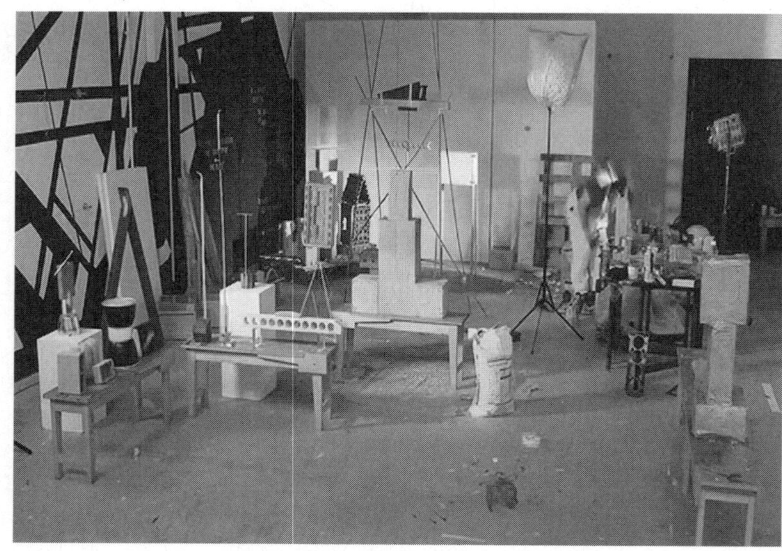

24 SCULPTURES IN 24 HOURS
first performed on October 4, 2014
Werk, Birmingham, UK
performed once in 2014

TERESA ALBOR

London, UK
alborteresa@hotmail.com
teresaalbor.com

24 SCULPTURES IN 24 HOURS
TERESA ALBOR

I made 24 sculptures over a period of 24 hours in Birmingham, in collaboration with Werk/Longbridge Public Art Project in October 2014. Residents of this working-class community contributed materials for the art "production line" on the site of the Longbridge Factory which closed ten years ago, putting thousands of people out of work. I was inspired by the heritage of the area, the working community and the production lines which ran for nearly a century.

The project raises questions about cultural production and labor, exposing both the similarities and the disconnects between the making of "art" vs. the making of other goods. It also plays with the concept of the "white cube" gallery scenario where art is a precious commodity consumed by the elite. In this case, we are in a project space, adjacent to a historical factory, the work is free and is produced openly, informed by "factory" processes, such as deadlines and mass production. Cultural production is depicted as an assembly line process. In summary: this is "task-oriented" performance art, about labor and art and the methods and systems of quantity-production.

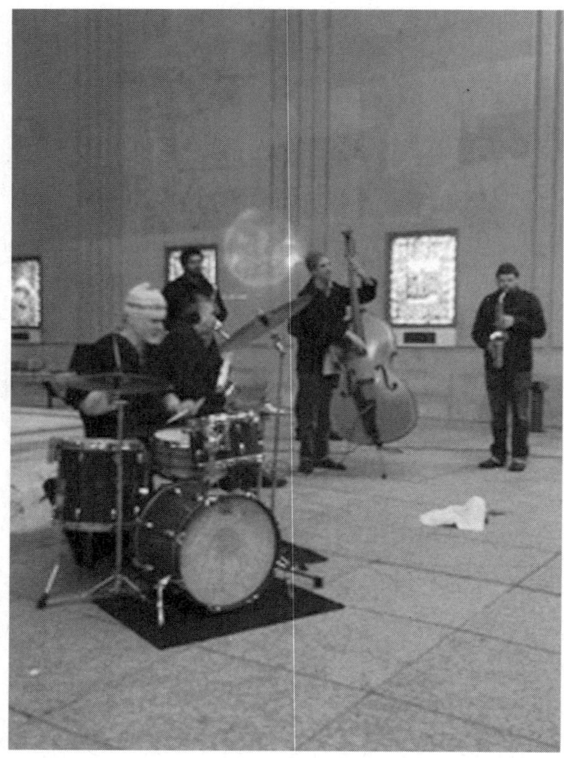

SUNSET WITH MIRO'S CHICAGO

first performed on October 4, 2014
In front of *Miró's Chicago*, Chicago, IL
performed once in 2014

SOUND ENSEMBLE / JON GODSTON, BRYAN PARDO, JOSH BEATTY, SPENCER HUTCHINSON, DAN GODSTON, BONBONFERA TIM KEENAN, DAN MCNAUGHTON

Chicago, IL
dan@borderbend.org
borderbend.org/blog/miro-sunset

SUNSET WITH MIRO'S CHICAGO
SOUND ENSEMBLE / JON GODSTON, BRYAN PARDO, JOSH BEATTY, SPENCER HUTCHINSON, DAN GODSTON, BONBONFERA TIM KEENAN, DAN MCNAUGHTON

"Sunset with Miró's Chicago" occurred in the plaza-alcove where *Miró's Chicago* is found; part of the performance also took place on the Chicago Picasso. This performance event—which included sound, movement and projections of NASA photos of the sun and moon—was presented in collaboration with the Chicago Temple. The Sound Ensemble members included Josh Beatty (tenor saxophone), Bryan Pardo (alto saxophone, clarinet), Jon Godston (soprano saxophone), Spencer Hutchinson (alto saxophone), Dan Godston (trumpet), Bonbonfera Tim Keenan (percussion) and Dan McNaughton (upright bass). This performance happened during the Ninth Annual Chicago Calling Arts Festival and in collaboration with the Chicago Temple, which gave us permission to perform in front of *Miró's Chicago.*

During one segment of the performance several Sound Ensemble members performed in front of the Miró sculpture, whereas several others performed on the Picasso sculpture (which has a slanted piece of steel that the public is encouraged to climb on). The improvised sounds of the ensemble members intermingled with the urban sunset and crepuscular din.

During this performance we were interested in exploring interrelationships between how performers improvise with each other, while doing so in a site-specific way as inspired by looking at the surrounding public art and projections of NASA photos. We also wanted to know what would happen to the sounds coming from the musical instruments as the physical locations of the musical instruments changed (from alcove, to open plaza, to having a saxophone horn face down on an urban avenue). We were also interested in messing with the sonic, visual and movement categories and boundaries that often become codified and ritualized in urban spaces. For instance, since part of the performance happened on both the south and north sides of Washington Street, this was an opportunity to question ways by which streets and the vehicles that use those streets often divide and cut off potential civic and creative activities that could happen in urban areas.

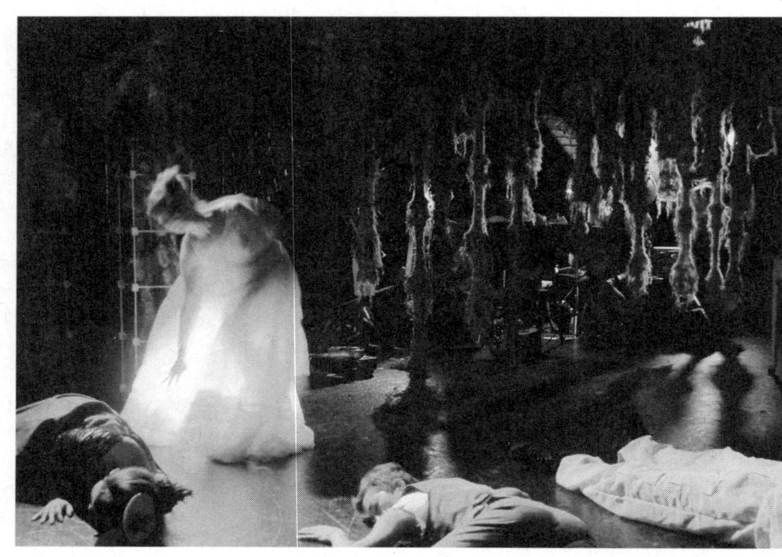

OBJECTS

first performed on October 4, 2014
Theater for the New City, New York, NY
performed four times in 2014

VAN REIPEN COLLECTIVE

Gary Heidt

Jersey City, NJ
gary@vanreipen.org
vanreipen.org

OBJECTS
VAN REIPEN COLLECTIVE

The construction of the actor-director dyad as practiced in Off-Off and Off Broadway is fraught. I had to direct "OBJECTS" because I wanted to be in it and I didn't want anyone to direct me. I had to play an authoritarian role as director to avoid submitting to authority. When I refused to exercise authority the members of our group who had been trained in theater sought to usurp my role.

The apotheosis of stage theater is an ersatz spontaneity, which deploys its synaesthetic array in subtle or surprising ways that frame a pre-existing text as if it were just bubbling forth from an actor's soul. As an improviser I have an aversion to direction because it often destroys spontaneity in order to create its simulacrum. Why not just present spontaneity? The cult of compulsory work sees this as lazy, arrogant idiocy. Worse, the ungainly techniques that have evolved to control theater sound and light are very difficult to adapt to the demands of improvisation.

Even in the most scripted performance a good performer finds a space for life. A habit of compliance with the dynamics of the director-actor relationship leaves theater-trained actors vulnerable to extreme anxiety in the face of less structured situations. While they want to find something that works and repeat it, I wanted to find simple situations and find out how many different ways they could be done.

Gertrude Stein's *Objects* is notoriously difficult to memorize. But as song lyrics, it's easier. I assigned each poem to a composer. Poems became songs. The songs became numbers.

My cast was mixed. Four musicians who were fun to watch on stage, all die-hard improvisers; two butoh dancers; a veteran modern dancer and two actors with a theater background. The musicians and dancers liked the idea of spending time living in and inhabiting the songs to see what they could discover. The theater actors, on the other hand, bridled. The idea that I didn't want to converge on one particular way of doing the performance was met with incredulity.

The musicians wanted to get just familiar enough with the material to improvise on it, and the actors wanted to master the material first before finding their regions of freedom. As a director I exercised my authority to protect the right of the freedom-loving performers to do their parts the way they wanted to.

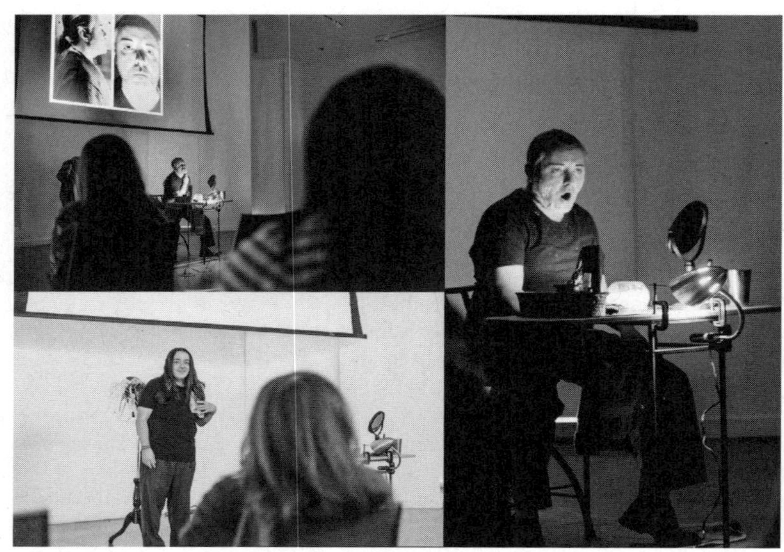

RAZOR'S EDGE

first performed on October 5, 2014
The Bronx Museum of the Arts, Bronx, NY
performed once in 2014

SEAN PAUL GALLEGOS

Bronx, NY / Albuquerque, NM
seanpaulgallegos@gmail.com
seanpaulgallegos.com

RAZOR'S EDGE
SEAN PAUL GALLEGOS

"Razor's Edge" addresses the factors that lead us to our perception of one's identity. The performance explores what makes up identity and how society defines it. Whether it be cultural or physical, deciding factors often are stereotypes used to simplify and categorize. I used the performative act of shaving, a perceived typical male activity, to stereotypically portray myself in my multiple ethnicities for the audience. My father is Tewa and Spanish of New Mexico and my mother is Cree and French of Canada, resulting in an internal battle with colonialism between my Native American and European ancestry.

The performance took place in three phases. In each phase I used my facial hair to denote a specific ethnicity from my own heritage. I chose to sing songs related to each ethnicity that I have been perceived as. At the beginning of the performance a photo was taken of my profile and then projected for reference on the wall above. Photos continued to be taken after each of the three times I shaved. These then projected photos became visual markers to aid in the understanding of my visible transformation.

I took my place at my shaving station complete with shaving mirror, razor, towel, electric clippers, lamp, crystal rinse bowl, stainless steel cup, tissue and shaving cream. I pressed play for the music to accompany my songs and started shaving. Gradually, my facial hair went from Anglo full hipster beard (Caucasian), to a sculpted Latin pencil-thin beard (Latino), and finished with no facial hair (Native).

The songs chosen were Neil Diamond, "They Come to America" for the Caucasian phase, Robbie Williams, "Angels" (Spanish version) for the Latino phase and for the Native phase I chose to sing Franz Schubert, "Ave Maria." Each of these songs hold deep time and space connections for me. "They Come to America" was a song from the white-washing era of my life of being adopted and changing my surname. "Angels" is a song that I learned first in English and then heard in Spanish years later in my travels with the circus through South America. This was my re-acquaintance period with being Latino. Finally, for the Native song I chose to sing "Ave Maria" as a comment on Catholicism's effect on Native culture, stemming from my own early childhood.

The facial hair chosen for each phase was a perception of how the world sees me. The doubts from one culture to the next, or the reassurance if my face is clean shaven and my hair is long and straight, suggests I must be Native. Or maybe, I am them all.

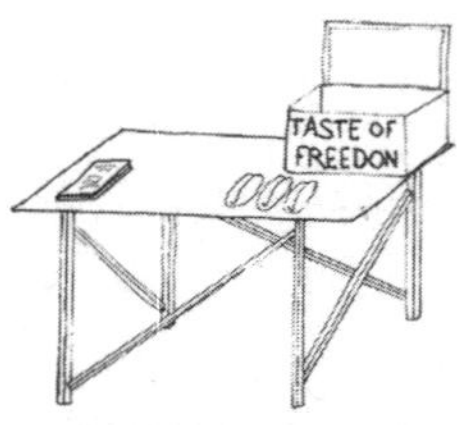

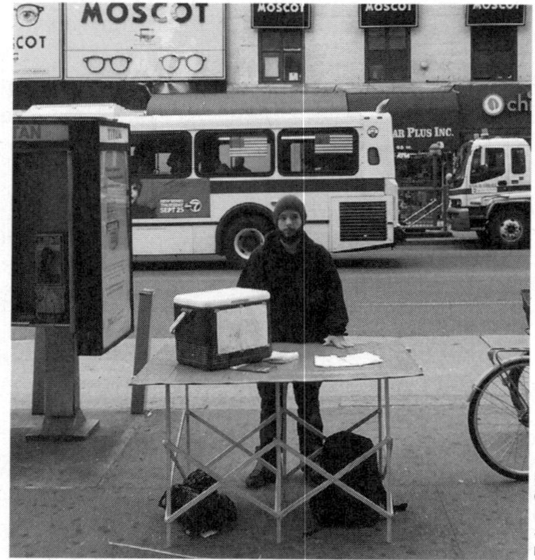

Felipe Cidade

TASTE OF FREEDOM

first performed on October 9, 2014
14th Street and Avenue of the Americas, New York, NY
performed once in 2014

FELIPE CIDADE

São Paulo, Brazil
f.cidade@yahoo.com
fcidade.wix.com/todoartistaeidiota

TASTE OF FREEDOM
FELIPE CIDADE

"Taste of Freedom" is a performance artwork which investigates diverse questions through the single act of serving a typical food from a specific region/culture with ingredients and condiments from another region/culture that was or still are in conflict/war. Epistemologically this work reflects on immigration, the metamorphosis between cultures and the ways in which politics can (but shouldn't) intervene in the transmission and comprehension of culture.

Using a table made specially for street food sellers (easy to carry and mount) with drawings and writings (that outline the logic of the work's proposal) and serving the food myself (neither acting nor pretending to play a role), "Taste of Freedom" positions the food and the junction between the ingredients as the most powerful elements at play.

In the same way that cultures/religions/political views can be at odds with each other but still develop mutual respect, "Taste of Freedom" outlines the ways in which specific regions in the world—while at odds traditionally—can ultimately come together.

Pascal says that God doesn't reveal to man the order of everything, but he also doesn't entirely hide it. There is access to partial truth in mathematics, physics, geometry and beyond. In this case, I like to think that the food operates as a kind of access point to a potential partial truth.

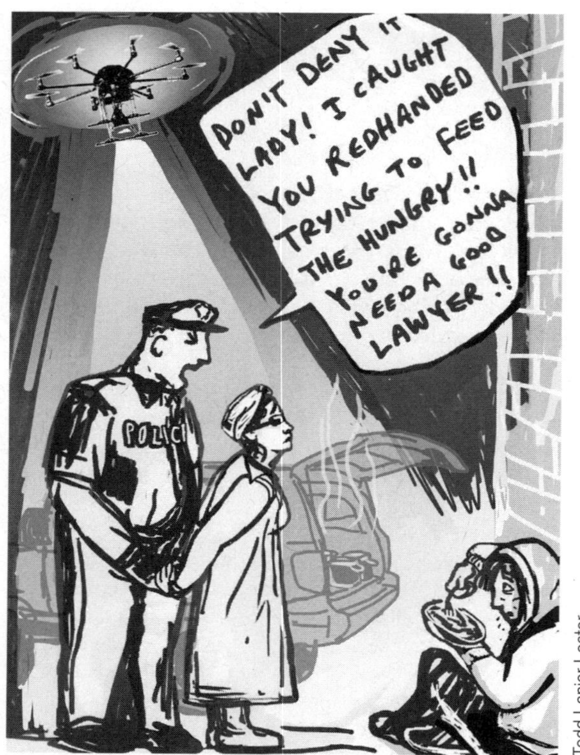

Todd Lanier Lester

QUALITY OF LIFE ENFORCEMENT: A ROVING INQUIRY
first performed on October 9, 2014
Roosevelt Avenue / Immigrant Movement International / Flux Factory, New York, NY
performed once in 2014

THIAGO CARRAPATOSO / NIKI SINGLETON / TODD LANIER LESTER
Public Ad Campaign, Queens Neighborhoods United

New York, NY / São Paulo, Brazil
quality-of-life-enforcement.tumblr.com

QUALITY OF LIFE ENFORCEMENT: A ROVING INQUIRY
THIAGO CARRAPATOSO / NIKI SINGLETON / TODD LANIER LESTER

"Quality of Life Enforcement: A Roving Inquiry" was a part of the Art in Odd Places/ AiOP festival in New York City. Concerned with how the broken window theory of policing is interpreted and enforced by NYC authorities—under the rhetorical guise of 'quality of life enforcement'—we are interested in a bigger frame of inquiry than simply how the city allows/accommodates human activity (including creativity). Moreover, we question how the city—as container to contemporary vectors of power—defaults to a legally closed (or closed off) societal space, thus stymying human activity (including creativity) at socio-economic or class levels different from the dominant culture.

The series of walks, subway rides and tours used three personal encounters as starting points for our collaborative inquiry and invitational research process:

[Saturday, October 11, 4-6 pm—Roosevelt Avenue walk with members of Queens Neighborhoods United; starting in Queens @ Immigrant Movement International]

I was visiting Tania Bruguera's Immigrant Movement International in Queens and witnessed some police stopping a food vendor and throwing away her food.
–Thiago Carrapatoso

[Sunday, October 12, 11:30 am—#4 train ride to the Hall of Fame for Great Americans (Bronx); starting @ Gandhi statue in Union Square Park]

I witnessed a panhandler and two buskers (the "it's showtime" kids) talking on the subway. The panhandler asked the young guys if, when the police stop them, "do they take your money away," to which the guys said "yes."
–Todd Lanier Lester

[Friday, October 10, 2:30-4:30 pm—street art walk; starting in Williamsburg @ El Puente / Espiritu Tierra Community Garden]

I was testing a batch of wheat paste in Williamsburg and was stopped by the NYPD anti-graffiti unit; I argued and spent a night in jail.
–Niki Singleton

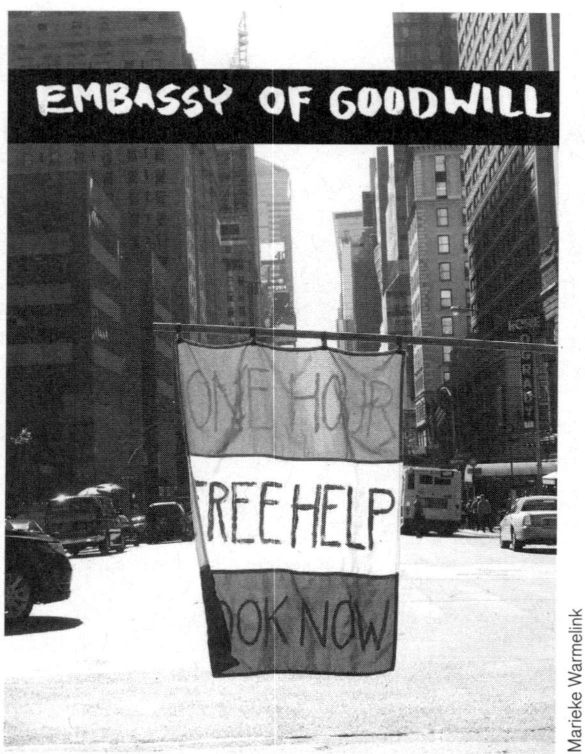

Marieke Warmelink

ONE HOUR OF FREE HELP

first performed on October 9, 2014
Art in Odd Places, Union Square, New York, NY
performed for ten days in 2014

EMBASSY OF GOODWILL / MARIEKE WARMELINK, DOMENIQUE HIMMELSBACH DE VRIES

Amsterdam, The Netherlands
info@mariekewarmelink.com
embassyofgoodwill.com / mariekewarmelink.com

ONE HOUR OF FREE HELP
EMBASSY OF GOODWILL / MARIEKE WARMELINK,
DOMENIQUE HIMMELSBACH DE VRIES

In the performance "One Hour of Free Help," Embassy of Goodwill offers one hour of free help.

The aim of Embassy of Goodwill is to raise the social image of the Netherlands by offering one hour of free help to locals and passersby in different places in the world. The Netherlands used to be known as a safe haven for individuals who think differently. However, in the past ten to fifteen years the country has been dominated by a growing fear of dissidents, which has resulted in a fertile ground for negativity. We, Domenique Himmelsbach de Vries and Marieke Warmelink, two socially engaged artists based in the Netherlands, share our expertise, experience and knowledge on a personal level to raise the social reputation.

By giving free help in different places in the world, we reach out to those in need, regardless of nationality, background, class, race or ethnicity. By doing so we collect vital experiences, personal stories and information that investigate the needs of local people. Our approach is based on the voice of the public. Through interaction and participation we analyze and map out these different needs. This working method has become an important source of information for policymakers. In this way the outcome is much more than just a performative work. It shows its positive effects in society on a day-to-day level.

Examples of free help we offer/perform:

Brainstorming, solving problems, renovating houses, gardening, vegetarian/vegan cooking for individuals or groups, designing posters, video editing, taking initiative, organizing, repairing bicycles, screen printing, glass cutting, welding, photography, sewing, teaching, basic computer help, welcoming guests at your house party, giving advice, playing New Wave at your party.

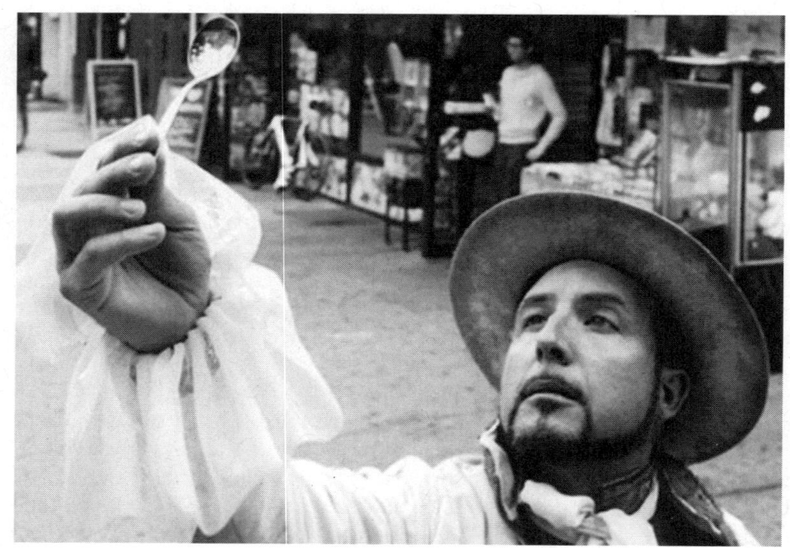

Enrique Ortiz

DUTY FREE RANGER
first performed on October 9, 2014
Art in Odd Places, New York, NY
performed eight times in 2014

RORY GOLDEN

Brooklyn, NY
rorynewyork@hotmail.com
rorygolden.net

DUTY FREE RANGER
RORY GOLDEN

"Duty Free Ranger" mashes a park ranger and a dandy in a roving public interactive intervention to awaken passersby on their day-to-day paths and to invigorate free use of public space. The Duty Free Ranger has no duties, holds no police powers, nor enforces laws or regulations. He uses a silver spoon (à la Charles II) as a mirror to walk backward and begs for donuts. He then transmogrifies into a baton twirler in a sequined singlet. Spontaneous exchanges inspire curiosity in this intervention exploring culture, class, privilege, fantasy and personal freedom.

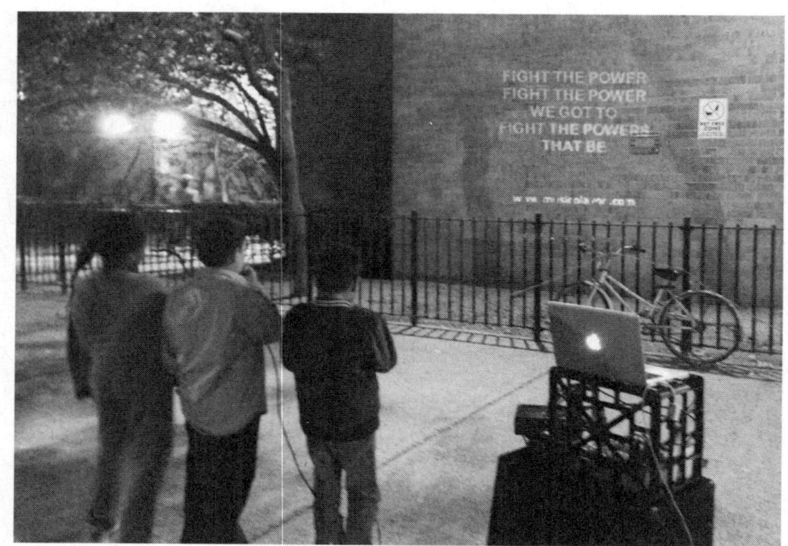

Stephen Sewell

A NEW SONG
first performed on October 10, 2014
Campos Plaza, New York, NY
performed twice in 2014

STEPHEN SEWELL

Brooklyn, NY
stephensewell.com

A NEW SONG
STEPHEN SEWELL

"A New Song" is a public performance in the form of a curated karaoke party. Taking inspiration from the International Workers Order's 1938 pamphlet of the same name, "A New Song" features a song selection composed entirely of protest songs. A flyer containing a list of available songs as well as a poem from the original IWO pamphlet is available for spectators and participants to take. The performance offers the opportunity for individual self-expression within a communal setting to underscore the role that music has played in encouraging collective activism.

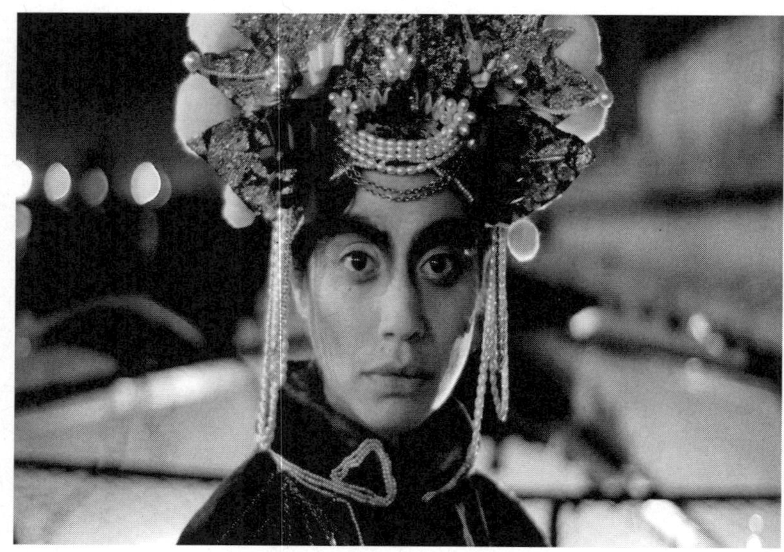

THE DREARY COAST

first performed on October 14, 2014
The Gowanus Canal, Brooklyn, NY
performed fourteen times in 2014

JEFF STARK

Sarah McMillan, Nick Chatfield-Taylor, George Graham, Chelsea Wagner, Caledonia Curry, Jason Engdahl, Suchan Vodoor, Ken Schatz, E. James Ford, Ava Eisenson, Zero Boy, Theresa Buchheister, Coco Conroy, Jo Firestone, Ryan Downey and many others.

New York, NY
jstark@nonsensenyc.com
drearycoast.org

THE DREARY COAST
JEFF STARK

"The Dreary Coast" is trespass theater. It is a show in a place where you do not expect a show—in this case on a raft on the Gowanus Canal, a horribly polluted Superfund site in New York. This original piece centered on the mythic character Charon, the boatman on the River Styx, and combined site-specific performance, guided tour, functional sculpture, handmade costumes, live music and pirate FM radio transmission.

At each show, audiences were robed in costumes and glided down the canal on a boat at night. These small audiences encountered actors and performances at bridges, docks and buildings along the way. We imagined the show as a kind of *Pirates of the Caribbean* ride amid a crumbling industrial neighborhood beset by pollution, flood and condo developers.

My projects blur the edge between fiction and reality, between narrative and non-narrative space, allowing audiences to question which parts of the event have been staged and which parts existed prior to the show. I am interested in risk, and in making explicit the relationship between artists and audiences. Our show did not ask for permission or permits. In this way, we remind each other that artists have a right and an obligation to participate in public space, a right to imagine what our cities can look like in the future—and the now.

The work was collaborative, featuring the efforts of 50 artists, designers and performers and was entirely self-produced.

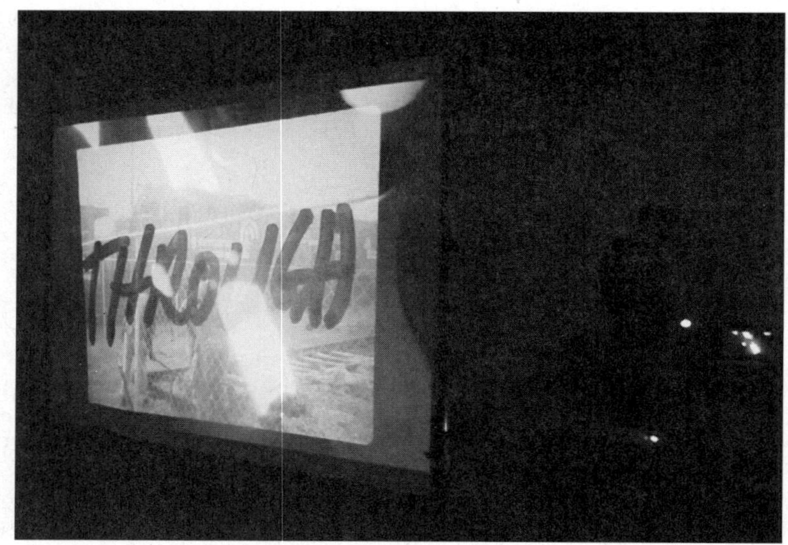

EXPERIENCE; TO EXPERIENCE (2.57142857143°)

first performed on October 15, 2014
Just Be Cause, Ithaca, NY
performed once in 2014

AHMED OZSEVER

Ithaca, NY
ahmedozsever.com

EXPERIENCE; TO EXPERIENCE (2.57142857143°)
AHMED OZSEVER

"Experience; to Experience" is a video, image and sound performance. The piece is in response to the idea of "experience" as a means of decoding history through memory—as opposed to merely chronological documents—and the resulting speculative evolution of the word "experience" from active to passive. The work is two simultaneous and choreographed (rear) projections; one digital video and the other 35mm slides. Both machines were operated live and the narratives told by both create a tension between the perceived passivity of the technologically contemporary video projection and the simultaneously memorial and discarded carousel slide projection. The soundtrack serves to syncopate the imagery and create an artificial timescale. The slide projector reverberated loudly throughout the space while a second audio track played through a PA built up as though generations of sound were piling on one another, creating a cacophony of rhythmic ambient noise. Each image in the slideshow has been reclaimed, written upon with the associations of the shifting language of experience, and when read together holds the structure of a concrete poem in three verses, each of which repeats. The rhythm of the slides holds steady (with the exception of human error) throughout the first reading, while upon second revolution each word holds a specific duration making it autonomous from the others. This serves as a way to associate the changing associations in the mind, an "after image" of association based upon the weight of the words themselves. The videos, which interact with the slide projection and sound elements, embody three different types of experience; from surprise to the collected or generational to transformative or long-term.

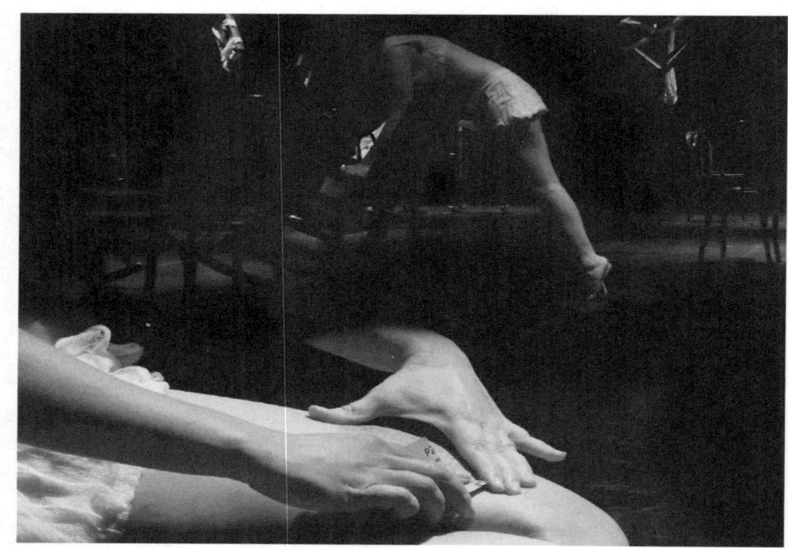

CITATION
first performed on October 15, 2014
Memorial Auditorium, Stanford, CA
performed once in 2014

RAEGAN TRUAX

San Francisco, CA / Berlin, Germany
rtruax27@gmail.com
raegantruax.com

CITATION
RAEGAN TRUAX

An act of remembering, "Citation" recalled performances by female artists from the 1960s onward, but avoided re-performance, exploring citations as recognizable yet ephemeral structures of meaning.

Transforming a proscenium theater into a site of memory, Truax filled the stage with rocking chairs and hung empty picture frames throughout the space. For 34 consecutive hours, she performed and repeated the following score: Rock/Remember/Unwrap/Write/Erase/Wrap/Rock.

To elaborate: Truax began by walking slowly through the space rocking chairs she came in contact with. Following her internal rhythm, she would engage in an off-balance duet with one chair that included twisting, lifting, falling and moving into memory. As remembering concluded, severing the final point of contact between her body and the chair, Truax revealed a bundle containing white gauze, a pen and a square of sandpaper and began writing on a section of her body about the present moment and the process of remembering. Audience members approached, trying to read the inscribed pen marks. With the sandpaper, Truax then sanded the writing from or further into herself. Ink disappeared as skin flakes and beads of blood rose to the surface of her body. Wrapping her wound in gauze and sitting with the audience, Truax then wrote the name of the female artist, title of a performance and date on the back of the sandpaper before standing to wrap a frame with the gauze, sandpaper and pen. Beginning again, Truax walked, rocked chairs and waited for a new sense or emotion to stir, catch and suspend.

Audience members entered at all hours and could come and go as they pleased. Many sat in rocking chairs, approached the performer, watched, engaged and came back.

Truax did not leave the space for the duration of the performance. She did not have a clock or other traditional markers of time on stage. She entered without food or water. She exited fifteen minutes after the 34th hour.

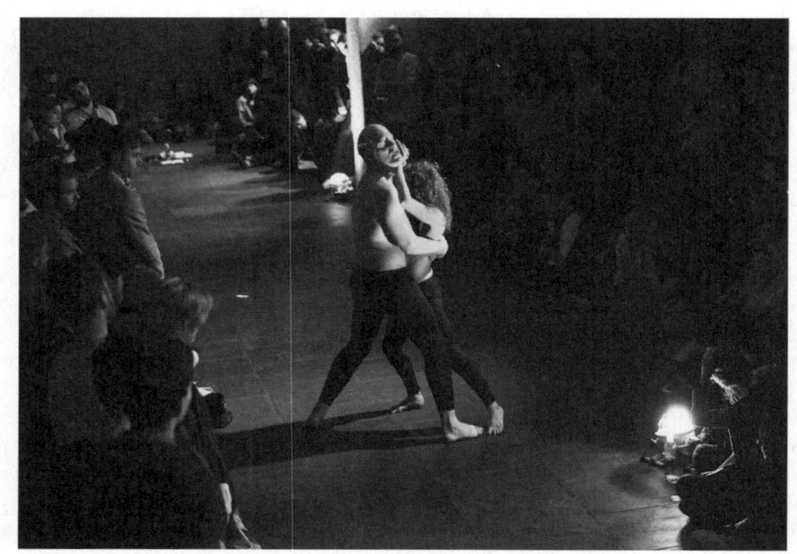

MORTAL KOMBAT
first performed on October 16, 2014
Gallery TPW, Toronto, Canada
performed three times in 2014

ARIANA REINES
Jim Fletcher, Edley ODowd

New York, NY
ariana.reines@gmail.com

MORTAL KOMBAT
ARIANA REINES

At a panel organized by Triple Canopy, Jim and I learned we had the same birthday. Having long admired his work with Richard Maxwell and Bernadette Corporation, I took our shared birthday as a sign we should collaborate. The idea of asymmetrical twinship was irresistible. Selfishly, I wanted to discover new ways of working with and through my body from a great actor whose power, it seemed to me, derived as much from his unique physicality and speaking voice as from his writerly sense of the materiality of language, the rudiments of words. I hoped Jim would get something out of working together too.

Before "MORTAL KOMBAT," Jim and I had previously written and performed a brief movement-heavy play together called "LORNA," inspired by Noh theatre and Butoh. With "LORNA," I went in with one goal: to generate the text together from experiments in deconstructed and slowed-down movement, rather than to pre-imagine a text whose duration, structure and meaning would later be inflected by staging, by Jim's and my physicality as performers.

"MORTAL KOMBAT" was an investigation of the structuring elements of physical aggression, by way of the popular 1992 video game. I wanted to take on and to challenge the notion of "a fair fight" and to explore how gender and size inflect questions and problems of physical dignity, active & passive resistance and styles of enmity. I wanted to generate language via the exploration of these physical states.

Jim and I developed "MORTAL KOMBAT" procedurally, by deconstructing movements as we had done for "LORNA," taking inspiration from Kathakali, krumping, judo grappling and basic jeet kun do along the way. Our rehearsals walked a strange and very fine line between martial arts sparring practice, double dutch, patty cake, improvisational dance, Youtube miming and a mirroring exercise we called "fake t'ai chi."

We presented a third iteration of "MORTAL KOMBAT" at the Whitney Museum's historic Breuer building before the museum moved to its new downtown location. For the Whitney performance, I wanted to add a sonic element to make the building itself, the very architecture, come alive. Drummer Edley ODowd of Psychic TV and Toilet Böys fame was the perfect third prong to the project, for at least 20 reasons, not the least of which being he too shared Jim's and my birthday.

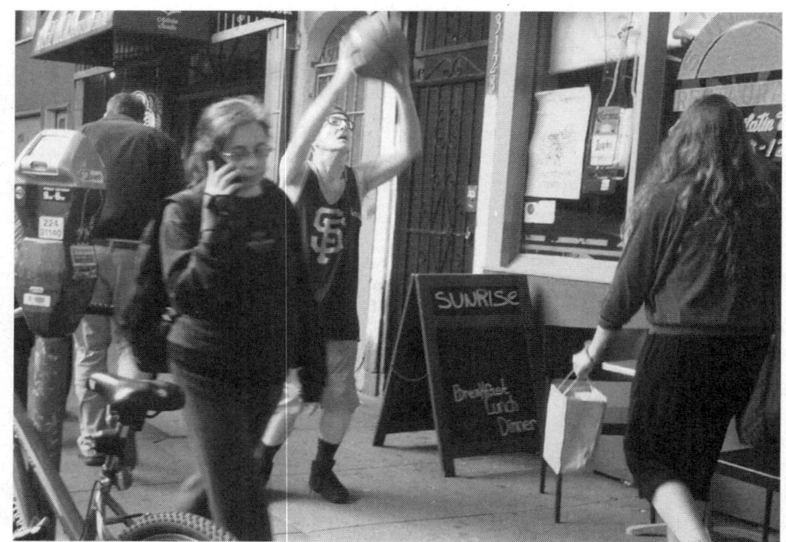

David Lawrence

THAT DOUCHEBAG WAS IN MY WAY (FTW)

first performed on October 17, 2014
In the public space of the Mission District, San Francisco, CA
performed six times in 2014

GORDON WINIEMKO

Los Angeles, CA
gordon@winiemko.com
winiemko.com

THAT DOUCHEBAG WAS IN MY WAY (FTW)
GORDON WINIEMKO

Contemplating the new wave of gentrification in San Francisco, which has driven up rents to the point where it would be truly impossible to live in the city again, it occurred to me that the root cause is that I live in a society that values winning at all costs. Tech workers would not be able to make so much money if we didn't value success and achievement. Government would not be a tool of corporations if we didn't love power and prestige. So I decided to play the game to win. I turned the Mission District of San Francisco into my own private basketball court. I donned the necessary clothing. I performed the appropriate gestures of the game. I engaged passersby either as teammates or used them as obstacles to overcome and to help me practice my ball-handling skills. I won.

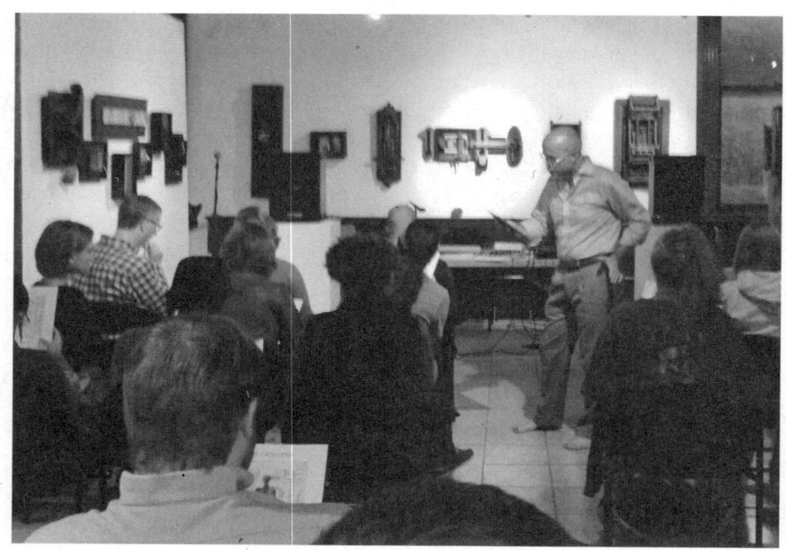

EYEVOICESCENSE

first performed on October 17, 2014
Albany Center Gallery, Albany, NY
performed once in 2014

GEOF HUTH

Schenectady, New York
geofhuth@gmail.com
dbqp.blogspot.com

EYEVOICESCENSE
GEOF HUTH

This performance consisted of seven sections to allow me to present seven different poetries for the audience to experience and to increase the possibility of reaching the audience with a tangible, memorable experience. The performance also had to engage within the space it inhabited, one filled with sculptural assemblages that worked similarly to the way that the performance accumulated disparate pieces of poetry into a cohesive but divergent experience.

I. Myology, Plate XIV: The performance began with a reading of a full-color visual poem, written in English and an asemic script.

II. Six Pwoermds: I then read six one-word poems slowly, allowing the audience to read and reinterpret these tiny poems.

III. Undelete: The only poem in the canonical form of a poem was a long textual poem filled with irregular repetition. I wandered through the audience while performing this, always moving their attention to another spot in the room.

IV. In Their Collected Beauty: I read aloud one small corked bottle filled with marbles and two metal letters (#9 of this sequence of bottle poems) and handed it to one member of the audience, motioning for her to pass the poem through the audience. I then picked up #10 from this series, filled mostly with glass, read its brief text, handed it to another audience member, and he looked at it and passed it through the audience.

V. Spokepoem: My next poem was merely a poem spoken extemporaneously and beginning with information from the biographies of the others performing that night, a poem made out of where my thoughts went.

VI. Four Polarrhoids: I read four poems, each in the shape of a Polaroid photograph with a single-word caption.

VII. Poemsong: I ended with a song, sung in no language at all, something loud that rang through the audience. At times, I pointed my voice to the ceiling of that small space so that its sound would fall back hard upon the audience.

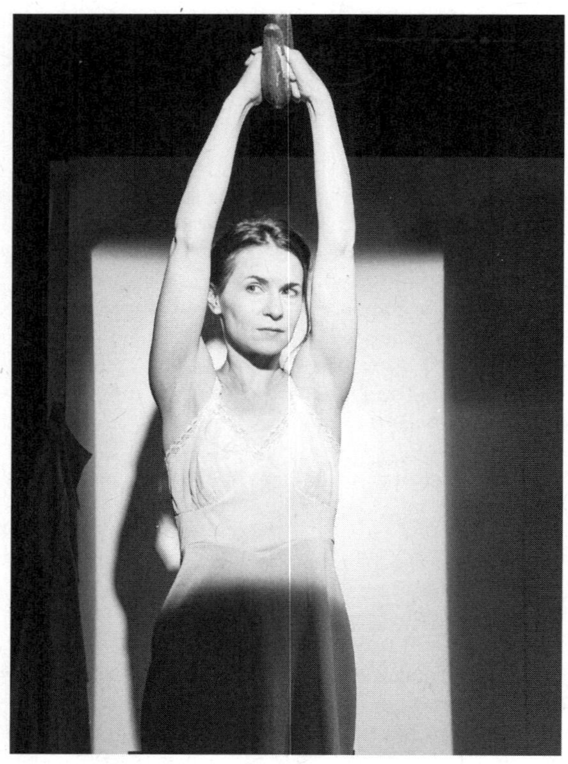

FROM PAGE INTO SPACE: DIRECTING GERTRUDE STEIN'S TENDER BUTTONS (FOOD)

first performed on October 17, 2014
Theater for the New City, New York, NY
performed four times in 2014

NIKI TULK

Cassandra Victoria Chopourian, Lauren Farber, Rich Gross, Mark Tulk, Gary Heidt

West New York, NJ / Jersey City, NJ
niki@smallhousecreative.com / info@vanreipen.org
vanreipen.org/work/tenderbuttons/food/index.html

FROM PAGE INTO SPACE: DIRECTING GERTRUDE STEIN'S TENDER BUTTONS (FOOD)
NIKI TULK

"Food" was a two-year performance project of Gertrude Stein's *Tender Buttons*, at Theater for the New City—an invitation to explore poetry through a spatial lens, a context in which I could experiment with visual, sonic and kinesthetic modes.

In approaching Stein's work, I felt strongly that we needed to respect the fact that the text does not "need" anyone to speak it; it has been speaking itself—with elegance and power—for 100 years. I crafted the rehearsal process accordingly; we responded to individual words and phrases in sound and physical improvisation for many months before bringing the entire text into the rehearsal room. Then, as you might call somebody by name in order to converse with them, we allowed the text to fill our mouths and movements.

Specifically, I placed a selection of Stein's phrases in empty frames around the space. We "listened" to them, conscious as we began improvising with the text through simple, scenic structures, that we move, breathe and only then speak. We observed with care as we handled/were handled by the words—what happened sonically? To our bodies? To the space? To the ways we interacted? We discovered (and used as our fundamental forms) rituals—the dinner party, preparation of food, courtship, seduction—both familiar, yet made newly strange by virtue of Stein's syntax, which deliberately and playfully cracks open the linguistic and ideological spaces that traditional sentences have marked out for us: "a sentence of a vagueness that is violence is authority and a mission and stumbling and also certainly also a prison."

The role of food in our culture, history and the landscape of social strata that is contained within (perhaps especially) the female body was an emerging theme as we worked within the patterns suggested by Stein's words: the female body as "juice and size and baking and exhibition and nonchalance and sacrifice..." with the paradoxical elements of woman as consumer of food, and also as the object of consumption and its attendant rituals.

As we explored those fissures, we discovered in a visceral way how deeply patriarchal and class/caste-based systems have regulated not only human relationships, but also the language of those relationships. The text, as it were, rose up in our midst and inspired us with how it was to be translated into three-dimensional, theatrical space—creating a playful, absurd and powerful process.

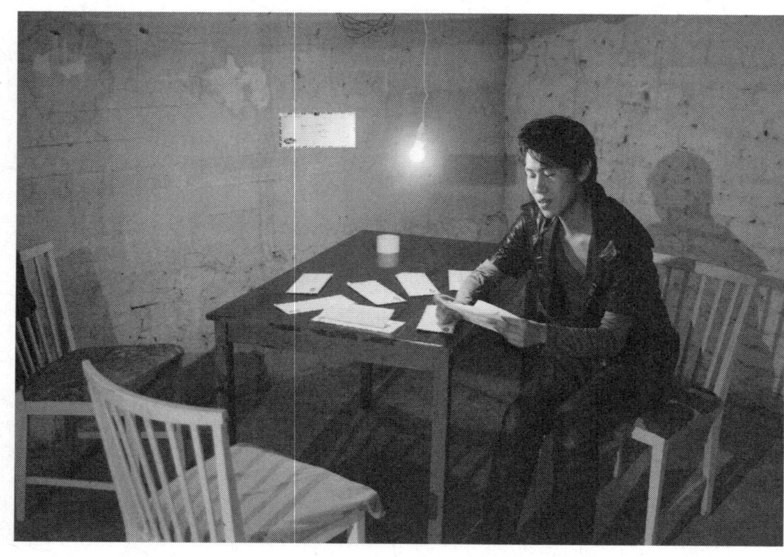

CORRESPONDING WITH DIFFERENCES
first performed on October 17, 2014
Annex of MUU Galleria, Helsinki, Finland
performed once in 2014

SHAWN CHUA

Singapore
shawnchuamr@gmail.com

CORRESPONDING WITH DIFFERENCES
SHAWN CHUA

"Dear you,

Letters take time, I am beginning to realize. They take time to traverse the distance separating you from me, they take time to be written and then they also take you in its time. By the time you read these words, I imagine you would have become a different 'you' and I may be a different 'me.' It seems that in letters, we are always writing to the future—a future, a certain possibility of what might be.

I'm thrilled that in a little more than a week from now, the Tom of Finland stamps will finally be released. Yes, the work of Tom of Finland has always provided a release for many (myself included)—a release of inhibited desire, of unfulfilled fantasies, of secret longings. Yet the launch of these stamps will stimulate another release—a setting free into the public realm of what once only belonged under the mattress, or in the furtive glances exchanged in dark alleys.

[...]

I sincerely hope that in reading this you, too, would write a letter to the future. It may be to your future self, or to someone who inhabits a future that you desire, or indeed to someone you don't know yet. It may be a confessional letter, a letter of advice, a love letter, a letter of apology, a personal letter of any form. From the multiplicity of personal stories, memories and longings, we begin to think and feel a 'community' that is perhaps not yet here, to galvanize in the present the concrete possibility of a there and then.

I would keep your letter anonymous, and it will be part of a performance installation for the Amorph International Performance Art Festival held on the 16-19 October. In exchange for your letters, I would send you a letter from someone else's future, along with a Tom of Finland stamp. If you are keen, do make sure that the letter would reach me by 25th September at the following address. [...]

I look forward to corresponding with you in the there and then of another world.

Yours,
[Signature]
30th August 2014"

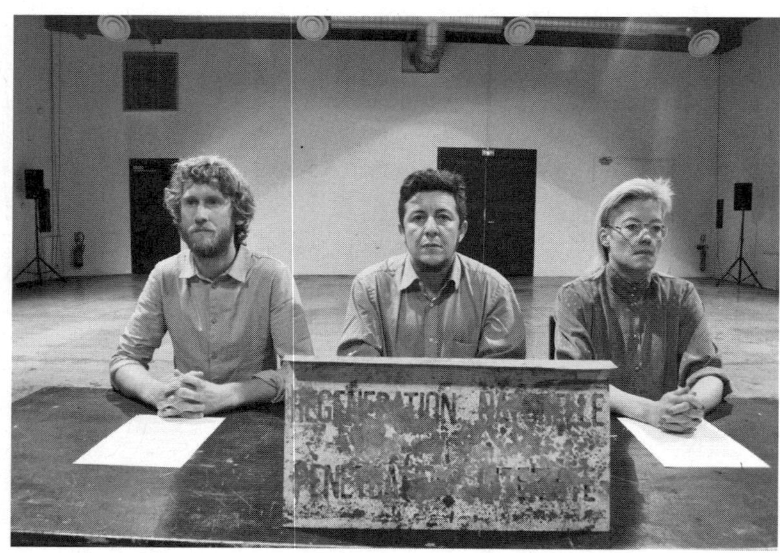

Eliane Akl

SHIP OF THESEUS
first performed on October 19, 2014
Le Generateur, Paris, France
performed once in 2014

DIMANCHE ROUGE

Paris, France
dimancherouge.org

SHIP OF THESEUS
DIMANCHE ROUGE

"The ship wherein Theseus and the youth of Athens returned had thirty oars, and was preserved by the Athenians down even to the time of Demetrius Phalereus, for they took away the old planks as they decayed, putting in new and stronger timber in their place, insomuch that this ship became a standing example among the philosophers, for the logical question of things that grow; one side holding that the ship remained the same, and the other contending that it was not the same." Plutarch, *Life of Theseus*.

Three of us sat at a table facing the public and read a text that we had written. Everyone of us read the same text once, using a microphone.

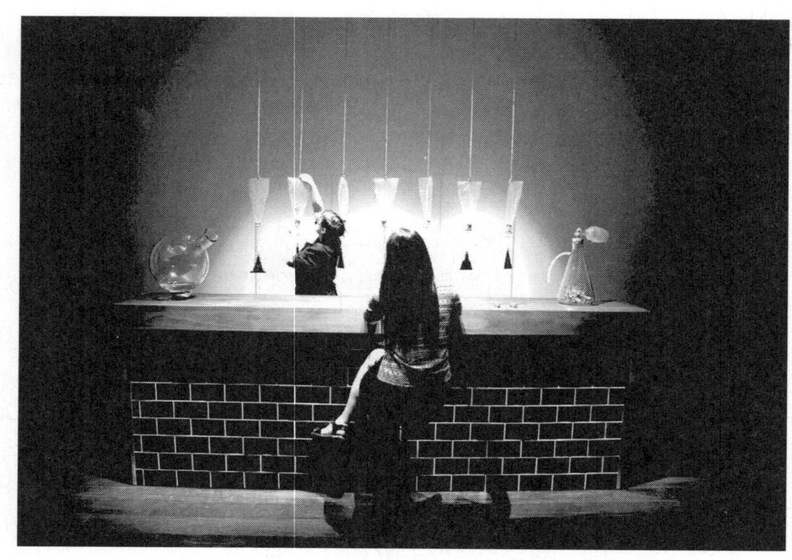

DIFFERENT KINDS OF AIR, A PLANT'S DIARY
first performed on October 22, 2014
Fremantle Arts Centre, Perth, Australia
performed 106 times in 2014

EMILY PARSONS-LORD

Perth / Sydney, Australia
e.parsonslord@gmail.com

DIFFERENT KINDS OF AIR, A PLANT'S DIARY
EMILY PARSONS-LORD

The purpose of the performance is to viscerally connect the individual to discourses surrounding climate change and the traces of the anthropocene in the air. Performed as part of the Proximity Festival, "Different Kinds of Air, a Plant's Diary" was a twelve-minute, one-to-one performance, installed as an air tasting bar that offered the audience member the opportunity to taste the air from different eras in Earth's history.

300-350 million years ago oxygen levels were nearly double what they are today, supporting mega flora and fauna. 252.5 million years ago, the Earth experienced its greatest extinction event with 93-97% of species on land dying out and a simultaneous spike in carbon dioxide levels. The history of the atmosphere on Earth is inexorably linked to the history of life.

"Different Kinds of Air, a Plant's Diary" offers the audience the opportunity to taste the air from some of these different eras in Earth's evolution. The gaseous composition, temperature, taste, and smell of air has changed drastically over the course of geological history; these differences affect human physiology, emotional states and consciousness.

What do these airs taste like? How do they make you feel? How do they affect your body, your consciousness and your memory?

Through physically breathing these air samples the audience experiences a visceral connection with the life that existed in the past, and a tactile and ethical encounter with some air of the future. It mediates on the scale of the earth and the scale of deep time.

The culmination of the work is the presentation to the audience of "future air." This air (actually sulphur hexafluoride, a seductively heavy, non-harmful to humans, human synthesised gas) is the most potent greenhouse gas that has yet been tested. It has the warming potential of 24,000 times that of carbon dioxide, and will be in the atmosphere for around 300-400 years. When inhaled, it acts as the opposite to helium—lowering the timbre of the voice. The immediacy of holding this seductive air in the hands of the audience member, and the invitation to try it, with the full knowledge of its warming potential, presents a real choice between desire and curiosity, and the sensation of responsibility and connection to the future of air.

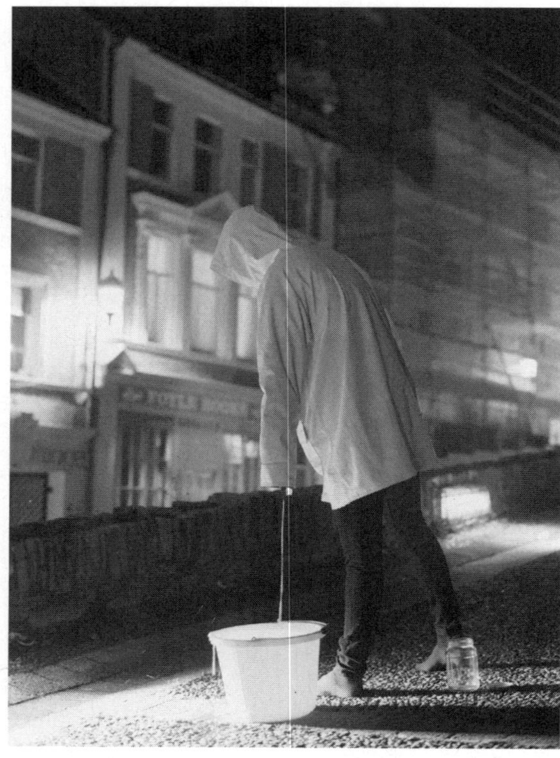

OHNE TITEL / WITHOUT TITLE
first performed on October 25, 2014
On the walkway of the city wall, Derry, Northern Ireland
performed once in 2014

MARITA BULLMANN

Essen, Germany
info@maritabullmann.de
maritabullmann.de

OHNE TITEL / WITHOUT TITLE
MARITA BULLMANN

1 yellow rain jacket

1 mini harmonica

5 eggs

1 bucket full of water

1 jar

1 inflatable dolphin

The performance took place outside on the walkway of the city wall of Derry, Northern Ireland. The only light came from the street lamps. During the whole performance my face is turned away from the audience. With the yellow rain jacket I become more a kind of character than a human. My movements are slow and methodical.

I lean against the wall and slowly blow into the mini harmonica till the sound gets really loud. From the right sleeve of my jacket three eggs fall on the ground. I gently move towards the bucket full of water. From the left sleeve I pour some water into the bucket until it overflows. Again with the right sleeve I let the other two eggs fall into the jar. I lay down and start to bang my head against the bucket till it tumbles over. With my right hand I reach for the jar and destroy it. I stand up and gently inflate the dolphin. While deflating the dolphin I slowly crouch. I put the dolphin down, stand up and disappear.

My intention was to research gestures, sign language and all kind of communications as an artistic and poetic vocabulary. The simplicity of the images and actions point to something beyond all layers of normal visual and perceptual mechanisms far away from their cultural coinages. Not only my character-like appearance but also the slow and determined movements became an emotional environment which touches memories and navigates between all kind of interpretations. With this performance I focused mainly on the creation of an intense situation, in a compressed and intimate but public space.

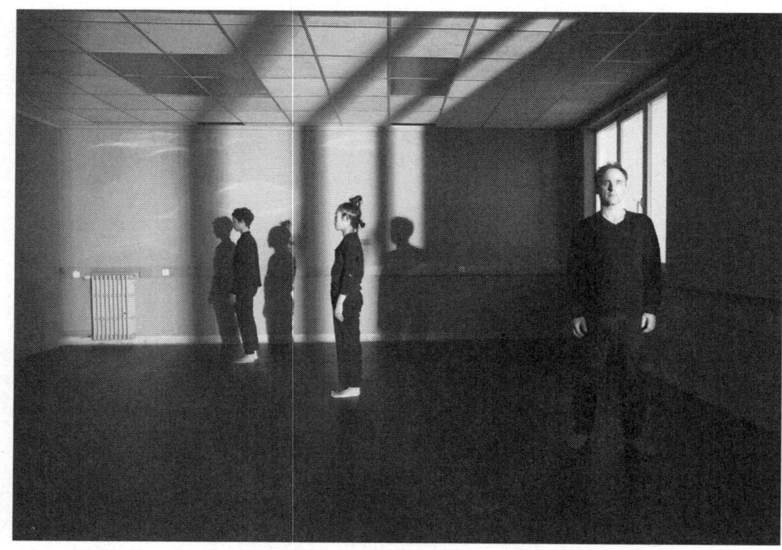

III (1)

first performed on October 29, 2014
KAAI Theater/Living, Brussels, Belgium
performed once in 2014

COLLECTIVE (3)

Jasmin Schaitl, Akemi Nagao, William "Bilwa" Costa

Berlin, Germany
performancecollective3@gmail.com
collective3.jasminschaitl.com

III (1)
COLLECTIVE (3)

III (1) is a site-relative performance, which combines three artists' individual practices including dance, task-based movements, performative actions and sound. It was developed over the course of ten days in KAAI Theater/Living while the collective was in residency at Work Space Brussels. Using limited materials, the trio execute movement, sound and visual scores, focusing on the points where their actions conjoin, sync, phase and/or oscillate in unison and simultaneity. Minimal, abstract and without narrative, III (1) leaves the audience space to assess the actions of the trio and interpret or propose her/his own meaning, content and thoughts.

The audience enters a silent and relatively dark space to an in-progress performance. A single light is coming through a row of windows along the back wall. This light shines through a cluster of three standing performers and spans the length of the space, creating a shadow on the far wall. The performers slowly move, one by one, perpetuating a gradual movement of the cluster. As they move towards the far wall, one performer, very slowly, peels away from the cluster and gradually moves to the floor, curling her body into a tight ball. This is repeated by a second performer, leaving the third to reach the far wall. A mirrored walking pattern duo spirals into the center of the space. Simultaneously, the third performer drops a trail of metal chopsticks as she follows a diagonal trajectory through the space. The duo end in close proximity and establish and hold a gaze. There is an abrupt break and they move into a series of movements and pauses, creating various triangles in the space with a white rubber line. One performer leaves the triangle, and then another, leaving a solo mover to create triangles. Using her body inside the rubber line, she creates triangles, which gradually become smaller and smaller, until she can no longer fit inside. The other two performers, standing far apart, establish and maintain a gaze. As the solo fades out, one performer breaks the gaze and walks to the chopsticks.

Picking them up one at a time, he tosses the chopsticks to the far wall. He is joined by another performer, as she begins tossing the chopsticks faster, from a kneeling position. The faster momentum creates a more complex sequence of sounds. She gradually tosses the chopsticks to another wall where they are picked up and tossed by the third member. She begins an even more rapid sequence, gradually tossing the chopsticks to the far wall, where she begins a very fast sequence creating an almost constant wash of sound. The other two performers stand very close to each other, on the far side of the space, where they are engaged in a duo of "non-touching"; a score which explores the point just before physical touch. The chopsticks stop abruptly, creating a silence, as the duo eventually fade out of the score and move apart.

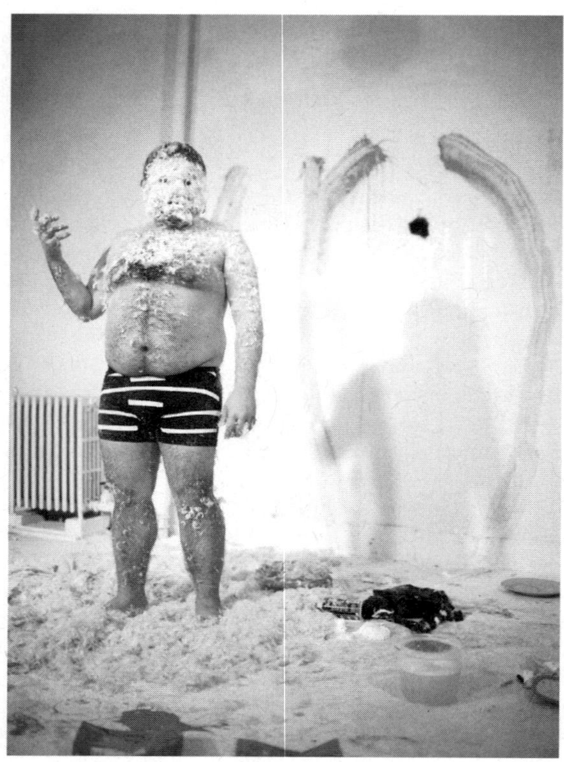

DO YOU UNDERSTAND ME?
first performed on October 31, 2014
Panoply Performance Laboratory, Brooklyn, NY
performed once in 2014

GERALDO MERCADO

Brooklyn, NY
info@geraldomercado.com
geraldomercado.com

DO YOU UNDERSTAND ME?
GERALDO MERCADO

This was a piece created for Empathy Play, the first exhibition of work by Social Health Performance Club, curated by Ayana Evans and Esther Neff. The bulk of my work is an exploration of empathy. "Do You Understand Me?" attempted to do this in a more abstract manner than I am accustomed to.

I spent two months growing a beard for this performance; I wanted to create a visible representation of my masculinity. I began the performance wearing my glasses, something I would never usually do. Like the change from Clark Kent to Superman, they are a part of my "normal self." I handed the glasses to an audience member and kept chanting the phrase, "You got me dawg," the double entendre here being a sign of gratitude and a declaration that "you are holding a part of me." Moving with big gestures I kept asking, "¿Tu me entiendes?" I began swallowing and spitting the contents of two boxes of tomato soup into a large bowl. I then removed my shoes and dipped my feet into the bowl of soup. I began walking around the space leaving red footprints in the performance area. I then dipped my sweater sleeves into the soup and used them to draw a symbol on the wall in one large motion, calling to mind two works by Regina José Galindo and Ana Mendieta, two Latina artists whose work has influenced my own. I switched my mantra to English: "Do you understand me?" I cut my beard onto a plate and used school glue to adhere it to the wall, an act meant to symbolize giving a piece of myself to the audience. Having shed an outer protective layer of masculinity, I took the rest of the glue and poured it onto my beardless face. I took a pair of scissors and cut open a down pillow (one belonging to an ex-girlfriend, though the audience wasn't told this). I took the feathers from the pillow and stuck them to my face, before asking one last time, "Do you understand me?"

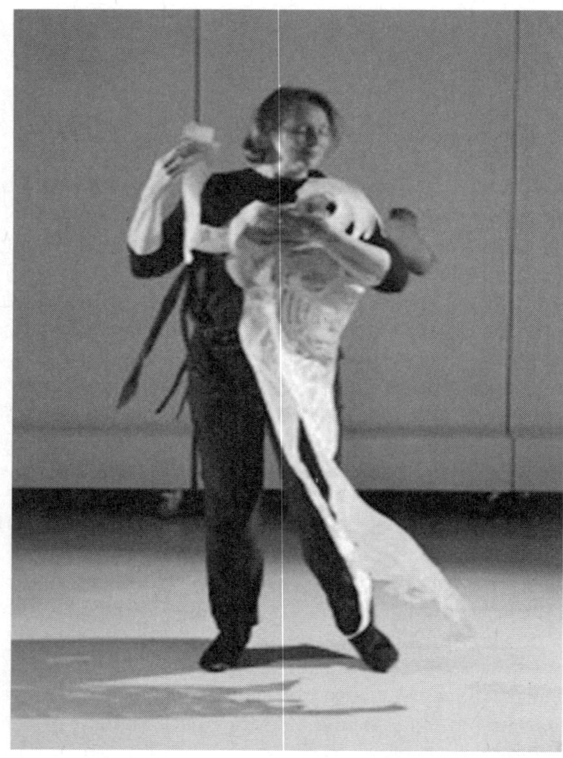

CALLING THE CUCKOO
first performed on November 2, 2014
Artscape Youngplace, Toronto, Ontario
performed once in 2014

LINDA RAE DORNAN

Sackville, New Brunswick, Canada
lrdornan@nb.sympatico.ca
lindaraedornan.ca

CALLING THE CUCKOO
LINDA RAE DORNAN

The desire to expand language as communication beyond words was my primary motivator for this performance. I used my body as an encoded text between words and silence, sound, actions and life stories. The absence of words at times and the fragmentation of structured language was evident in some actions while poetry emerged in others.

"Calling the Cuckoo" was a series of short and long actions about language as body, voice, space and movement, with a healthy dose of humor. Each performance short built into the next using chanting, song, extended vocal techniques, speech and actions from daily routines and life cycles where verbal and gestural languages intersect. Some of the processes performed included building a poem phonetically through repetitive song, reading a story backwards, bodily spelling words, telling a story with words and onomatopoeia effects and dancing with a fabric cut-out of words/sentences as a body. Some props were used such as a large red stuffed anatomical heart, three-foot drawing sticks and a body/word cut-out. The support structure of video projections and audio tracks were programmed in Isadora.

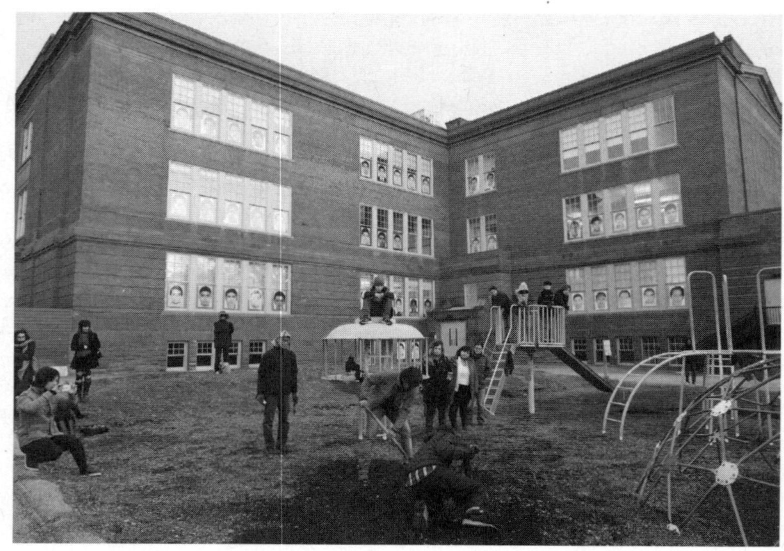

AYOTZINAPA / SEARCH, DEATH AND RESURRECTION
first performed on November 2, 2014
FADO Performance Art Centre, Toronto, Canada
performed once in 2014

ROBERTO DE LA TORRE

Mexico City, Mexico
delatorre.rob@gmail.com / robdelatorre@yahoo.com.mx
robertodelatorre.com / issuu.com/robertodelatorre/docs/de_la_mordida_al_camello

AYOTZINAPA / SEARCH, DEATH AND RESURRECTION
ROBERTO DE LA TORRE

The proposed theme is linked to the disappearance of the 43 students of the Rural School of Ayotzinapa, "Raúl Isidro Burgos," which occurred on September 26, 2014, in Iguala, Guerrero. This project makes reference to the many graves that have been found throughout the country with hundreds of bodies of deceased people.

During this performance, I explored the interior and exterior of the performance space (a former public school) through the use of different tools of various shapes and sizes that I found in the space while exploring. At the beginning of the event I had a small spoon that I found inside of a potted plant, then under some bushes I located a shovel that I used to dig the earth, which then revealed a set of buried shovels which I offered to the public so that they could help me dig.

Later on, with the support of other volunteers we moved to the playground area and began to remove the earth until we discovered beneath the surface, dirty and torn clothing. I took the buried garments and hung them on the metal structures at the recreational park as if they were human skins.

Finally, standing on a compact mound in front of two of the facades of the building, I focused on one of the windows where the photographs of the missing students were placed. I repeatedly banged the edge of the shovel against the dirt, the same way other participants had started to do with their own tools—and as a result, a synced, deep, metal sound emanated around the room. While this was happening, hundreds of printed sheets of paper were thrown down from one of the windows, which represented the awakening of a large segment of the Mexican population that has gone out on the streets to demonstrate repudiation of such atrocious events.

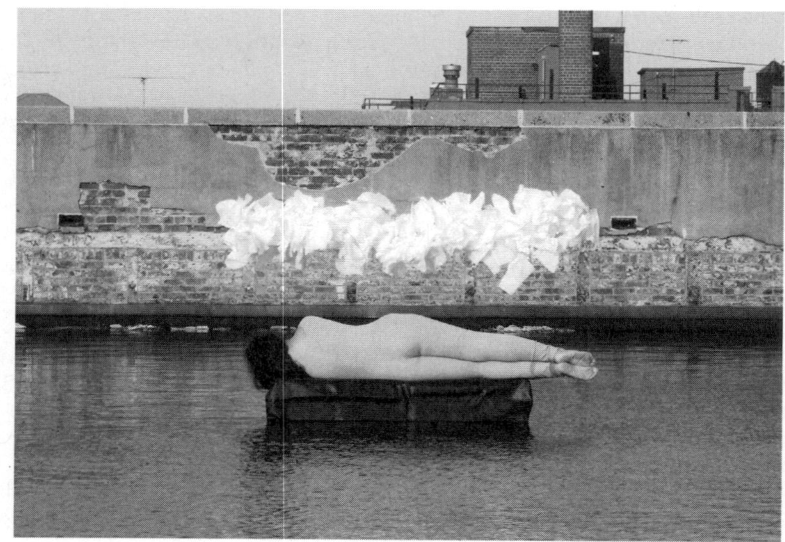

SKY BURIAL | SURVEILLED

first performed on November 7, 2014
Andrew Freedman Home, Bronx, NY
performed once in 2014

MELISSA CALDERON

Brooklyn / Bronx, NY
melissaacalderon@gmail.com
melissacalderon.com

SKY BURIAL | SURVEILLED
MELISSA CALDERON

Presented as commentary on the constant helicopter surveillance of communities of color, "Sky Burial | Surveilled" melds the ancient Buddhist burial practice with the concept of the death of privacy, solace and trust of government. The 30-minute silent performance visually and audibly captures the steady flux of police helicopter surveillance of The South Bronx, a historically known community of color. The artist lies under a reflective pool of water and a cloud made of tissue to represent the symbiotic relationships of power and fragility, futility and necessity. The reflecting pool activates the roof as a mirror, "as above, so below," addressing the constant cannibalization of bearing witness to tragedy while the Body of Community is being picked apart through ever-watchful eyes.

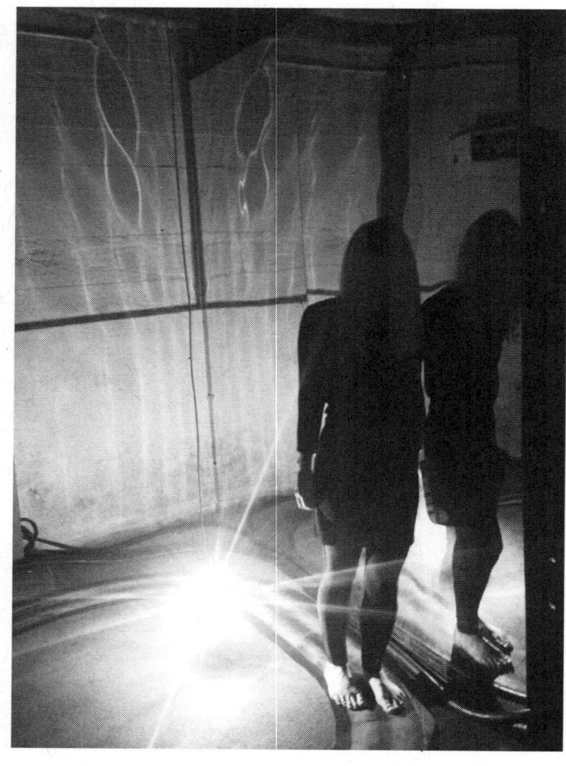

PHASES

first performed on November 7, 2014
The Island, Bristol, UK
performed once in 2014

CHELSEA COON

Boston, MA
chelsea.e.coon@gmail.com
chelseacoon.info

PHASES
CHELSEA COON

Over the duration of five hours, I slowly walked barefoot on a circular track of sandpaper until the soles of my feet wore away. I am interested in the way this image represents our position in space; our beginning and our eventual end.

In time, we will all disappear (only for a moment before we reappear again).

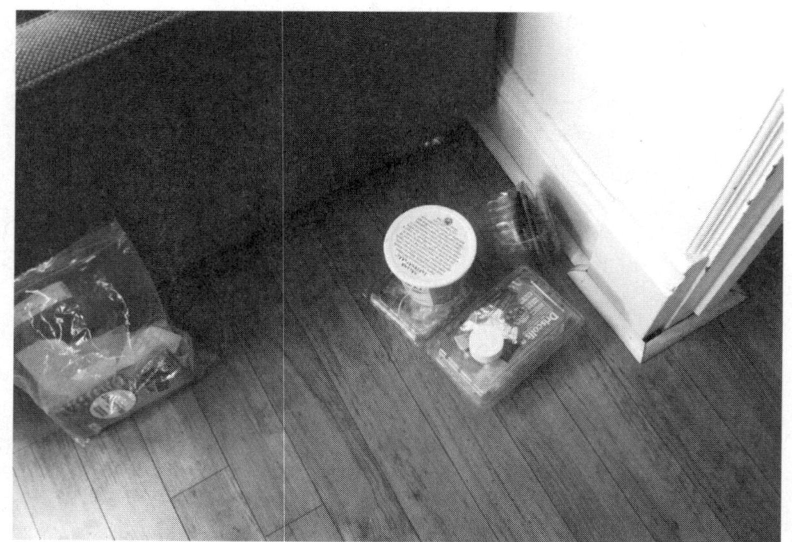

PLASTIC MARTYR
first performed on November 8, 2014
Total Human, Iowa City, IA
performed once in 2014

MAYA WEEKS

Cayucos, CA
mayaweex@gmail.com
anaturalhistoryofcolours.tumblr.com

PLASTIC MARTYR
MAYA WEEKS

This is a performance in which i surround myself sitting with most of my weight on my left buttcheek and legs folded to right side in a "Moomins" dress, not trying to play up my gender but not trying to look as masculine as every other day of the three months that i have lived in Iowa, where, encouraged by lack of single-stream recycling i made an attempt to quit single-use plastic cold turkey, excepting yogurt which, due to too many digestive issues & yeast infections i was more than reluctant to quit[1] and, because i am a glutton remaining to be convinced by my frangible relationship with the Iowa river that veganism is the only acceptable reaction to factory farming & industrial agriculture cheese; and, because i am an ARTIST and i have to save things, tape, and pens, and lip balm i carried with me from California, Cornwall etc. and my tool kit from the Shellmound IKEA ca. 2011 and the iPod that broke after my last trip to San Francisco, to arrange all these various plastics the likes of which are accumulating in the oceans[1] various gyres and more of which are shipped to China than recycled domestically[2] on the wooden floor of this full house in which Cassandra Gillig has just told me at our first meeting about the plastic-making machines of her suburb to read this poem ("AMTRAK FUCK THE POLICE") unable to tell if anyone is feeling anything on the evening of November 8 2014.

---

1. i tried to make my own yogurt from milk in glass bottles as i had in the Bay but because in Iowa City there was no milk to be bought in glass bottles and the organic milk was only sold in plastic-coated cartons, it was actually most ecological to buy yogurt by the (giant, plastic) tub—although i quickly found that i preferred the organic yogurt made WITHOUT pectin which only came in a smaller tub and myself making more and more an exception.

2. Did u know: the rounded triangle "recycling" symbol does not necessarily mean that an item is recyclable but rather is a "resin identification code" whose number indicates which polymer/s it is made from?!

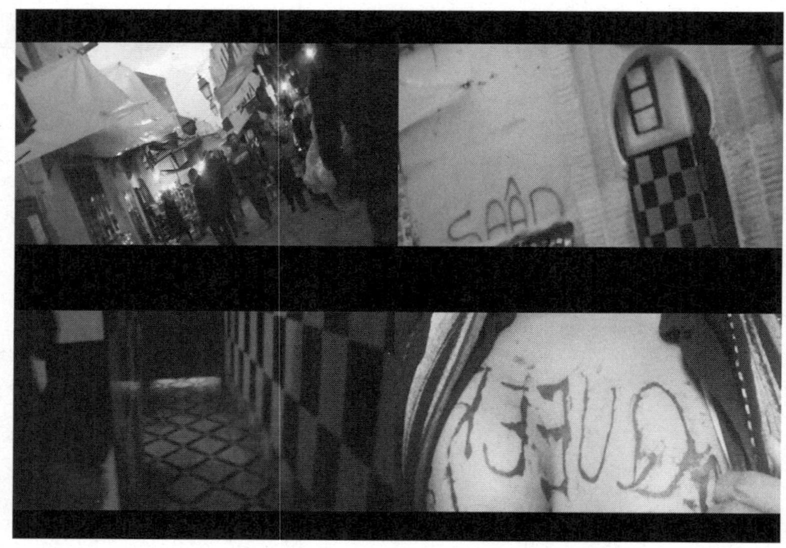

Elizabeth Steen

NO QUEER BODIES—A PUBLIC SCRUBBING
first performed on November 8, 2014
A public hammam in the Medina of Fes, Morocco
performed once in 2014

ALEX BERRY

Atlanta, GA / Seattle, WA
amberry03@gmail.com
amberry03.wix.com/portfolio

NO QUEER BODIES—A PUBLIC SCRUBBING
ALEX BERRY

The scrubbing took place in a local female hammam (public bathhouse) in the Medina of Fes. The English word queer was tagged with henna on my knuckles, arms, back, broadly across my chest, neck, feet and legs. After drying, my body was publicly scrubbed by an attendant—an elderly Moroccan woman—with a rough brush, traditional black soap and rinsed with buckets of hot water.

Blinded by steam, bodies became just breasts and buttocks, toes and teeth; where each naked body forfeited her identity by undressing and entering. The transformation of my marked queer body—as it was awkwardly flipped on the slippery tile floor— is an ephemeral and seemingly humorous spectacle. The vigorous scrubbing and consequent searing sensation irritated and further embedded the henna into my skin. Body parts tagged queer became red and triumphant upon the spectacle's end. But I was no one. Finally, my skin retained residue through minimal scarring several weeks after the performance.

Queer is progressively used by (not for) individuals choosing to use the term in a broader category of self-identification. It is a re-owned contemporary label by a community who embraces its usage as unconventional and eccentric while also acknowledging its derogatory history. Queer can be utilized as an umbrella term, not just for LGBTQ but any refusing a binary. It is inclusive and—as I intend to use the term—fluid, global and resilient.

"No Queer Bodies—A Public Scrubbing" addresses the visibility of self-identity. I endeavor agency, uniqueness with acknowledgment of cross-cultural barriers and likenesses. Emphasis is also placed on symbolic space—as the hammam is both public and private. As a queer tourist, I pursue solidarity and attempt inclusion of global truths and equality.

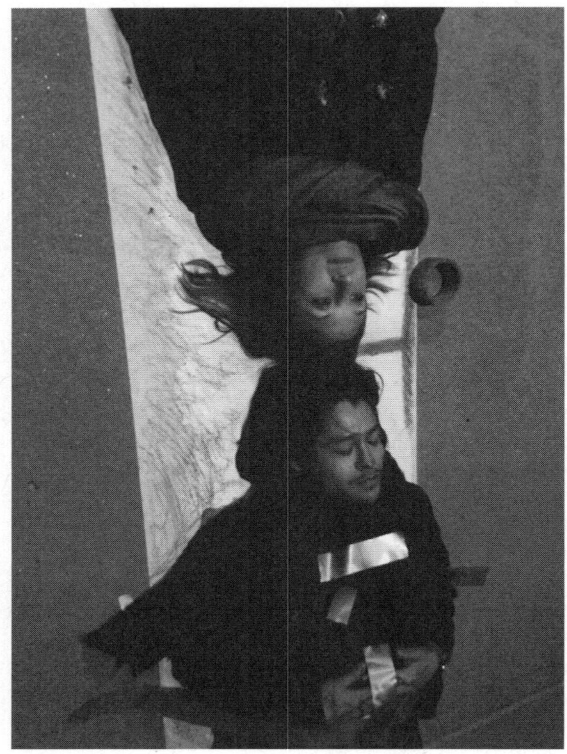

CONVERSING UNDER A BLANKET WITH A PATCH OF SKY STUCK IN A MIRROR

first performed on November 8, 2014
The perimeters of Madelife Art Gallery, Boulder, CO
performed once in 2014

DREAM TIGERS / HANNAH KEZEMA, ANGEL DOMINGUEZ

Boulder, CO
dreamtigersss@gmail.com

CONVERSING UNDER A BLANKET WITH A PATCH OF SKY STUCK IN A MIRROR
DREAM TIGERS / HANNAH KEZEMA, ANGEL DOMINGUEZ

DREAM TIGERS sought to perform a conversation of failure within the context of the 2014 Failure Festival curated by HOARDED STUFF, who said of FF: "This is a celebration and an acknowledgment of the fact that when things inevitably don't go as we plan, somehow, we must adapt." We learned to adapt.

In preparing for the performance, we realized that the performance itself was in a continuous state of preparation. In this way we never began. We faced the paradox of the plan: how does one prepare to fail? Furthermore, how does one perform failure?

We set out to perform for three hours (the length of one festival night); the actual duration became closer to five hours in total. Recordings of previous conversations of failure were to play continuously throughout the performance. The disembodied voices became a prop-like object. On the day of the festival, we were informed that we could no longer hold the space in the parking lot. This failure would precipitate the nature of the rest of the performance as a series of trials and errors. By eliminating that space, everything became our space.

Every thirty minutes a timer would go off and be restarted. We would announce "DREAM TIGERS WILL BEGIN IN 30 MINUTES," while writing these words in charcoal on sheets of butcher paper. We would get undressed and redressed in front of mirrors. We became acutely aware of time within our bodies: it was only through duration and repetition that we were able to predict when the timer would go off. We utilized a table with wheels—this meant that the demarcations of time were also demarcations of space. Time affected our mobility. For each increment, we mapped out a "station" on the periphery of the Madelife building where we would attempt to trace our shadows in charcoal: one of us would hold a floodlight while the other attempted to trace their silhouette.

The audience members initially participated before becoming the directive force of the performance. They decided our props were their props; they decided our bodies were props. The conversational aspect of the performance was abandoned in favor of direct interaction. A failure to be silent allowed the performance a voice of its own. In the end the performance performed us. The performance of failure and planning to fail inevitably invites more failure; as if the performance could exist both inside and outside of a beginning, in a perpetual state of becoming.

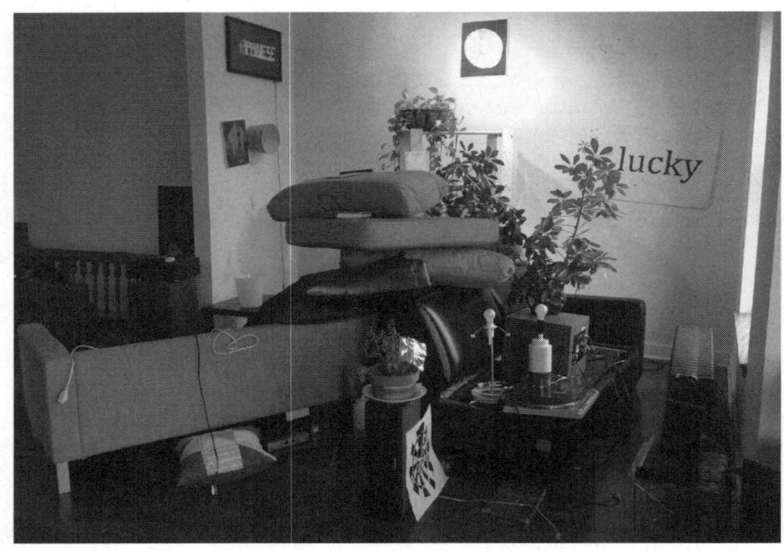

Shir Ende

LIVING ROOMS PROJECT
first performed on November 10, 2014
Various living rooms, Chicago, IL
performed seven times in 2014

SHIR ENDE

Chicago, IL
shirende.com

LIVING ROOMS PROJECT
SHIR ENDE

The duration of each intervention varies from 10 to 30 minutes.
The participants and I gather all the objects in their living rooms (objects on the wall must be taken down as well), to create a border in the middle of the frame of the camera.

Then we settle.

We then each take objects from the border to claim a space in a predetermined side. As we disassemble the border, we gradually start entering each other's side, erasing the separation and creating a shared territory.

The performance is done when all objects have been moved and have claimed a space. (If I, the guest/artist, touches an object that should not be touched or moved a certain way throughout this interaction, participants are allowed to intervene.)

The "Living Rooms Project" is the negotiation of space through the placement of objects. I create interventions in living rooms of different individuals as a guest, intruder and settler. As we strategically rearrange their domestic space within the frame of the video camera, the participants become my collaborators and opponents. Considering the politics of the domestic space, the roles and power dynamics shift as I attempt to inhabit and occupy the space of others by implementing my own rules. Through this non-verbal negotiation, a temporary border is constructed and disfigured as we divide and share the space.

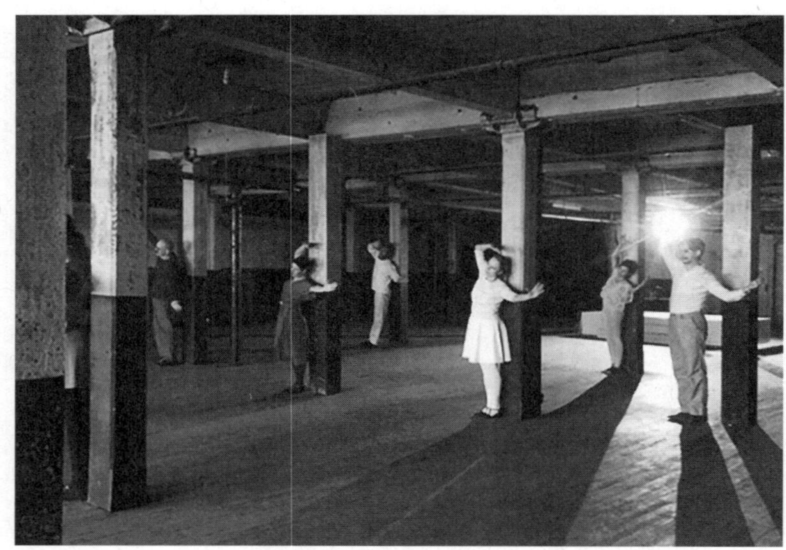

I LIKE YOU BETTER NOW
first performed on November 12, 2014
Hi-Temp Fabrication, Buffalo, NY
performed once in 2014

PATRICIA BRACE, RITA LEDUC // BCIJPG / NANCY HUGHES, SCOTT SLOCUM, GRETTA SOWYRDA
Lori Brett, Cynthia Cadwell Pegado, Laura Jean Castelluzzo, Leslie Fineberg, Michelle Joy, Henry Raes, Meagen Tucker, Dale West

Brooklyn, NY / Buffalo, NY
ilikeyoubetternow@gmail.com
ilikeyoubetternow.com

I LIKE YOU BETTER NOW

PATRICIA BRACE, RITA LEDUC // BCIJPG / NANCY HUGHES, SCOTT SLOCUM, GRETTA SOWYRDA

On November 12, 2014, we joined the Buffalo Contact Improvisation Jam Performance Group (BCIJPG) in a performance that integrated itself with our 14,000 square foot multi-media exhibition, "I Like You Better Now." Through improvisation and premeditated sensory movement, BCIJPG choreographed a piece in each of the two rooms, joined together by our own, third performance. In an inversion of the traditional theatrical process, the abstract narratives of these performances were dictated by the physical and conceptual languages of the surrounding installation and video, i.e., narrative was born from design rather than design based off of narrative. In this way, BCIJPG created a performance that physically expressed compounded, derivative responses to the intersection of exhibition, site, performers and present.

The performance began in a windowless room with four videos projected on eight by eleven feet screens that, by leaning on four massive columns, created a rectangular room-within-a-room. In this first act, principal BCIJPG members Nancy Hughes, Scott Slocum and Gretta Sowyrda initiated a contact-improvisational dance that seamlessly merged with our on-screen narrative. As we flittered digitally on the four screens, Hughes, Slocum and Sowyrda tumbled, writhed, floated and twirled in response. At the conclusion of the twelve minute video, Hughes and Slocum led the crowd by song into the second room where they were greeted with our intermezzo performance. In this act, Leduc read a poem with woven impressions of her spatial ideals from atop a stage-like overlook. Before long, she made room for Brace who performed a dance representation of her emotional ties to the site. As soon as she leapt off the platform, act three began with BCIJPG and guest dancers joining to flood the space. Within a forest of faux, forced perspective columns in-between two 100 foot forced perspective walls, six glowing windows at the far end appeared to be farther away than reality. Throughout the next twenty minutes, BCIJPG improvised a loosely-choreographed dance dictated by the opposing 100 foot walls, the diametrically opposed windows and the expansive (but interrupted) floor space. The performance came to an end as the dancers assumed their perches at the base of each column.

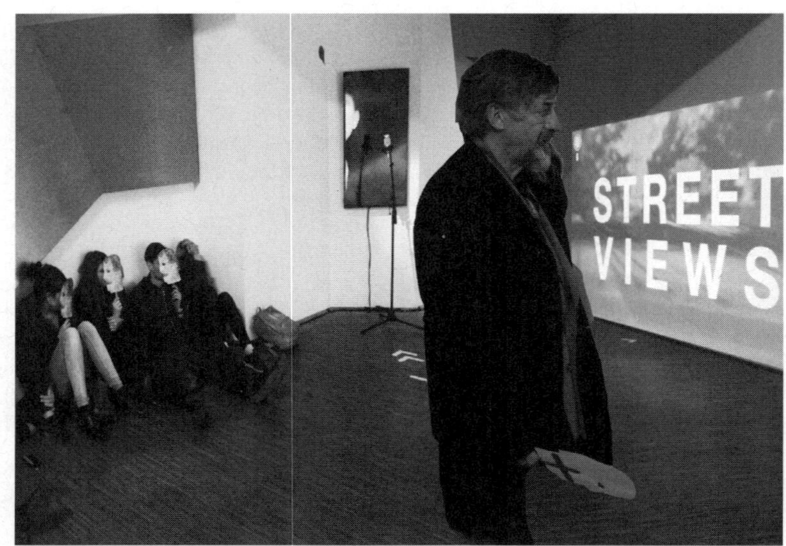

Annie Berman

STREET VIEWS
first performed on November 12, 2014
KulturBahnhof Kassel, Kassel, Germany
performed once in 2014

ANNIE BERMAN
Goto80 and the Uwe Schenk Band; Ghost Hunter; Augustus Bro & Gallery Six, Diana Trushell,
Mariya Chelova

New York, NY
twitter.com/ANNIE_BERMAN

STREET VIEWS
ANNIE BERMAN

This piece concerns presence and performance and plays with the idea of a virtual presence. The artist was invited to Kassel to exhibit work. The artist's presence is marked by a sign that reads, "The Artist is Present." A red Google location identifier appears on the sign. This same icon appears above a flat screen monitor among the viewers. The monitor is oriented vertically and displays a portrait of the artist, her face blurred out. A microphone points towards the screen. Emanating from the screen is the artist's voice. She is narrating the piece projected on the opposite wall. The projected piece entitled "STREET VIEWS" is an eight minute loop of scenes from Google's mapping application. The projected image meets the floor. The navigation arrows continue on the floor into the space itself. On the wall is an offering—brightly colored hand-cut masks on colored sticks made by enlarging a small figure from Seurat's *Sunday in the Park*. A handwritten sign reads: "Take one. Privacy masks." Visitors take masks; a group of art students wear the masks, watch the piece, sit on the floor and photograph themselves wearing the masks. They then ask someone nearby to take their photo. The person obliges. They then recognize this person's face and identify her as the artist. The artist confirms their suspicion and takes a seat among them to engage in a dialogue about the piece. It is only because of this chance interaction that the virtual and physical presence merge.

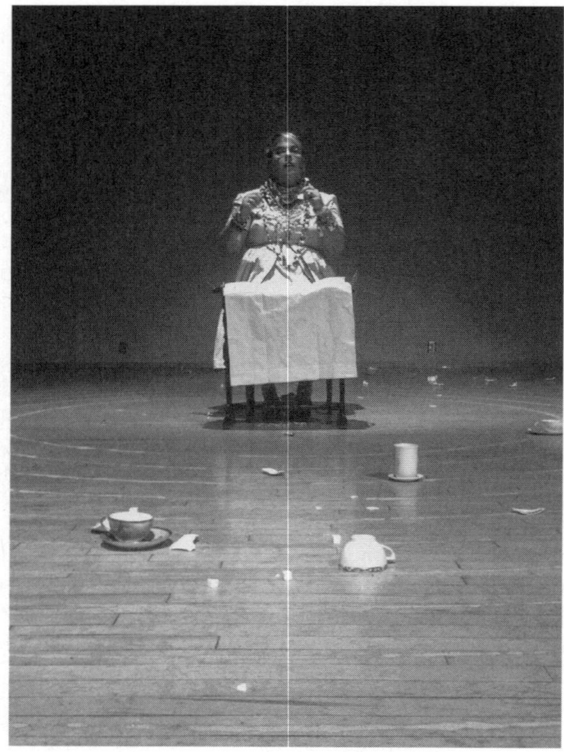

BROACHED TOPICS

first performed on November 14, 2014
Waterloo Center for the Arts, Waterloo, IA
performed once in 2014

LIBBY ROWE

San Antonio, TX
libby.rowe@me.com
libbyrowe.com

BROACHED TOPICS
LIBBY ROWE

For "Broached Topics," I pronounced four statements in sets of ten related topics while putting on accessories. Each set of pronouncements began with a crass or socially unaccepted statement, followed by rewordings that became increasingly palatable (though contained, equivalently questionable content). While pronouncing the most disgusting statements, I put on many pieces of jewelry. In each set of pronouncements, I decreased the amount of accessorizing necessary to beautify the ugliness of the words. By the end of the performance, my décolletage was encrusted with necklaces, broaches, rings, earrings and tiaras to a claustrophobic extent. This performance was conceptualized to draw attention to the power of words and the lengths people will go to be able to accept ideas that are socially unconscionable by changing the language used to present them rather than changing their actions or belief systems.

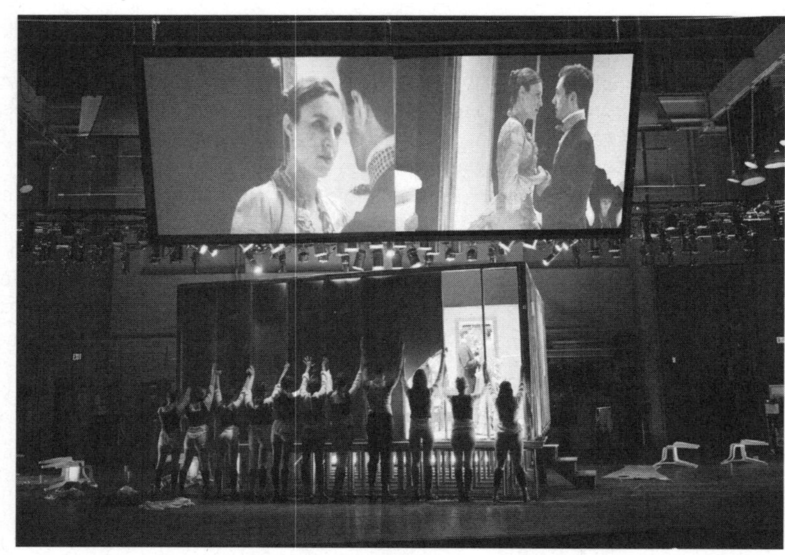

Caite Hevner Kemp

MISS JULIE

first performed on November 14, 2014
Sharp Theater, Ramapo College, Mahwah, NJ
performed seven times in 2014

PETER A. CAMPBELL

Anne-Charlotte Harvey, Laura Ward, Rachel Budin, Caite Hevner Kemp, Jennifer Paar, Steve Fallon, Justin Propper, Angie Turro, Nick Walsh, Stephanie Gonzalez, Sam Simone, Ryan McGilloway, Amber Walker

Mahwah, NJ / New York, NY
peteracampbell.weebly.com

MISS JULIE
PETER A. CAMPBELL

"Doctors say I'm the illest, cuz I'm suffering from realness." —Kanye West

This production of August Strindberg's "Miss Julie" was inspired by a desire to explore high naturalism. We wanted to create a highly naturalistic space for the actors to work in, but wanted it to be available to the audience mostly as film. We created a box set that, at the beginning of the play, was a closed drywall box within which is a mostly fully realized kitchen. The action inside was captured on two handheld cameras following the actors creating a two-camera live film that was projected on two large screens above the set. Over the course of the play, much of the drywall was knocked down, opening up and revealing the "live" space as the play progressed.

Strindberg was compelled by film's potential and limitations:
"Notice how many shots must be taken in sequence by the cinematograph to reproduce a single movement, and even then the image is still shaky. There is a missing transition in every vibration. Where a thousand shots are needed for one movement of an arm, how many would now be needed to depict the movement of a soul?"

In 1908, nearly twenty years after he had written "Miss Julie," Strindberg encouraged his collaborator and director August Falck "not to stick to the letter" of the text of the play "but to adjust it to the demands of the contemporary stage." Where Strindberg used extreme intimacy between characters and close-up psychological theatricality, in this production we used close-up film shots. Where he called for pantomimes and ballets, we created music videos. The production outside of this box set was informed by contemporary pop culture—specifically the music and videos of Kanye West, Beyoncé and Miley Cyrus. These references spoke to me, and to my primarily college-age collaborators and audience, about the sexual and class issues of the play. We used the servants on the estate as a chorus that provided a contemporary "frame" to engage the spectators in a contemporary world of clear-cut and complicated misogyny, violence and violent sexuality.

"Miss Julie" takes a hard look at a couple of human souls, and finds them wanting. This production attempted to manifest moral and psychological confusion through the mixing of media presentations, making the struggle of the live and the mediated an expression of the moral dilemmas of our own time.

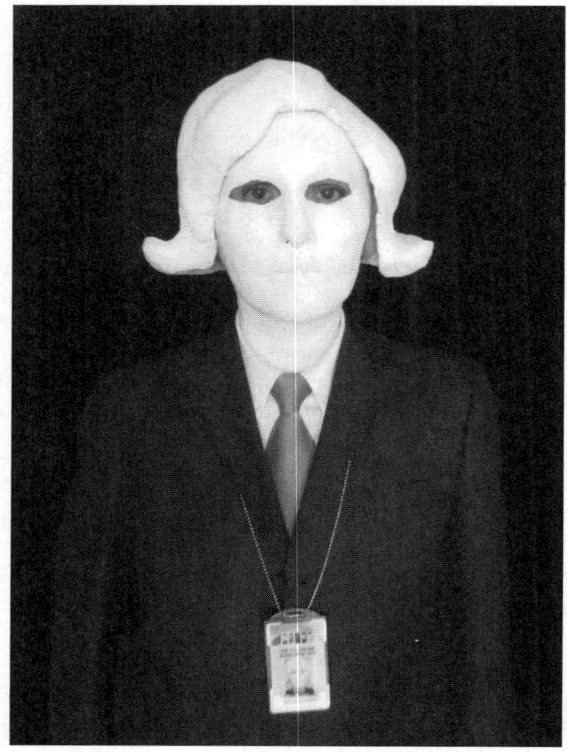

ART GUARD (EN GARDE)

first performed on November 15, 2014
The Baltimore Museum of Art, Baltimore, MD
performed once in 2014

LAURE DROGOUL

Baltimore, MD
lauredrogoul@gmail.com
lauredrogoul.com

ART GUARD (EN GARDE)
LAURE DROGOUL

Solo performance with recorded tape (audio guide), plaster mask and museum guard uniform. The museum guard has been an essential fixture of the art museum from past to present. They are ubiquitous and largely invisible while simultaneously being highly visible in the gallery. Unwittingly, they frame and create the museum visitor's experience. With this performance, I suggested that the guard be considered the art of the museum. Masked (in a mask I created which allowed me only to see—my mouth was sealed) and uniformed as a BMA museum guard, I offered lessons in self-defense with a pre-recorded audio guide. In this scenario, where the museum guard is at once the art and the guard, it seemed important to me that the art in the museum practice self-defense. This performance lasted approximately five hours.

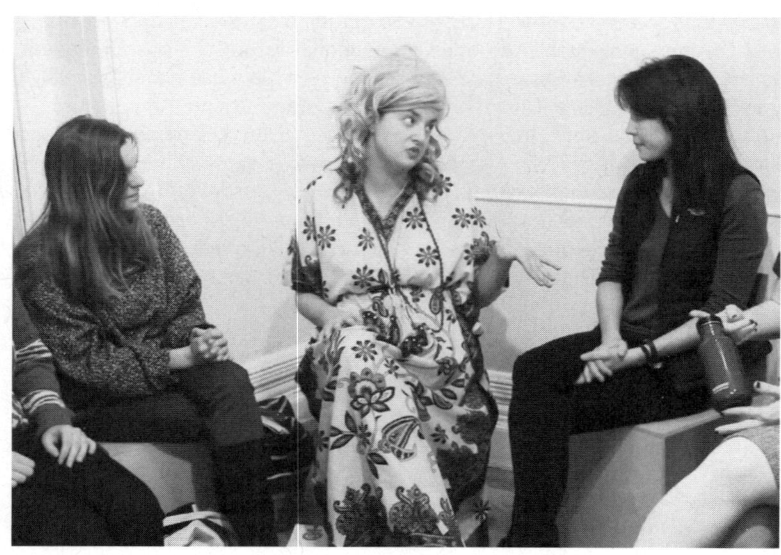

KARAN DEVINE RETURNS #1: WOMEN'S GROUP
first performed on November 15, 2014
PARMER, Brooklyn, NY
performed once in 2014

CHLOÉ ROSSETTI
Mikaela Assolent, Flora Katz, PARMER

New York, NY / Brooklyn, NY / Paris, France
chloerossetti@gmail.com
chloerossetti.com / sinouscontinuons.blogspot.fr

KARAN DEVINE RETURNS #1: WOMEN'S GROUP
CHLOÉ ROSSETTI

I was invited by Mikaela Assolent and Flora Katz, two French curators, to participate in a "feminist working group." Each invitee was asked to bring an element, prepared beforehand, that is as close as possible to their own area of expertise. The element, such as a text, anecdote, performance, video, object, etc., would be up for discussion according to the conversation format and staging chosen by its presenter. Listening, commenting and contributing would be open; participants would be free to speak spontaneously whenever possible. Each individual would thus be able to negotiate their own contribution to the session.

I decided to bring one of my characters, Karan Devine, and make my contribution to the group by way of an embedded performance. Unlike the other nine members of this particular session at PARMER, Karan Devine, a 28-year old downtown "art star" on the tail-end of severe burnout, is not at all clued into feminism, intellectual affairs of any kind of the liberal arts at all.

Karan Devine sat down, thanked everyone for letting them be a part of her "women and art group," and then launched into her story, telling them that she had broken up with her long-term boyfriend, Mickey Future (of the post-glam rock-era band Mickey Future and the Presence, active from '82 to '92), and had sought refuge recently at the Center for Difficult Womyn, a womyn-only half-way house in the Catskills, at the purported behest of her best friend Indi Warthole, the world's first and only 24/7 female Andy Warhol impersonator, who had spent some time in rehab there the summer before. Though the environment was occasionally deeply troublesome, Karan had learned the love and companionship of women there, and was looking for something similar back in New York. Karan then demonstrates her "art projects" to the group which include holotropic breath work, synonymous to hyperventilating or "pregnancy breathing"; a deafening, guttural scream that she had learned at a mandatory Primal Scream Therapy workshop at the Center; and a cover band—of her ex-boyfriend's band—called Dickey Future and the Absence, in which Karan gets all of the other members of the feminist working group to sing a very misogynistic refrain with her.

I documented this intervention and later incorporated it into a video, titled, "KARAN DEVINE RETURNS #1: WOMEN'S GROUP," from which this embedded performance now takes its name.

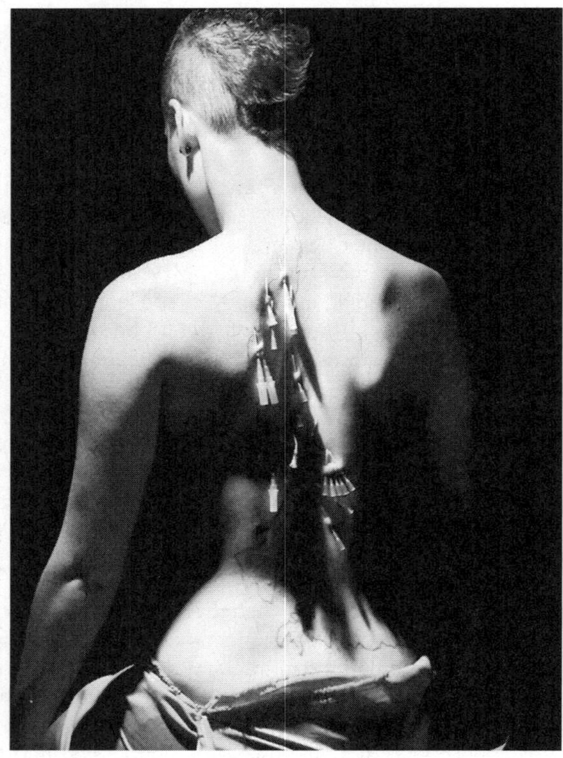

QUISIERON ENTERRARNOS...NO SABÍAN QUE ÉRAMOS SEMILLA

first performed on November 18, 2014
El Paliacate Espacio Cultural, San Cristóbal de las Casas, Mexico
performed once in 2014

DANIEL BRITTANY CHÁVEZ

Javier Escudero

San Cristóbal de las Casas, Mexico / Santiago, Chile
brittanydchavez@gmail.com / javier.esc@gmail.com
brittanychavez.org / javieresc.wix.com/javierescudero/vimeo.com/113031080

QUISIERON ENTERRARNOS...NO SABÍAN QUE ÉRAMOS SEMILLA

DANIEL BRITTANY CHÁVEZ

"Quisieron Enterrarnos...No Sabían Que Éramos Semilla" is a political performance art body piece that addresses the state violence of Ayotzinapa and the 43 disappeared students and puts it in conversation with widespread violence in the Americas in the year 2014, such as femicide and other state disappearances that have received less mainstream attention. Using an inverted map of the Americas (from Canada to Chile) that is tattooed on my back, I had 27 needles inserted into the skin on my back in the geographical areas most affected by these various violences in the year 2014. The first insertions happened in Guerrero, Mexico, with five needles. The rest of the needles were inserted one at a time with a couple locations carrying two needles. After insertion, scarification cuts were made alongside each needle. Then, the needles were removed one at a time while the blood ran over the map. The performance intends to present the body as a living archive for historical memories of violence across many bodies.

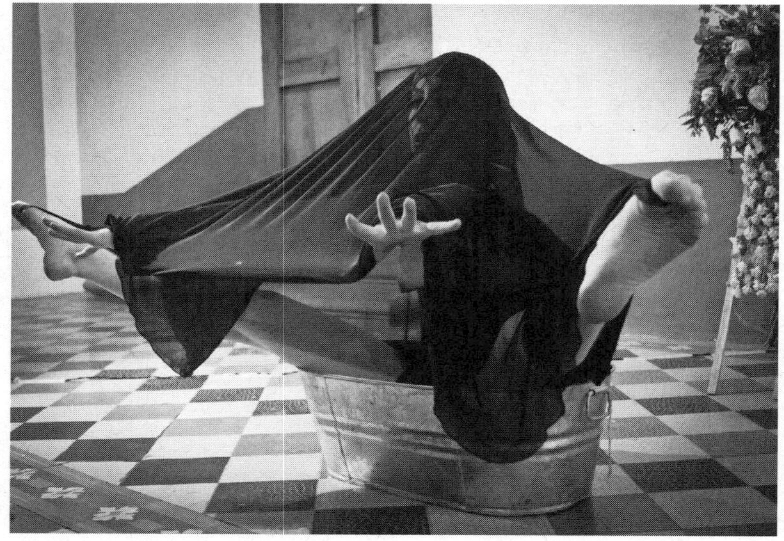

43 SHROUDS

first performed on November 22, 2014
Museo de la Ciudad de Querétaro, Querétaro, Mexico
performed once in 2014

ANÚK GUERRERO

Lechedevirgen Trimegisto

Guadalajara / Querétaro, Mexico
anukguerrero@gmail.com / nigredolab@gmail.com
anukperformer.blogspot.mx / lechedevirgen.com

43 SHROUDS
ANÚK GUERRERO

A hand-in-hand work where we deal with the harsh reality that our country is immersed—namely, Mexico—in an atmosphere of violence, impunity and death. This work is a tribute that recalls the recent tragedy that occurred in Ayotzinapa as evidence of a state crime that deprived 43 students' lives.

Symbolically, we take the image of Christ and Magdalena to resignify a passion duet where pain and drama are protagonists to set in context the current situation in this country, where disappearances increase everyday and the society is paralyzed by the narco-state with cruelty. Uncertainty is a lifestyle that we as new generations reject; we demand justice.

"43 Shrouds" is an contemporary incarnation of the deaths made with traces of 43 imprints of our bloody faces carried out by the public as a registration. It is an installation in memoriam of those boys whose freedom and dreams were deprived.

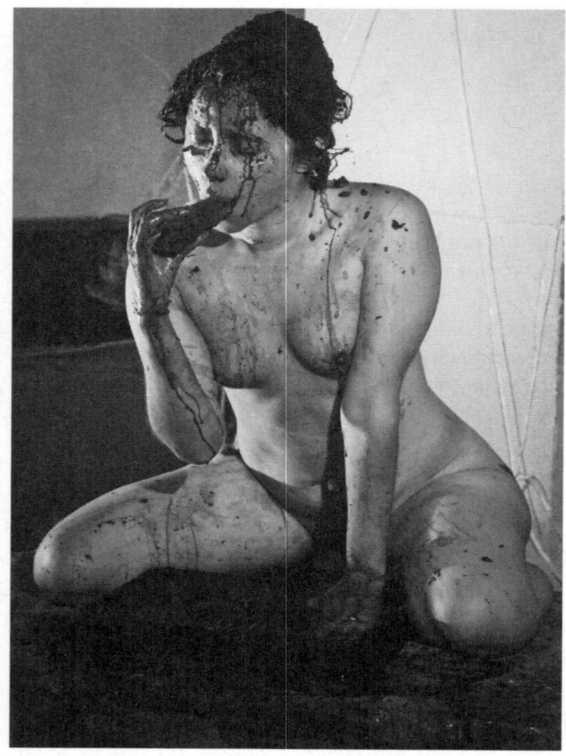

EXPRESS TORTURE PROCESS

first performed on November 22, 2014
Museo de la Ciudad de Querétaro, Querétaro, Mexico
performed once in 2014

BLANCA ANGÉLICA VELEZ NAVARRETE

Anúk Guerrero

Mexico
blanca_angelicavelezn@hotmail.com

EXPRESS TORTURE PROCESS
BLANCA ANGÉLICA VELEZ NAVARRETE

The latent suffering of a kidnapped or missing person is something beyond our perception and understanding, unless we are immersed in such a situation, or a similar one. In this sense, self-submission to torture, which is what comprises the performance piece "Express Process Torture," has been a way of approaching the pain of the kidnapped—in this case being the tying of hands and feet and drowned in blood and excrement—to protest and demand justice for the disappeared from all corners of the republic and the world who expect a release that might never arrive.

Living—albeit in an approximate and laconic way—through despair, helplessness, fear and the terrible pain of being constrained, helpless, submissive and tormented, is how you can achieve widespread empathy with those who have been unable to recover it.

Fellatio to turd shows how easy it is to taste and eat my own excrement dissolving in my mouth, compared with the repulsive, abhorrent and intolerable shit that people swallow every day as far as economy, religion, racist geopolitics, industry pharmaceuticals and obsolescent capitalism are concerned. The "big fucking lies" are harder to digest and do more harm to humanity that this eschatological element through which the masses are scandalized. And, especially, the act of "fellatio" is a raw and strong protest that in a nutshell says: "I'd rather lick my turds than your filthy dick"; in a clear manifestation against the pusillanimous macho and the misogynist rapists who only exist in order to show their bestiality, uselessness and rational and emotional inability to interact with beings different to them. So, with this piece I positioned myself, from the most stigmatized, against abuse of power in all his many forms, to show that these values are reversed.

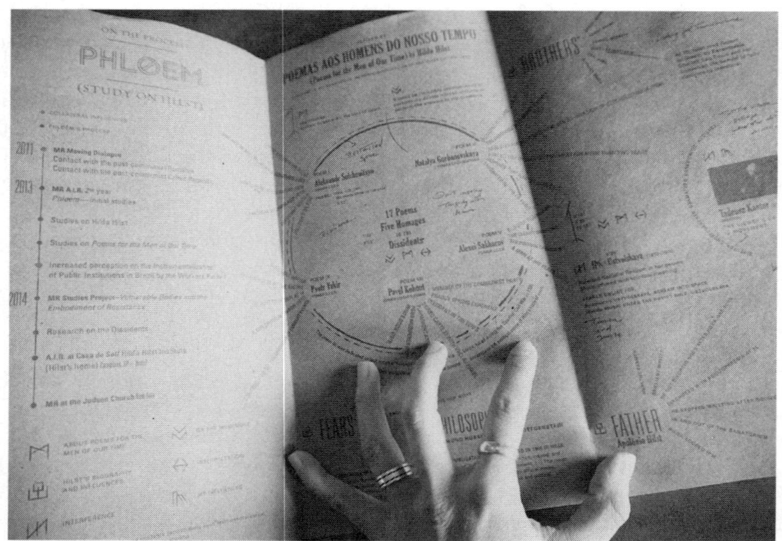

Cristiane Bouger

ON THE PROCESS—PHLOEM (STUDY ON HILST)
first performed on November 24, 2014
Movement Research at the Judson Church, New York, New York
performed once in 2014

CRISTIANE BOUGER
Johann Stollmeier, Bruna Michelin, Larissa Brandao

New York, USA / Curitiba, Brazil
cristianebouger@gmail.com
cristianebouger.com

ON THE PROCESS—PHLOEM (STUDY ON HILST)
CRISTIANE BOUGER

"On the Process—Phloem (Study on Hilst)" was the first installment of an expanded performance project influenced by the poetry and life of Brazilian writer Hilda Hilst (1930-2004). Inspired by *Poems for the Men of Our Time* (*Poemas aos Homens do Nosso Tempo*), I conceived this movement-based performance lecture as a way to consistently share the strategies, doubts and concerns around the construction of my work. Before the performance presentation, a diagram of the work process was distributed to each viewer.

When Hilst wrote *Poems for the Men of Our Time* in 1974, Brazil was under a military dictatorship, which, arguably, suppressed the insurgence of Communism in the country. It came to my attention that five poems in Hilst's series were dedicated as homages to dissident writers of the communist regime in the former Soviet Union and Czechoslovakia: Aleksandr Solzhenitsyn (I), Natalya Gorbanevskaya (III), Alexei Sakharov (V), Pavel Kohout (VII), and Pyotr Yakir (IX). These five poems guided the creation of "Phloem."

By intertwining and overlapping the performance lecture with the diagram and a video with the duration of the 16-minute performance, I crafted the core of my exposure on sharing *process*. The lecture focused on commentary about the performance score and content related to the work references; the diagram exposed the political persecution of each dissident, allowing the viewers to tap into their works, as well as to get a glimpse of "Phloem's" structural aspects and further influences, which included the theater work of Tadeusz Kantor and the music of Russian composer Galina Ustvolskaya. It also pointed out aspects of Hilst's biography and a timeline of the events that brought me to the creation of "Phloem." The video, filmed in a single sequence frame, showed me in the role of the director who observes, and by this means, captured the movement of the viewer/critic as choreography. While my projected image on the background wall observed the performance, my uncertainties concerning the work were listened to as voice-over narration on the video. Close to the end of the performance, my feedback coming from the video interacted with my actual presence on the scene, exposing the multilayered roles implicit in my work (writer, director, video artist, and performer). The video cinematography was designed by Johann Stollmeier with editing by Bruna Michelin. I designed the diagram in collaboration with Larissa Brandao.

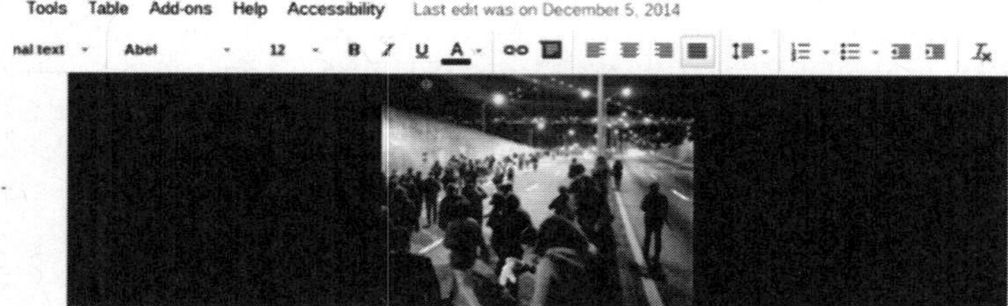

The role of the lover is exactly the same as the role of the artist.
If I love you, I have to make you conscious of the things you can't see.
— James Baldwin

Dear America,

Black lives matter. Black lives matter, and you do not yet understand that. It is Thanksgiving Day of 2014, and you do not yet understand how devastating your confusion is. You do not yet understand that the grief emanating from your insistent ignorance is not located solely within those you murder, incarcerate, drug, rob, starve, depress, impoverish, and refuse to educate. The grief among those you so treat is continuing to shake loose. It is continuing to become wild—as wild as the land now called your name once was. The wilderness of this grief is as sublime and as potent as was the land whose material promise you so violently devoured in your flight from the oppression you could no longer tolerate back home in England.

The emerging (and ongoing) grief of those you murder, incarcerate, drug, rob, starve, depress, impoverish and refuse to

Adjua Greaves

DEAR AMERICA (2014)
first performed on November 27, 2014
Google Docs / Internet, New York, NY
ongoing performance for nine days in 2014

ADJUA GARGI NZINGA GREAVES

Brooklyn, NY
adjuagreaves@gmail.com
agng.info/dearamericablacklivesmatter.tumblr.com

DEAR AMERICA (2014)
ADJUA GARGI NZINGA GREAVES

Because Thanksgiving Day of 2014 fell just three days after a grand jury's decision not to indict Ferguson, Missouri's then-officer Darren Wilson for killing unarmed human being Michael Brown, and because just six days later another grand jury decided not to indict New York Police Department officer Daniel Pantaleo for choking to death unarmed human being Eric Garner, I found myself unwilling and unable to celebrate the origins of this country with the traditional gestures prescribed for the holiday.

Instead, I performed a catharsis of my grief online—writing through my thoughts and concerns about my homeland's lack of love for itself via the publicly shared Google Doc available at bit.ly/1pr4yPC, a link I shared on my Facebook, Twitter, and Instagram accounts Thanksgiving morning.

Thinking and creating publicly within the same channels and devices that conveyed this news to me, and alongside other grieving and reportage, the performance was chiefly concerned with the potency of immediate publication, and the power of baring once-secret grief.

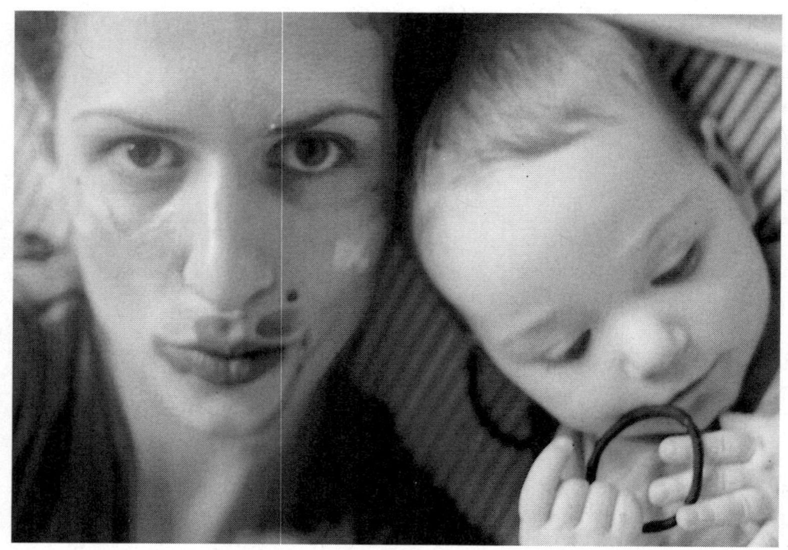

BABY HELP
first performed on December 2, 2014
at home, Brooklyn, NY
performed once in 2014

GENEVIEVE WHITE
Margo Laurelie Skreber White

Brooklyn, New York
genevievewhite@rocketmail.com
genevievewhite.com

BABY HELP
GENEVIEVE WHITE

This piece is an exploration of my relationship towards beauty in connection with my daughter. What do I want to show her? What do I value? How does she perceive me as seen through the eyes of a baby? Also, this piece is a response to a lack of time and pressure to do too many things at once, as a mother. Often, this results in chaos. By asking my baby to "help" me put on my make-up during this recorded performance, she makes a mess of my face, which in turns makes me look like a monster about to go out in social life. Incorporating my daughter in my work helps me actually make work, which is very private as it is filmed at home as an active performance without an audience but filmed and recorded for its own sake. Going back to the history of early performance work, this is a way of filming reality for me as a mother and an artist.

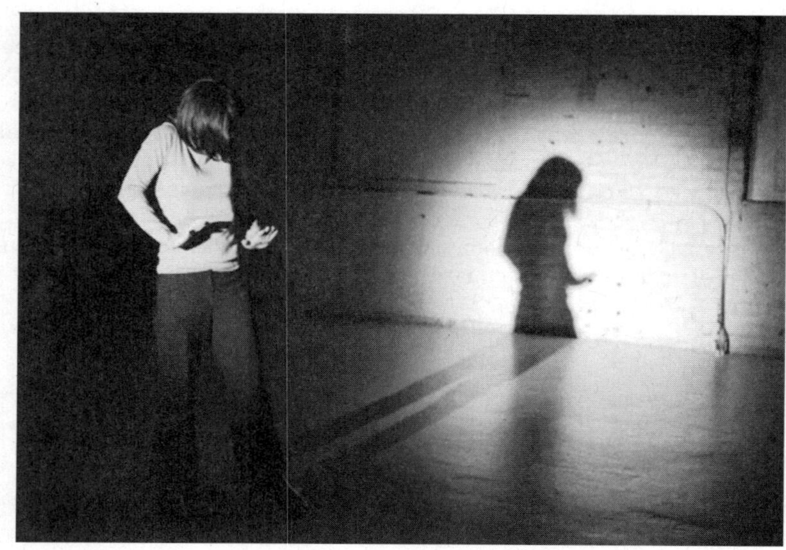

SCREENING ROOM, OR, THE RETURN OF ANDREA KLEINE

first performed on December 3, 2014
The Chocolate Factory Theater, New York, NY
performed four times in 2014

ANDREA KLEINE

Bobby Previte, Michael Kammers, Paul Langland, Anya Liftig, David Overcamp, Vicky Shick

New York, NY
andrea@andreakleine.com
andreakleine.com

SCREENING ROOM, OR, THE RETURN OF ANDREA KLEINE
ANDREA KLEINE

After having continually made performance work since the early 1990s, in 2002 I stopped performing for a variety of reasons. With a few exceptions, I also stopped creating performances. Invited by The Chocolate Factory to return, I was confronted with my own absence, disappearance and negation.

"Screening Room…" begins as a re-imagination of an episode of Screening Room, a 1970s talk show about film. The particular episode I used featured choreographer/filmmaker Yvonne Rainer and her 1976 film *Kristina Talking Pictures*. The piece transforms as "Andrea Kleine," the performance artist suffering from stage anxiety and agoraphobia (and also portraying Rainer) as she integrates herself into the 1970s interview and becomes a new character in Rainer's film, thus changing the story of the film and the direction of the interview. The piece becomes an exploration of the conflicted relationship of performer to performance through a hybrid of dance, theater, television, documentary and group experience illuminating the intersections of fiction and autobiography.

"Screening Room…" is the third project in a series of pieces exploring reenactment. "Memoir" (2010) re-created my 1999 piece "Memoir Never Was" with the original dancers/actors performing remotely from their homes over video-chat. "Rationality" (2011) was a reenactment of a 1992 live call-in cable-access philosophy TV show re-staged in my apartment. "Screening Room…," marked my return to the traditional performance stage/venue after more than a decade. Unlike the other works in the series, "Screening Room…," (although it used part of a verbatim TV interview) was tasked with defining itself. As both performer and subject, I am all but forgotten by the performance community. By using Yvonne Rainer as a device/mask, I not only (re) placed myself within the continuum of dance history, but also within another person who shed dance for other art forms, as well as within a past era when things were not obsessively documented, which in part allowed me to disappear. Can performance ever truly be documented? Can a life truly be documented? Who are we? Where are we going?

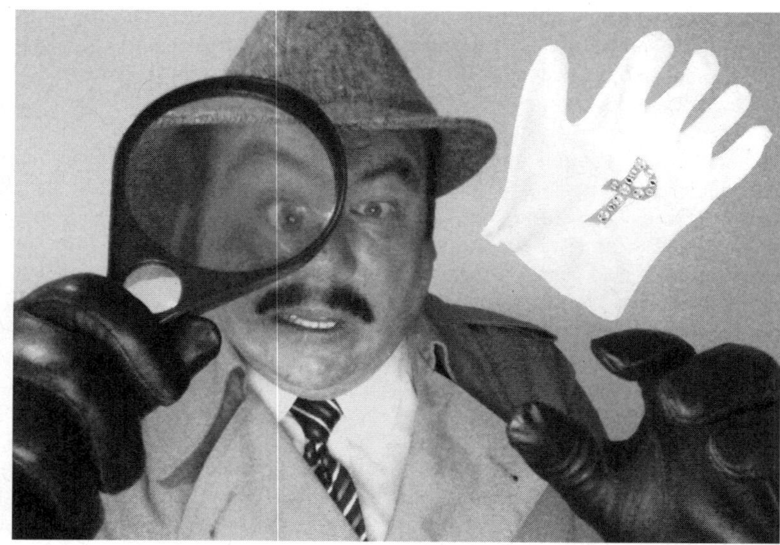

THE INK PANTHER
first performed on December 3, 2014
Ink Miami Art Fair, Miami, FL
performed five times in 2014

VINCENT J. KRAL

Tampa, FL
vince@vincekral.com
vincekral.com

THE INK PANTHER
VINCENT J. KRAL

I was invited to curate an exhibition at the Ink Miami Art Fair during Miami's Art Basel. I was given a suite dubbed the Pulp Lounge and was given the task of curating one work from each of the thirteen exhibitors. As I started my research of the exhibitors' websites I wrestled with trying to come up with a cohesive theme for selecting works. I had limited time to coordinate with exhibitors as to what works they were bringing. I wanted to make it as simple as possible. I did not like trying to select works from the websites, I wanted to hand pick the works onsite and take them for my show. That's when I conceived the art heist scenario but I didn't want visitors to believe there had been an actual theft, it had to be over the top and funny so I came up with the title "The Ink Panther" and switched from curator to performance artist.

I created fourteen monogrammed art-handling gloves like those left by the Phantom in the *Pink Panther* movies. I took one piece from each room allowing the exhibitors to help decide which piece could be taken. In return I left a glove and a clue that could be displayed at their discretion that indicated a piece was missing from their collection. In the Pulp Lounge I hung all of the stolen artworks in the main living space and created an installation in the bedroom that was filled with clues as to the identity of the thief: Vincent J. Kral. The title cards for each work also read as clues telling where each piece was taken from and provided the name and room number of each exhibitor. The performance aspect began as I wandered the fair as Inspector Jacques Clouseau complete with trench coat, hat and a large magnifying glass. I spoke with patrons in character and explained that I was on the case and would have it solved by the end of the fair. This performance piece was important because it became the solution to my curating predicament and added an amusing way for patrons to explore the fair.

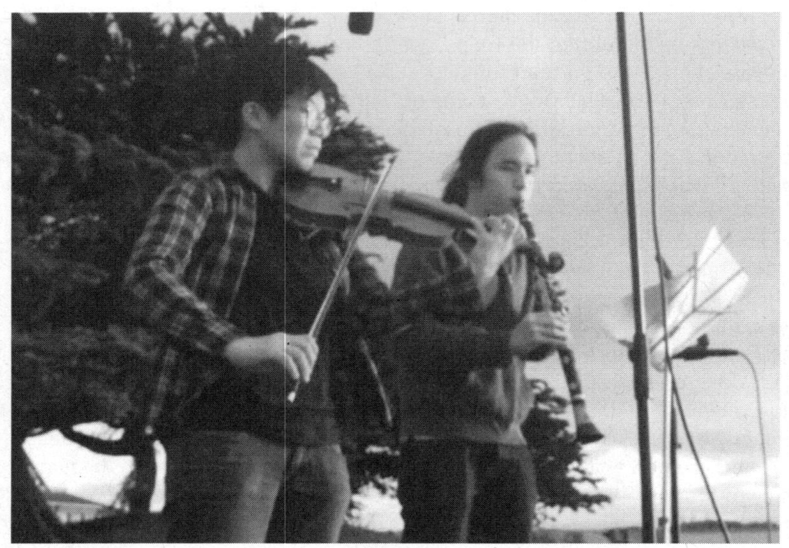

MUSIC FOR BODIES OF WATER
first performed on December 5, 2014
Berkeley Marina, Berkeley, CA
performed twice in 2014

ADAM ADHIYATMA / ADRIA OTTE
Shawn Chua Ming Ren

Oakland, CA / Singapore, China
aadhiyatma@mills.edu / aotte@mills.edu
adamadhiyatma.com

MUSIC FOR BODIES OF WATER
ADAM ADHIYATMA / ADRIA OTTE

While modern air travel has rendered large bodies of water quickly traversable, our histories and ancestries as travelers/immigrants have been shaped by their danger and impassibility (physically, culturally and economically). The experience of difference, alienation and distance by travelers/immigrants is not just a manifestation of abstract cultural separations; it is the physical imprint of bodies of water on our bodies and selves.

We began to develop a collection of scores focused on one's relationship with bodies of water. Eventually, a meta-score arose from this collection: "Perform music on one side of a body of water. When you get to the other side, perform it again." Using this directive as a starting point, we decided to establish a series of performances. The first performance, at the Berkeley Marina and Land's End, consisted of three pieces.

The first piece, "Imaginary Continent #7" by Adam, was a short composed score for violin and clarinet that moves into an improvisation. We performed this piece at the Berkeley Marina and at Land's End, on opposite sides of the San Francisco Bay. Performers were asked to be present with themselves and their environment before playing, and to take note of how their embodiment of the music changed from one side to the other.

The second piece, "Pacific Resonance" by Adria was an improvisation to be performed specifically while looking out at the Pacific ocean and had simple text instructions: "Look out at the ocean. Try to see the other side. Send a message." I would spend time by the ocean, imagining what was on the other side and wondering how my thoughts and intentions might be carried by the waves. To prepare for this, we improvised together by the Bay and discussed the possible resonances of performing by the water.

The third piece was a realization of Adam's "The Spirit Hovered Over the Water #1." This graphic score addressed the interface between multiple feelings: the warmth and comfort of community and the tranquility/violence of existing by the sea. I (Adam) decided that it was a useful score for embodying the conflicting emotions brought on by large bodies of water.

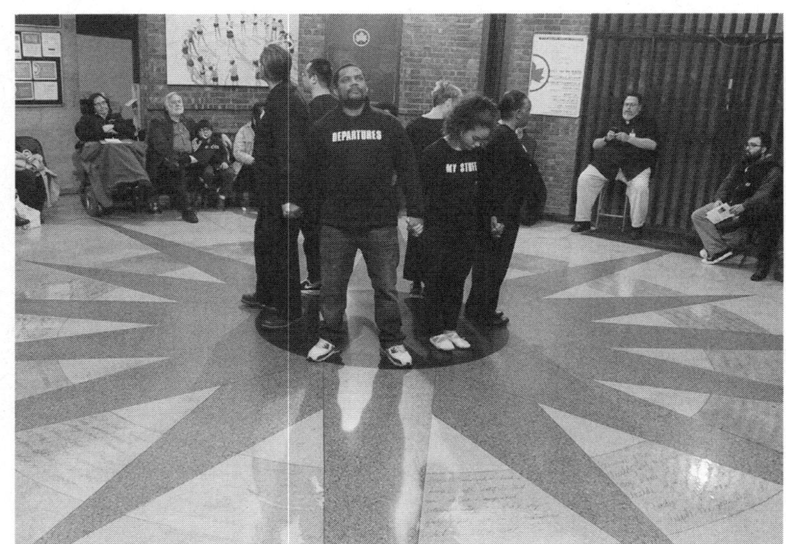

Merve Kayan

100 DAYS
first performed on December 7, 2014
Lyons Recreation Center Rotunda, Staten Island, NYC
performed once in 2014

MANDY MORRISON
Gabriella Dennery, Lori Greene, John Greene, Angelo Angelas, Terry Bennett, Rachel Carson, Lauren Denitzio, John Foxell

Staten Island, NY / Brooklyn, NY
mandymachine@gmail.com
mandymachine.com

100 DAYS
MANDY MORRISON

"100 Days," a spoken word and percussion performance, was initially conceived to capture the elliptical nature of daily thought and language, from a diverse range of perspectives. Ever since Roosevelt pioneered the 100 day concept taking office during the Great Depression, the phrase has been used by the U.S. media and scholars as a gauge of political success and activism. In the lives of ordinary people however, the number is often an arbitrary time frame that can demarcate incremental changes in the flow of daily life or a dramatic shift in one's personal landscape through unforeseen events. With funding in 2014, from the New York State Council on the Arts, I planned this performance to include a small diverse group of local (Staten Island, NY) residents where I live, to be presented in a prominent community space. Select participants, including myself, were given a notebook with 100 pages in which to capture an observation for each day that passed over a three plus month period. The idea was that we would weave these divergent singular observations together and perform them as a group. Then, in late July, Eric Garner's death occurred within blocks of the performance location which is a historic WPA, New York City Parks building.

This event and those that followed shifted the initial idea for the performance to that of experiences based on the participants' personal lives. It was also becoming clear as my meetings with these individuals progressed that a different type of expression would be a more accessible way for them to put forward their thoughts to an audience. One of the participants had been on Welfare, one had been to prison and another had overcome addictions. They all had great story-telling abilities and had been through varying types of ordeals; as I got to know them, I felt that giving them the opportunity to share their stories in a public space should take precedence. This provided them the ability to 'own' their narratives with confidence. As I gave them ideas about how to present themselves, they became 'dramatists' in a manner that would have not have been possible initially. The first incarnation of the performance lasted 30 minutes, and was presented on December 7, 2014. Through interwoven narratives, this version illuminated a range of insights that took into account a specific timeframe (often tumultuous) from each participant's life, as a point of reference. My dilemma as an artist is that while I often have difficulty with many aspects of social practice and socially engaged art, from an aesthetic perspective I am deeply appreciative of the need for arts culture to embrace differing voices and attitudes. This project is my way of entering into a dialogue within a contemporary art practice that attempts to address the problems and dissonances that face us as a people. I view this piece as an initial exploration in a process that has the potential to grow and expand into a larger form of performative expression.

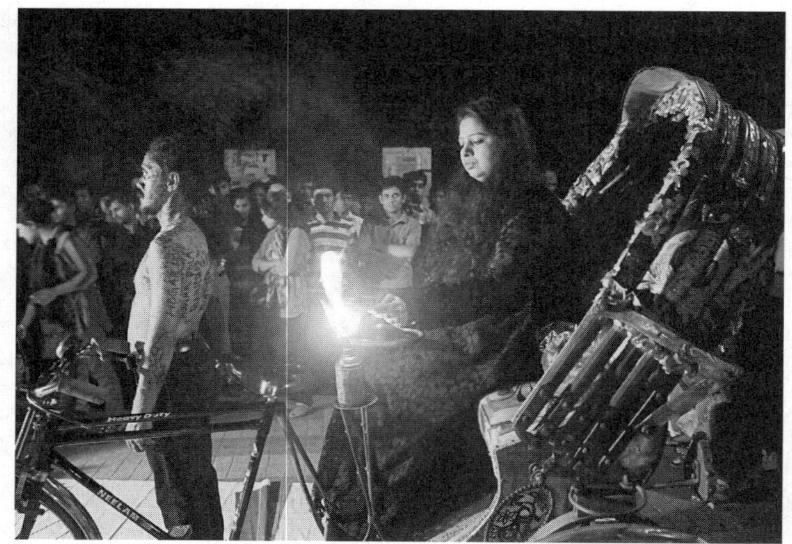

IMPRINTING THE DARK PERIOD

first performed on December 11, 2014
Chhobir Haat, Kazi Nazrul Islam Avenue, Dhaka, Bangladesh
performed once in 2014

DIMPLE B SHAH AND AUDIENCE

Dhaka, Bangladesh

IMPRINTING THE DARK PERIOD
DIMPLE B SHAH AND AUDIENCE

This performance I conceived as I was entering Dhaka through the roads from the airport to a friend's place. I saw a very big cluster of tricycle wala taking the road by storm and in a road fully packed with traffic; I could only see the struggle and pain in their bodies which they take constantly to survive in everyday life. For me, as a third person who is looking at whole thing as silent observer, I had to swallow the fact that this is way of life in Dhaka to work hard and survive. This got me thinking two things: one is the position of the "Victim" (the cycle wala) and other one is me, the "silent observer." I wanted to bring both these elements into my performance work.

In this performance my main concern is to bring into being various social issues which act like boundaries for action and for justice. We are constantly consuming this pressure/tension of society on an emotional and mental level and we keep on absorbing these so-called negativities in the form of Darkness, which accumulates in our system like carbon; if we don't burn out and convert this into energy, it will totally take us to depth of its darkness. My performance will be an attempt to eject all the negativities of our society in the form of bodily actions.

The act was ritualistic process for both my audience and me. I asked my audience to vent out their negative emotions—which are negative imprints of society—by writing on the paper which was supported by dozens of sheets of carbon paper. I also also asked them to write these thoughts on the body of my friend who became a part of the performance who was standing in position of "Victim." I took a third position of observer, but not silent this time. I did a ritualistic act sitting in a very dominating position where I burnt slices of bread on a kerosene lamp and tried to eat all burnt bread without water. It was metaphorically symbolizing that we in the third position also absorb a lot of negativity if we are sensitive. Later, the paper, on which the negative words were written, was also burnt as incense to spread positive energy. Imprinting the dark was the overall performance where I (observer), "the victim," and audience all went through the process of taking away negativity in their own way.

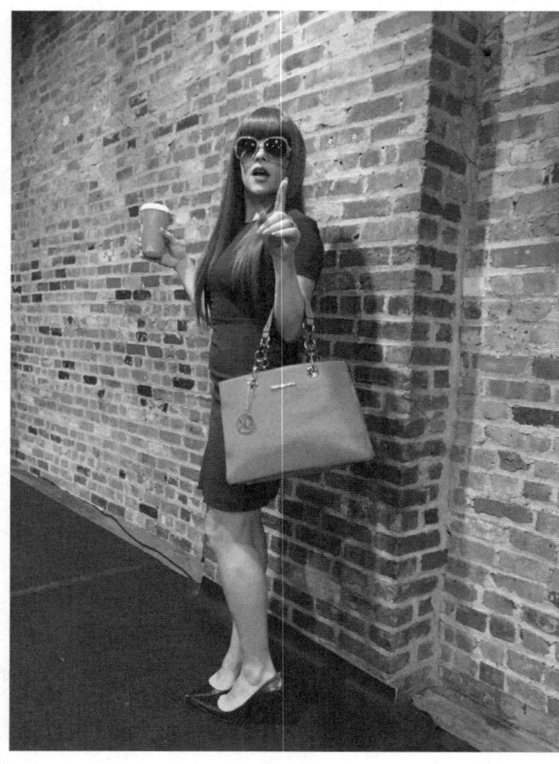

PULL YOURSELF TOGETHER! (A STUDY #OSHA)
first performed on December 12, 2014
The Brick Theater, Brooklyn, NY
performed twice in 2014

WAXFACTORY
Ivan Talijancic, Gillian Chadsey

New York, NY / Brooklyn, NY
hq@waxfactory.nyc
waxfactory.nyc

PULL YOURSELF TOGETHER! (A STUDY #OSHA)
WAXFACTORY

In 2014, WaxFactory began a multi-year developmental process of a new work titled "PULL YOURSELF TOGETHER!" through a series of studies which will comprise a team of six designers and thirteen performers engaged in an in-depth investigation of Anton Chekhov's iconic play "The Seagull." The process is focused both on dramaturgical and design research, but also on developing kernels of choreography, staging, sound score and video design in an exploration of inter-personal relationships amongst the play's cast of characters. Through this exploration, the WaxFactory team (under the helm of the director Ivan Talijancic) is exploding as many ways in which this century-old play resonates in the 21st century America, and specifically a metropolis that is the New York City. Contemporary parallels will be drawn and incorporated in this work to examine our society's destructive obsession with celebrity, excess and hedonism. The first showing was a character study for Shoshona Sands, a real estate manager in the Hamptons, developed by the performer Gillian Chadsey in collaboration with the director.

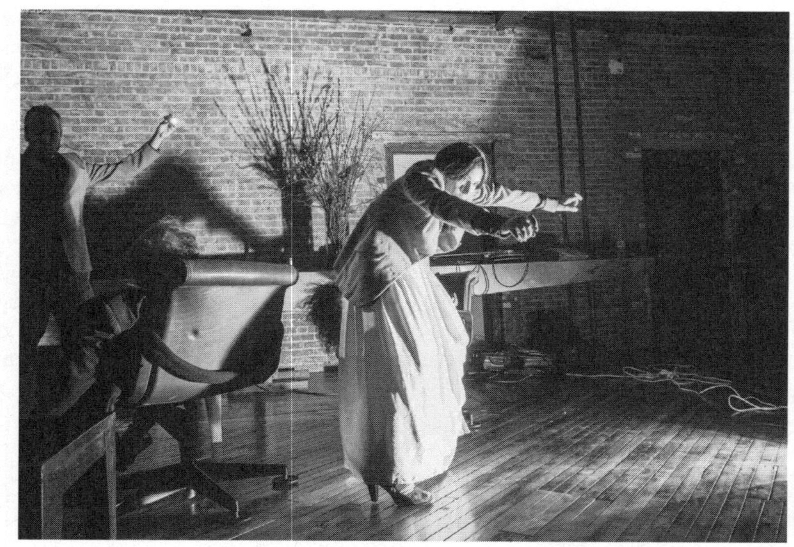

THE UNCARVED BLOCK

first performed on December 14, 2014
The Old American Can Factory, Brooklyn, NY
performed once in 2014

THE UNCARVED BLOCK

Gary Heidt, Lauren Farber, Kyungmi Lee, Cupcake Gross, Steven Dworkin, SHARE

Jersey City, NJ / New York, NY
cassandra@vanreipen.org
vanreipen.org/work/ub/index.html

THE UNCARVED BLOCK
THE UNCARVED BLOCK

The Uncarved Block is a group of artists intent on exploring the range of possibilities for improvisation as performance. I personally come from primarily a theater background, though in recent years have become involved in music as well. I have been amazed by the way musicians are able to gather together and play music with little discussion. Whereas with theater, it's just different. Of course, there's that sketch variety of improv that has lots of games and things that people do, and that's wonderful but not what interests me. I was curious about an improv practice that sits more in the realm of abstraction than situation. And so Uncarved Block was born in 2012. And of course there are schools to draw from, such as Viewpoints and such, and that is wonderful. I am not interested in reinventing the wheel, no, but I am also interested in other objects besides wheels.

Many of the artists of Uncarved Block come from the land of Music more than Theater, and that's great. But I will tell you now that these are folks not interested in being schooled or learning someone's technique, and so we find our way through, and discover what works best for us. We make up exercises where we focus on a particular thing, and that attunes our attention to it.

Another thing that we practice—and this comes from David Finkelstein, who has his own deep practice that I have learned a great deal from (and he has led several workshops with Uncarved Block)—is giving ourselves a set of directions before the improv begins.

More and more, I have come to believe that the key is to learn what instructions to give oneself to yield the juiciest results and the greatest concentration.

The Uncarved Block's powers were used throughout the year mostly in rehearsals. And that is something real and applicable. And I do believe that the best rehearsals are treated as improvisations, which involves exploring within a given set of circumstances, rather than endless repetition.

However, we shared a final 2014 'performance' at SHARE at the Old American Can Factory in Brooklyn, collaborating with the mixed media artists who were there—who were both audience and participants as we were to them that evening. They echoed some of our vocals, provided sonic landscapes for us to move through, and other times, simply witnessed our efforts.

Working thusly with this group of (primarily) musicians felt right and just and brought it all home, altogether.

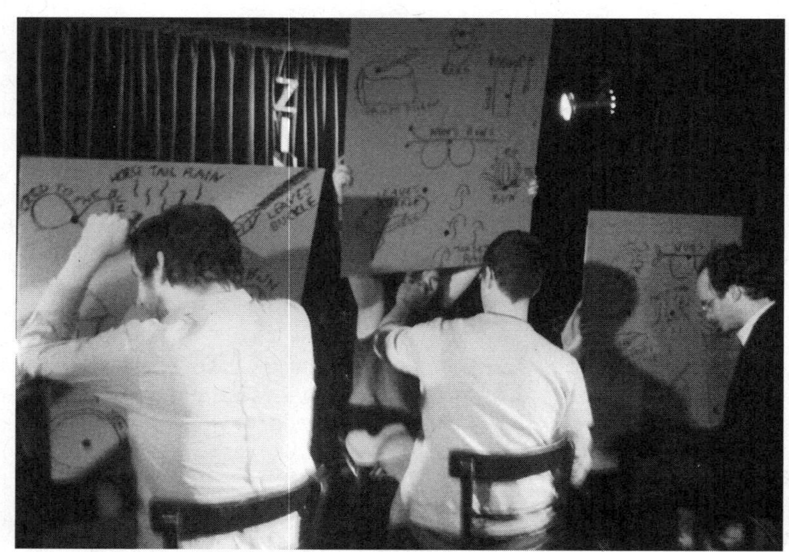

Lindsey Boldt

FAAL-E-FF, THE AUTO-RHAPSODOMANCER
first performed on December 14, 2014
Zinc Bar, New York, NY
performed once in 2014

FARNOOSH FATHI

New York, NY

FAAL-E-FF, THE AUTO-RHAPSODOMANCER
FARNOOSH FATHI

The inspiration for this performance comes from the ancient practice of rhapsodomancy—divination through poetry or song—and specifically from the popular Persian tradition of reading Hafez's poetry, known as *Faal-e-Hafez* (*faal* is Farsi for "divination" or "fortune"), as a means of divination. If you visit Shiraz, especially anywhere near Hafez's tomb, you'll likely encounter people (often children) with canaries who, for a couple dollars (and once you've thought up your question or wish to yourself) will pick out with their beaks, from hundreds of tiny scrolls, a poem from Hafez that becomes your *faal*. The FFFAAL Auto-Rhapsodomancer consists of three cardboard divination stations with two chairs per station, one in front of the "oracular divide" and one behind. Six poems are taped to the back of the divide, where the one who delivers the *faal* sits. On the front side of the divide, drawn in charcoal on the cardboard, are six images with names. Each image has a hole in it—these are the poetry glory holes through which you hear and speak the *faal*. Each image corresponds to a particular poem it appears in; for example, the image of the "dandelion door" corresponds to a poem ("Home State") in which it appears. To receive your reading, you let some burning feeling or question arise in silence for you. Once it has, you poke your finger through one of the holes, and the person on the other side reads you the corresponding poem.

The purpose of this simple performance machine is, first, a more complete engagement of the text (you read it—you see the poem—and you are also read to— you hear the poem) and this is done with the ease of relative anonymity (the board is between participants and those remaining in the audience see no faces). You are divined and you divinate too, which not only approximates the actual process of reading, but amplifies it. That is, the purpose of performing poetry as rhapsodomancy is presenting poems as mediums of divination, as potential fortunes. It says, these poems are intended to serve you; they exist primarily for your personal interpretation. What you want to read in it, finding what connects or resonates for you is the point and in fact, whatever you have—a private concern, an ineffable feeling—a poem in its capaciousness and generosity can engage and in the exchange you find yourself holding your own experience differently. I imagine that this is actually what we do naturally (consciously or subconsciously) when we pick up a book of poems and flip to a random page and decide if it speaks to us, or turn to a book we love. So this rhapsodomancy machine works to acknowledge, allow and make overt that process.

Beginning with myself and one volunteer, this machine starts a chain. The one who has received a *faal* has the option of coming behind the board and offering a *faal* for another audience member. Soon enough, the auto-rhapsodomancer is in full rotation, which, for the poet (reclined for a moment in the audience) can just watch.

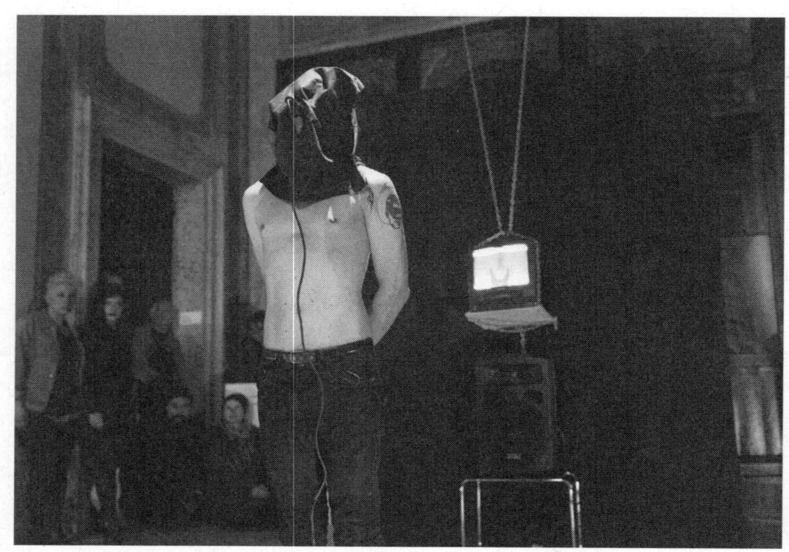

Monika Sobczak

I.W.B.E.

first performed on December 16, 2014
2nd Venice International Performance Art Week, Palazzo Mora, Venice, Italy
performed once in 2014

GABRIELE LONGEGA

Venice, Italy
gabrielelnggrl@gmail.com

I.W.B.E.
GABRIELE LONGEGA

The work is part of an ongoing research about Power.

Power is investigated on different levels and forms: political, social or personal and by using various media like performance, video or visual art.

The main aim behind this performance is to question the audience about the meanings of the actions, symbols and images they are seeing.

1st image: I enter the stage with a flag sewn on my body and I start to remove the pins and set myself free. The flag, black and empty, is an archetype, that can be read in many different ways: as a symbol for nationalism, social identity, ideology, restriction, tyranny, oppression, corruption. But it also symbolizes classification, boundaries, both innate or imposed, that wrap our mind and body and that are hard to get rid of. Then I start to wave the flag, stomping the boots, with sounds of drum rolls in the background. The movements are paramilitary, as a black army parade, predicting the next actions. I put down the flag on the ground, I tear it up and start to sew it.

2nd image: the flag, the object, becomes an execution hood. I put it over my head and finish to sew it around my neck. Following the rite of execution, I attend my gallows speech, my last opportunity to speak. So I pull out a knife and cut a hole for my mouth and put a microphone inside, holding it with my teeth.

3rd image: I am being executed, black hood over the head, microphone inside my mouth I start to shout a statement 'The power is necessary,' 'The power is necessary'. My words are distorted with loud and noisy voice effects. At the same time a television hanging behind me runs a video where I am saying the same sentence but using sign language, to create a dualism, a contrast and conflict of communication. The gestural sign language is also very animated, based on facial expressions, while in front I am a static person, blank, standing still.

The statement is ambiguous. Is power necessary or not? And what kind of power are we talking about? The shout goes louder and unclear, louder and louder, in continuous loops, louder and louder. BANG. The sounds cease, the performance is over.

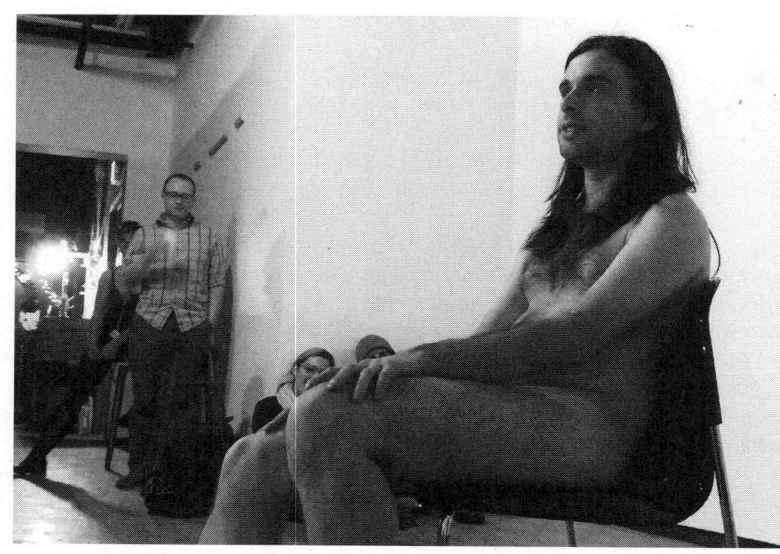

GENDER DROPOUT
first performed on December 17, 2014
Gallery Sensei, New York, NY
performed once in 2014

MITCHELL MURDOCK

New York, NY
mpm290@gmail.com

GENDER DROPOUT
MITCHELL MURDOCK

This mixed-media performance, entitled "Gender Dropout," is a weekly piece that combines live performance with a still photography documentary series. It is shot by one different person per performance, and edited by myself.

Within the space of fifteen minutes, I ask a photographer, chosen beforehand, to direct or position me in five positions or roles that reflect my gender. The photographer does not have to be a professional—they just have to be comfortable using the camera within that space of time, and communicating with me while doing so. For the first position, I am clothed. For the final four, I am nude.

The positions correspond to how I see myself, or how the photographer sees me. The audience is encouraged to participate and join in the direction, provided that it does not stray off topic. Within that time, we hope to glean new ideas about how an individual's identity rests on a spectrum, rather than two binary points.

This piece was first performed at Performance Anxiety. I avoid the word "intimate," but it is a transparent performance, in that I remain honest to the photographer and audience while respecting their requests. There are no materials required other than a working camera.

I intend the project to be both useful to myself as an individual artist; as well as a tool for discussion among the variety of people who choose to observe and/or participate verbally. It is an exploration of the identity I present—male-bodied while identifying as non-binary. And it is a study of the socially prescribed ideas on gender that manifest within a given space of time.

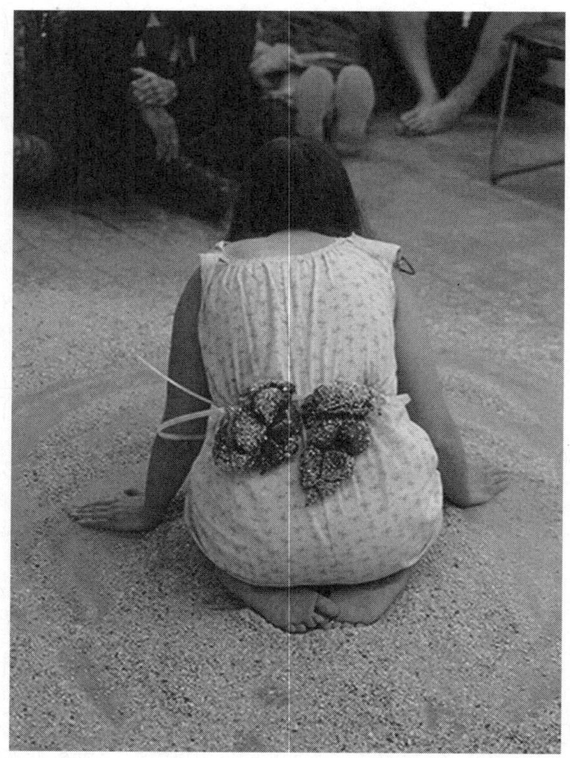

Davi Barbosa

MEMORIES
first performed on December 17, 2014
Gallery Sensei, New York, NY
performed once in 2014

JENNA KLINE

Brooklyn, NY
jenna.g.kline@gmail.com
jelliebeers.com

MEMORIES
JENNA KLINE

With "Memories," I attempted to prepare myself for an imminent death in my family. The performance enabled me to express what I experienced while observing the steady decline of a loved one from terminal cancer. I sought to prime myself for the future tragedy by simulating and experiencing symptoms that occur prior to death: dizziness, nausea, disorientation, exhaustion, and unsteadiness; conditions which I have observed with this type of cancer. My grief fueled the intensely physical actions.

I began by entering the space. A stereo repeatedly played the song "Memories" from the musical *Cats*. All the versions used were originally played on music boxes. Some of the iterations were highly distorted, while others were slow and tragic. I began by spinning as if I were inside of a music box and hummed along to the tune. I held my hands gracefully as if dancing ballet. Over my shoulder, I held a 14 lb. bag of cat litter. The litter spilled around me and caused a large cloud of strongly perfumed dust to fill the space. For a moment, I stopped spinning to attach a pair of beef kidneys to my back, near my own kidneys, with industrial strength zip ties. This is the organ that will ultimately fail as a result of this particular cancer.

Eventually, the spinning becomes faster and the humming becomes louder and more erratic. The audience became a blur as I rotated which caused me to lose my balance and fall to the floor several times. It became difficult to continue spinning after each fall as I was becoming increasingly dizzy and nauseous. I dumped the remainder of litter over myself and kept the empty bag over my head. I breathed in the dust that remained inside and began gagging violently.

When I felt I had spun enough, I began collecting the litter with a small dust pan into a central pile. The performance ended shortly after the thirteen minutes of recorded music though I continued cleaning through the intermission until there was no trace of litter in the space.

Rest peacefully
J — 1996–2014
S — 1997–2013

INDEX: TERMS

INDEX: CONTRIBUTORS

  INDEX OF CONTRIBUTORS AND COLLABORATORS

INDEX: PLACES

NOTES

NOTES

NOTES

NOTES

SUBMIT YOUR 2015 PERFORMANCE FOR VOL. 5

WWW.EMERGENCYINDEX.COM

BECOME A SUBSCRIBER

WWW.UGLYDUCKLINGPRESSE.ORG/SUBSCRIBE

BECOME A PARTNER ORGANIZATION
AND SHARE YOUR *INDEX* WITH ARTISTS

EMERGENCY@UGLYDUCKLINGPRESSE.ORG